Democracy's Think Tank

Democracy's Think Tank

The Institute for Policy Studies
and Progressive Foreign Policy

Brian S. Mueller

UNIVERSITY OF PENNSYLVANIA PRESS

PHILADELPHIA

Published by
University of Pennsylvania Press
Philadelphia, Pennsylvania 19104-4112
www.upenn.edu/pennpress

Printed in the United States of America on acid-free paper
10 9 8 7 6 5 4 3 2 1

A catalogue record for this book is available from the Library of Congress.
ISBN 978-0-8122-5312-2

For Izzy, Austin, and Evelyn

CONTENTS

Peace Intellectuals Against Cold War Liberalism

On September 21, 1976, the former defense and foreign minister of Chile under socialist Salvador Allende, Orlando Letelier, joined by Michael Moffitt and his wife, Ronni Karpen Moffitt, drove to work in Washington, D.C. At 9:35 a.m., near Sheridan Circle, a bomb exploded underneath their car, sending it flying into the air. Letelier lost both of his legs in the explosion and remained trapped under the car. The blast severed Ronni's carotid artery. The explosion ejected her husband, Michael, from the back seat of the car. Twenty-five-year-old Ronni and forty-four-year-old Letelier later died as a result of their injuries.[1] Terrorism had struck the nation's capital. Within two years of the bombing, FBI officials named an associate of the Chilean National Intelligence Directorate (DINA), American-born Michael Vernon Townley, along with several members of the Cuban National Movement, as suspects in the killings. Manuel Contreras, who headed DINA, orchestrated the plot, with the backing of Chilean dictator Augusto Pinochet. Had no explosion occurred on that September morning, Letelier and his two colleagues would have arrived at the Institute for Policy Studies (IPS), a think tank in Washington, D.C., founded in 1963 by two disenchanted former Kennedy administration officials, Richard J. Barnet and Marcus G. Raskin.

Less than a week after the murder, the *New York Times* posthumously published a letter written by the slain diplomat regarding Pinochet's recent Decree No. 588, which deprived Letelier of his Chilean citizenship. Letelier described the actions of Pinochet as representative of the "totalitarian logic" of the regime, which relied on "terror and vengeance" to silence its critics at home and abroad. Why did Pinochet seek to "erase" Letelier and other dissidents from existence? According to the former diplomat, "What the junta is fighting is not so much the men who three years ago led a democratic

Government but rather the ideas we represent. What they are denying is the nationality of values, such as Chilean democracy, that for 150 years constituted an example for Latin America and for the world."[2] Thus, Letelier represented a danger to the Pinochet regime because he spread certain "ideas" in an effort to educate the world, average citizens and political leaders alike, about the undemocratic and brutal methods of Pinochet.

The membership rosters of prestigious think tanks like the Council on Foreign Relations, the Carnegie Endowment for International Peace, and the Brookings Institution are filled with former diplomats like Letelier. However, given his perspective on the power of ideas, when used in an educative capacity, to destroy totalitarian regimes like Pinochet's, it is not surprising that Letelier found a home at IPS after escaping the clutches of the Chilean dictator. In the early stages of planning for IPS, Raskin envisioned the institute as a promoter of "a democratic society." He lamented the "authoritarian nature of the twentieth century," where technological advances, growing nuclear arsenals, and "the seeming complexity of social and political problems have distorted the concept of democracy to the breaking point." A genuine democracy required an informed citizenry "to help formulate and choose real rather than pseudo-alternatives," according to Raskin. The alternative involved relying on the "little objective information and mostly invented or colored views" of experts in an "authoritarian government." In such a system of governance, "the citizen recoils, becomes apathetic and allows the Government (the few) to make the choices for the society." The intellectuals at IPS "would consider the types of information and knowledge needed by the citizens to make rational choices and help to prepare the kinds of pamphlets that would state in clear terms the alternatives and implications of alternatives that exist in the solution of problems in readily understandable language."[3] In short, IPS would serve as democracy's think tank, working for the citizenry rather than military or government officials.

The survival of democracy required an end to the Cold War, which gave birth to and sustained the authoritarian governments and domestic national security state so reviled by Letelier, Raskin, Barnet, and their colleagues at IPS. Before he considered establishing an independent research institute, Raskin worked as an assistant to National Security Advisor McGeorge Bundy. Even then, the future cofounder of IPS voiced concerns over the arms race and its effect on democracy. "In the context of the Twentieth Century the only loser is the free democratic society since it is the most delicate kind of system of government; the kind which an arms race, or a limited war or a general nuclear war cannot support without changing or corrupting in a very basic sense the meaning of freedom and democracy," he wrote to his superior.[4] Raskin blamed the Cold War for democracy's dormant state. To achieve its twin goals of ending the Cold War and reviving democracy, the institute offered a blueprint for a post–Cold War foreign policy.

Descendants of Dewey: Democracy and
a Post–Cold War Foreign Policy

IPS's story shows that another path to peace existed during the Cold War, one that did not depend upon amassing huge stockpiles of nuclear weapons or foreign intervention to stop the spread of communism but rather required the strengthening of democracy instead of its diminution. Politicians and the "defense intellectuals" they relied on for strategic advice too readily accepted sacrificing democracy on the altar of global supremacy. IPS sought to flip the maxim of "peace through strength" on its head with its suggestion that achieving peace required the rebirth of democracy. To this end, IPS looked for ways to dismantle the national security state and make the world safe for all kinds of democracies, not just those of the liberal capitalist variety.

IPS's vision for a post–Cold War foreign policy depended on a reawakened citizenry using the knowledge and insights provided by "public scholars." Such a perspective recalls the well-known debate between Walter Lippmann and John Dewey in the 1920s, when the two liberal progressives argued over questions of expertise, education, the public, and democracy. In *Public Opinion*, published in 1922, Lippmann offered a pessimistic assessment of democracy. "For the real environment is altogether too big, too complex, and too fleeting for direct acquaintance" by the average citizen, he concluded. Thus he suggested a greater reliance on "the responsible administrator," an expert tasked with providing the citizenry with the necessary facts to make informed decisions. Dewey considered *Public Opinion* "perhaps the most effective indictment of democracy as currently conceived ever penned."[5]

As Lippmann became even more dismissive of democracy in subsequent works, most notably in his 1927 book *The Phantom Public*, a rebuttal came from the pen of Dewey in the form of *The Public and Its Problems*, also published in 1927. Dewey, too, expressed concerns over whether the "public," as he called the citizenry, could carry out its prescribed role. He blamed, among other things, "the machine age," reliant on specially trained administrators and experts, for transforming America into a "Great Society [that] has invaded and partially disintegrated the small communities of former times without generating a Great Community," where the hallmark of democracy, face-to-face deliberation, occurred. Dewey believed that the average citizen possessed the knowledge necessary to sustain a democracy. "But that intelligence is dormant," Dewey explained, "and its communications are broken, inarticulate and faint until it possesses the local community as its medium." It was through these local debates that citizens cultivated "the ability to judge" the advice of the experts prior to making political decisions.[6] In other words, a "participatory democracy" required a "Great Community."

Lippmann's negative views regarding the capacity of citizens to make rational and informed decisions prevailed, if not immediately, then certainly during the Cold War. Still, "as the most important advocate of participatory democracy," as Robert Westbrook has argued, Dewey inspired scores of followers, among them the New Left of the 1960s.[7] Few imbibed the spirit of participatory democracy as much as IPS. The institute carried Dewey's torch into battle against midcentury realists of the Lippmann tradition.

IPS wanted to embed the principle of participatory democracy within the foreign policy machinery of the state. For IPS, the enemies of democracy included the unaccountable defense intellectuals housed in defense-related think tanks like the RAND Corporation, whom U.S. officials turned to for policy advice, and the unelected members of the National Security Council (NSC). These shadowy figures provided the lifeblood for the national security state. IPS looked to "the people" as an antidote. The institute aimed to bring foreign policy decision making into the public arena. Echoing the sentiments of one of liberalism's founding fathers, John Locke, IPS viewed the legislature as central to a flourishing democracy. The Cold War thrived amid secrecy. As IPS saw it, classified reports discussed among faceless bureaucrats behind closed doors was not only anti-democratic but also destructive of global peace. Conversely, an empowered Congress, acting at the behest of "the people," could restrain the bellicose machinations of U.S. officials, both elected and unelected, and chart a new path forward for U.S. foreign policy.

By weakening the national security state and its foot soldiers, IPS hoped to end America's constant meddling in other nations' affairs and usher in a new post–Cold War order based on democratic and republican principles. Rather than try to remake the world in the image of the United States as so many other liberals had advocated since Woodrow Wilson, IPS supported "ideological pluralism," which meshed perfectly with its pragmatic sensibilities. Pragmatism is inherently anti-ideological in the sense that it refuses to affix immutable and all-embracing labels on objects, leading to its celebration of diversity. Remarkably, IPS refused to advise other nations on how to configure their political and economic systems; only its citizens, after much experimentation, could make such a decision. Moreover, according to IPS doctrine, ideology was not conducive to a post–Cold War world. Intent on preserving their respective political and economic systems, the United States and the Soviet Union spurred conflict and used overt and covert measures to weaken and replace foreign regimes. On the other hand, "ideological pluralism," achieved through military and economic non-intervention and nuclear disarmament, promised the creation of a global community of nations and the survival of democracy abroad in all its manifestations.

This book uses the story of IPS as a lens to explore the role of intellectuals, whom I call the "peace intellectuals," involved in the battle to end the Cold War. Though not always on the front lines of the much-publicized antiwar protests, the peace intellectuals at IPS provided invaluable information for activists. Information about the role of research institutes in the social justice and peace movements of the Cold War era is sorely lacking. Students for a Democratic Society (SDS) had a Peace Research and Education Project; the Student Nonviolent Coordinating Committee formed its own Research Department; and the American Friends Service Committee (AFSC) relied on investigative reports from its in-house National Action/Research on the Military-Industrial Complex (NARMIC). None of these, however, had the same degree of success and longevity as IPS, due largely to the latter's ability to find an audience both within and outside the corridors of power in Washington, D.C.

The story of the American Left cannot be told without discussing the contributions of IPS. During the Cold War, there was no shortage of radicals willing to speak truth to power, but IPS went a step further by building an institution to challenge Cold War liberalism and the bipartisan foreign policy consensus. Looking at the second half of the twentieth century, the American Left experienced peaks and valleys, but the permanence of IPS as an institution ensured that radical ideas remained part of the conversation in Washington and across the nation. Apart from IPS, the American Left lacked the institutions needed to have an impact. Conservatives understood the importance of institution building and its significance in terms of changing the direction of the country, which led them to imitate IPS by creating new think tanks like the Heritage Foundation. Yet, even as conservatism dominated American politics, IPS remained a fixture, finding an audience among grassroots activists, foreign policy elites, and politicians, much to the chagrin of conservatives.

Though not as well-known as the defense intellectuals who inhabited think tanks like the RAND Corporation, the peace intellectuals who take

center stage here merit attention. Undoubtedly, their influence is more difficult to gauge with precision. Unlike their counterparts at RAND and Brookings, they did not develop the ideas that guided America's Cold War mission.
But to weigh the success of these peace intellectuals on whether their views
found a hearing in the hallowed halls of Washington fails to capture the
other ways in which their ideas mattered. Briefly given access to persons of
influence, Barnet and Raskin soured on John F. Kennedy's New Frontier and
chose instead to blaze a new trail in search of an innovative way to connect
"the people" to the power brokers. Though IPS would always speak truth to
power, the institute never wanted to become another RAND or Brookings
Institution. As the gadfly journalist I. F. Stone observed, IPS existed as the
"institute for the rest of us." After all, like Dewey, IPS's founders held "the
people" in much higher regard than elites. In the chapters that follow, I examine how the peace intellectuals associated with IPS helped mobilize opposition to the Cold War among government officials and grassroots peace
activists alike, both domestically and internationally.

This book also considers what happened to liberalism during the Cold
War. After its founding in 1963, the institute quickly became an outpost for
liberals disenchanted with Cold War liberalism. IPS attracted those individuals unwilling to follow the path taken by so many others who by the late
1940s had become anti-communist Cold Warriors and disposed of their social
democratic communitarian values. They included New Dealers like financier
James Warburg and antitrust lawyer Thurman Arnold but also various representatives of the New Left, such as Lee Webb, an early leader of SDS. This
commingling of past and present liberalisms, usually seen as rivals, is what
makes IPS's story significant. Guided by an anti–Cold War sensibility and a
fidelity to citizenship and democracy, IPS rejected both liberalism and Marxism. In pursuit of a "Third Way," the institute developed a theory of social
reconstruction, which offered a blueprint for the revitalization of democracy
through the decolonization of both the United States and the world.

This book does not shy away from the limitations of IPS's activism and
the difficulties involved with "speaking truth to power." IPS had an ambiva-
lent and often combative relationship with liberals in power, which made the
left-liberal alliance envisioned by the institute's founders an enormously challenging task. Initially committed to bringing intellectuals into contact with
policymakers, IPS went on to find its greatest success among grassroots peace
activists, whether by creating the most recognized anti-draft statement of
the Vietnam War era or aiding anti-nuclear activists in small-town America

in the 1980s. That is not to say that politicians and officials in Washington ignored IPS entirely. In the political arena, IPS worked closely with progressive members of Congress, but it never overcame its distrust of liberals and the Democratic Party, both of whom remained too wedded to a Cold War mentality. Thus, unlike defense intellectuals, IPS aimed to use its knowledge and expertise in the service of "the people." IPS's failure to redirect U.S. foreign policy is as much a result of the conservative ascendency in the United States and the increasingly centrist Democratic Party as it is a product of its own shortcomings.

A Postmortem: The Death of Democracy at the Hands of Liberals

The fate of democracy during the Cold War is at the center of this study. The United States pursued its totalitarian enemies to the far corners of the globe to safeguard democracy. Yet, from IPS's perspective, the global anticommunist struggle only strengthened totalitarianism. Liberal Cold Warriors erred in salvaging Woodrow Wilson's brand of liberal internationalism, with its circumscribed understanding of democracy and disregard for self-determination and diverse political and economic systems.[8]

World War II rejuvenated Wilsonian liberal internationalism. Despite the efforts of thinkers in the United States and elsewhere to construct a global order premised on democratic and egalitarian principles, the Cold War produced a world divided into socialist and liberal democratic capitalist camps.[9] With containment as the centerpiece of postwar internationalism, the United States used illiberal means—the massive stockpiling of nuclear and conventional weapons, the formation of military alliances, and collaboration with ruthless dictators—to restrict the growth of communism. Advocates of "liberal democratic internationalism" staked their hopes on recently decolonized nations seeking cooperation through membership in international bodies and military alliances and by engaging in free trade as part of the global capitalist system. To this end, the United States created economic institutions (the International Monetary Fund [IMF] and the World Bank) and collective security organizations (the United Nations and the North Atlantic Treaty Organization [NATO]) to aid in the creation of this new American-led global order. Though meant to preserve democracy and extend the benefits of capitalism to all nations, these organizations had the opposite effect.[10] The Cold

War consensus undergirding containment guided U.S. foreign policy for the first two decades after the end of World War II, until the Vietnam War led to increasing doubts regarding its principal features. Even then, the cracks were more apparent than real as the United States remained committed to safeguarding the liberal international order, albeit in less confrontational and visible ways.[11]

Democracy fared no better on the home front. The rise of fascism followed by the looming threat of communism led liberal intellectuals and policymakers to look for ways to constrain democracy. The rise and popularity of the demagogue Joseph McCarthy only added to liberal elites' distrust of the masses. As the theologian Reinhold Niebuhr referred to the "children of darkness" and historian Arthur Schlesinger Jr. spoke of humankind as "imperfect," Cold War realism took hold in America, and with it the citizen came to be replaced by the rational expert as the guarantor of democracy.[12] Liberalism became more technocratic, resulting in the growth of "managerial liberalism" by the 1960s.[13] In foreign policy, defense intellectuals associated with the growing numbers of think tanks, academic institutions, and government-funded research centers used their expertise in the social and natural sciences to devise the strategies used in waging the Cold War and implementing managerial liberalism. Together, these foreign policy intellectuals composed what historians have called a "military-intellectual complex." Many of these defense intellectuals came to the United States as exiles from Hitler's Germany, including influential figures like Henry Kissinger but also lesser-known academics like Hans Speier and Karl Loewenstein. As witnesses to the rise of totalitarianism, they came to distrust the masses. Locked in a life-and-death struggle with the Soviet Union, which for these German émigrés appeared reminiscent of the clash between democracy and fascism in Germany in the 1920s and 1930s, democracy's long-term survival required its temporary abatement. Guided by such an outlook, these intellectuals organized the national security state and developed war plans and nuclear strategy. Besides think tanks, they established a presence in the National Security Council, which allowed them a privileged seat of power behind closed doors.[14]

With the onset of the Cold War, defense intellectuals fashioned a new enemy, the Soviet Union. The existence of an insurmountable threat required military preparedness and constant vigilance to protect against a surprise attack, giving rise to a national security state. Even in the absence of actual conflict, perpetual "wartime" resulted in the militarization of the United States, from the highest levels of government down to neighborhoods.[15]

More Dewey than Wilson or Marx: IPS's Native Radicalism

As the architects of the Cold War, liberals were responsible for the retrench-ment of democracy and for consigning the more progressive features of lib-eralism to the graveyard. By bringing together a unique amalgam of old and new radical traditions, IPS hoped to put liberalism back on the right track. Two varieties of liberalism appealed to IPS intellectuals: early twentieth-century progressivism and the New Left. IPS aimed to breathe new life into the former and keep the latter vibrant well into the future.

In seeking an alternative to Cold War liberalism, IPS looked to early twentieth-century voices for inspiration. Dewey, Wisconsin senator Rob-ert M. La Follette and other "peace progressives" sought to halt the growing militarism of the United States, which they blamed on industrial and finan-cial interests, in the run-up to World War I through more active participa-tion and oversight by the citizenry. Most importantly, the peace progressives assumed the vernacular of democracy in opposing U.S. militarism. Of all the peace progressives, IPS had the most affinity for Dewey, despite the philos-opher's much-criticized decision to support U.S. entrance into World War I. Dewey's lifelong crusade to create a more robust democracy, both at home and abroad, appealed to IPS's founders, especially Raskin.[16]

To build a more democratic, egalitarian, and peaceful society and world, Dewey embraced the pragmatic tradition, as did IPS, which is fitting given the philosophy's native roots in America. The traumas of the Civil War inspired a group of thinkers to develop a new theory. They blamed the hardening of abo-litionist and pro-slavery ideas into ideologies for the outbreak of the Civil War. William James, a psychologist, adapted the ideas of Charles Sanders Peirce, a scientist and logician, identifying the philosophy as pragmatism. In James's hands it served as a counter to the rampant scientism of the era that through rationalism and abstraction denied the possibility of change. James promised "no dogmas, and no doctrines save its method." Though opposed to scientism, James employed the scientific method and used experimentalism to determine the truth, by which he meant the idea that best conformed to reality.[17]

By the mid-twentieth century, a new threat appeared as an iron curtain descended across Europe and the world, dividing both into East and West or communist and democratic. Once again ideology threatened the survival of not only Americans but humankind as well. By this point, pragmatism, and with it the democratic ideals inherent in the philosophy, was nowhere to be found.[18] The Cold War, however, failed to extinguish the pragmatic spirit entirely. IPS served as the guardians of the pragmatic tradition.

At the same time, through its efforts to reanimate active citizenship with the creation of a "participatory democracy" in the United States, IPS epitomized the ideals of the New Left, especially those found in the 1962 Port Huron Statement, the manifesto of SDS. This intellectual kinship should come as no surprise given that both IPS and SDS borrowed heavily from Dewey's writings.[19] Yet unlike the New Left of the late 1960s, IPS did not imitate Third World revolutionaries spouting Marxist dogma. Many disenchanted activists gave up on "participatory democracy" in favor of Marxism-Leninism, which looked to a vanguard cadre of professional revolutionaries to lead the unknowing and undisciplined grassroots protestors in armed revolution in solidarity with Third World peoples against the American imperialist capitalists. IPS, on the other hand, remained committed to a more democratic and native form of radicalism with its roots in the late nineteenth and early twentieth centuries. Reminiscent of the "Yankee radicals" of the 1870s or the "adversary tradition" of reformers like Henry George, Edward Bellamy, and Henry Demarest Lloyd in the late nineteenth century, IPS kept its distance from Marxist theory in favor of a republican ideology concerned with the preservation of small-d democracy. Though IPS's radical republicanism made it difficult at times, the institute remained committed to working with liberals within the existing political system, much like earlier reformers who retained their critical edge while still participating in a left-liberal coalition. As a result, IPS avoided the fate of the Weathermen and other revolutionary groups and survived to continue the fight against Cold War liberalism while also keeping the flame of the New Left burning for a new generation.[20]

IPS's Post–Cold War Foreign Policy by and for the People

Peace activists, of course, did not stand idly by as political and military leaders in the United States and the Soviet Union threatened the survival of humankind with unending conflicts and the buildup of massive nuclear weapons stockpiles. Yet, such resistance to the Cold War is often portrayed by scholars as ephemeral, involving a quick burst of activity before receding into the shadows. For instance, after anti-nuclear activists helped secure the Partial Test Ban Treaty of 1963 and anti–Vietnam War protestors forced an end to U.S. involvement in Southeast Asia, both movements dissipated.[21] A lull in activism did occur, but IPS intellectuals remained committed to ridding the world of nuclear weapons and stopping U.S. imperialism. In the process, IPS continued in the tradition of New Left internationalism of the 1960s.[22]

IPS's battle to save democracy and strengthen republicanism extended beyond the borders of the United States to the farthest reaches of the globe. To achieve world peace, IPS argued that the United States needed to restrain its selfish nationalist and hegemonic tendencies. The only way that the world might be "made safe for democracy" would be if the United States stopped interfering in the political and economic affairs of other nations. As their initial task, IPS's cofounders set out to distinguish the institute's brand of internationalism from that of the liberal Cold Warriors. In their first book after the institute's founding, *After Twenty Years: Alternatives to the Cold War in Europe*, Raskin and Barnet targeted one of the building blocks of the Cold War, NATO. Over the next quarter century, IPS intellectuals built on Raskin and Barnet's analysis to construct a new kind of internationalism premised on "ideological pluralism."

Just as early pragmatists blamed ideology for the Civil War, IPS claimed that the conflict between the United States and the Soviet Union stemmed from the contest that pitted liberal democracy against Marxism. Such dualism bothered the pragmatic minds at IPS since it placed artificial constraints on nations looking to develop innovative economic and political systems. Democracy flourished only if allowed to develop organically from the grassroots. Without a promise of non-intervention by the United States and the refashioning of economic and political arrangements, self-determination would remain a hollow promise, as the Vietnamese discovered. In short, ideological pluralism required an end to U.S. interference abroad, in all its forms, and an openness to non-capitalist and non-Western ideas. The institute's promotion of ideological pluralism paralleled that of the earlier progressives, particularly Randolph Bourne. He too looked to transcend the nation-state and its predilection for going to war and to replace it with a cosmopolitan community of nations with diverse political and economic systems.[23]

Following the Vietnam War, a wide-ranging debate occurred over the future of nationalism and the possibility of a new post–Cold War order in the face of American national decline.[24] With ideological pluralism, IPS hoped to propel the latter to the forefront. Carrying out the educative role envisioned by Dewey, IPS intellectuals acted as stewards for Third World peoples and nations in pursuit of a drastically amended international political and economic order. In doing so, IPS joined a plethora of other nongovernmental organizations (NGOs) involved in the international arena in the 1970s.[25]

Jimmy Carter's victory in the 1976 presidential election seemed to signal a turn toward a new post–Cold War paradigm and with it a rejection of Cold War liberalism. After all, Carter's promotion of human rights seemed like a dramatic break with past strategies.[26] In fact, the incoming president could not avoid the issue. The rise of totalitarian governments across Latin America in the 1970s led to an explosion of human rights activism, especially after the violent overthrow of Salvador Allende in Chile in 1973, which precipitated a renewed focus on U.S. intervention abroad. Carter's actions, however, failed to match his campaign rhetoric. Intent on maintaining pressure on the Chilean government, Carter angered human rights activists when he refused to cut ties with the military junta. Carter also clashed with Congress over military aid and government and commercial arms sales.[27]

Meanwhile, activists rarely agreed on what sorts of human rights merited attention. Not surprisingly, IPS favored a "maximalist" definition that included protection of social and economic rights. In doing so, IPS staked out a position that went far beyond the "minimalist" position of organizations like Amnesty International that focused on political and civil rights. The latter groups tended to act out of moral outrage and took an apolitical approach to human rights activism. Above all else, Amnesty International and its like-minded allies sought to bring attention to individual cases of torture and fought to preserve the victims' bodily integrity. By focusing on the physical harm done to individuals, these activists ignored how economic and political structures created the environment that made such abuses possible.[28]

IPS, on the other hand, subscribed to the notion of the "indivisibility" of human rights, which held that the preservation of political and civil rights required the protection of all rights, including economic, social, and cultural. The institute did not frame its opposition to capitalism in strictly Marxist terms. Rather, IPS intellectuals insisted that capitalism was inimical to the preservation of human rights. Such thinking put IPS squarely in line with the authors of the 1948 Universal Declaration of Human Rights, who had waged an exhaustive fight to include social, economic, and cultural rights. Yet, from IPS's perspective, despite the promulgation of the indivisibility of rights in the 1948 Universal Declaration, the United States, human rights organizations, and postcolonial states still acted as if an invisible wall separated the various rights.[29] IPS, like many human rights activists in the 1960s and 1970s, brought its concerns to the U.S. Congress rather than to the United Nations. The institute found several allies in Congress, most notably Edward Kennedy and Tom Harkin. Yet, while many human rights advocates expressed a newfound concern for human rights to atone for the sins committed by the United States in Vietnam, others, including IPS, had another purpose in mind. The institute looked to reveal how U.S. support of foreign dictators emboldened these regimes to carry out human rights abuses.[30]

Thus, as Carter promoted his human rights program, IPS sought to expose its less attractive underbelly. IPS's efforts focused on U.S. complicity in Chile and elsewhere, particularly arms sales by the U.S. government and the extension of private bank loans to authoritarian leaders. The institute's staunch opposition to Carter highlights a recurring theme of this book: IPS's post–Cold War liberalism often put it at odds with liberals in and outside the Democratic Party. Carter, along with several other top administration officials, belonged to the Trilateral Commission. The Trilateral Commission and its members, both past and present, recognized the importance of reorienting U.S. foreign policy to allow for a greater consideration of North-South issues, especially economic matters. At the same time, it held elitist views regarding the role of the citizenry and remained centrist in its overall perspective of the world, as evidenced by its desire to keep the United States at the top of an interdependent world. In short, the United States adapted to the tectonic shifts of the 1970s, but its goal remained the same: global superiority.[31] IPS would have to look elsewhere for support for its post–Cold War vision.

While its criticism of Carter shattered any hopes of influencing the Democratic administration, IPS's expansive understanding of human rights forced it to look beyond congressional circles as well. To achieve its goal of ideological pluralism, IPS felt that it needed to offer a strategy for the Third World to remove the chains placed on undeveloped nations by the IMF, the World Bank, and multinational corporations. Unlike the defense intellectuals who remained wedded to the power brokers in Washington, IPS intellectuals could appeal directly to "the people."[32] The Third World Left that emerged during the "long 1960s" linked activists of color in the United States and anticolonial movements abroad based on common racial and ethnic identities into a transnational solidarity movement.[33] IPS, composed mainly of white intellectuals, saw its involvement with the Third World differently. Race and ethnicity mattered far less to IPS than a shared global citizenship. To an extent, such an approach limited the institute's ability to reach the Third World. A certain blindness prevented IPS's founders from recognizing this deficiency. For instance, when the institute obtained a large grant in 1974 for a new center abroad to strengthen the relationship between Westerners and Third World peoples, Barnet and Raskin chose Amsterdam as the site for the Transnational Institute. Still, other peace intellectuals at the institute forged strong ties with Third World leaders and activists in Chile, Jamaica, and Cuba. Thus, despite its whiteness, IPS constructed an "imagined solidarity" with Third World peoples, who no doubt realized the institute's ability to publicize and amplify the voices of the unheard that normally escaped the attention of policymakers in Washington.[34]

From Chile to Jamaica, IPS struggled against the anti-democratic tendencies of the liberal internationalist order. Just as the Cold War led to the division of the world into East and West blocs and prevented experiments in new forms of governance, the ideological contest that pitted capitalism against communism precluded countries from seeking alternative paths to economic development.[35] Third World nations received expert-driven modernization plans that safeguarded the liberal capitalist order and ensured that the international economy remained unfair and undemocratic.

The unapologetic Cold Warrior Walt Rostow, who wrote *The Stages of Economic Growth: A Non-Communist Manifesto* in 1960 and later pushed for a more aggressive U.S. policy against Vietnam as Lyndon Johnson's national security advisor, popularized modernization theory. His blueprint, along with the many other similar proposals making their way around Washington, favored top-down, expert-led programs with a penchant for scientific and technological solutions, much like its domestic variant, managerial liberalism. Modernization theorists sought to extend the liberal world order to the far reaches of the globe and dissuade nationalists from carrying out noncapitalist forms of development. To ensure that Third World nations stayed on the proper course, the United States sacrificed democracy by turning to dictators who used violence and intimidation to discourage active political participation and activism. Only rarely did the U.S. government or international institutions like the World Bank fund development plans that did not accord with Western-style modernization schemes.[36]

IPS excoriated liberal models of modernization and development. Under the guise of helping Third World countries, IPS considered it all a facade. Modernization theory, IPS intellectuals believed, served as liberal capitalism's handmaiden. Many Third World nations recently freed from the yoke of colonialism shared IPS's anti–Cold War perspective and its preference for looking at the world in terms of North and South. The decolonization movement represented a fight against the Cold War, with its bipolar orientation, as much as against colonialism. Third World nationalists keenly understood that the Cold War placed nearly as many limits on a nation's sovereignty as had the demolished colonial system. Actual self-rule required an end to the Cold War, which drew attention away from fundamental North-South economic issues that impinged on a nation's sovereignty.[37]

In its crusade against Western-oriented modernization theory, the institute shared the international stage with actors from the Global South in search of a New International Economic Order (NIEO). By the mid-1970s, the United Nations approved four resolutions related to economic development in the Third World. These included the Declaration of the Establishment of a New International Economic Order, the Program of Action on the Establishment of a New International Economic Order, the Charter of the Economic Rights and Duties of States, and Development and International Cooperation. These documents offer a glimpse into the most pressing issues from the perspective of the Third World. Improving North-South relations required stabilizing and fixing commodity prices; tariff reductions in the North to allow for more equitable trade, especially industrial goods from the Third World; increased foreign assistance as a form of repayment for historically low commodity prices; debt reduction measures; reform of the World Bank, IMF, and other multilateral institutions to make them more sympathetic to the grievances voiced by the Global South; protectionist trade policies to help Third World industry; and additional technology transfer.[38]

Though in agreement on most matters, the institute offered its own program that differed, in some cases fundamentally, from the demands put forth by the Global South. Advocating self-reliance, IPS encouraged undeveloped and underdeveloped nations to separate from the international capitalist economy. Only through the establishment of participatory democracy in the Third World could the region's poorest citizens fulfill their basic needs, most notably, access to food, which IPS hoped to elevate to a human right. IPS's ideas found a welcome reception in several Third World nations, including Julius Nyerere's Tanzania and Michael Manley's Jamaica. IPS wholeheartedly supported the socialist projects undertaken by Nyerere and Manley in their respective countries and, more importantly, their attempts to tear down the edifices that buttressed the liberal world order. IPS, of course, did not act alone but rather belonged to a larger "NGO International" critical of current development models premised on capitalist economic theories that fostered continued global inequality and further divided the world into rich and poor classes.[39]

By the 1980s, hopes of creating a post–Cold War order had diminished even more with the election of Ronald Reagan. Convinced that the Soviet Union represented an "evil empire," Reagan initiated a massive nuclear weapons buildup resulting in a "Second Cold War" between the superpowers.[40] Confronted by such a reality, IPS looked once again to "the people" to help with the transition from a politics of power to a politics of peace. For a decade in which conservatism reached its apex, the "Age of Reagan" witnessed a groundswell of activism, especially anti-nuclear protest.[41] IPS worked with well-established anti-nuclear organizations and relative unknowns to promote its program of general and complete disarmament and to dismantle the infrastructure propping up America's nuclear stockpile. Unlike most liberals,

IPS offered only tepid support for arms control measures, which fell short of general and complete disarmament and relied too heavily on expert negotiators.[42] At the same time, IPS found itself on the fringes of the anti-nuclear movement, which by the 1980s had become more concerned with public relations and political lobbying than citizen activism. Thus, while the middle-of-the-road nuclear freeze mobilized thousands against Reagan's nuclear policies, more radical ideas, including general and complete disarmament, which had found support in certain government circles as far back as the 1950s, remained beyond the pale.[43]

IPS's efforts to reorient U.S. foreign policy and put it on a more democratic footing are highlighted in the thematic chapters that follow. The first chapter follows IPS as it set out to define its role as a base for "public scholars" while constructing a new liberalism, known as social reconstruction, meant to ease the transition to a post–Cold War order. Next, the narrative focuses on the institute's proposed blueprint for a post–Cold War order premised on the idea of ideological pluralism. Then the spotlight turns to IPS's involvement in the anti–Vietnam War movement. Working through official circles and street protests, the institute looked at Vietnam as a test site for its theory of ideological pluralism. Despite its best efforts, IPS failed to convince the U.S. government to allow nations to follow their own economic and political trajectory. In response, the institute investigated how domestic factors impeded the implementation of ideological pluralism abroad and offered suggestions for empowering U.S. citizens to determine U.S. foreign policy. From there, the book examines IPS's involvement in the human rights movement of the 1970s and its related efforts to transform the global economy to allow for ideological pluralism in the economic realm. The two concluding chapters excavate IPS's attempts to dismantle the military-industrial complex and abolish nuclear weapons through grassroots protest and transnational activism.

IPS's unbridled faith in the virtues of democracy—rooted in an expansive understanding of citizenship—led the think tank to formulate a new vision for both America and the world, one that transcended the national security state and the Cold War. Despite the peaceful resolution of the Cold War, many of the issues behind the campaigns engaged in by IPS and profiled in these pages remain a problem. IPS's story offers evidence of an alternative from the not too distant past that can offer guidance for citizens concerned with the current crises threatening democracy.

CHAPTER 1

On a Mission to Save Liberalism

"Liberal thought and liberal leadership in politics leaves much to be desired," a young aide to Representative Robert Kastenmeier wrote in 1959. The author, Marcus Raskin, lamented the paucity of liberal programs put into place since the 1930s. "Consequently," he argued, "what remains is the vocabulary of liberalism which gives the semblance of thought and action but is more the reflection of the present American societal pattern of 'drift,' 'apathy,' and the 'American malaise.'"[1] By the late 1950s, liberalism lacked substance as it endured a prolonged period of stasis. Over the previous decade, liberals had followed the advice of Arthur Schlesinger Jr. to seek out the "vital center," which required strengthening liberal democracy and avoiding totalitarianism from both the Left and Right.[2] From the perspective of IPS cofounders Raskin and Richard Barnet, postwar liberalism had forsaken its radical heritage when it sought to conserve the domestic and international liberal order.

With Republican Dwight Eisenhower in the White House and liberalism under the spell of Schlesinger's "vital center," intellectuals and activists embarked on a journey to find a "Third Way," an alternative to liberalism and Marxism. These voices in the wilderness attempted to breach the Cold War consensus and chart an entirely new course for the Left. Besides liberalism and Marxism, their discussions broached such topics as the role of intellectuals and their interactions with activists, democracy and citizenship, how to frame opposition to the Cold War, and the importance of alliances with American youth and international leftists. Barnet and, to a much greater extent, Raskin participated in these ongoing conversations. Raskin's paradoxical experiences in government—first as a legislative assistant to Kastenmeier, one of the most liberal members of Congress, and then as an aide to McGeorge Bundy, John F. Kennedy's national security advisor and a major architect of America's expanded involvement in Vietnam—forced him, along with Barnet, to acknowledge the limits of politics and begin the process of building a new institution premised on the notion of intellectuals speaking truth to power. With the creation of IPS, Barnet and Raskin rejected the model developed by other think tanks that housed defense intellectuals and sought access to the halls of power. Instead of speaking for the influential and powerful, IPS aimed to amplify the voices of "the people" by serving as "public scholars." Raskin and Barnet hoped to lay the groundwork for a new politics and a new liberalism. Doing so put IPS on a collision course with Cold War liberals. In many ways, IPS carried on the tradition of the New Left, but as "radical liberals" remained far more willing to work within "the system" and condemned youthful protestors' calls for revolution. IPS preferred a different approach, one that involved a major transformation of liberalism through social reconstruction. Ultimately, IPS occupied a gray area between activist and intellectual while synthesizing certain liberal, radical liberal, New Left, and progressive ideals.

The Search for an Alternative
to Cold War Liberalism, 1956–1963

With "A New Liberalism in the Democratic Party," Raskin joined a whole coterie of intellectuals, activists, and politicians looking to take advantage of a temporary lull in Cold War tensions to forge a new path forward and bring an end to the conflict before nuclear annihilation destroyed humankind. An early salvo in the campaign against Cold War liberalism originated with the appearance of *Liberation* magazine in March 1956. Its editorial staff included such heavyweights from the radical pacifist movement as A. J. Muste, Bayard Rustin, David Dellinger, and Roy Finch. In the inaugural issue, the editors assailed existing ideologies and promised to use *Liberation* as a vehicle to develop new theories. They felt that liberalism lacked the capacity to respond to the most pressing issues of the day, and when it did, offered only half measures that failed to attack the root of the problem. "Essentially the liberal accepts the existing order," the editors complained, while also making sure that it is known that "he is troubled and wants the good conscience of repudiating its wrongs." In the end, such rhetorical outrage produced only inaction. Meanwhile, Marxism belonged to an "outmoded bourgeois epoch" that no longer existed in the twentieth century. Nor did the radical pacifists approve of Marx's affinity for war and violent revolution in pursuit of a socialist utopia. Thus, instead of relying on liberal and Marxist creeds, the editors spoke about decentralization, participatory democracy in the workplace and the political and social realms, and employing technology only for humane purposes.[3] In the aptly titled "Tract for the Times," the editors at *Liberation* perfectly encapsulated the concerns that inspired IPS and others to look beyond liberalism and Marxism to a "Third Camp" or "Third Way."

The involvement of Muste, viewed by many activists as the elder statesman of American pacifism, in the launching of *Liberation* points to the importance of ideas to the peace movements of the 1950s and 1960s. At the same time, his participation in the venture also highlights the tensions that existed between intellectuals and activists. Muste wanted *Liberation* to act as a sounding board for ideas meant to inspire readers to carry out direct action protests. Writing policy proposals, conducting political lobbying, and peace education had all failed to stop U.S. militarism. Thus, even as he worked closely with some of the great minds of the peace movement, Muste repeatedly coaxed them to act, not just think, write, and make appeals to politicians.[4] Despite the difficulties involved with bridging the gulf separating intellectuals and activists, the former often informed the latter, and vice versa, making both central to the creation of a "Third Camp."

As liberals clung to the "vital center," a new group of thinkers looked to renew America's democratic tradition and reinvigorate the welfare state. Inspired by John Dewey's "democratic public," in which "the people" participated in the decision-making process after talking with their fellow citizens, social critic Paul Goodman, sociologist C. Wright Mills, and others formulated a "radical liberalism" that laid the groundwork for the New Left of the 1960s. These thinkers tasked themselves with educating the public in preparation for carrying out the duties required of citizens in a "democratic public." To this end, Mills encouraged academics to write for a wider audience, Goodman eventually joined IPS, and University of Michigan philosopher Arnold Kaufman, who was the first to use the moniker "radical liberal," helped organize the first teach-in against the Vietnam War. In the end, however, Mills, Goodman, and Kaufman struggled with the same difficulties that bedeviled Muste when he tried to link theory to action, mainly how to engage with protest movements without sacrificing their responsibilities as critical intellectuals.[5] Though critics of Cold War America and liberalism, Mills and Goodman remained committed to both, so long as each underwent significant transformations. The abiding faith in liberalism shown by Mills and Goodman also appeared in Kaufman's later book, *The Radical Liberal*, which will be discussed in relationship to IPS in this chapter. Despite heated disagreements, Mills and Goodman remained committed to the democratic ideal.

A month after the first issue of *Liberation* appeared on the newsstands, Mills's newest book, *The Power Elite*, arrived on the scene. In it, Mills documented how a "power elite" slowly disabused local political and economic leaders of their power as it became concentrated among a group of national leaders. Mills's power elite included the "corporate rich," the "warlords," and the "political directorate." These power brokers effectively made democracy a sham by denying citizens a role in decision making. Mills, anticipating later calls by the New Left for "participatory democracy," argued that "publics" could counter the power elite. Yet, as Daniel Geary has argued, Mills's "disillusioned radicalism" imbued his work with a sense of despondency about whether "publics" could rise from the ashes. Nor did liberalism, at least in its current form, offer a solution. As Mills wrote a year prior to publishing *The Power Elite*, "administrative liberalism" had relied on "a set of administrative routines," with decisions "made by God, by experts, and by men like Mr. [Secretary of Defense Charles] Wilson," which precluded the involvement of the democratic public.[6]

For Goodman, solving America's social ills required a return to a small-d democracy. Goodman despised Marxism. He preferred to scour the American past for homegrown radicals. Randolph Bourne's anarchist sensibilities intrigued Goodman, as did Muste's pacifism. He developed his views on democracy by looking to the republican ideology popular in the eighteenth and nineteenth centuries. Goodman, to a far greater extent than Mills, embraced a decentralized "participatory democracy" reliant on localism to balance the centralized national government.[7]

Goodman's 1960 book *Growing Up Absurd* cemented his place as one of the premier social critics in midcentury America. Yet, the conformity and alienation that came under ridicule in the book were of secondary importance to Goodman. While rampant consumerism and mundane jobs led the Beats and counterculture to reject U.S. society and seek refuge in communes and elsewhere, Goodman exhorted his readers to take political action.[8] Among other things, Goodman lamented the fact that even as voting requirements diminished, "the ideal of the town meeting" disappeared, along "with the initiative and personal involvement that alone could train people in self-government." Moreover, "the self-determination won by the American Revolution for the regional states" that "should have made possible real political experimentation" was replaced by "a deadening centralism," he claimed.[9] Goodman's unique blend of anarchism, republicanism, and decentralization eventually gained the attention of the New Left.

On November 15, 1957, the Committee for a Sane Nuclear Policy (SANE) entered the debate over nuclear weapons with a full-page ad in the *New York Times* with the provocative headline "We Are Facing a Danger Unlike Any Danger That Has Ever Existed." The statement expressed alarm at the widespread consumerism and lack of morals evident among the U.S. populace. It went on to implore Americans to exhibit a "greater concern for the human community of the whole," which required fighting for world peace. To this end, SANE encouraged the readers of the *New York Times* to advocate arms control and a nuclear test ban.[10]

By the time SANE arrived on the scene, the anti-nuclear movement had undergone a transformation. As the size of nuclear explosions grew with the introduction of the hydrogen bomb in 1954, so too did fears over radioactive fallout. To make their concerns known, radical pacifists participated in events organized by Lawrence Scott's Non-Violent Action Against Nuclear Weapons, later known as the Committee for Non-Violent Action (CNVA). The first such protest, a Hiroshima Day demonstration on August 6, 1957, at a Nevada nuclear test site, involved a twenty-four-hour "Prayer and Conscience Vigil." Authorities arrested some of the protestors after they attempted to gain entrance to the testing grounds. In April 1957, one of SANE's founders, *Saturday Review* editor Norman Cousins, had convinced Nobel Prize–winning physician Albert Schweitzer to issue a statement about the effects of radioactive materials on the human body. The following year, biologist Barry Commoner helped found the Committee for Nuclear Information (CNI) to publicize the dangers posed by nuclear fallout to children. In the end, these environmental concerns found widespread support and led to the passage of the 1963 Limited Test Ban Treaty, which had the unintended effect of dampening appeals for general and complete disarmament.[11]

Though they shared concerns about the health and environmental effects of nuclear fallout, CNVA and SANE agreed on little else, underscoring the problematic relationship between radical and liberal activists in the peace movement. For instance, Muste, writing in 1962, praised "early Christians" for their "quality of looseness from the world-that-is, of experimentation, creativeness"—in short, their refusal to accept the status quo. He advocated a similar approach to dealing with the nuclear age. "Mankind *has* to find the way into a radically new world," Muste explained. Advocating much more than reform, Muste and other radical pacifists refused to conform to the parameters laid down by the nation's military and political leaders. Instead, they would build a new society in the shell of the old. Though speaking from a Christian perspective, Muste sounded very much like a Deweyan pragmatist.[12]

In their early years, SANE and CNVA had a shared membership, but the former's moderation always rankled the radical pacifists. To begin with, SANE supported the Eisenhower administration's rejection of a test ban agreement that lacked preliminary inspections. CNVA members accused SANE of turning its back on grassroots activists fighting for the treaty by siding with the president. More significantly, Cousins and several other SANE board members capitulated when in May 1960 Senator Thomas Dodd, the chairman of the Senate Internal Security Subcommittee, demanded SANE close its doors to communists. Rather than oppose Dodd's witch hunt, the SANE board developed new chapter membership requirements. Appalled by SANE's red-baiting, many radical pacifists abandoned the organization. The group's obsessive anti-communism dismayed Muste, who blamed both the United States and the Soviet Union for the Cold War.[13] Still, Muste spent the remaining years of his life—he passed away in 1967—attempting to bridge the divide between liberals and radicals in search of a Third Way.

Shortly after Mills published *The Power Elite*, he became less pessimistic. Increasing calls for an end to the arms race and a relaxation of Cold War tensions prefigured the emergence of new "publics" to counter the power elite. A refreshed Mills became associated with radical pacifists in the United States and peace activists in Britain. Because of these relationships, Mills focused less on academic sociological studies and more on writing "pamphlets" for activists, including *The Causes of World War Three* and *Listen, Yankee*. The latter, published in 1960, points to the international scope of the peace movements of the late 1950s and early 1960s, especially concerning Cuba. Influenced by Latin American leftists he met during brief trips to Brazil and Mexico, Mills became enamored with Fidel Castro's Cuba and its efforts to develop a Third Way. Based on a series of interviews Mills conducted with Cuban revolutionaries while visiting the island for two weeks in 1960, *Listen, Yankee* included a collection of letters written by a fictional Cuban revolutionary. Intent on preserving Cuba as a "third force," Mills downplayed the dictatorial features of the Castro regime and dismissed the burgeoning anti-Castro campaign led by the United States in response to Cuba's close ties to the Soviet Union.[14] Mills's writings on U.S. foreign policy and Cuba found an audience with the still nascent New Left.

Of all the Cold War battlegrounds, Cuba held a special place in the hearts of leftists. While SANE remained silent about deteriorating U.S.-Cuban relations, preferring to focus on nuclear disarmament rather than U.S.

intervention abroad, radical pacifists, including Muste, Dellinger, and James Peck, formed the Non-Violent Committee for Cuban Independence. Yet even more than older pacifists, young Americans became ardent defenders of the Castro regime. Groups like the Fair Play for Cuba Committee (FPCC), which formed in the spring of 1960, instilled in the embryonic New Left the ideals of anti-imperialism and Third World solidarity. CBS reporter Robert Taber and Alan Sagner, a New Jersey contractor involved in Democratic Party politics, formed the FPCC to counter the misinformation being circulated about Cuba. The FPCC quickly gained the support of university students, especially at the University of Wisconsin, home of the journal *Studies on the Left*, an early purveyor of New Left thought. *Studies* devoted an entire issue to Cuba in late 1960 that included a lengthy editorial statement proclaiming solidarity with the Cuban revolutionaries. Under the auspices of FPCC, hundreds of students visited Castro's revolutionary Cuba before the U.S. government put a travel ban in place in 1961.[15] U.S. obsession with the tiny island of Cuba unintentionally birthed New Left internationalism, which would outlive the most recognizable New Left organization of the 1960s, Students for a Democratic Society (SDS).

By 1960, American youth had begun to awaken to the dangers of nuclear Armageddon and the stultifying existence that awaited them in adulthood. Mills noticed the change before most others. In his "Letter to the New Left," published in the British *New Left Review* in 1960, Mills excoriated liberal defenders of the "vital center," whom he called "NATO intellectuals," and appealed to the "young intelligentsia" to break free from the confines of the Cold War liberal consensus.[16] Radical pacifists also recognized the appeal of direct action protests for youthful activists. Throughout 1960 and 1961, hundreds of young protestors took part in CNVA's Polaris Action, which targeted the U.S. Navy's newest and most powerful nuclear submarine, the Polaris. Intent on boarding the watercraft, activists used makeshift boats to block the Thames River off the coast of New London, Connecticut. Others took part in leafletting, picketing, and marching in major cities, at the naval yard, and in front of the factories where the submarines were being constructed.[17] While American youth continued to flock to radical pacifist organizations like CNVA, a new organization stepped in to speak for the New Left.

SDS existed at the center of the variegated universe that made up "the movement." Alan Haber, a student at the University of Michigan, turned the Student League for Industrial Democracy, which, like its parent organization, espoused anti-communist, Cold War liberal views, including support for the labor movement and a welfare state, into SDS in 1960. That same year,

Kaufman published an essay that would have profound implications for SDS and the New Left more generally. With "Human Nature and Participatory Democracy," Kaufman, a teacher to many of the University of Michigan students involved in SDS, gave a name to the inchoate ideas developed by Goodman, Mills, and others. He argued that participatory democracy made possible "the development of human powers of thought, feeling, and action." Kaufman encouraged the creation of a participatory democracy to overcome the "pessimistic assessment of man's nature" offered by Reinhold Niebuhr and Schlesinger, both of whom questioned humankind's capacity for self-rule.[18]

Not until 1962, however, with the release of the Port Huron Statement, did American youth take notice of SDS and, consequently, Kaufman's theory of participatory democracy. The primary author of the manifesto, Tom Hayden, agreed with liberalism's goals but thought its program for obtaining them inadequate. SDS's founding document indicated a willingness to work within the political system, albeit with some modifications to its institutions. While generally in agreement with liberals, SDS sought wholesale, as opposed to piecemeal, reform.[19] The question of how to rectify the problems facing the United States led SDS to Kaufman's "participatory democracy," which, as understood by SDS, required "that decision-making of basic social consequence be carried on by public groupings" of citizens. This phrase is among the most memorable in the entire Port Huron Statement, but beyond providing a handful of "root principles," SDS struggled to offer a definition over the ensuing years.[20] Specifying the steps necessary to develop a participatory democracy fell to others, including IPS.

In 1963, SDS published "America and the New Era." Though it was written only a year after the Port Huron Statement, SDS's attitude toward liberalism underwent an appreciable transformation. Any hope that liberals might come to their senses had all but disappeared. SDS's pessimism stemmed from the realization that liberalism had come under the control of corporations, resulting in the former's growing conservatism. "America and the New Era" bemoaned the growth of "corporate liberalism," which led liberals to shun protest tactics and reject demands for substantive reforms. Eventually, New Left theorists blamed corporate liberalism for U.S. intervention abroad. *Studies on the Left* popularized the idea that further domestic liberal reform hinged on the continued control of foreign markets and resources. In refusing to disentangle liberalism from imperialism, the New Left eliminated any possibility of future collaboration between liberals and radicals.[21] These suspicions only grew as the 1960s progressed, leaving revolution as the only means to transform America.

The journal that had helped launch the reexamination of liberalism and U.S. foreign policy in 1956, *Liberation*, exemplified the partnership between radical pacifists and the New Left. SDS leaders Hayden, Paul Booth, Carl Oglesby, and Todd Gitlin all contributed to the magazine, which served as a key forum for many of the youthful activists looking to exchange ideas and strategies with radical pacifists. At the same time, *Liberation* offered older activists, such as Muste and Dellinger, a venue to promote nonviolent civil disobedience as younger protestors increasingly turned to guerrilla violence.[22] IPS's emergence in the midst of these debates meant that it too would have to declare where it stood on such consequential matters as liberalism versus radicalism, the role of intellectuals and activists, the meaning of democracy, Third World liberation movements, and the Cold War and the nuclear arms race.

The Progressive Origins of Raskin's "New Liberalism"

Raskin spent just sixteen years in his birthplace of Milwaukee, Wisconsin. Yet, it is fitting that he was raised in the state that gave birth to the "Wisconsin Idea" and in the city where "sewer socialism" developed and remained influential into the 1950s. The Wisconsin Idea tasked the American public university with carrying out two related objectives: educating the public to prepare them for the obligations of citizenship and producing knowledge for use by the government. As result, Wisconsin became known as the "laboratory of democracy." Raskin took the Wisconsin Idea very seriously. Indeed, when institutions of higher learning failed to carry out their duties during the Cold War, Raskin took it upon himself to create IPS as a stand-in for universities. The Wisconsin Idea grew out of the progressive views held by three leading figures in the history of the University of Wisconsin, two of them presidents, John Bascom and Charles Van Hise, and the other an economist, Richard T. Ely. Progressivism in Wisconsin, whether Raskin knew it or not, resembled his own views in the sense that it brought together people from different social, economic, ethnic, political, and religious groups into what one historian has described as "the new citizenship." Milwaukee socialists followed a similar strategy, speaking only rarely about economic classes and workers controlling the means of production. Such rhetoric, these "sewer socialists" understood, prevented them from working with other radicals and reformers, including progressives, seeking alternatives to revolution.[23] In short, Raskin borrowed from his progressive and socialist forebears in Wisconsin a desire to transcend divisions in search of the common good.

In 1958, one year after earning a law degree at the University of Chicago, Raskin entered the political arena, becoming a legislative assistant to several congressmen, among them Representative Kastenmeier.[24] The time spent with Kastenmeier likely had an indelible impact on Raskin's thinking about politics, intellectuals, and the Cold War. As Kastenmeier's legislative aide, Raskin met Arthur Waskow, a graduate student in history at the University of Wisconsin. In 1961, Waskow described Wisconsin Democrats in the post-McCarthy era as "one of the most idea-centered parties in the country." Sensing this change in the party, "university people, channeled by the [Robert M.] La Follette tradition of the social sciences in politics," joined the Democratic Party in droves. As a result, Waskow explained, "it was the most natural thing in the world for me to assume that Bob Kastenmeier, when he ran in 1958, could use and would want, respect, and pay attention to somebody who had firm ideas on the issues, knew how to do research on them, and would act more as an independent thinker than as someone just assigned to answer questions about data merely to dress his ideas up nicely." At the same time, Waskow continued, "it was also natural for Bob to assume that politicians should listen to scholars, not merely use them as research tools."[25] During this formative time, Waskow and Raskin received a political education that guided them for the rest of their lives. Both men carried with them the belief that all public officials would welcome the advice of an "independent thinker."

During his stint as roving legislative assistant, Raskin composed "A New Liberalism in the Democratic Party" in April 1959. Though predominant in American thought and politics, liberalism lacked "operational usefulness," according to Raskin. Consequently, he called for "a basic restatement of the meaning of liberalism," in terms of both its domestic and international components, since it was "formulated for a different time and in the face of a different kind of threat." Essentially, Raskin wanted to update liberalism so that "it applies to the social and political condition of Man in the Twentieth Century." Domestically, this meant something "broader than the kind of economic liberalism promulgated in the 1930s by the New Deal." In regard to foreign policy, Raskin argued that a new liberalism needed to move beyond the strategies developed by Dean Acheson. This meant taking into account "the political and social revolutions of rising expectations of the Twentieth Century" among the people in Asian and African nations, which he viewed as "a credible and operational alternative to communism." In short, Raskin aimed to make liberalism into an ally of insurgencies abroad. He wanted a new liberal theory to "emphasize the revolutionary character of the twentieth century" and dispel the notion that such uprisings occurred because of communist interference.[26]

With "A New Liberalism in the Democratic Party," Raskin laid bare his debt to pragmatism, which required flexibility in thinking, and his desire to see the emergence of ideological diversity and a Third Way.

Impressed with Raskin's paper, Kastenmeier organized a meeting with Democratic congressmen George Kasem, Frank Kowalski, Byron Johnson, George McGovern, William Meyer, and Charles Porter to discuss it. Formation of the Liberal Project followed shortly thereafter.[27] Explaining the rationale behind the endeavor, Kastenmeier stated, "We felt that part of the weakness of liberalism was that its older policies had grown outdated in the radically new conditions" of the 1960s. Sounding like his legislative aide Waskow, Kastenmeier compared the effort, which involved a partnership between academics and politicians, to the work conducted by economist John Commons for Robert M. La Follette Sr. during the Progressive Era.[28] Waskow later explained that this group of intellectuals and politicians intended to construct a "participatory liberalism" to counter the flawed worldview of Cold War liberals.[29]

The Liberal Papers appeared in 1962 and included essays derived from the conversations among Liberal Project members. In his introduction to the volume, Congressman James Roosevelt of California pointed to a growing disillusionment with the policies developed in the late 1950s and early 1960s, which promised only "decline and catastrophe for the United States both as a free society and first-rate world power." Roosevelt blamed a "breakdown in communication in politics between the intellectual and the politicians" for the dearth of new policies and ideas. As a result, liberals clung to concepts developed during the New Deal, repackaging them into "cliché-ridden, formalistic, and sloganized" programs.[30] Raskin shared with Roosevelt a desire to see intellectuals and politicians working in concert to rejuvenate liberalism. Vicious attacks on the Liberal Project, however, led to the endeavor being short-lived.

Using a prepublication copy of *The Liberal Papers* supplied by the Republican National Committee, Republicans in Congress, including Senator Everett Dirksen of Illinois and Representative Charles Halleck of Indiana, assailed the congressmen involved with the study. While the *New York Times* praised the book for offering "a formidable series of proposals for changing the status quo of the 'cold war,'" Republicans saw only a blueprint for U.S. appeasement. Minority leader Dirksen protested that the book "could well be renamed 'Our American Munich.'" "Chamberlain," Dirksen continued, "surely never did as much for Hitler as is proposed here under the name of liberalism to be done for Khrushchev and Mao."[31] More than two years later, the Republican

Congressional Committee Newsletter revived the campaign against *The Liberal Papers*. The newsletter agreed with previous critics who described the study as "A Blueprint for Surrender." Of all the essays in the volume, Waskow's earned special notice from Republicans, who found it "brimming over with ideas for placating the Communists."[32]

Besides leading the Liberal Project, Raskin also traveled in the same milieu as David Riesman, author of the landmark 1950 sociological study *The Lonely Crowd*. An original trustee of IPS, Riesman also served as Raskin's mentor. The future IPS cofounder took part in a March 1960 retreat at Bear Mountain Inn in New York organized by radical pacifists associated with the American Friends Service Committee. Other attendees included psychologist Erich Fromm, pacifists Muste and Stewart Meacham, and SANE's Robert Gilmore. Out of this meeting came the idea for the Committees of Correspondence. Riesman became the driving force behind the new organization. Along with Riesman, Michael Maccoby, who received a Ph.D. in social relations from Harvard in 1960, presented a paper at Bear Mountain titled "The American Crisis." Raskin liked the essay so much that he invited Riesman and Maccoby to discuss it during a Liberal Project gathering and included it in *The Liberal Papers*.[33]

Riesman and his Committees of Correspondence shared with Raskin an anti–Cold War sensibility critical of liberal Cold Warriors and liberal peace activism alike. Following the Berlin crisis in 1961, Riesman explained that he left Washington "feeling that the ex–New Dealers now in the government were like people at the court of Versailles, loving the parties and the excitement but not really worried about nuclear war." Similarly, while trying to understand the influence of Secretary of State Dean Rusk on Kennedy's foreign policy, Riesman grouped Rusk with other "bomber liberals" who used their identity as well-meaning liberals to offset their quite reactionary anti-communist views. So as not to be confused with these liberals, Riesman and Maccoby demanded modifications to America's foreign policy. They also criticized SANE's support of a partial test ban treaty as too timid and claimed that it "provided no adequate basis for a critique of American foreign policy, let alone of the domestic consequences and concomitants of that policy." Riesman intended to use the Committees of Correspondence to keep pressure on liberals to end the Cold War. The organization's initial statement of purpose, drafted during the Bear Mountain meeting, offered a far-reaching proposal involving the "destruction of thermonuclear weapons" and supported "independent American initiative." A later statement, which appeared in the *Harvard Crimson* on September 30, 1960, did not go as far but nonetheless remained committed to the idea of the United States undertaking "unilateral steps toward disarmament" as a necessary component of "tak[ing] risks in pursuit of peace."[34] Ensconced in these debates over the future of liberalism and nuclear disarmament, Raskin received a unique political education that remained with him for the rest of his life.

On the Edge of Kennedy's New Frontier

When several of the congressmen he served lost their seats in the 1960 election, Raskin began looking for a new job. Riesman recommended Raskin to Kennedy's national security advisor, McGeorge Bundy, who welcomed the addition of Raskin to his staff. "Marc Raskin has a remarkably powerful and lively mind. We shall probably have some disagreement, but I shall feel a lot better for knowing that certain problems have passed by his critical eye on their way to resolution," Bundy wrote to Riesman.[35] Republican critics, however, did not agree. As he prepared to join Bundy's staff, Raskin's past work under Kastenmeier came back to haunt him. In yet another Republican attack against *The Liberal Papers*, Representative Robert Stafford of Vermont argued that Raskin's participation in the Liberal Project made him unfit for a position involving decisions on America's national security. Stafford pointed to Raskin's "amazing record of illogical statements in the past," including publicly doubting America's ability to defeat the Soviet Union and encouraging Americans to avoid military service. According to Stafford, Raskin's position as a special staff member of the National Security Council put him "inside one of the more vital areas of our defense organization today," ostensibly allowing the fox into the Cold War henhouse.[36]

Accustomed to the free thinking encouraged in Kastenmeier's office, Raskin, to the detriment of his career, did not shy away from offering controversial advice. On his first day on the job, not long after the failed Bay of Pigs invasion, Raskin, in front of Schlesinger, Walt W. Rostow, and other top advisors, questioned Bundy about whether the United States learned any lessons from overthrowing Guatemala's Jacobo Árbenz in 1954. Not long after this, Raskin received a phone call from Bundy's assistant informing him that he no longer needed to attend staff meetings and that Bundy would meet with him personally at another time. Raskin, however, remained a thorn in Bundy's side. In a memorandum written in May 1961, Raskin called for "fundamental changes" at Guantanamo in Cuba. While he opposed closing the base, because it "would appear as an indication of weakness both at home and to the Communist world," Raskin thought the United States needed to repurpose it. "We might endeavor to turn it into a series of hospitals and technical institutions for the Cuban people, staffed by U.S. personnel. This will change the nature of the threat toward Cuba and make our presence there more palatable."[37] It did not bother Raskin that when he made these suggestions relations between the United States and Cuba were at their lowest point.

Raskin also refused to shy away from far-reaching proposals on matters pertaining to nuclear disarmament. Even as he lamented the likely difficulties associated with reaching agreement on such issues, Raskin recommended undertaking a "completely new and bold policy" to create an atmosphere more conducive to disarmament. He had in mind "the initiation of unilateral acts of a *tension reducing nature.*" Raskin did not consider unilateral disarmament a radical approach. As he saw it, both superpowers had unilaterally increased their nuclear stockpiles, so why not do the same but in reverse. Nor did he consider his plan utopian. "The real *idealists* are those who actually believe that the arms race can be conducted indefinitely without something going wrong, who actually believe that the men behind the nuclear weapons are super-rational and will behave just like so many computers," Raskin proclaimed.[38]

Writing to Bundy and Deputy National Security Advisor Carl Kaysen after participating in a series of meetings between delegates from seventeen nations to discuss nuclear disarmament, Raskin advised against taking part in subsequent multination talks. The resumption of nuclear tests by the United States and the Soviet Union meant that any future conference would involve "group breast beating on nuclear testing and recrimination by others against the United States." In place of the seventeen-nation talks, Raskin recommended that representatives from the United States and the Soviet Union meet privately, or else "the disarmament discussions will continue on a ritualistic and propaganda basis." At the same time, successful bilateral negotiations necessitated "getting rid of some of our pet shibboleths," as Raskin phrased it in an earlier memorandum. Improving relations with the Soviet Union required a realistic assessment of America's rival, "rather than thinking of it as some kind of Leviathan" intent on global domination. A more accurate portrayal of the Soviet Union would show that the nation faced economic difficulties and struggled to spread its communist ideology. Raskin concluded with a warning, stating that "the notion of standing fast is the notion of the dinosaur; the world changes, problems become more complex, but the dinosaur, unable to adjust himself, destroyed himself."[39] Here, in nascent form, is the pragmatism that guided both Raskin and IPS for the remainder of the Cold War.

During his time on the National Security Council staff, moreover, Raskin implored Kennedy, through Bundy, to listen to the anti-nuclear protestors. When the Student Peace Union (SPU) picketed in front of the White House in November 1961, Kennedy sent out his disarmament advisors to converse with the students. The following February, SPU organized a "Washington Action" protest that brought five thousand concerned Americans to the Capitol. Writing just prior to the February SPU action, Raskin tried to persuade his superiors to take the student protestors seriously. "To some extent the way this group will be treated by the Administration will decide whether this group and others like it will take a more violent turn," Raskin wrote to Bundy. He also suggested that public protests might give Kennedy "greater flexibility in foreign policy matters in ways he otherwise feels he might not have." As a result, Raskin believed the administration had "something to learn from these people" and wholeheartedly recommended that the protestors be "treated courteously, with sensitivity, with understanding" by all government officials.[40] Here is evidence that the faith in the American people that Raskin and so many other intellectuals at IPS exhibited throughout the entire period of this study predated the construction of the institute.

Within a year, Raskin's controversial views led to his ostracization. In an April 1962 memorandum to the president, Bundy referred to Raskin, in jest, as a "young menace," though "a good staff officer in spite of—and perhaps partly because of—his insistent effort to find ways of making progress in this most unpromising field" of disarmament. Amid the continuing uproar over Raskin's role in *The Liberal Papers*, Bundy refused to bow to pressure to remove his embattled aide. However, constant bickering between Kaysen and Raskin eventually led to the latter being sent to the Bureau of the Budget. In recommending Raskin for a grant from the Carnegie Corporation, Bundy acknowledged that "his [Raskin's] views would not be yours and mine" but nevertheless praised his former staff member. "He did very lively, brilliant and energetic work for me," Bundy explained, "but in the course of this effort it became clear that he was much too independent and determined in his own ways of thinking to be a perfect staff man so I let him go to Budget."[41] Though not surprised by his excommunication, Raskin likely felt disappointed that Bundy, unlike Kastenmeier, discouraged free thinking.

Meanwhile, Raskin's future collaborator, Barnet, also gained the attention of Kennedy officials. After earning a law degree from Harvard University in 1954, Barnet served as a U.S. Army officer in Europe in the Judge Advocate General's Corps from 1955 to 1957. Following a three-year stint at a private law firm, Barnet became a fellow at the Harvard Russian Research Center in

1960. From 1961 until 1963 he held the position of special assistant for disarmament in the State Department.[42] As a fellow at the Russian Research Center, Barnet studied disarmament issues, which led to the publication in 1960
of *Who Wants Disarmament?*

Seeking to understand why the various attempts to achieve disarmament
foundered after World War II, Barnet refused to lay the blame solely on the
Soviet Union and exonerate the United States. For Barnet, the rejection of
the Baruch Plan, a 1946 U.S. proposal regarding the regulation of nuclear
energy, represented an important juncture in the history of disarmament
negotiations. According to Barnet, both superpowers were responsible for
the failure to reach an agreement, though he understood the Soviet Union's
reluctance. He surmised that Stalin likely realized that rejecting the proposal
would not lead to "ultimatums or a rain of bombs, but unending debate."
After all, the United States had demobilized its armed forces in 1946, opening
the door for the Soviet Union to expand into Europe. Thus, Stalin had no
incentive to agree to the proposal. Moreover, Barnet considered the Baruch
Plan extremely one-sided in favor of the United States. It was "designed to
be a riskless adventure" for America, according to Barnet. Besides allowing
the United States to increase the size of its nuclear arsenal, the plan required
"economic control by a group of capitalist nations" and used "moralistic talk"
about punishing countries that refused inspection. For all its faults, Barnet
still considered the Baruch Plan significant since it represented "the only
time in the post-war period when the American government seriously considered giving up its nuclear stockpiles."[43]

Instead of looking for ways to rid the world of nuclear weapons, Barnet accused the United States of hindering disarmament efforts in the 1950s.
For instance, when the Soviet Union conditionally accepted a 1954 plan put
forth by the French and British linking disarmament to conventional troop
reductions, the United States suddenly lost interest in ending the arms race.
In fact, beginning in 1956, it sought "ways to reduce the peculiar danger of
modern weapons rather than the means to eliminate them entirely."[44] By the
1960s, arms control replaced disarmament as the goal of officials in Washington and Moscow. Although quite critical of the United States in his studies, Barnet gained the attention of John J. McCloy, one of the foreign policy
establishment's Wise Men and a disarmament advisor for Kennedy. As an
aide to McCloy, Barnet helped set up the Arms Control and Disarmament
Agency (ACDA). He no doubt hoped that the agency might breathe new life
into general and complete disarmament, but disappointment awaited Barnet.

A Think Tank for a "New Liberalism"

As Waskow joined the staff of the Peace Research Institute (PRI) in Washington, D.C., and Raskin took a position on Bundy's staff, the two remained in contact. Meanwhile, Barnet, working at the ACDA, participated in various conferences and meetings at PRI and recommended an ACDA grant for PRI to conduct a study on an international police force. Barnet and Raskin became acquainted during a meeting led by McCloy with State Department officials and military leaders, among others. During the discussion, McCloy apparently remarked, "If this group cannot bring about disarmament, then no one can," which led to Barnet and Raskin exchanging skeptical glances.[45] With Waskow's PRI struggling to keep its doors open due to fundraising shortfalls and Barnet and Raskin disenchanted with Kennedy's New Frontier, their future remained uncertain. According to Waskow, Raskin acted as the "spark" that ignited discussion about forming a new institute in Washington, D.C.[46]

IPS opened its doors on November 3, 1963. Its founding trustees were Riesman, Barnet, and Raskin, with the latter two also serving as codirectors. The IPS board of trustees included Thurman Arnold, a former judge on the Court of Appeals known for his strong antitrust views; David F. Cavers, professor of law at Harvard; Hans J. Morgenthau, professor of political science at the University of Chicago; Steven Muller, director of the Center for International Studies at Cornell University; Gerard Piel, publisher of the *Scientific American*; Freeman Dyson, physicist at the Institute for Advanced Study in Princeton, New Jersey; James Dixon, president of Antioch College; financier James P. Warburg; and Philip Stern, a Democratic Party activist and heir to the Sears, Roebuck fortune.[47]

Shortly after SDS's 1962 national convention, in a prospectus for IPS sent to the president of Haverford College, Raskin offered a portrait of America that mirrored the one found in SDS's Port Huron Statement. The cofounder of IPS impugned government officials for exhibiting a "paralysis of will, imagination and energy, a fatalistic conviction and assumption that nothing much can be done, an acceptance of the belief that to live is to be imprisoned." Raskin observed that a "philosophy of nihilism . . . serves as a backdrop for those who would rather shirk their social responsibilities than accept them." He painted IPS as a curative. The proposed institute would carry out a broad investigation of existing domestic and foreign policies, looking at the ways in which they overlapped, and develop new programs and structures meant to "encourage the ethic of individual responsibility in group or social action" that the current environment lacked. Beyond these tasks, Raskin envisioned IPS as a center for "a kind of education which will not only arouse people's concern for public problems, but show them how their intellectual training bears on the solution of these problems." Analyzing government policies and programs, formulating alternative plans and strategies, and educating citizens to play a greater role in governance remained central features of IPS's outlook.[48]

The prospectus also castigated existing think tanks. It referred to the intellectuals at these institutions as "men [who] live by grace of the individuals or departments they advise, and therefore tend to confine their criticism and suggestions to making existing policy more 'efficient,' in terms of already accepted objectives. Their advice is almost always technical and procedural, and rarely ethical and substantial."[49] In contrast, IPS prided itself on its autonomy, which allowed it to offer moral rather than technical solutions to America's problems. Raskin's hostility toward think tanks like the RAND Corporation stemmed from a deeply held belief that intellectual independence and government funding were incompatible.[50] His suspicions were valid. For instance, in the twelve years preceding debate over the antiballistic missile (ABM) system in 1968, the Pentagon spent $4.5 billion for research conducted by think tanks. In the end, the intellectuals at these institutes helped government officials justify the ABM system. To protect against a similar outcome for IPS, the codirectors put a clause in the IPS bylaws prohibiting the think tank and its fellows from accepting government funds. As a result, Paul Dickson includes IPS among a group of "truly independent, nonprofit, self-determining think tanks" with "clients" coming from various "publics" rather than from the government.[51]

Raskin received tremendous pushback from the heads of other think tanks, which only strengthened his resolve to go ahead with his plans for IPS. Not ignorant of the likely obstacles that lay ahead, Raskin met with officials from the Brookings Institution, a leading Washington, D.C., think tank. During the meeting, Robert Calkins, the president of Brookings, worried about oversaturation. He claimed that existing institutions already lacked "adequate financing, adequate manpower and none of which felt it was able to do an adequate job." With these difficulties in mind, Calkins suggested that Raskin and his colleagues scrap their plans and join Brookings, or another think tank. In an addendum to the minutes of the meeting, Barnet and Robert B. Livingston of the National Institute of Mental Health described Calkins as "positively frightened by the competition," a fear that stemmed from the Brookings Institution's "definitely lesser quality of personnel and product." Barnet and Livingston offered a harsh appraisal of the research coming out of

Brookings, describing its reports as "a description of the state of affairs written in conspicuous detail but without much evaluation." In a letter to Hallock Hoffman of the Center for the Study of Democratic Institutions in California, Raskin characterized Brookings as "not first rate" since it offered only "minor alterations" or "procedural criticisms" and refused to look for "possible alternatives."[52] Calkins's counsel, therefore, served as additional proof for IPS's cofounder of the timid approach of existing think tanks.

As Raskin gauged the interest of educators and intellectuals about a new institute, he and a group of his closest associates took the initial steps toward making IPS a reality. According to Waskow, these early conversations envisioned IPS as a "home for the kind of learning that I had in Kastenmeier's office, or that Raskin had from Bundy's office." (Waskow crossed out this sentence in his draft of the letter.) IPS would conduct "research in the basic problems of policy formation in the present world crisis, using Washington as a laboratory of sorts." Besides taking part in policy research, students would have the opportunity to work in congressional offices, lobby for groups such as SANE, or serve in executive offices.[53]

It is worth noting that several of the figures initially involved with IPS had previously worked as congressional aides or as lower-level bureaucrats. In a letter asking the historian C. Vann Woodward to join IPS as a visiting fellow, Waskow described himself and the other architects of IPS as "a league of frightened men." These early IPS supporters, Waskow wrote, had "all been close enough to the government to realize how unable it is to examine itself or its policies clearly or carefully, and how impossible any change in direction will be without such a basic re-examination."[54] The past political experiences of the founders make it all the more remarkable that these men felt that IPS could have a meaningful effect on government officials.

The Intellectual and Activist as One: The Public Scholar at IPS

Though IPS was classified as a think tank, the intellectuals at the institute vehemently rejected this label. Much of the work undertaken at IPS involved developing new theories. At the same time, inspired by the likes of Dewey, the institute formulated ideas not just for government officials but for the citizenry as well. IPS intellectuals assessed an idea based on its relevance to society and the possibilities it offered for the reconstruction of America. Simply put, IPS did not want to replicate the stuffy and staid atmosphere of universities or follow the lead of think tanks that formulated ideas tailored to the needs of their sponsors. Nonetheless, IPS's ambiguous relationship with liberal politicians greatly added to the institute's difficulties as it sought to devise a course of action that straddled the line between offering policy advice to officials in Washington and bringing ideas directly to the people.

IPS, not surprisingly, held defense intellectuals in low esteem. Raskin, in a *New York Review of Books* essay, set off a debate by labeling social scientists and other intellectuals working at the behest of the federal government "megadeath intellectuals." Discussing the growth in government-funded military-related research among university professors, Raskin claimed that "their most important function is to justify and extend the existence of their employers." As nuclear weapons replaced conventional armies, Raskin argued that "military and industrial leaders needed some kind of theory to rationalize their use" and make nuclear war "a practical enterprise which could serve the political ends of the state." He denounced scholars who made their services available to the government, not only defending nuclear war but also drawing up nuclear strategies. According to Raskin, only by "examining the motives of the men" involved in defense-related research could the conversation on arms control begin. "A useful arms debate," he explained, "can take place only when we are willing to recognize who is capable of thinking independently and who is not, and why."[55] There was no doubt in Raskin's mind that the "megadeath intellectuals" lacked the critical distance necessary to speak truth to power and seek a nuclear-free society.

Raskin received immediate blowback for his portrayal of nuclear strategists as "megadeath intellectuals." Albert Wohlstetter, an influential defense intellectual in his own right, chided Raskin for his "self-righteous chiliasm," especially his division of the academic community into the virtuous and the wicked. Raskin's attempt to distinguish the "good guys" from the "large conspiracy of the insane, the insincere and the impure, worthy not of refutation but only of exposure," did not hold up to scrutiny, Wohlstetter claimed. As proof, he pointed to scholars like Jerome Wiesner and George Kistiakowsky, who "consulted" or "advised" the military or "had investments of their own in defense industry" yet still spoke out against the arms race. Wohlstetter refused to believe that defense intellectuals formulated strategies for nuclear war solely as a cover for America's expanding nuclear arsenals. "This fantasy," he claimed, "has all the veracity of the Protocols of Zion and rather less than that of De la Hodde's conspiratorial *Histoire des Sociétés Secrètes*."[56]

Regardless of such criticism, IPS sought to distinguish itself from think tanks filled with Raskin's "megadeath intellectuals" and serve as a base for peace research. IPS came onto the scene amid a movement to make social science a tool for peace rather than war. In 1954 the Ford Foundation provided the seed money for an interdisciplinary research lab at Stanford University, the Center for Advanced Study in the Behavioral Sciences (CASBS). At the CASBS, psychologists, economists, biologists, mathematicians, and political scientists aimed to prove that the same quantitative methods used to support a war system could prepare the way to peace. Kenneth Boulding, an economist who spent a year at the CASBS, met with other fellows to discuss the possibility of a new journal devoted to peace research. Out of this initial conversation came the idea for the *Journal of Conflict Resolution*. The first issue of the new journal, which was housed at the University of Michigan, appeared in the spring of 1957. Two years later, in 1959, the university became the home of the Center for Research on Conflict Resolution. These early efforts laid the groundwork for myriad other peace research institutes and journals in the United States and around the globe, including the Peace Research Institute in Washington, D.C., the predecessor to IPS.[57]

Not everyone agreed that peace researchers differed all that much from defense intellectuals. One critic, for example, argued that the former "created an informal but nevertheless useful counterweight in government circles to the New Civilian Militarists and their more saber-rattling allies" but remained an appendage of the establishment. In trying to impress political leaders, peace researchers ignored the average citizen. The critic accused peace researchers of speaking for the "masses" instead of allowing them "to intervene themselves, as people." Concerned with "helping the elite adjust the system," peace researchers tended to hide "the real roots of international conflict" and thus prevented disarmament, the commentator argued.[58]

Waskow set out to disprove such allegations. In the process, he revealed how IPS intended to distinguish itself from traditional think tanks. Referring to peace researchers, Waskow wrote that "these men do not think that just because they have refused to be whores of the Establishment they must undergo a shotgun wedding with one or another revolutionary party. Most peace researchers are not prepared to mouth anyone's slogans. They demand to find out." To show how peace research "would be made useful," Waskow described the techniques used by scholars in the field. After developing a theory or hypothesis, peace researchers turned to "model-building" and "small-group research" to gauge the likely response by officials to possible crises. Researchers then placed these models alongside historical events that mirrored the circumstances of the model to determine the likely success of the hypothetical plan. Once researchers obtained "considerably higher confidence" in their hypothesis, they could then begin "action experiments" in a much-reduced scale. Following a successful trial run, it would then be "politically and intellectually possible to create new world policies." This process ensured that peace researchers abstained from supporting revolutionary proposals fashionable at any given moment.[59] In other words, while IPS would not grovel before the government, neither would it pander to activists seeking scholarly approval for outlandish ideas. Additionally, Waskow's description of "action experiments" highlighted how he and IPS intended to present their ideas to the public.

References to practicality and real-world applicability pepper the work and correspondence of almost every intellectual at IPS. This aspect of IPS makes classification of the institute as a think tank problematical. Intent on not becoming a collection of academics isolated from society, IPS wanted its ideas to transcend seminar rooms. In fact, IPS intellectuals did not care if other scholars found their work stimulating. All that truly mattered was whether their ideas found traction in society and resulted in concrete change. Writing in 1968, Waskow made a strong case for what differentiated IPS from other think tanks. IPS was "committed to the idea that to develop social theory one must be involved in social action and in social experiment. And therefore, the institute stands on the bare edge of custom in the United States as to what an educational research institution is, as against what a political institution is. By standing on that bare edge, it creates tension." In other words, Waskow did not believe that theory could exist on its own. Rather, once formulated, it had to undergo experimentation to see if it stood up to reality. By carrying out its research in such a way, IPS dissociated itself from other institutes. As a result, "rather than going to universities and arguing for it, rather than going into foundations and suggesting that they set up study committees to create, we *did* it." Once academics and politicians witnessed how IPS's ideas played out in real-world situations, they would have no choice but to accept the proposals put forth by the institute, Waskow claimed.[60] Moreover, using small-scale experiments to test their ideas protected IPS intellectuals from charges of utopianism.

Existing at "the bare edge," IPS proudly stood apart from other think tanks. Waskow, as an example, held the label itself in disdain, claiming years later that it made IPS "mad" to be classified as such. "The think tanks were political, very political," he remarked, and "they were all in [the] service of the government," whether Brookings on the Left or the Hudson Institute on the Right. Conversely, at IPS, Waskow explained, "we were not dependent on the government, we would not take money from the government. We were critical of the government and our constituency was basically the people, the Movement even more than the people."[61] While such blanket statements necessarily circumscribe the activities of think tanks, the fact that Waskow and his colleagues felt the way they did goes a long way in explaining why IPS distanced itself from these other research institutes.

The peace intellectuals at IPS believed strongly in the pragmatic ideal, ever conscious of the need to keep ideas in the realm of probability. Detailing IPS's approach to "institutional reconstruction," Barnet pointed to the construction of alternative institutions as the first step toward changing America. Once the public saw the benefits of the new structures, support would follow. In Barnet's opinion, without "public support for an alternative vision I see no way of enlisting the political strength to unseat the obstructionists in Congress or to change the rules under which they perpetuate the collapsing status quo." Taking ideas from the page and making them real prevented intellectuals from developing outlandish theories with no practical application. Waskow argued that "if one imports into the present an image of the future so threateningly alien that it is not allowed to persist more than a week and a half, then one is not likely to have done much to change the future." This does not sound like a revolutionary seeking the destruction of America. Rather, Waskow's thinking resonated with Deweyan pragmatism. In fact, Waskow claimed that his strategy was "like the process of science at its best: hypothesis, experiment, new hypothesis—always knowing that no theory is 'the truth,' but only a useful and beautiful way of understanding and reshaping the complex reality." A 1968 promotional statement described IPS as "try[ing] to be radical in perceiving the need for change, visionary in conceiving alternatives to present policy, and practical in developing alternatives."[62] Pragmatism guided IPS intellectuals and kept the institute from straying too far from the American grain.

To contest the gloomy predictions and doomsday scenarios prepared by the "megadeath intellectuals," IPS became a haven for "public scholars." Speaking before the Senate Subcommittee on Constitutional Rights in 1971, Barnet distinguished the "public scholar" at IPS from other kinds of researchers. "He is a trained observer and analyst of the operations of government who communicates his findings to the public," Barnet explained. Not working directly for the government or relying on funding from the government, the public scholar's "constituency is not the government itself." Nor did the public scholar speak primarily to other academics. Instead, he or she sought "to make available to all citizens information helpful to them in making up their own minds on critical public questions," Barnet told the senators.[63]

Barnet considered this task of great importance, especially as the problems facing society became more perplexing and difficult for ordinary citizens to understand. Reminding the subcommittee of the founding fathers' insistence that America have a protected free press, Barnet claimed that public scholars sustained journalism. As domestic and foreign affairs became more complex, public scholars could use their deep wellspring of knowledge to keep the public informed. "The operations of government have become so vast, the issues so intertwined that the investigative reporter with a daily headline cannot adequately serve the public's right to know," Barnet told the subcommittee.[64] IPS clearly wanted to influence the thinking of government officials, but intellectuals at IPS felt they had a duty to educate the public and bolster their ability to make informed decisions as citizens.

At the same time, IPS saw itself acting as an intermediary between government officials and activists. As IPS critic Joshua Muravchik astutely observed, the institute served "as a bridge between radicalism and the liberal establishment." IPS's cofounders acknowledged as much, explaining in 1965 that "it is the Institute's task to create those alternatives [to revolution] while serving as the link between the most disaffected and disadvantaged parts of the society and the highest levels of government." In 1966, Waskow happily reported that two columnists from the mainstream press described IPS as "the intellectual arsenal of the New Left" while a student activist called the institute "the vanguard of the status quo." He felt "proud of them both."[65] For IPS intellectuals, statements such as these served as proof of the institute's complete independence.

While cognizant of the need to seek alliances with politicians and grass-roots activists to remain relevant, the cofounders always cautioned against the institute becoming too close to either. Barnet and Raskin repeatedly made it clear that they did not want the tail, or social movements, to wag the dog, meaning IPS. During a "needs assessment" meeting in 1986, Raskin described IPS as "an island of freedom in the movements of the past two decades," continually making itself available to activists. He pointed to "Aristotle's Academy, the Frankfurt Institute in Weimar Germany, which failed because it didn't really relate effectively to society." Nonetheless, Raskin referred to a "tension between critical engagement and critical distance from those movements [that] will continue to be before us." During an interview conducted in the late 1990s, Raskin reiterated this point. He explained that "we viewed ourselves as not being of the movement, not being part of any particular movement." With an eye toward the future, he described social movements as temporary "fashions" that changed with the times. And while IPS supported various causes, the institute's survival mattered most at the end of the day. He argued that "you have to find a way of protecting them [IPS and other institutes], so that in fact those movements, and ones to come in the future, will have a place to be." Barnet agreed, claiming that "the independence of the institute was the most critical factor" in deciding how to relate to the various campaigns. "If we were part of the movements, or 'serving' the movements, we would be hurting the institute, and ultimately we would be hurting the movement."[66] In the end, as the protests died down, IPS remained to fight the next battle.

Still, particularly in the 1960s, the codirectors faced a lot of pressure to relinquish all ties to policymakers in favor of "the people." Writing in the mid-1960s, Robb Burlage, a member of SDS prior to joining IPS, expressed concern "about making practical proposals to government without their emerging from and relative to political movement." Burlage advised against working too closely with the government, claiming that IPS's most innovative ideas resulted from close contact with activists. IPS needed the support of movement people because, Burlage asserted, "without feet, ideas become the rhetoric of co-optation." Moreover, Burlage offered an early word of caution against IPS becoming too intellectual and losing touch with everyday people. "We must declare our purpose to be the study and demonstration of the policy of publics, not Public Policy in the old, clogged, established channels which are at best only potential arenas if they relate to the people not vice versa," Burlage explained. Another former SDSer, Don McKelvey, agreed with Burlage, writing in 1966 that "organizing people is more important than peddling ideas."[67]

IPS struggled to maintain its critical edge while still remaining relevant in the halls of power. In its early years, according to a 1987 discussion memo, IPS was "founded on the theory that ideas have their own legs, that challenging perspectives would draw interest and energy from liberal legislators and executive officers." The emergence of various social movements in the 1960s caused additional problems. IPS had to achieve a balance between serving as policy advisors to government officials and carrying out its role as the people's think tank. IPS "became a bridge between the demands of citizen movements and Washington." Karl Hess explained the unique space IPS filled by imagining how the institute might have conducted itself during America's revolutionary era: "If this were 1773, and the city were Boston, the Institute would be holding a seminar on British Imperialism. There would be tables and charts to show the injustice of the tax on tea. Probably some-body from the Governor's office would be invited. Then, independent of the Institute, six or seven of the fellows would go out and dump a shipload of tea into Boston Harbor."[68] IPS largely succeeded in balancing the demands of its diverse audience; both politicians and activists streamed through the institute's doors.

IPS's Uneasy Relationship with Liberalism

Attempting to define liberalism is no easy task; classifying IPS is nearly as difficult. That said, the institute shared many characteristics with Kaufman's "radical liberal."[69] Kaufman believed that the radicals of the 1960s had gone too far in their denunciation of liberalism, so he set out to show these crit-ics its radical character. "For the need to deepen and enrich the quality of the democratic process, to make it both more deliberative and more participatory flows directly from the central doctrines of liberalism," Kaufman declared.[70] At the same time, he found the current incarnation of liberalism distasteful and lacking in radicalism. As a fix he suggested implementation of the programs liberal politicians had promised but never delivered. Despite "rhetoric" to the contrary, liberals supported an "illiberal allocation of America's vast resources" and an "illiberal use of America's vast power."[71] Put simply, Kaufman believed that liberal politicians had drained liberalism of its most radical components by advocating programs contrary to the tenets of the liberal creed.

Kaufman realized that the transformation of liberalism required outside pressure from activists willing to work within the system in an oppositional manner. He dismissed "the politics of self-indulgence" favored by many in the New Left because "in rejecting the system he also forfeits access to insti-tutional resources which he must control if liberal ideals are to be effectively pursued. Thus, he sacrifices the prospects of political success for the sake of his soul." Why did he describe the movement's desire for "authenticity" as a form of "self-indulgence"? Kaufman argued that "even if loss of authenticity were the inevitable result of the calculation and compromise that effective action requires, damage to one's self ought to be balanced against the resulting sacrifices imposed on others."[72] IPS shared with the New Left a yearning for authenticity, but this did not preclude involvement in politics.[73]

The quite different reaction to the 1964 Free Speech Movement at UC-Berkeley by IPS trustee Riesman and the institute's peace intellectuals helps to demonstrate further the latter's ability to straddle liberalism and radicalism.

Riesman never wavered in his belief in the system's ability to respond to reasoned analysis from critical voices, which explains why he devoted so much time to the Committees of Correspondence. Yet, when the "creative tension," as Daniel Geary has described it, between liberalism and radicalism veered out of control, as it did during the free speech protests in 1964, Riesman disavowed the New Left.[74] IPS responded to the uprising at Berkeley in an entirely different manner. Three peace intellectuals from the institute visited the campus to speak to different parts of the university community. Christopher Jencks, an expert on educational issues, received an invitation from Clark Kerr, the president of the University of California system, to "brief the trustees, the regents, and upper administration folks." The student government called on Waskow to give a talk. Meanwhile, Goodman spoke before the Free Speech Movement protestors. "So there were these three levels of different political brands, you might say," Waskow later remembered.[75] During the 1960s, at least, the liberal establishment, students, and radical activists all looked to IPS as the voice of reason.

The New Left flocked to IPS. Writing in 1965, Riesman, who considered IPS "a center for discussion and influence among the young radical students," pointed to Goodman's name as being "magic" among the younger crowd. In his opinion, the institute appealed to student radicals because many at IPS were "close enough in outlook to the radical and dissident young to evoke their responsiveness" but also "help educate the young beyond some of the naïve paranoias they now hold about American society." Of all the fellows, Riesman surmised, Waskow had "a real feeling for the young people and close ties with them while, at the same time, he is more scholarly and detached." According to Waskow, Raskin and Barnet were "more outside the new left" than others at IPS, which explains their reluctance to align the institute with the various activist organizations in the 1960s and 1970s.[76]

Though "corporate liberalism" already permeated SDS by 1963, not all liberals came under such intense scrutiny. In 1966, journalist Jack Newfield, who himself had taken part in antiwar and civil rights protests, wrote *A Prophetic Minority*, which provided a portrait of the New Left, and liberalism, midway through the decade. In it, he described "humanist liberals," among whom he included IPS intellectuals, as "improvisational pragmatists" less beholden to Marxist theory and not as "anti-American" and fatalistic as certain elements of the New Left. Humanist liberals sought to maintain a critical distance from the New Left. Consequently, the former "retained enough of its own rationalistic identity to see the flaws of the new movements with piercing clarity." At the same time, Newfield suggested that IPS existed "midway between the

insurgent movements themselves and the Establishment." From such a position, humanist liberals did not vilify liberals, leaving the door open for future
collaboration.[77]

Given the shared humanist sensibilities between IPS and student activists, it should come as no surprise that SDSers sought refuge at the institute.
Inquiring about the possibility of joining IPS for the fall of 1964, Tom Hayden
confessed that he knew little about the institute except the writings of certain
fellows but nonetheless liked "that it creates a new role opportunity for intellectuals to become involved in the process of social change while maintaining critical independence." SDS's president, Todd Gitlin, wrote to Raskin in
1964 asking for a recent article written by the codirector on the Vietnam War.
Gitlin promised wide coverage of Raskin's piece since "we [SDS] have better
access to the campus than almost all other student organizations, maybe all."
That same year, SDS invited Raskin to speak at the organization's annual convention. Gitlin's successor as SDS president, Paul Potter, wrote to Waskow in
1965 suggesting that IPS and SDS jointly sponsor an institute in the summer
for SDS members. Potter envisioned a sort of radical summer school with
IPS intellectuals as teachers. Several other SDS members inquired about joining IPS's student program as well. In March 1966, Lee Webb, past national
secretary of SDS, wrote to Waskow to say that he "would very much like"
to become a student at IPS. Describing the letter as his "formal application,"
Webb told Waskow that IPS appealed to him because the fellows and students were "complementary and stimulating" and the institute allowed free
thinking.[78] Thus, as IPS's founders had hoped, a close relationship developed
between the institute and American youth.

IPS's Third Way: Social Reconstruction

IPS objected to liberalism because of its authoritarian and undemocratic features. Raskin castigated liberal "reformers" for looking at "the world as something to make over and believed that they had the power, the will and the right
to do so." In the process, they remade the world in the image of the United
States.[79] Raskin noticed a similar dynamic taking place within the United
States. He claimed that a form of internal colonization precluded the development of a truly democratic society. As he explained during a 1971 interview on
Pacifica Radio, "What I have in mind is taking the geographic notion that is that
we go abroad to colonize others and moving it internally in the United States
structurally so that people see" how even "leaders" had their lives structured

by external forces.[80] Raskin's hierarchical pyramid included four "colonies." The Violence Colony turned citizens into "hostages" as nuclear war threatened humankind and a select few political and military leaders controlled the levers of power. America's economic system represented a Plantation Colony in which large businesses and corporations determined the type of work people did. At a very young age, people came to accept colonization due to the Channeling Colony, by which Raskin meant the educational system, and the Dream Colony, in which media, particularly television, encouraged placid acceptance of the status quo.[81]

Raskin and IPS had several tools at their disposal to begin the dismantling of the pyramidal state. One approach involved the application of the pragmatic method, but Raskin, pointing to Dewey's paradoxical support for World War I, explained that undoing the pyramidal state required a new knowledge, both more humane and less reliant on existing scientific and technological tools.[82] Nor could Marxism offer a way out of the pyramidal structures constructed by "liberal authoritarians." Raskin considered it folly to "stay enamored of the Soviet system or other socialisms which assert that a revolution of social relationships has occurred, when all that has happened is that those within one country assign themselves the name of commissar and those in another call themselves manager."[83] Writing about the Soviet dissident Aleksandr Solzhenitsyn, Raskin stated, "If socialism is to be a progressive social formation, it must consolidate the gains of past revolutions, not bury them." In the Soviet Union, Raskin wrote, "practical politics and revolutionary program, the Higher Principle, took the place of natural and decent feelings." Thus, socialism committed the same transgressions as democratic capitalism by denying a place at the table for humane values. Claiming that "Solzhenitsyn has thrown down the gauntlet to the world's Left," Raskin implored leftists to support the Soviet dissident's efforts because "he acts as an artist who is the custodian of the chain of our inner humanitarian spirit." If pragmatism, Marxism, and socialism lacked the attributes necessary to overcome "liberal authoritarianism," what then?

Unsatisfied with existing theories, Raskin developed a new philosophy that promised to preserve an individual's humane qualities while also promoting democracy. The IPS cofounder favored combining the philosophies of Dewey and Jean-Paul Sartre into a single theory Raskin called existential pragmatism. He described Sartre as being involved in a search for a third way, neither socialism nor capitalism, where democracy existed without crushing the "individual." Moreover, whereas Marxism focused too heavily on class and the role of intellectuals as the vanguard of workers, existential pragmatism,

Raskin wrote, "assumes the humanness of all within the situation and the pain of all within it."[84] While existentialism tended to favor individualism and solitary acts of rebellion, there also existed a more outward form known as existential humanism, which transcended the inner-directed individual working to change himself or herself. As evidenced by Sartre's arguments in "Existentialism Is a Humanism," the very act of changing oneself required an understanding of how such actions would lead to a larger societal transformation. Raskin agreed with such an interpretation, arguing that Sartre's individualism did not mean isolation from the larger community and society. "Where freedom is not linked to the group, it is transformed into a subjective feeling of being alone and lost. Sartre understood the danger that in modern societies freedom can deteriorate into oceanic loneliness," Raskin wrote in 1980.[85]

Beyond theoretical considerations, what did social reconstruction look like in practice? In his 1971 magnum opus, *Being and Doing*, Raskin explained how to overcome the "liberal authoritarianism" that created the multilayered colonizing arrangement within the United States. Social reconstruction involved "the initiation of projects, social inventions, analysis and a new political party that will reconstruct the body politic in a nonhierarchic direction with shared authority." The most important instrument for Raskin was the "project," which served as the mechanism through which the colonized achieved freedom. Predicated on the idea that a reconstructed society required "horizontal, interdependent relationships," projects represented a series of experiments undertaken by individuals at their own initiative. To avoid taking on the characteristics of the colonized society, however, projects needed to remain committed to democratic decision making and equity between the various groups involved. Raskin offered several examples of projects, including food cooperatives, alternative schools, and even the aforementioned Liberal Project. Despite the pyramidal structures in the United States, Raskin argued that "the colonies are not in such a way so overwhelming that they cannot begin to be moved aside, that they themselves are not beginning to collapse little by little, which then always develops new space."[86]

Unlike revolutionaries who promised radical change overnight, IPS's more pragmatic social reconstruction required patience. As Jencks explained in a 1971 "Reconstruction Project" proposal, "A major transformation which makes society significantly more humane, more egalitarian, more participatory, and less expansionist will take at least a generation."[87] Readers of Raskin's treatise on social reconstruction understood as much. Famed economist John Kenneth Galbraith described Raskin as a Fabian, in reference to a British democratic socialist organization, though "even the Fabians would regard him as very gradual, perhaps unduly so." The pragmatism that undergirded IPS's activism required experimentation over time, which revolutionary thinking did not have the patience for and thus did not allow. Yet this begs the question: Did Raskin's theory of social reconstruction differ all that much from liberal reform? Several commentators pointed to a resemblance between the two. A review in the *New Republic* suggested that *Being and Doing* would be "comforting" to liberals seeking incremental and slow-paced reform.[88] While the means employed in pursuit of social reconstruction appeared identical to those used by "liberal reformers," the ends desired by IPS differed greatly. Whereas liberals accepted the pyramidal society, IPS sought its replacement with a participatory democracy.

Given that liberal authoritarianism gave rise to the colonization of America, it should come as no surprise that Raskin and IPS left no place in their blueprint for liberals. According to Raskin, the "liberal reformer" did not possess the necessary perspective to tear down the pyramidal structures. "The liberal reformer in the United States assumes that the basic hierarchic structure of the society is correct," he wrote. Thus, liberals denied the need for systemic change, preferring instead "adjustments" developed by "the mandarin class of experts" and premised on the idea of equality of opportunity as the primary means of improvement. Raskin held the "insurgents" of the various social movements of the 1960s in much higher regard and looked to them for help with the decolonization of America.[89] In short, the success of social reconstruction hinged on the replacement of liberal reformers with the citizenry.

Not surprisingly, the Democratic Party became a favorite target of IPS. The peace intellectuals at the institute shared with large segments of the American populace in the late 1960s a disdain for Democrats. As racial strife led to riots and as thousands marched against the war in Vietnam, support for Lyndon Johnson deteriorated. In such an environment, the "Dump Johnson" movement gained momentum. Even after Johnson shocked the nation in March 1968 by announcing that he would not seek reelection, the "Dump Johnson" movement continued to support Minnesota senator Eugene McCarthy over Vice President Hubert Humphrey.[90] In October 1968, "dissident Democrats," including the organizer of the "Dump Johnson" movement, Allard Lowenstein, came together under the New Democratic Coalition (NDC). The NDC hoped to take control of the party machinery away from the allies of Johnson and Humphrey. For this reason, and hopeful that a victory for Richard Nixon in November might accelerate changes within the Democratic Party, the NDC did not support Humphrey.[91] Others looked beyond the Democratic Party. Raskin, expecting the Democrats to nominate Humphrey, organized several meetings with "a few Kennedy and McCarthy types" in June to discuss the formation of the New Party. At the Democratic National Convention in Chicago in August 1968, Raskin used the University of Chicago as the headquarters for the New Party. From there, he sent out "20 full-time cadres" to persuade "dissident Democrats" to abandon the Democratic Party.[92]

Raskin conceived of the New Party as a vehicle for social reconstruction. He supported placing McCarthy at the top of the ticket, though various state New Party organizations preferred comedian Dick Gregory and Black Panther Eldridge Cleaver. As he told a *Washington Post* reporter, the New Party would aid in the creation of new legal, health, and educational institutions "to show what the alternatives are, to show what things could be like."[93] Conversely, Raskin argued that "the Hubert Humphrey of 1948 has won the liberal battle within the Democratic Party." As a result, activists needed to temper any hopes about the Democrats undergoing any further transformations. Liberal reform undoubtedly benefited many Americans, but Raskin warned that liberalism threatened American democracy. Writing in September 1968, he compared Humphrey to "the right wing Social Democrats in Germany who espoused piddling social services through authoritarian bureaucracy while accepting the power and legitimacy of the military-corporate elites." Therefore, an insurgent candidate like McCarthy, even if he had won the nomination in Chicago, would likely face several roadblocks in his efforts to overhaul the Democratic Party as an insider. Raskin believed that in order "to change the Democratic Party from within by 'capturing' it would require a purge of the entire congressional leadership in Congress—an event unknown in the history of American politics."[94]

At the same time, Raskin's interest in the New Party transcended electoral politics. The survival of "projects" required a political party not allied to "liberal authoritarianism." The *New York Times* mentioned how the organizers of the New Party "tend[ed] to see the party in long-range, rather abstract terms," mostly concerned with making society more inclusive and democratic by abolishing racism and bureaucracy. Raskin did not disagree. He told the paper that his purpose in forming the New Party went beyond the election of an individual candidate. He suggested that the New Party made it possible to "transform society peacefully." "The other course is revolution," he explained, "which would end in repression and Fascism." Raskin counseled strategic involvement in electoral politics, and not necessarily based on the chances of victory. Rather, he argued that periodic participation helped sustain the "political space" necessary for advocates of social reconstruction to "simultaneously challenge colonizing groups and define its own position through dialogue with those people who are viewed by the colonizers as immobile and quiescent."[95] In short, Raskin recognized the futility of using the existing political machinery for social reconstruction, but he also refrained from calling for a revolution.

Raskin's New Party had to contend with the NDC, which had the backing of Kaufman, who served on the NDC's steering committee. Kaufman remained committed to working within the Democratic Party, resulting in a clash between the two radical liberals. In Kaufman's opinion, the New Party represented a pipe dream with no realistic chance of competing with the established Democratic Party. Neither African Americans nor independent voters appeared likely to join the New Party, and Raskin "delud[ed] himself" to claim otherwise, according to Kaufman. He described these as "enormous electoral disabilities." The NDC, on the other hand, found much greater success. Kaufman claimed that delegates at the 1968 convention "forced meaningful concessions and gave the nation a sense of liberal ferment." Moreover, "a wedge of insurgency" placed NDC members in important positions in the Democratic Party's state organizations.[96]

Besides questioning the electoral strength of the New Party and sounding the alarm about its minimal influence within the Democratic Party, Kaufman took umbrage with the group's anti-liberal stance. Unlike the NDC, which espoused "the moral rhetoric of liberalism," the New Party chose a different approach. According to Kaufman, "a large part of the New Party's claim to newness is based precisely on its rejection of the language and tradition of American liberalism." Kaufman refused to give up on liberalism. He believed that "liberal ideals can have an explosive impact on policy," if only Democrats implemented the far-reaching programs advocated by groups like the NDC. Kaufman accused Raskin and his New Party allies of living in the past by choosing "to identify American liberalism with the Old Coalition that kept the Democratic Party in power for some 35 years." Thus, in his final judgment, Kaufman found the New Party lacking in both radicalism and pragmatism. "An authentic radicalism does not dismiss unpleasant institutional facts by wishing them away," Kaufman exclaimed.[97]

Kaufman failed to convince Raskin that the NDC sought fundamental change and that it could occur within a transformed Democratic Party. In fact, the IPS cofounder accused the NDC of belonging to the Cold War liberal camp. He described its program as being "much more in tune with what might objectively be regarded as a reformed ADA [Americans for a

Democratic Action]." Moreover, Raskin downplayed the NDC's influence within the Democratic Party. With the NDC only "a distinct minority," the Democratic Party still relied on voters "whose class interests at this moment appear to demand a law-and-order mentality." Thus, he predicted that the NDC's future involved being "co-opted to accept the new authoritarian basis of Democratic leadership." In Raskin's opinion, the Democratic Party remained wedded to "the national security state which it built and was responsible for since the 1930s" and military Keynesianism.[98] Raskin, and in turn IPS, embodied the ideals of radical liberalism as developed by Kaufman. Yet the different approaches to electoral politics in the late 1960s point to the institute's existence on the "bare edge," to borrow a term from Waskow, of liberalism that kept it from ever fully embracing the Democratic Party. In many ways, IPS's skepticism of the Democratic Party proved warranted, as evidenced by its rightward lurch in the final decades of the twentieth century.

The failure of the New Party forced Raskin and his IPS cohorts to remain within the Democratic orbit. Even so, IPS maintained a critical distance from the party. When McGovern, a senator from South Dakota whose views on liberalism and the Cold War were nearly identical to those of the IPS cofounders, looked to lead the Democrats against Nixon, Barnet could not fully endorse such a strategy.[99] In a letter congratulating Senator McGovern, a stalwart IPS ally and future trustee at the institute, on his announcement to run for the Democratic nomination in 1972, Barnet "wonder[ed] whether a serious political movement to make the kinds of changes you are talking about can emerge from that Party." Interestingly, in a letter to McGovern regarding the upcoming Democratic nominating convention, which came to epitomize New Politics liberalism and identity politics, Raskin implored the presidential candidate to include in his acceptance speech a call for a "new citizenship." For Raskin, citizenship involved far more than the protection of individual rights. As he wrote in a speech that he encouraged McGovern to use when he accepted his party's nomination for president, "Unless we remove the impediments to citizenship for all of our people, unless we learn how to think and cooperate together, unless we see ourselves as having more in common with each other than against each other, unless we clearly understand our obligations to each other," the United States would falter. The Democratic Party's exploitation of identity politics greatly troubled Raskin, who sought a "beloved community" in pursuit of the "common good."[100]

In the years following McGovern's drubbing by Nixon in 1972, Raskin continued to castigate the Democratic Party and its attraction to identity politics. Writing to the former candidate in 1977, Raskin encouraged

McGovern to disregard "the principle of coalition-building" in favor of the "principle of programmatic development." According to Raskin, while the former involved "those with particular interests press[ing] their own point," the latter represented "a common point of view that is more than the addition of individual interests." With the New Party no longer in existence, Raskin became a supporter of the NDC. During a speech he gave at its 1978 national conference, Raskin referred to the numerous "cause groups" on the Left, which rarely found the common ground necessary to mount a strong offensive. Arguing that the Democratic Party failed to reconcile the viewpoints of the various interest groups, Raskin called for a new party.[101] Thus, long after his failed attempt to create a new party in 1968, Raskin still sought an alternative to the Democratic Party.

With the Left in an anemic state and the United States set to elect the conservative Ronald Reagan, Raskin looked to the past for inspiration and direction regarding the future of liberalism. In its May 17, 1980, issue, the *Nation* brought together several commentators to debate "What's Left?" Raskin argued that liberalism needed to eschew "the antipragmatic imperial discipline of geopolitics" in favor of a system of relations based on international law. Liberalism in the 1980s had to focus on bringing the economy back under the control of political and democratic forces, according to Raskin. He castigated intellectuals, especially Schlesinger, for lazily calling for the revival of "vital center" liberalism. The IPS codirector claimed that the center had become too conservative for it to serve the liberal cause.[102]

Searching for a philosophy more appropriate for the 1980s, Raskin turned his attention to two opposing "modes" of liberalism from earlier in the twentieth century. According to Raskin, "establishment liberalism" placed power in the hands of the executive, who acted as an arbitrator between the corporations and the American people. While regulating corporations, the president ensured continued economic growth through economic pump priming. At the same time, the president pushed for passage of social programs in the 1930s and 1960s in order "to stop 'the unruly classes' from burning down the cities." Establishment liberalism succeeded so long as the economy prospered, which it did until the 1970s. A second form of liberalism, "progressive liberalism," also existed in America. Raskin described this alternative as "liberalism's most vibrant form, suffused with the restless energy of Americans in pursuit of justice and happiness." Progressive liberalism demanded "a dualsector economy of cooperatives, public enterprise and small businesses" with a "noninterventionist and independent foreign policy." According to Raskin, the "philosophical roots" of progressive liberalism extended far and wide to include a variety of voices not usually considered in the same category. He sought a return to the "pragmatism of John Dewey, the politics of Robert La Follette Sr. and the legal thought of William O. Douglas." Progressive liberalism would continue the fight of Eugene Debs, Upton Sinclair, Walter Weyl, Charles Beard, Jane Addams, and John L. Lewis, "all of whom believed that workers should exercise control over their places of work, and evinced a deep suspicion toward unaccountable wealth privately held, unaccountable government and politicians who led their people into war or on imperial ventures."[103]

*   *   *

For IPS intellectuals, liberalism had gone astray beginning in the 1930s, taking on a more authoritarian, undemocratic, and bureaucratic hue. The most significant point to glean from the preceding discussion is that democracy stood at the center of IPS's belief system. Therefore, the lack of democratic features found in Cold War liberalism greatly concerned the institute, so much so that Barnet and Raskin created IPS in the hope that its existence might assist with the creation of and show the way toward a more democratic society. The peace intellectuals at the institute, unlike so many defense intellectuals, refused to kiss the ring of power in Washington. Instead, as "public scholars," Raskin and Barnet set out to make IPS into I. F. Stone's "institute for the rest of us," which had as its goal the social reconstruction of America. As radical liberals, the peace intellectuals at IPS disapproved of revolution. At the same time, liberalism in its current state led only to colonization at home and abroad. According to Raskin's theory of social reconstruction, renewing democracy required decolonization within the United States. Without a doubt, the greatest threat came from the "violence colony," which led to the nuclear arms race and endless wars. Democracy, in America or elsewhere, withered when faced with a prolonged state of war.

World War I sounded the death knell for progressivism. Henry Wallace attempted to revive it in the years immediately after World War II, but another conflict, the Cold War, stopped the movement in its tracks. A common theme emerged throughout the twentieth century: the survival of progressivism required the absence of war. A similar logic applied as well to democracy, a key component of Raskin's "progressive liberalism." American imperialism begot the authoritarian national security state. Though already understood by IPS, Watergate brought this fact home, especially for Raskin. As he wrote in 1974, "It was clear that to administer an empire, the methods used abroad were ones that would be used within the United States."[104] Thus, doing away with the internal colonization of the United States described by Raskin in *Being and Doing* required a decolonization of the entire world, which would happen only if the United States renounced empire and its role as guardian of the liberal capitalist international order. IPS, itself a "project" and "social invention," attempted to remake liberalism and pave the way for a post–Cold War order. A key element in this new playbook involved the concept of "ideological pluralism," the topic of the next chapter.

CHAPTER 2

A World Safe for Diversity

IPS's Road Map for a Post–Cold War Order

"The world must be made as safe as possible for American economic growth by discouraging or aborting anti-capitalist revolutions wherever possible." IPS cofounder Richard Barnet wrote these words in early 1976 as the United States prepared to celebrate its bicentennial. Despite the debacle in Vietnam, U.S. officials still clung to the idea of containment, which, among other things, meant the continued reliance on military alliances and foreign intervention to prevent the spread of communism and keep underdeveloped nations from upsetting the international economic order.[1]

It was in this context that IPS sought a new internationalism premised on a populist and pluralist vision for the world that required non-intervention, militarily and otherwise, by the United States. To achieve this goal, IPS confronted a key structure of the Cold War, the North Atlantic Treaty Organization (NATO). IPS's criticism of NATO stemmed from the institute's disagreement with the internationalism of its liberal Cold Warrior architects. IPS blamed NATO for begetting and sustaining the bipolar world that demanded allegiance to either capitalism or socialism. While liberal internationalists regarded the United States as the world's premier democracy, and thus the only nation capable of leading others toward the same destination, the institute deplored such hierarchy. In its place, IPS sought a "world community" guided by populist principles. Opposed to the elitist and technocratic leadership model favored by Cold War liberals, IPS sought globalization for "the people," which entailed their empowerment and the transcendence of national borders.

By the 1970s, population growth, energy shortages, and economic stagnation forced a reappraisal of the existing world order. Jimmy Carter's ascension to power seemed promising. However, guided by associates of the

Trilateral Commission, the purported first post–Cold War president disappointed IPS, leading to an unlikely alliance with the libertarian Cato Institute. Though opposites on the ideological spectrum, the two think tanks agreed on the necessity of placing limits on U.S. power abroad. Greater restraint did not mean a turn toward isolationism but rather a different way of interacting with the world. Embarking on this new path required the redefinition of realism. IPS sought a realism divorced from balance-of-power dynamics, the nation-state, and the use of force. A key component of IPS's "new realism" was a recognition and acceptance of the diverse political and economic systems of Third World nations. From IPS's perspective, the United States had to make the world safe for diversity to prevent interdependence from becoming a mockery. Without the former, the latter retained the worst features of Cold War internationalism, including a hierarchical system of nation-states dominated by industrialized countries, uniform political and economic systems tethered to the East or the West, and a repudiation of self-determination. In an ultimate display of IPS's willingness to let "the people" of the world determine their own fate, the institute supported national liberation movements and the rise of Eurocommunism. First, however, the United States had to step aside.

IPS's Battle Against a Pillar of the Militarized Cold War

Beginning in the 1960s, internal divisions within NATO aroused public interest in the future of the Atlantic alliance. In the section "What Is Needed" of the Port Huron Statement, the Students for a Democratic Society (SDS) offered a thorough critique, written almost entirely by a German exchange student who attended the meeting as a representative from the Sozialistische Deutsche Studentenbund, of U.S. foreign policy vis-à-vis Germany and NATO. Fearful that any attempt to reunify Germany might lead to a nuclear confrontation between the superpowers, SDS called for the maintenance of the "status quo" until Cold War tensions subsided. As for NATO, SDS considered it part of an "outmoded European defense framework" premised on the fear of a Soviet invasion of Europe. Yet, for the remainder of the decade, both the U.S.-based New Left and its German equivalent focused almost entirely on the Vietnam War.[2] Others, though, continued to look for ways to either obliterate or salvage NATO. One commentator, Ronald Steel, who pointed to the original purpose of NATO as a temporary structure, already in 1964 doubted whether the alliance deserved rescuing. Henry Kissinger, too, worried about the future of NATO. He blamed U.S. hegemony for causing dissension within its ranks and encouraged the United States to adapt to new conditions in Europe by allowing the emergence of "a united Europe" to act as a more equal partner in the Atlantic alliance, and thus preserve NATO.[3]

IPS's internationalist vision required the dissolution of NATO. Even before the institute existed, Marcus Raskin wrote to his former boss, McGeorge Bundy, to express his distaste for NATO. Describing the ties between the United States and West European nations as "not pragmatic and almost wholly ideological," Raskin called on U.S. and Soviet officials to agree on troop reductions in Europe, leaving France to shoulder a greater share of the defense burden. He based his advice on what he perceived as a growing anti-NATO sentiment in the United States. Before long, Raskin predicted, Americans would turn against NATO due to "isolationism, UNism, and the fact that a significant portion of the American people, notably Negroes, will become more vocal and will show that they have little if any commitment to either the ideals or the goals of West Europe."[4] In short, Raskin contended that "the people" no longer, if they ever did, supported the logic undergirding the military alliance and officials in power needed to take notice.

Signaling their intentions to strike at the heart of the Cold War and bipolarity, Raskin and Barnet targeted NATO in their first book released after IPS's founding. In *After 20 Years: Alternatives to the Cold War in Europe*, Raskin and Barnet castigated the United States for seeing NATO "as an end in itself," unlike America's allies, who considered it merely "a temporary expedient." While Europeans "accepted and occasionally repeated the rhetoric that fired American statesmen, most European statesmen thought it possible to be both against communism and for negotiations with Moscow" in order to reunite Europe, Barnet and Raskin wrote.[5] Thus, with its first shot across the bow, IPS left no doubt that it sought a new internationalism with something other than NATO as its centerpiece.

IPS intellectuals argued that NATO had outlived its usefulness. The Soviet Union no longer posed a threat to Europe. As evidence, Raskin and Barnet pointed to several Soviet proposals meant to speed NATO's demise. Most notably, the Soviets accepted a non-nuclear and reunified Germany as a neutral self-governed nation outside of NATO. U.S. obstinance, however, stood in the way because the Soviet proposals "undermined the rationale of the Atlantic Community and might weaken the ties between the United States and Western Europe," Barnet and Raskin explained. Barnet made a similar argument when he testified before the Senate Foreign Relations Committee in 1966. He pointed to a growing unwillingness by Western European nations, now less dependent on the United States for aid and military protection, to follow America's lead when it came to Cold War politics.[6] From the perspective of IPS's cofounders, U.S. officials feared the loss of American influence and thereby delayed a settlement promising greater autonomy to Europeans.

As pragmatic realists, Barnet and Raskin warned U.S. officials not to allow ideological considerations to serve as a distraction from the changing situation in Europe and stand in the way of a relaxation of tensions between the East and West. The realism of IPS's cofounders, however, differed starkly from that of Kissinger, a rising star in foreign policy circles. Reviewing the book for the *New York Times*, Kissinger claimed that *After 20 Years* far exceeded the pessimism of earlier critiques of NATO. Kissinger found the book's obsession with the tremendous costs involved with creating and maintaining NATO puzzling since U.S. officials had few other options available to defend Europe against a Soviet invasion. The future secretary of state berated the authors for discounting NATO's role in tempering the Soviet Union's expansionist tendencies and preserving a free Europe. Barnet and Raskin "refus[ed] to admit that the freedom of Europe may be due to America's Atlantic vision," Kissinger exclaimed. Instead, the authors used the Soviet Union's restraint as evidence to support their claim that Europe no longer needed NATO's protection. Kissinger worried that Raskin and Barnet had a "tendency to base policy on the most favorable assumptions," which led them to put too much trust in the Soviet Union.[7]

For the peace intellectuals at IPS, too much mistrust had led to a militarization of the Cold War. Thus, in *After 20 Years*, Barnet and Raskin called for the creation of a new "collective security arrangement" so that "the problem of European security would once again be treated as a political problem, not as a military one." Barnet and Raskin wanted to require UN approval of any military action undertaken by NATO, and even then "only as an extreme *ad hoc* measure in the case of gravest urgency." In other words, under Barnet and Raskin's proposal, NATO could act only when "deputized by the UN."[8] As the Cold War intensified, NATO took prominence over the United Nations. Barnet and Raskin sought to reverse the roles, giving the United Nations the position of senior partner in the relationship.

What about the threat of a Soviet invasion of Europe? IPS intellectuals dismissed such fears. Writing in the early 1980s, Barnet claimed that NATO served as "an elaborate insurance policy" dependent on a U.S. nuclear shield. Yet "the only workable deterrent," and one that, unlike the threat of nuclear retaliation, actually prevented a Soviet invasion of Europe, involved "permanent popular resistance," according to Barnet. "A dynamic Europe that is

modernizing its institutions, managing its economy and establishing mutually advantageous relations with resource-producing countries" would do
more to repel a Soviet invasion than arming Europe to the teeth. Conversely,
if Europe chose to focus on a nuclear buildup to the detriment of economic
and social progress, it would "risk the same sort of social dissolution" as
France had in 1940, Barnet warned.[9] Of course, when Barnet wrote this in
1981, officials had already decided to introduce modernized nuclear weapons
in Western Europe.

IPS understood that German reunification stood as the primary roadblock to a peaceful conclusion of the Cold War. Therefore, Barnet called on
the superpowers to step aside and allow the two Germanies to determine
their own futures, which required greater dialogue between the residents of
East and West Germany. He predicted that such exchanges would likely result
in a non-Communist reunified Germany since the West Germans possessed
superior skills and numbers in comparison to their neighbors. With the German question no longer an issue, Barnet foresaw a new "regional organization" taking shape in Europe in which the United States, the Soviet Union,
and all European nations "would be obligated to respond to any threat to
European security from any direction," both East and West.[10]

While IPS was in favor of having "regional" blocs replace NATO, the
institute's cosmopolitanism led Barnet and his cohorts to look for ways to
bring these disparate alliances together into a single community under the
watchful eye of the United Nations. In a sense, IPS hoped to transform the
United Nations into the organization originally envisioned by British and U.S.
officials, including Prime Minister Winston Churchill and President Franklin Roosevelt, who preferred having the new international body act as an
umbrella organization for smaller regional units.[11] In a 1968 report for the
UN Association Panel on Atlantic Relationships, Barnet proposed a European Security Commission—composed of all European nations, the United
States, and the Soviet Union— as a replacement for NATO and the Warsaw
Pact. The new alliance's forces would be "aimed at no single enemy but at
potential disturbers of the peace from either East or West." As Europe took
on more responsibility for its defense, Barnet anticipated a reduction in U.S.
and Soviet troop levels on the continent, but only after the superpowers
reached agreements on arms control and the German question. The fact that
"regional organizations . . . have fallen considerably short of earlier expectations and hopes" did not concern Barnet. Nor did the rising tensions between
Greece and Turkey or the robust nationalism in France and West Germany.
To deal with these issues, Barnet recommended that the European Security

Commission "be integrated as closely as possible with the security concerns of the rest of mankind through the United Nations."[12] Thus, Barnet sought a unique blending of regionalism and internationalism, with the former allowing for the advancement of local interests and the latter curtailing nationalism's destructive tendencies.

Building a "World Community" and the End of American Hegemony

Universalist sentiments guided the architects of the United Nations. At the same time, its limited membership and the unequal separation of powers between the Security Council and the General Assembly illustrates the wide gulf between rhetoric and reality. In fact, for much of its history, the United Nations served as an instrument of the most powerful nations.[13] IPS recognized as much. While the United States began turning its back on the United Nations in the 1960s over disagreements related to Vietnam and the growing presence of the Third World in the General Assembly, IPS sought to transform the international body for a new age.

The peace intellectuals at IPS celebrated the dramatic growth of the UN General Assembly in the 1960s. In a 1965 letter to Assistant Secretary of State Harlan Cleveland, Arthur Waskow argued that the United Nations needed to create a "special role" for underdeveloped nations in the General Assembly. He pointed to the growing enmity toward the United States and other powerful nations among "the small and large but weak and poverty-stricken powers, as a kind of 'world populism' that needs some sort of legitimating and peaceful focus if it is not to erupt in violence," as it did in China in 1949. Allowing these diverse voices to take part in UN debates "might provide a safety valve for this explosive 'populism,'" Waskow explained. At the same time, a larger role for the smaller, less developed nations did not necessarily threaten U.S. leadership. American industry, Waskow explained using a historical analogy, survived despite the measures enacted by Populists in America in the late 1800s.[14] Waskow sought a middle way between the status quo and the outbreak of violence. He continued to pursue the issue in a conversation with former SDS president Todd Gitlin. He encouraged the SDS leader to focus on the General Assembly, and the United Nations more generally, to improve conditions in the Third World. Waskow recognized that many nations distrusted the United Nations and saw it as an "instrument" of the United States, but he suggested that "the small, the weak, and the poor" could reclaim the Assembly for their own purposes. Waskow's vision for the United Nations required, however, the presence of a "pro-small-and-poor, pro-Assembly, pro-new-kind of UN, pro-Third-World voice" in the United States, which he felt SDS could provide.[15]

Even with an expanded roster of Third World nations in the General Assembly, the UN Security Council held much of the decision-making authority, especially when responding to international disputes. Cognizant of this fact, Waskow sought to alter the way the United Nations determined when and where to send its peacekeeping forces. Under Waskow's proposal, the size of the peacekeeping force depended on the number of nations voting. He suggested using a "threshold," based on the amount of money, the quantity of troops, and the types of weapons, to determine how many UN members could participate in the vote. Thus, while large-scale UN missions would require approval and funding from nations in the Security Council, the General Assembly could sanction smaller operations, with all nations voting in favor paying for the undertaking. Waskow claimed that his plan allowed smaller countries to "pool their power" to stop the actions of the great powers. Since it accepted the rise of a "world populism," which he described as a "hostility to *all* the rich, whether capitalist or communists, and a fierce determination to resist them," Waskow expected widespread support for his plan.[16]

At times, IPS intellectuals argued in favor of something far more grandiose than a mere dismantling of NATO. Instead, they sought the reconfiguration of the global order into a world without borders. In calling for the replacement of NATO with regional collective security arrangements connected to the United Nations, IPS intellectuals accepted the fact that the United States might lose its ability to control world affairs. Furthermore, they openly acknowledged that their plans for a post-NATO world involved doing away with the tidy hierarchical structure built into the existing alliance system. Writing in the early 1970s, Barnet argued that the United States had to accept "a high degree of disorder and instability" in the world and allow nations to choose their own political and economic systems. Nor could the United States stand above the rest of the world community as it had done in the past. He appealed to Americans "to identify with the people of other countries as members of the same species with the same basic problems" and not "as abstractions to be manipulated for our own psychological and political needs" to ensure continued American dominance.[17] Global supremacy, in short, precluded the development of a world community.

NATO interfered with IPS's plan to create a truly egalitarian world order. The idea of an Atlantic Community, which stood at the heart of NATO, aroused the ire of Raskin, who viewed it as too myopic and too dismissive of the rest of the world. By positioning itself as part of the Atlantic alliance, Raskin claimed that the United States chose to "identify itself with the 'cult of the blood' notions which dominate the ideology of the Atlanticists [and] it will appear as nothing more than a 19th century Holy Alliance" intent on preserving the status quo in the image of the powerful. Therefore, Raskin favored the United Nations, which, he claimed, "will give the power of participation and choice to the poor in the development of their own nations." Only by creating a world community, acting under the purview of the United Nations, could America avoid nuclear annihilation. Raskin put so much faith in the United Nations because, in his words, "it is not based on the assumption of permanent enemies or attachments, except the permanent attachment to the survival and dignity of all mankind."[18] Thus, the ability to respond to changing conditions rather than seeing the world as black and white, or communist and non-communist, is what made the United Nations attractive to the peace intellectuals at IPS.

Disturbed by what nationalism had wrought, Barnet put forth a vision for a global beloved community of citizens rather than nations. Asked during an interview if "a corresponding decline of the nation-state" had to follow the strengthening of international law, Barnet responded in the affirmative. He argued that only through "a limitation on the rights of individual nation-states" would it become clear what path offered the best hope for each nation's "security or for the promotion of their 'national interests.'" By the early 1970s, he argued, various events made the nation-state "obsolete"—it could not, for instance, protect its citizens against nuclear decimation, achieve "world order" through military or other means, promote development in foreign nations, or secure foreign markets. Barnet did not seem disturbed by the decline of the nation-state. While he feared that "managers of nation-states" might "become more frustrated by their inability to solve urgent problems" and turn to "authoritarian and militaristic methods" to try to retain influence, Barnet wanted to do away with the nation-state. "Planetary survival will depend upon how quickly the power of the nation-state can be contained and a wider human identity can be established," he argued.[19]

By the late 1970s, Barnet became even more emphatic about the need to create what he called a world community. Writing in 1978, he argued that the nation-state lacked the means to deal with political and economic problems in a decolonized and globalized world. "The reality of interconnectedness is forcing us to think beyond the religion of nationalism and to work toward political structures that are obedient to the biblical injunction that mankind is one," Barnet exclaimed.[20] It is not clear, however, what Barnet hoped to replace the nation-state with since he never came out in favor of world government. Rather, he seemed to think that the United Nations could carry out most of the decision-making functions previously held by the nation-state.

Not everyone at IPS could foresee a future where the nation-state did not exist. Raskin, for instance, accepted that treaties and international law often failed to rein in the worst habits of countries, but he also rejected other alternatives. Using the U.S. Civil War as an example, Raskin feared the appearance of similar fissures under a world government. Therefore, even as Raskin and Joseph Duffey argued in 1975 that "the UN could be the major forum for carrying out the business of foreign policy" and encouraged the United States to "take some responsibility in developing a world common law," world government did not appeal to the pragmatic minds at IPS.[21] At best the United Nations might deter the most egregious acts committed by nations. Believing "that there must be an international political framework for conducting national foreign policy," Raskin looked to the United Nations as an institution that could "help each nation set limits to nationalistic behavior" in an increasingly multipolar world.[22] Thus, strengthening the United Nations took precedence over creating a world government.

After Vietnam: U.S. Foreign Policy in an Age of Limits

As the nation's two-hundredth birthday approached, historians, political scientists, politicians, and the American public took notice of the transformed global environment. "Two centuries ago our forefathers brought forth a new nation; now we must join with others to bring forth a new world order," historian Henry Steele Commager proclaimed in the preamble to his 1976 Declaration of Interdependence. Concerned primarily with planetary survival in the face of the seemingly insurmountable ecological and economic crises facing the world in the 1970s, Commager's declaration symbolized the growing appeal of interdependence.[23]

Before interdependence became fashionable in the mid-1970s, Lester Brown called for a "world without borders," but most commentators offered a more circumscribed blueprint for how the world should respond to the changing conditions.[24] Much of the analysis of interdependence originated from the pens of policy advisors and government officials. For instance, Joseph Nye held positions in the State Department and the National Security

Council under Carter. In 1977, with the publication of *Power and Interdependence*, Nye and Robert Keohane introduced the concept of "complex interdependence." Their theory allowed for the involvement of non-state actors concerned with more than just national security, such as economic, ecological, and social issues. Complex interdependence put far less faith in brute force to resolve problems, which meant a change to the "distribution of power" as military and economic strength no longer guaranteed global supremacy. These non-state actors, furthermore, including multinational corporations, made it more difficult for states to dominate international affairs, as did the growing importance of international organizations like the United Nations, which allowed smaller states to join together in pursuit of similar aims. It is important to distinguish Keohane and Nye from other advocates of globalism, including Lester Brown, whom the authors labeled "modernists." As they wrote in a retrospective ten years later, "We emphasized that interdependence would not necessarily lead to cooperation, nor did we assume that its consequences would automatically be benign in other respects." In making such an argument, Keohane and Nye hoped to make explicit their linkage between the power politics of realism and interdependence, primarily through their discussion of "asymmetries in military vulnerability," which acknowledged the continued relevance of military superiority in an interdependent world.[25] Thus, for all the discussions about interdependence requiring a new approach to foreign affairs, power and the use of force remained central to U.S. foreign policy.

The peace intellectuals at IPS championed a "new internationalism" that required fundamental changes to how the United States interacted with the rest of the world. As U.S. officials vacillated about what strategy to follow in Southeast Asia, Earl Ravenal, formerly a division director in the Department of Defense from 1967 until 1969, and later the Libertarian Party's 1984 presidential candidate, offered a dramatic break from past foreign policy. For Ravenal, the debacle in Vietnam proved that the United States could no longer dominate the world as it had done since the end of World War II. In a paper written for Senator Mike Gravel in 1971, Ravenal offered a glimpse into what he meant by a "new internationalism." Ravenal's plan called for "military nonintervention"; a "withdrawal from the false imperatives of 'collective security' in the preservation of a Metternichian rigidity"; a greater reliance on "international law and international institutions"; "the tolerance of revolutionary politics"; and a greater awareness of the Earth's limited natural resources.[26] Most, if not all, of the policies advocated by Ravenal found favor among the peace intellectuals at IPS.

America's defeat in Vietnam elicited much soul-searching. While most commentators and politicians despaired over waning American power abroad, IPS found a silver lining in the outcome of the Vietnam War. "Our allies, and the whole international system, ought to settle down to a lower order of expectations of American response," Ravenal concluded. Among other things, this new reality made possible the reduction of America's defense budget. However, Ravenal opposed mere "efficiency cuts, or token cuts" favored by "liberal critics," which he argued did not go far enough.[27] Despite IPS's high hopes for a "new internationalism," America's Cold War mission persevered. Writing in the *New Republic* in early 1976, Barnet lamented the "bipartisan silence" following the war: "Far from reexamining the world view that led a generation of American leaders, and the rest of us with them, into the famous quagmire, they have rededicated themselves—and us—to that same world view." He blamed the "bureaucracies" and "bureaucratic inertia" for the continued adherence to what he labeled "the cold war model of reality." Consequently, the aims of U.S. policymakers remained the same: achieve military supremacy over the Soviet Union and maintain U.S. economic dominance. The lack of debate within the corridors of power resulted in officials losing a sense of "reality," Barnet argued. Not surprisingly, he posited that "the best hope of restoring a sense of reality to foreign policy is to challenge and test official wisdom through democratic debate."[28]

As the United States adapted to the post–Vietnam War era, many liberals, including those at IPS, were intrigued by a relatively unknown politician from Georgia offering a new vision for America's foreign policy. According to notes taken by Saul Landau during a foreign policy discussion held at IPS in March 1976, Raskin felt "it would be possible now to present an alternative foreign policy and get wide support, because there is a widespread feeling that going back to the same well of ideas and people that have given us foreign policy in the last 30 years would be a mistake."[29] Carter, however, ran in 1976 as a moderate, which precluded a massive overhaul of U.S. foreign policy, at least to the extent desired by the peace intellectuals at IPS. At one point during the presidential campaign in 1976, Carter's chief speechwriter, Patrick Anderson, brought the candidate a couple of books, including one of Raskin's. As he gave Carter the book, Anderson asked, "Do you know IPS? It's a left-wing think tank. They're usually ten years ahead of everybody else in Washington." Carter replied cheekily, "Maybe we can cut that down to five."[30] Carter's off-the-cuff comment hints at the future president's more limited ambitions, which clashed with IPS's hopes that America's new leader might pursue a post–Cold War foreign policy.

Officials within the Carter White House soon discovered just how wide a gulf separated the new president from IPS. Zbigniew Brzezinski, Carter's national security advisor, sent the president an article written by Barnet for *Harper's* in August 1977. In this "first major assessment" of Carter's foreign policy, as Brzezinski described it, Barnet attacked his human rights rhetoric as nothing more than an attempt to justify U.S. involvement abroad, serving a purpose similar to that of anti-communism in the first two decades of the Cold War. Therefore, Carter fit the mold of past Democrats like Woodrow Wilson, Harry Truman, and John F. Kennedy. "Like Kennedy," Barnet wrote, "Carter projects moral fervor and a sense of mission. In the tradition of Woodrow Wilson, he believes that America's destiny is to be the architect of a new world suffused with American values." Brzezinski described Barnet as a "left-oriented critic who has obvious axes to grind."[31] Thus neither party viewed the other as an ally, despite sharing with one another similar views, especially in terms of Latin America.

Amid a purported post–Cold War presidency, Barnet, along with Richard A. Falk, an international law scholar, lamented the continuation of the Cold War consensus. They argued that the Left, except during the Vietnam War when it achieved a "temporary influence" over policymakers, rarely had a voice in matters of foreign policy. Instead, conservatives in Congress and within the government bureaucracy ensured that "dissent from the right is taken seriously by the White House while dissent from the left can usually be ignored with impunity." What concerned Barnet and Falk most was that "managers of the official consensus" ignored the transformed global environment and continued to believe in the "myth of continuity." This "myth" held "that the next 25 years will be like the last 25 and that, therefore, the fundamental policies of the last generation can be extended over the lives of our children."[32] In short, IPS doubted Carter's desire to transform U.S. foreign policy.

The president's ties to the Trilateral Commission, home to Barnet and Falk's "managers of the official consensus," did little to assuage IPS's skepticism. Before serving as Carter's national security advisor, Brzezinski played a key role in the commission's formation. Brzezinski, who had called for a strengthening of the relationship between industrialized nations in his 1972 book *The Fragile Blossom*, set out to create a forum for business and government leaders and academics from Japan, Europe, and North America to develop new policies for an interdependent world. To this end, he contacted the financier David Rockefeller, who had undertaken his own campaign for an "International Commission for Peace and Prosperity." Meeting at Rockefeller's home in Pocantico Hills, New York, in July 1972, representatives from the United States, Western Europe, and Japan established a new think tank, the Trilateral Commission, with Brzezinski as its first executive director when operations began in 1973. Apart from producing studies on topics ranging from energy, trade, and the international monetary system, the commission also fostered ties to government officials, including Secretary of the Treasury George Shultz, Kissinger, and Carter.[33] The commission held views not too dissimilar from those espoused by IPS. More concerned with North-South issues than East-West tensions, and therefore less inclined to support militarized containment, the commission sought to reduce economic disparities between industrialized nations and the Third World and an easing of U.S.-Soviet hostilities through improved trade relations.[34]

Yet in pursuing such goals, the commission remained committed to a U.S.-led world order, with industrialized nations, themselves under the supervision of technocratic experts, guiding Third World nations toward economic development. Self-determination did not figure into the thinking of the commission. In fact, at least according to a 1975 Trilateral Commission report titled *The Crisis of Democracy*, the commission frowned upon the expansion of democracy. In a chapter written by Samuel Huntington, the political scientist concluded that "some of the problems of governance in the United States today stem from an excess of democracy," comparable to what occurred during Andrew Jackson's presidency and ultimately led to the outbreak of the Civil War. As a result, Huntington called for "a greater degree of moderation in democracy."[35] IPS intellectuals, of course, abhorred such thinking. Too little democracy, not an abundance, led to militaristic containment during the Cold War.

The influence of the Trilateral Commission on Carter led IPS intellectuals to doubt the new president's eagerness to transcend the Cold War paradigm. Writing in 1978, Raskin portrayed Carter as a stooge for the wealthy individuals ensconced in the Trilateral Commission, who also bore responsibility for U.S. intervention in Vietnam. Raskin argued that the trilateralists sought as their candidate "a man who could restore allegiance to the old system and knew how to co-opt liberal forces who otherwise might overturn the entire checkerboard." Once in the White House, Carter brought with him more than a dozen members of the Trilateral Commission, guaranteeing "the restoration to power of the war imitators," Raskin claimed. Near the end of Carter's presidency, Barnet compared the "Trilateral agenda" to the Nixon Doctrine, since both strategies had the same goal of preserving American supremacy.[36] In the end, therefore, the worst elements of trilateralism combined with a Cold Warrior mentality to make Carter a false prophet of a post–Cold War order.

Carter's military budget confirmed for IPS the president's allegiance to Cold War liberalism. Speaking before Congress in 1978, Ravenal raised objections to Secretary of Defense Harold Brown's budget for the upcoming fiscal year and called for progressively lower defense spending. He recommended immediate cuts of $9 billion, with most of the savings coming from arms reductions and the dismantling of the alliance system. In place of deterrence and the forward basing system, Ravenal proposed a strategy of "war avoidance" and "self-reliance." In regard to the former, he described it not as "any gleeful predilection for disengagement" but rather a realistic understanding of the state of the world in the late 1970s. "We have to get used to a world that we cannot control, a world where we don't have the ability, let alone the right, to act out our needs for national self-esteem," Ravenal declared. "We need a better sense of these limits." Protecting America's shores from a military strike and takeover by a foreign enemy mattered most to Ravenal. For him "national security" meant the preservation of self-determination against attacks from external foes.[37] After defense intellectuals had transformed "national security" into a strategy for world domination, IPS intellectuals sought to reclaim and return it to its traditional purpose of protecting the homeland.[38]

Though Ravenal's understanding of national security involved the United States playing a diminished role in world affairs, IPS never advocated a "Fortress America" policy.[39] Nearly a decade before the debates surrounding America's role in the world reached a crescendo following the withdrawal of the last U.S. officials from Vietnam, Waskow defended SDS activists participating in a 1965 sit-in at the Chase Manhattan Bank in New York City. He concluded that despite being tarred "as 'neo-isolationists' for opposing the war in Vietnam," these activists "were actually deeply concerned with the correct and worthwhile use of American power to make the world more decent—a kind of 'neo-interventionism.'" These "neo-interventionists," unlike the architects of the Vietnam War, possessed the foresight to see "that only an intervention using nonmilitary, libertarian means can hope to produce a democratic result." Barnet, too, decried the charge of "neo-isolationism" used by Secretary of State Kissinger and President Ford to impugn critics of U.S. foreign policy. The growing economic links between nations meant that the United States could never return to a Fortress America strategy, Barnet explained. "The choice is not whether the United States is to be integrally involved in the international system but the terms of the involvement." In fact, Barnet claimed that America's "self-perpetuating elite" favored isolationism, as proven by their "resistance to sharing power" with other nations. "The

hostile reaction of the Ford Administration to the efforts of the poor countries to create a more equitable 'new international economic order' reflects a
deep-seated isolationism," Barnet alleged.[40]

Nor did IPS intellectuals question the need for the United States to pursue its interests abroad. Michael Klare and a coauthor, for instance, supported "the principle of non-intervention," especially in civil wars in the
Third World. At the same time, they accepted that the United States needed
to ensure that the world's sea lanes remained open. With this goal in mind,
Klare and his coauthor encouraged a refashioning of U.S. forces. This involved
the U.S. Navy replacing "its giant, attack-oriented aircraft carriers and bat-
tleships" with "smaller but more numerous sea-control vessels" to maintain
open waters.[41] Non-intervention did not mean building a wall between the
United States and the rest of the world. America would continue to play a
role in international affairs but while living in harmony with other nations,
not as an aggressor or hegemon.

Exasperated by Carter's continued adherence to the Cold War liberal
creed, IPS sought an alliance with a group of strange bedfellows: libertarians. The institute opened its doors to people like Karl Hess, a former speechwriter for Senator Barry Goldwater and prominent libertarian interested in
self-reliance and local autonomy. In his autobiography, Hess explained the
shared proclivities that united the institute and libertarians: "The moderate
IPS people such as Raskin and Barnet, not the Utopian Marxist sloganeers at
the institute, understood that there had been an Old Right in this country—a
faction that was isolationist in foreign policy and supportive of competition
rather than privilege in business. I was welcomed to the institute by at least
those two as a representative of that Old Right who could engage in fruitful
dialogue with the New Left."[42] It was not unheard of to see the two groups ally
in the 1960s. The New Left worked closely with the conservative youth organization Young Americans for Freedom on certain campaigns in the 1960s,
especially in opposition to the draft and the Vietnam War.[43]

As IPS welcomed libertarians into its community of scholars, it also forged
ties with the Cato Institute. Ravenal, for instance, split his time between the
Cato Institute, a leading libertarian think tank, and IPS. Beyond sharing personnel, IPS agreed with libertarians on several substantive issues domestically
and internationally. Moreover, Cato's founder, Edward H. Crane III, purposely
set out to attract disenchanted liberals to libertarianism, as evidenced by how
he introduced his think tank's new journal, *Inquiry*, where IPS intellectuals
published frequently during the Cold War. Crane promised "investigative
reporting and analysis on such topics as enforcement of victimless crime

laws, civil liberties and threats to the Bill of Rights, government underwriting and subsidizing of corporations, the abuses by the U.S. domestic and foreign intelligence agencies, and U.S. government interference in the affairs of other countries." IPS's cofounder Raskin recognized the difference between Cato and other conservative think tanks. Referring to a meeting he had with Cato staff, Raskin predicted, "They *will* be very successful." He seemed to rejoice over the fact that they "follow[ed] the Vienna school (von Mises, Hayek—and *not* Friedman)." He also claimed that Cato "want[ed] all sorts of associations with us [IPS]," including cosponsoring sessions on isolationism and U.S. foreign policy.[44] Cato's leadership did, in fact, court IPS.

Much to the chagrin of conservatives, Cato repeatedly looked to strengthen its ties with IPS and did not shy away from publicly praising the leftist institute. In late 1978, for example, a conservative syndicated columnist expressed dismay over a pamphlet he received from Cato announcing "a major on-going joint project with the Institute for Policy Studies in Washington, D.C." The partnership involved the "study [of] the military, financial and political implications of strictly non-interventionist United States foreign policy." The columnist predicted that "friends of the respectable free market people on the Cato Institute board will be shocked to learn of the linkage" and claimed the think tank was "in over its head" partnering with IPS. He did not understand Cato's decision to collaborate with IPS since "there's nothing libertarian about the Institute for Policy Studies in any sense."[45] Crane disagreed with the columnist. He favorably compared IPS to his institute during a 1985 interview, noting that both were "interested in stretching the boundaries of the debate, of changing our assumptions about politics and economics." Despite the grumblings of conservatives, Cato remained committed to working with IPS, even going so far as to fund IPS programs. Cato gave IPS a $2,500 grant in 1977 and another $7,500 the following year.[46]

"New Realism" and "Ideological Pluralism"

The 1970s is known as an age of limits. Domestically, the United States faced oil shortages and "stagflation," while internationally defeat in Vietnam sagged American ambitions and self-confidence. Richard Nixon and Kissinger, despite their proclivity for realism, sought to transcend such limits to maintain what Daniel Sargent has called "Pax Americana."[47] From IPS's perspective, such thinking did not accord with existing conditions. Barnet blamed America's foreign policy debacles in the 1970s on "obsolete analysis, obsolete style, and obsolete goals." The Kissinger viewpoint, Barnet wrote, "assumes that any world problem can be managed if the right five people get together. It is a 19th Century view of world politics based on the assumption that when princes and potentates meet, they can deliver their subjects." This antiquated understanding of world affairs, however, kept "the most obstreperous forces" from the negotiating table. Even when denied a political voice, these forces could still "ensure that the status quo will not be pleasant," either by committing terrorist acts or by acting as a thorn in the side of the superpowers, Barnet explained. With the 1976 election less than a year away, IPS intellectuals met to chart a new path forward for U.S. foreign policy. Barnet argued that any strategy needed to include democracy promotion. "In the long run the survival of democracy in the U.S. depends on our actions abroad. We can't create democracy abroad, but we can influence it. Our opposition to democracy abroad on the other hand weakens and imperils our own institutions because there is an interrelation between foreign and domestic policy, between resources and geopolitics, between costs and who pays the costs," Barnet explained.[48] In other words, Kissinger's strategy, which involved bringing together a small group of elites to make the global rules, may have worked in the past, but conditions in 1976 did not resemble those of 1946. The United States had to acknowledge the new actors on the world stage and assist them in their march to democracy.

IPS did not reject realism per se but rather how its practitioners, especially Kissinger, misused it to pursue global supremacy for the United States. The peace intellectuals at the institute, whose board of trustees included international relations scholar, and a "founding father" of realism, Hans Morgenthau, belong to the unique assemblage of "pragmatic realists," in the words of Jackson Lears, who stood in opposition to U.S. empire. These dissenters derided thinking based on "abstraction" rather than lived experiences and the accumulation of evidence. Moreover, pragmatic realists possessed a "cosmopolitan spirit" that required a recognition and acceptance of non-American ideas and ways of life.[49] Morgenthau clearly helped shape the foreign policy perspectives of IPS's cofounders. Claiming that "exposure to Hans Morgenthau's teaching at a crucial stage in my own development [has] been influential in shaping my own thinking," Barnet offered several "conclusions" that he reached using a realist approach. He determined, for instance, that America represented the "latest of the modern world empires" and would remain so for only a "brief" moment, while the Soviet Union viewed itself as a "nation-state" rather than "the embodiment of a revolutionary ideology."[50] In short, the realist perspective allowed Barnet to see U.S. hegemony as fleeting and the Soviet Union as just another nation-state interested in pursuing its national interests rather than spreading ideology. Such views, in turn, led him to see the Cold War as obsolete.

The IPS cofounders' revisionist reading of Morgenthau's realism led to a major new understanding of the role of morality and the national interest in foreign affairs. Raskin went to great lengths to show that realism, as developed by Morgenthau, did not disregard moral considerations. Even before the Vietnam War, most notably in his 1951 book *In Defense of the National Interest*, Morgenthau regarded morality and restraint as significant aspects of realism.[51] "The principle of logical and moral symmetry is crucial to the realist's position," Raskin wrote in an essay on Morgenthau. Citing Morgenthau's work as exemplary of this kind of thinking—especially *Politics Among Nations*, where Morgenthau calls on the United States to "judge other nations as we judge our own" and thus "respect the interests of other nations, while protecting and promoting those of our own"—Raskin scolded other realists for ignoring this aspect of Morgenthau's political theory. He also chided those who "perverted [it] to mean expedient measures, gratuitous and dangerous." "The practice of realism is reduced to what Power intends," Raskin complained, and therefore lacked "the moral underpinnings" central to Morgenthau's worldview. Likewise, IPS's cofounders lamented the use of "national interest" to defend U.S. military intervention abroad. Barnet sought to domesticate the term, taking it "to mean the welfare of the majority of citizens of the U.S." unconnected to U.S. security interests abroad.[52]

Given the unique situation facing America in the mid-1970s, IPS intellectuals called for a "new realism." Barnet warned U.S. officials that "empires collapse because they lose touch with their own time and employ self-defeating strategies for maintaining their power." Thus, he cautioned against "trying to perpetuate the era of American hegemony after the conditions for it have passed" and suggested that the United States needed to begin "building a more equitable international economic order and a less militarized international political order." Moreover, the United States lacked the means to preserve American global supremacy. As Barnet explained to his fellow IPS thinkers, "The new realism recognizes that each instrument for maintaining domination is failing," which meant that the United States could no longer rely on nuclear weapons, counterinsurgency, covert activities, and coups to achieve its goals.[53] If present conditions no longer allowed for U.S. hegemony, realism necessitated a new approach to foreign affairs. To this end, IPS introduced the idea of "ideological pluralism."

Under the direction of Roberta Salper, IPS's Working Group on Latin America produced *The Southern Connection: Recommendations for a New Approach to Inter-American Relations*. Though focusing on Latin America, the 1977 study offers insight into the sort of internationalism IPS thought necessary in a post–Cold War order. *The Southern Connection* aimed to convince officials and ordinary Americans of "the broader need to free U.S. policymaking from the outmoded assumption of U.S. hegemony" shattered by Vietnam. The success of ideological pluralism hinged on the United States "not interven[ing] to shape governments and societies to our views and preference." Accepting ideological pluralism meant that the United States needed to disabuse itself of "narrow, short lived definitions of national interest and national advantage that have sometimes led to punitive action," the report claimed. In Latin America, ideological pluralism necessitated the return of the Panama Canal to Panama and an end to America's "policy of restrained hostility toward Cuba." The report argued that Cuba should not have "to make amends for its decision to follow a socialist development alternative."[54]

IPS's study on Latin America brought the think tank attention, both positive and negative. By early 1978, IPS had sold 1,800 copies of *The Southern Connection*. Additionally, the Overseas Development Council held a dinner in which members of Congress, diplomats, and government officials "directly involved in determining U.S. policy in Inter-American affairs" used the report. Due in part to the participation of well-known policymakers and academics, conservatives took notice of the study and lambasted its contents.[55]

Neoconservative Jeane Kirkpatrick, a future UN ambassador under Ronald Reagan, spoke out against *The Southern Connection*, believing that the report served as a blueprint for Carter's Latin American policy. According to Kirkpatrick, "No sooner was he [Jimmy Carter] elected than he set out to translate them [the report's findings] into a new policy for dealing with nations of the hemisphere." The contents of the IPS report made this possibility especially distressing, particularly its "sweeping indictment of past U.S. policy," its promotion of self-development in Latin America, and its linkage of human rights to economic rights, which Kirkpatrick labeled a "fight for human rights with socialism." Kirkpatrick had no doubt that America's enemies had infiltrated the Carter White House. The parallels between IPS's recommendations and the president's Latin American policies confirmed for Kirkpatrick the New Left's admission into the foreign policy establishment and that "new liberalism" squared nicely with "revolutionary 'socialism.'" More worrisome for Kirkpatrick, the "utopian globalism" espoused by these liberals could easily turn into "anti-American perspectives and revolutionary activism."[56]

Did IPS's ideas find their way into Carter's White House? According to Vanessa Walker, internal debates over Presidential Review Memorandum 17 (PRM 17) in early 1977 point to similarities between the proposals in *The Southern Connection* and the Carter administration's blueprint for the region. For instance, officials acknowledged that looking at events in Latin America through the lens of the Cold War only exacerbated problems. Thus, PRM 17 sought to prioritize North-South issues and even announced that "we can accept more ideological pluralism in 1977 than we could in 1962."[57]

Regardless, Kirkpatrick overstated the role of IPS within the Carter White House, but the institute went too far in the opposite direction, downplaying its influence. A 1987 talking paper boasted that IPS "played a significant role in defining the Carter Administration's human rights initiatives," but this contradicts a statement made later by one of the cofounders of IPS. Raskin admitted to journalist Sidney Blumenthal that IPS, to its own detriment, "paid very little attention to the Carter administration." Raskin explained that IPS thought Carter offered no hope, but also confessed, "We [IPS] were moral snobs." Writing one year after Carter's election victory, Landau agreed with Raskin's later recollection. Although the Carter presidency offered IPS the opportunity to formulate policy, the institute did not take advantage of the new environment. Landau blamed this on the fact that IPS was so "blinded by the glitter of opportunity in the future" that its fellows could not "collectively pull ourselves out of the past muck."[58] More likely, IPS and Carter simply did not share the same outlook when it came to foreign policy, which would have made a partnership difficult to sustain. Though Carter offered rhetorical support for ideological pluralism, such approval did not extend to revolutions in Latin America.

Fear of Soviet expansionism blinded U.S. officials to the economic explanations for revolutionary actions in Latin America. Not so for Barnet and Landau, who recognized the uprisings in Central America as "expressions of desperate economic and political conditions of the countries themselves" caused largely by underdevelopment. Self-determination drove Central Americans to revolt, not, as Cold Warriors charged, the Soviet Union: "Revolutionary leaders do not sacrifice their lives to turn their country over to a superpower 8,000 miles away." What, then, did the authors want America to do in response to Nicaragua and other revolutionary states in the region? "A consistent commitment to human rights and support for political pluralism everywhere is likely to achieve better results than punishing shaky new regimes for their excesses by stepping up the pressure and making a state of siege appear unavoidable," Barnet and Landau concluded.[59] U.S. hostility toward revolutions only made small Latin American nations cling tighter to the Soviet Union.

Like the revisionist historian William Appleman Williams, who advocated an "open door for revolutions," IPS understood that supporting self-determination meant a greater acceptance of Third World insurgencies. To this end, Barnet encouraged American officials to take a more pragmatic approach and review its relationships with foreign nations. "Examining old habits of mind and passionate attachments to 'friends' and 'enemies' would enable the United States to bring commitments and resources into balance," he explained. As part of this process, he implored the United States to take a less reactionary approach to revolutions abroad. Officials needed to realize that these uprisings did not threaten America's security. Such events merely changed the dynamics of foreign relationships. "To live in security in a revolutionary world the U.S. will have to cope with the unpleasant truth that Americans cannot continue to grow richer while millions starve and still feel safe," Barnet argued. He claimed that the United States needed to "be much less ideological in relating to revolutionary nationalist regimes" and seek opportunities for cooperation, especially economic, with decolonized nations. Doing so would "have a moderating influence on revolutionary governments," Barnet predicted.[60] In short, ideological pluralism meant working with revolutionaries as equal parties as opposed to treating them as pariahs and seeking their destruction.

Though supportive of revolution, IPS refused to countenance the use of violence. As Frantz Fanon and others celebrated armed rebellions, Barnet criticized the "psychological devices" used by revolutionaries to support violent acts. He rejected the argument that overthrowing repressive governments required the use of force. "Just as the National Security Manager justifies the use of napalm, personnel bombs, and crop destroyers as the necessary preparation for a peaceful society so the Revolutionary shares the same guilt-assuaging illusion," Barnet claimed.[61] Ideological pluralism would come through persuasion, political means, or social protest, not by taking up the gun.

Beyond NATO

NATO in Europe, the Southeast Asia Treaty Organization (SEATO) in Southeast Asia, and the Baghdad Pact in the Middle East all existed to prevent the spread of communism. Convinced that these treaties provided only nominal

benefits for the United States, Barnet called for "no formal alliances." In place
of the alliance system, he wanted the United States to follow "a consistent
policy of being a supporter, not a guarantor, of existing boundaries and then
making clear that we have a very strong nonintervention policy on internal disorder," which would prevent the United States from taking sides in
other nations' domestic disputes. America needed to concern itself only with
"the preservation of the existing territorial status quo or . . . orderly peaceful
change," Barnet explained. The present alliance system, on the other hand,
existed primarily "to stabilize regimes in the face of internal subversion," as
opposed to stopping foreign aggression.[62]

By placing limits on U.S. actions abroad, IPS hoped to make the world
safe for diverse political and economic systems, including communism.
Concerned about the rising U.S. military budget in the late 1970s, Ravenal
embraced a policy of "unilateral disengagement" of U.S. forces from Europe.
He acknowledged that U.S. withdrawal might result in communist gains
in places like Italy, France, Spain, and Portugal, but he suggested that the
United States could "establish contacts" with the new governments. By the
late 1970s, several IPS intellectuals came to support Eurocommunism. In
November 1977, IPS held a seminar led by Santiago Carrillo, the general
secretary of the Communist Party of Spain and a leading advocate of Eurocommunism. During introductory remarks, Raskin offered his support for
Carrillo and his ideological doctrine. Besides strengthening the prospects
of both participatory democracy and national socialism, Raskin suggested
that Eurocommunism increased the likelihood "of a Europe united across
transnational lines without bending the knee to either the Soviet Union or
the United States."[63] In short, IPS hoped to tear down the "iron curtain" and
create a post–Cold War Europe.

IPS remained committed to dismantling NATO and the Warsaw Pact
well into the 1980s, though the obstinacy of the superpowers made such
efforts difficult. As a means "to investigate the possibilities of greater
autonomy in both Eastern and Western Europe, from the USSR and USA
respectively," IPS's Transnational Institute undertook a New Europe Project.
A report documenting the "New Europe" conference held in Amsterdam
in April 1983 noted that "the Project seeks to identify those points of weakness in the bloc system that are developing and to analyse the forces most
capable of advancing such a process of dissolution." The project, needless to
say, faced an uphill battle. Robert Borosage, who took over as IPS director in
1977, claimed that a paper he presented at the conference, which dealt with

the issue of superpower disengagement, caused "the Russians [to] hit the roof. They saw a European settlement as both impossible and undesirable." U.S. officials, furthermore, showed no inclination to dismantle NATO. Since the United States viewed NATO as "the least risky projection of American military power and the least difficult to justify," Barnet understood the difficulties that lay ahead for IPS.[64]

*   *   *

In setting its sights on NATO and asserting that the military alliance inhibited ideological pluralism, IPS sought to demolish a primary apparatus of the Cold War. Yet IPS tended to place too much of the blame for NATO's existence on the United States. Despite Europe's constant complaining, European leaders remained committed to a close relationship with the United States.[65] The Soviet Union, too, preferred NATO to the alternative, a unified and militarized Germany. In fact, IPS intellectuals, particularly Barnet, attached too little importance to the issue of German reunification, believing that both superpowers would accept the political and economic systems chosen by a reunified Germany. Even SDS favored a divided Germany out of concern that any moves in the opposite direction might instigate a nuclear exchange between the superpowers. Perhaps, as IPS argued, the unwillingness of the participants of the Cold War to move beyond the status quo explains the longevity of NATO. Loath to seek an alternative to NATO, both East and West preferred sticking with what they knew, refusing to conduct experiments on possible alternatives. As champions of pragmatism and ideological pluralism, IPS could not condone the defense of the status quo. In attempting to preserve the liberal international order, the United States denied what it sought to promote, democracy, by depriving nations of the ability to develop indigenous alternatives to Western-style democracy and capitalism. Military alliances, most notably NATO, ensured that the iron curtain across Europe remained a barrier to the world community envisioned by IPS.

The institute's advocacy of a world community should give pause to the notion that populism is primarily inward-looking and nationalist in orientation. While populist voices have advocated both isolationism and foreign intervention to further national interests, IPS favored a populist internationalism. In calling for a world community, the institute sought to erase distinctions based on national boundaries and create a truly global citizenry. Thus, peace intellectuals at the institute supported isolationism only insofar as it involved U.S. military intervention. In pursuit of a post–Cold War order,

IPS allied with libertarians at the Cato Institute rather than the liberal in the White House: Jimmy Carter. The institute struggled to counter the truncated vision for an interdependent world advocated by liberals associated with the Trilateral Commission. IPS's troubled relationship with Carter demonstrated just how wedded liberals were to the Cold War. A refusal to allow ideological pluralism not only led to the diminution of democracy but put the United States on a path toward disaster in Vietnam.

CHAPTER 3

Let the Dominoes Fall Where They May

Ideological Pluralism in Vietnam

Appearing on NBC's *Today* show on November 25, 1969, Richard Barnet, who had recently visited North Vietnam and spoken with government officials there, including Prime Minister Pham Van Dong, accused the United States of preventing a peaceful settlement of the Vietnam War. "What they are saying," Barnet explained in reference to North Vietnamese leaders, "is that the United States must not stand in the way, as it is now doing, of the natural evolution of South Vietnamese politics, which is moving more and more toward a desire on the part of everybody—Catholics, Buddhists, non-Communist forces—toward a neutralist government in South Vietnam that would make peace."[1]

The Vietnam War made it crystal clear to IPS that anti-communist ideology and the guardianship of the liberal world order barred the United States from following a strategy that allowed for ideological pluralism. Guided by Dwight Eisenhower's domino theory, U.S. policymakers continued to devote blood and treasure to the cause of defeating communists in Southeast Asia. IPS embarked on a campaign to prove that the United States intervened in Vietnam to stop the spread of communism and preserve its hegemony over the liberal world order rather than to defend Vietnamese independence and democracy. As a solution, IPS demanded that the United States commit to negotiations with all warring sides. Yet it did so not out of ideological solidarity with the National Liberation Front or North Vietnam. Rather, the institute's perspective on Vietnam conformed with the tenets of ideological pluralism, which held that "the people" should determine their own form of government without outside interference. In the end, IPS failed to sway U.S. officials, so, as it did in other campaigns, the institute sought to influence "the people." The institute's involvement in the draft resistance movement highlights the tensions between the activists and peace intellectuals at IPS regarding whether to focus on draft resistance or its relationship to the war system.

Hitler's Ghost and America as an Imperial Hegemon

IPS intellectuals held no compunction about condemning U.S. actions in Vietnam, both publicly and privately, to government officials and the American people. Following the passage of the Gulf of Tonkin resolution, Marcus Raskin offered a wide-ranging critique of U.S. policies in Vietnam and the domestic response to them. In an unpublished paper written in November 1964, Raskin proclaimed, "The silence on the part of American intellectuals regarding the American tragedy is quite deafening." Listing the many immoral and deadly acts committed in Vietnam by U.S. troops, he lamented, "Like Sisyphus we work with stone so much we become stone ourselves." To preserve what remained of America's humanity, Raskin called on the United States, as well as its South Vietnamese allies, to "stop its brutality, its use of napalm, torture, and other crude un-American forms of behavior." He also insisted that Lyndon Johnson remove those administration officials "who have foisted this miserable situation on ourselves and others." Lastly, Raskin proposed a meeting between the United States, France, China, and the Soviet Union to lay the groundwork for a negotiated settlement in Vietnam.[2] The irresponsibility of intellectuals, official accountability for war crimes, and the need for negotiations remained central elements of IPS's critical stance against the Vietnam War for the duration of the conflict.

In calling for the resignations of Johnson administration officials, Raskin hoped that bringing new blood into the government might eliminate the tendency to equate events in Vietnam with Hitler's expansionist policies in the 1930s. Johnson's assistant secretary of state, William Bundy, among others, warned against repeating the mistakes of World War II when U.S. and British officials appeased Hitler. Such thinking colored the perspective of Bundy, who criticized a paper written by Raskin on the Vietnam War for dwelling on the atrocities committed by South Vietnam while overlooking North Vietnam's use of the same harsh tactics. He compared Raskin's views to pre–World War II anti-interventionists who ignored Hitler's expansionist policies in Europe in the 1930s. "Your whole handling of this aspect reminded me all too painfully of attitudes in Europe in the 1930s that equated every police measure by Beneš against the Sudetens morally to the whole course of Hitler's conduct," Bundy wrote. Replying to Bundy's criticisms, Raskin chided the assistant secretary of state for his use of "false historical parallels which are totally irrelevant." Bundy's all too familiar analogy of Vietnam as a domino poised to fall under the weight of communism seemed to Raskin "far too ideological, emotive, conclusive and reductive." "The apocalyptic view saves us the trouble of forging a sophisticated foreign policy for Asia which requires diplomatic skill and prowess," Raskin explained.[3] Once again, the pragmatism of IPS led Raskin to excoriate U.S. officials for refusing to adapt to current realities.

Barnet, too, sought to expose the errors of the Munich analogy. He reprimanded U.S. officials for overstating the threat communism posed to U.S. security. To think, Barnet wrote, "that the Castros of the future will muster an army of millions, transport them by sampan and burro, and loose them on our cities is nothing less than a psychotic phantasy, so absurd in fact that it is never explicitly stated, only hinted at in vague anxiety producing historical analogies" with no relevance to present conditions. Unlike U.S. officials, who blamed the war in Southeast Asia on communist interference, the IPS cofounder likened the conflict to a civil war, with Ho Chi Minh leading a nationalist revolution. Moreover, by looking for fictional enemies abroad, U.S. officials ignored the growing unrest at home. Barnet argued that "the diversion of money and energy to fight which is supposed to keep Asian Communists from landing on our shores helps perpetuate the conditions which have created native insurgents and guerrilla warfare in American cities."[4] In other words, if the United States truly wanted to slow the growth of communism, it needed to redirect some of the money it spent on defense to improve the lives of its own citizens.

While critical of American involvement in Vietnam, IPS did not support an isolationist foreign policy. Waskow, speaking at the University of Michigan teach-in in March 1965, warned the crowd against allowing a "neo-isolationist arrogance" to guide their thinking. He encouraged his listeners not to become "the man who simply shuts off his living room with walls and security locks, takes a cab to the office so as not to see the poor, and leave them to rot in their misery." Rather, returning to ideas he pursued earlier in his career, Waskow argued that the United States should fight communism with "Unarmed Forces," like the Peace Corps, and "win unarmed victories for liberty." However, with Vietnam decimated, Waskow had doubts as to whether America could win any sort of victory, "unarmed" or otherwise. Therefore, he called for an immediate military withdrawal from Southeast Asia. In a 1966 letter to *War/Peace Report*, Waskow demanded that the United

States "withdraw militarily without conditions." Although he knew that it was unlikely that his proposal would gain public support, Waskow contended that "we should accept a local defeat that resulted from our own stupidity and moral blindness, rather than make the Vietnamese pay for our stupidity by destroying what is left of their country."[5] The United States, in other words, had so tarnished its image and caused such great physical destruction in Vietnam that it could never fix what it had done.

Yet hegemonic responsibilities, mainly the preservation of the liberal world order, required the United States to remain in Vietnam. Cold War power politics encouraged a growing interest in the Third World, without an accompanying concern for the people living in the region. Barnet blamed the obsession of power on the "national security manager," a figure described in greater detail in the next chapter. For the bureaucrat, Barnet explained, "the acquisition of power is both a necessity and an end in itself."[6] Yet, as the old adage goes, power corrupts. Raskin, along with well-known war correspondent Bernard B. Fall, who had previously supported the American war effort in Vietnam, released an edited collection of essays in 1965 in a book titled *The Viet-Nam Reader*, which sold 44,000 copies by November 1966. It included writings by U.S. officials and documents from the South Vietnamese National Liberation Front (NLF).[7] In the introduction, Raskin and Fall wrote, "Power, where it is used without wisdom and only in the name of one nation, will result in the ultimate corruption of the good ends that nation originally might have wished to achieve—and in the corruption of that nation itself."[8] Preserving U.S. global supremacy necessitated the continued involvement in Vietnam—but at a tremendous cost to the United States that Raskin thought both unwise and foolhardy.

From IPS's perspective, U.S. officials considered Vietnamese interests only as an afterthought. Using a photocopy of the Pentagon Papers that the institute obtained from Daniel Ellsberg, Ralph Stavins aimed to show readers in 1971 that neither communism nor national security led the United States to intervene in Vietnam. Instead, Johnson chose to escalate the war in 1965 to preserve America's status as "Number One Nation." According to Stavins, McGeorge Bundy and other officials tolerated the failure of Operation Rolling Thunder because the bombing helped America preserve its position atop the world. For Bundy, Stavins claimed, "the way he [America] plays the game becomes as important to him as the result of the game." Concerns over preserving U.S. credibility led Bundy to advocate continued bombing of Vietnam, much like, in the words of Stavins, "a gamester [seeking] to bring about an imperial goal." Raskin had made a nearly identical argument not long after the bombing of Vietnam began in earnest in February 1965. In his "A Citizen's White Paper on American Policy in Vietnam and Southeast Asia," Raskin alleged that the United States bombed Vietnam to send a message to China. Being "goaded by Chinese propaganda and psychological feelings of impotence," U.S. officials feared being branded "paper tigers" if the United States failed in Vietnam.[9] Thus, for IPS intellectuals, U.S. involvement in Vietnam had little to do with the nation itself or its people. Rather, U.S. officials put the prestige of the country on the line to enhance, and later preserve, its position as "Number One Nation."

At the end of *The Viet-Nam Reader*, Raskin and Fall offered several proposals for ending the Vietnam War. Since America's bombing campaign failed to "break North Vietnamese morale" or "boost South Vietnamese morale," the editors called for an immediate halt. According to Raskin and Fall, the United States needed to accept the "hard reality" that any coalition government in South Vietnam would have to include the NLF. To calm the minds of U.S. officials concerned about this eventuality, the editors explained that "the NLF program does not, at least *formally*, clash with basic United States objectives." Raskin and Fall also called for the removal of all U.S. and North Vietnamese troops from South Vietnam that had arrived after February 7, 1965. Troops deployed prior to 1965 would remain until an international control commission agreed on a date for withdrawal. As a next step, Raskin and Fall suggested that all sides sign an agreement modeled on the Austrian State Treaty of 1955, which granted Austria its independence and allowed the sovereign state to remain neutral. The proposed treaty called for the eventual unification of North and South Vietnam.[10] For the most part, Raskin and Fall's "diplomatic alternatives" guided IPS's thinking on the war until its end.

The Viet-Nam Reader succeeded in capturing the attention of student protestors more than government officials. Raskin claimed that he and Fall received "a great number of letters" from university faculty and their students. "The book hardened up the lines, started people thinking about fundamental American policy," Raskin noted. In fact, the reader served as the authoritative text at teach-ins on campuses across the nation. Raskin took part in several of these events, debating Abe Fortas, Walt Rostow, and other pro-administration voices.[11] *The Viet-Nam Reader* achieved exactly what the codirectors had wanted for IPS publications: it became an alternative source of information to help the public reach its own conclusions regarding U.S. policy in Vietnam.

Negotiations Now! "Ideological Pluralism" in Action

Despite the destruction wrought by Operation Rolling Thunder, the United States continued bombing Vietnam. Secretary of Defense Robert McNamara believed the air war strengthened America's negotiating position. Future events proved McNamara wrong. When the United States initiated the first bombing pause in early 1966, the North Vietnamese refused to carry out talks with foreign nations on matters pertaining to Vietnam's political system. North Vietnam's defiance increased public support for an expanded air war and encouraged Johnson to expand the bombing to end the war more quickly.[12]

When it became clear that the United States had to find a way to extricate itself from Southeast Asia, liberal opposition to the war generally split over the issue of what to do with U.S. troops stationed in Vietnam. Whereas radicals called for their immediate withdrawal, liberals wanted to wait until the two sides reached a negotiated settlement. IPS stood somewhere in the middle of these two approaches. While Waskow demanded the immediate withdrawal of U.S. forces from Vietnam, other IPS intellectuals, most notably Raskin, called for the drawdown to occur in stages. Repeatedly throughout the 1960s, Raskin proposed reducing the number of U.S. troops in South Vietnam to 38,000. By 1967, even Cold War liberals like Arthur Schlesinger Jr., John Kenneth Galbraith, and Joseph Rauh came around to supporting negotiations. They created Negotiations Now!, which called for a bombing halt and the opening of talks with all sides involved in the fighting. While against escalation, this group also opposed unilateral withdrawal of any kind.[13]

For the length of the Vietnam War, IPS intellectuals urged the United States to not only negotiate but, more importantly, invite the NLF to the bargaining table. For many at IPS, only the NLF, rather than the North Vietnamese, could speak for the Vietnamese people. At the same time, Raskin warned in an unpublished paper that prolonging the war strengthened the position of communists in the NLF. On the other hand, beginning negotiations in 1966 meant that "serious differences in the NLF will [still] show up," empowering the diverse non-communist elements in the political organization. Therefore, Raskin concluded that "end[ing] the war on terms which would have served the American national interest" meant meeting with "the principal belligerents," especially the NLF. To do otherwise "would be similar to Great Britain attempting to get peace during the American Revolution by negotiating with France since the revolution was supported and dominated by the French." Ending the conflict required U.S. officials to acknowledge the actual participants in the war. Barnet contended that "the State Department's whole script for 'negotiation' takes on an air of fantasy" in thinking that Ho Chi Minh controlled the NLF guerrillas, an attitude he blamed on the wrong-headed belief that the Vietnamese civil war might end as did the Greek civil war, with defeat of the communists.[14]

From day one, IPS argued for the inclusion of the NLF in negotiations because the institute, unlike U.S. officials, did not despair over the possibility of a communist government in Vietnam. Barnet described the NLF's "program" as "deliberately moderate and non-communist" due to the local conditions the NLF faced in South Vietnam. According to Barnet, the NLF understood that "their only hope of bringing effective rule to South Vietnam is to attract a coalition of the many diverse elements which make up what is, historically, a nation but, organizationally, a collection of duchies." U.S. policies, however, weakened the very groups that compelled the NLF to moderate its program. Barnet accused the United States of "undercutting the independent power of non-communist nationalists by giving full backing to the military junta." He called on Johnson to press South Vietnam's president, Nguyen Van Thieu, to welcome nationalist and communist voices into his cabinet. Additionally, Barnet argued that successful negotiations required an end to U.S. political and military interference in the affairs of South Vietnam. Barnet repurposed the domino theory by suggesting that disengagement from the region would have a positive effect on the nations surrounding Vietnam. Using Thailand as an example, Barnet wrote that the Thai government would realize that it had to "follow a strategy of conciliation in dealing with the guerrillas rather than a strategy of pure repression."[15]

The ability of the North Vietnamese to persevere despite American bombs raining down on them only increased the respect Barnet and others at IPS had for the people of that country. Following his trip to Hanoi in 1969, Barnet drafted a glowing report of North Vietnamese society. Surprised by the tenacity of the North Vietnamese, he wrote that "they have shown that they can take punishment and even thrive on it." Though the country had been torn asunder by war, Barnet boasted that university enrollments in North Vietnam had grown, rice yields had increased, and deaths from infectious diseases had declined. He also spoke highly of their "decentralized" industry, school administration, agriculture, and health care. These "changes are popular and have raised morale," Barnet reported. The North Vietnamese exuded an "extraordinary spirit of determination and light heartedness," in his opinion. Telling the story of how the North Vietnamese seemed more concerned with the infestation of mosquitoes in the craters left behind by U.S. bombs than anything else, Barnet reached the conclusion that "Vietnam appears to be one of the countries in the world least vulnerable to massive air bombardment."[16] Like many other antiwar activists in the 1960s, IPS intellectuals were prone to see only the best in the North Vietnamese.

Still, IPS intellectuals differed from other critics of the Vietnam War who paid inordinate attention to the ideological propensities of the North Vietnamese and the NLF. For instance, Staughton Lynd and Tom Hayden, who visited North Vietnam in 1965, waxed poetic about the "possibilities for a socialism of the heart" in Vietnam. As one historian has argued, Lynd and Hayden "presented the war very much from an American viewpoint," meaning that for them it became less about Vietnamese survival and independence and more about building support for a particular theory or cause in the United States.[17] IPS intellectuals took a different approach. The ideological proclivities of the North Vietnamese and NLF mattered far less to IPS intellectuals whose main concern was that the Vietnamese people had the ability to determine their own political fate without foreign interference. Representative of this sort of thinking, Barnet, in a memorandum for National Security Advisor Henry Kissinger in 1969, made clear that any plan needed "to provide the greatest possible self-determination and protection for all political elements in South Vietnam after the complete withdrawal of U.S. forces."[18]

IPS's advocacy of inclusive peace negotiations found few backers in Washington, D.C. No matter their disdain for the war, White House officials refused to accept the possibility of a communist Vietnam. Pragmatists at IPS, however, realized that no other alternatives existed. Denied a political and military victory in Vietnam, Barnet argued in an unpublished article, "the U.S. must act in a way to make it credible that we are prepared to leave and to permit the play of local forces in Vietnam to determine their political future, even if it means a communist government." Otherwise, negotiations served merely as a holding pattern "to outwait the patient warriors of Vietnam." While underscoring the need for the administration to exert greater pressure on Thieu to bring more non-communists into his cabinet, Barnet did not obscure the fact that the communists might still take over the South Vietnamese government. No matter how quickly the United States withdrew its forces from Vietnam, Barnet, in reference to the possibility of a communist takeover, admitted that "we cannot prevent it if it should turn out that the non-Communist elements are too weak to play a significant independent role." Still, Barnet claimed, if the United States stopped trying to achieve the "unattainable goal of determining the character of the South Vietnamese Government," Thieu's government would be able to "better use its power to promote objectives that are both more in its own interest and more realistic."[19]

In other words, America's continued presence in Vietnam weakened non-communist voices and increased the likelihood of a communist conquest.

The Vietnam War put Cold War liberalism on the defensive. Still, the idea that the United States should extricate itself from Vietnam knowing full well that the nation might go communist proved too much for many foreign policy elites. The intransigence of policymakers bewildered IPS intellectuals. Hoping for a change in policy with Richard Nixon in the White House, Barnet encouraged the president, then sixty days into his term, to "look coldly at the real choices open to the U.S. and prepare to redefine U.S. war aims in terms of political realities rather than the optimistic fantasies that so misled his predecessor." The fact that thus far into his presidency Nixon did not invite the NLF to participate in negotiations served as evidence of the administration's lack of knowledge about Vietnamese politics, Barnet charged. He argued that "the communists represent the best organized political force in the country and have the allegiance of the largest single minority, if not a majority, of the population." Nor did Barnet accept half measures, or what he called an "imposed coalition" in which "the United States would try to interest them [the NLF] in the Ministry of Tourism." Rather, Barnet preferred that "the U.S. Embassy in Saigon [devote] its full attention to packing" and leave the construction of a coalition government to "indigenous Vietnamese forces" to begin the process of repairing the political and environmental destruction of their nation. Barnet claimed that should the NLF achieve dominance it would "have to accommodate the various factions or else continue a bloody civil war which it is in the interests of no Vietnamese to prolong." The Buddhists, Cao Dai, Catholics, and "semiautonomous groups" like the Hoa Hao would all make it difficult for the communists to take total control of the country, Barnet predicted.[20] IPS intellectuals accepted the spread of communism in Southeast Asia if it allowed native people to determine their own fate.

Throughout 1969, Barnet reached out to American and Vietnamese officials to promote his views on a coalition government. He suggested to the NLF that it create a "peace cabinet" composed of communists and non-communists. Writing in February 1969 to Nguyen Thi Binh, who later served as the representative for the NLF at the Paris Peace Conference, Barnet proposed having an American delegation visit Vietnam to promote the "peace cabinet." Such a tour would exhibit for the rest of the world that the only "real obstacles to negotiation" remained in the U.S. government, which "continu[ed] to support puppets against the desires of an ever-growing majority of the Vietnamese people."[21]

From IPS's perspective, America's "puppets" in South Vietnam also stood in the way of ideological pluralism. Along with troop withdrawals and a bombing halt, Barnet encouraged U.S. officials to put increased pressure on Thieu to begin negotiations with the NLF, when the presence of U.S. troops still afforded him an advantage. Next, Barnet suggested that Thieu create a Provisional Commission for National Reconciliation. This commission, with input from the NLF, Buddhists, Saigon government officials and citizens, and exiles, would organize and plan for national elections. Barnet's proposal aimed at "ensuring maximum participation and protection for all elements in South Vietnam" and strived to limit America's role to "lend[ing] whatever support it can to demands from the Vietnamese themselves for international inspection and specific assurances for amnesty." In the end, success hinged on Nixon's willingness to "candidly tell the public that we cannot guarantee or even predict what the future political development of South Vietnam will be."[22] Though disconcerting to many Americans, ideological pluralism required a high degree of uncertainty.

Notwithstanding IPS's pleas, U.S. policy remained unchanged. Invited by the North Vietnamese Jurist Association to visit Hanoi in December 1969, Barnet met with "former soldiers" from the South Vietnamese army and "middle class professionals." "The destruction and uncontrolled inflation in Saigon are building a nationalist coalition for peace," Barnet contended. Therefore, U.S. and South Vietnamese officials had to come to grips with this reality. According to Barnet, America's understanding of the war, which differed dramatically from that of the North Vietnamese, precluded a successful conclusion of the conflict. Having spoken with North Vietnam's prime minister, Premier Pham Van Dong, during his trip to North Vietnam and then to National Security Advisor Kissinger and other U.S. officials upon his return to the United States, Barnet exclaimed that "it became clear to me that Hanoi and Washington are not fighting the same war."[23] Much to the dismay of IPS intellectuals, U.S. officials still considered Vietnam the front line in the battle against communism. The Vietnamese, on the other hand, sought a return to normalcy and an independent Vietnam.

With the onset of détente and Nixon's trip to China in 1972, Barnet could not fathom why the United States continued to pour money and troops into Southeast Asia. According to Barnet, North Vietnamese and NLF leaders had their doubts as to whether a reunified Vietnam would come under the control of a communist government. Even so, Barnet wondered why Americans found such an outcome disconcerting. Unlikely to ally with either the Soviets or the Chinese, "the successors to Ho Chi Minh would become the Tito of Asia and would in all likelihood court the friendship of the United States as counterweight to the nearby communist giants," Barnet claimed. Why, he asked, "when the President clinks glasses in the Kremlin and the Great Hall of Peking" did the United States continue to expend blood and treasure in pursuit of a non-communist Vietnam? Barnet implored the United States to accept a proposal from the Provisional Revolutionary Government (PRG) for a "government of national reconciliation" that included "any Vietnamese politician or political group who put national independence first." According to Barnet, the PRG's proposed government would be "two-thirds non-communist" and guided by a "liberal, nationalist, and neutralist" perspective. He predicted a "deliberately moderate" approach to governance that included "independence and neutrality" in foreign affairs and, domestically, continued "guarantees [for] private ownership of agricultural land and industrial property."[24]

IPS's fidelity to ideological pluralism led it to downplay the threat of North Vietnamese reprisals against South Vietnam following U.S. withdrawal from Southeast Asia. The North Vietnamese had practiced "pragmatism" in their previous efforts "to survive by adjusting to political reality," according to Barnet. He predicted that following the exodus of Americans from Vietnam, "their [North Vietnamese] political goal will be reconciliation and reconstruction of their tortured country." At the same time, he cautioned that the North Vietnamese's willingness to forgive had its limits. The United States needed to immediately withdraw its personnel and troops. "The more 'our Vietnamese' are identified with the brutality of the U.S. war effort and the longer the war goes on, the likelier targets of public anger they become," Barnet explained.[25]

As it turned out, reconciliation between the opposing sides did not go as smoothly as Barnet predicted. Following the reunification of Vietnam in 1976, the North forced South Vietnamese soldiers into communist reeducation centers, where some of the prisoners stayed until the early 1990s.[26] Despite this reality, Barnet remained committed to the communist experiment in Vietnam. This controversy split the American Left. Barnet, along with seventeen other activists, academics, and religious leaders, cosigned an "appeal," written by socialist Corliss Lamont and published in the *New York Times* on January 30, 1977, that called for improved relations between the United States and Vietnam. Recalling concerns about a "bloodbath" following the withdrawal of U.S. troops, the appeal suggested that nothing of the sort occurred. "Peace has come to Vietnam without any bloodbath and without any cruel policy of reprisal. It is time for Americans of good will to recognize and applaud this achievement." The appeal accused critics of Vietnam's human rights record of "distortion and exaggeration," even while acknowledging that the Vietnamese government sent forty thousand "Saigon collaborationists" to reeducation camps, a "surprisingly small" figure given the total population in South Vietnam. Moreover, the appeal claimed that the South Vietnamese government committed much worse "savagery" during the war. "The present government of Vietnam should be hailed for its moderation and for its extraordinary effort to achieve reconciliation among all of its people." In the end, the appeal continued, "responsibility" for human rights abuses in Vietnam belonged to the United States for creating regional instability after more than a decade of warfare.[27]

Two years later, singer and antiwar activist Joan Baez penned an "Open Letter to the Socialist Republic of Vietnam," which was signed by eighty-three others, including Daniel Berrigan, Allen Ginsberg, Cesar Chavez, Bradford Lyttle, and Staughton and Alice Lynd. The letter referred to the present as "a time for grieving" because of the denial of human rights in Vietnam, which led to "the current number of political prisoners between 150,000 and 200,000." Among the atrocities listed in the letter were mass imprisonment, disappearances, forced relocation to reeducation centers, and the use of humans to clear mine fields. The letter demanded an end to such practices and urged the Vietnamese government to invite "an international team of neutral observers to inspect your prisons and re-education centers." Noting "a deep philosophical split over the issue," Baez admitted that many leftists refused to sign the statement. As for Barnet, he continued to defend the actions of the Socialist Republic of Vietnam. In an exchange with conservative commentator Patrick Buchanan on a local Washington, D.C., news program in 1981, during which Buchanan compared Vietnam's actions "to what Hitler did to the Jews," Barnet strongly disagreed. "I would describe it [Communist Vietnam] as a regime that was trying, under the most incredibly difficult circumstances, to bring about a reconstruction of the country. I don't think they've done a very good job of it. I don't approve of many of the things they've done," Barnet conceded. At the same time, he accused Buchanan of hypocrisy for ignoring similar atrocities being carried out by right-wing governments in Argentina and Chile.[28]

Speaking for the Draft Resistance Movement

In no other war before or since have Americans spoken out in as large numbers as they did during the Vietnam War. Much of the outcry centered on the draft. The burning of draft cards began in 1964 and became more common as the war progressed.[29] Raskin became interested in conscription while still a legislative assistant for Representative Robert Kastenmeier. As an aide, he authored a report in advance of a congressional hearing on the extension of the draft law, which opened his eyes to the relationship between the Selective Service System and American empire. Describing his moment of sudden awareness, Raskin explained, "The argument we had to beat was that if we don't have permanent conscription our worldwide commitments will become meaningless. This was my first attempt to get at the issue. I began to see the draft as a mechanism to perpetuate a permanent warrior-like mentality in this country."[30] Thus, from early on, Raskin linked the draft to militarism.

As Raskin and Waskow wrote "A Call to Resist Illegitimate Authority" in 1967, they looked to organize a group of influential intellectuals to support young draft resisters. Noting a "groundswell of revulsion against the war," Waskow appealed to John R. Seeley of the Center for the Study of Democratic Institutions and famed linguist Noam Chomsky to join with other intellectuals in "a solemn act of civil disobedience by the nearest we have to moral leadership" in America. As "the tightest link between the war and people's daily lives," Waskow and Raskin targeted the Selective Service System. Though opposition to the draft existed at universities across the country, Waskow warned that without the participation of intellectuals "there will be no one to speak for the legitimacy of draft resistance by the kids," which weakened the movement. Prepared to go to jail for his beliefs, Waskow intended to defend his actions "on the grounds of the illegitimacy under international law and unconstitutionality under American law of the present uses of the draft, and therefore on the grounds that under Nuremberg there is a positive duty of good citizens to resist its operations." Waskow and Raskin explained in another letter, this time to philosopher Herbert Marcuse, that they hoped to bring together at least fifty "rather well-known intellectuals" to take part in a sit-in at the Selective Service headquarters in Washington, D.C., possibly involving civil disobedience.[31] Raskin and Waskow's appeal to intellectuals to stand together and speak out against official wrongdoing conformed to the role IPS imagined for itself as public scholars.

Despite previous statements in support of draft resistance, the movement lacked a declaration that offered a philosophical rationale for anti-draft actions. This changed in 1967 when the *New Republic* and the *New York Review of Books* published "A Call to Resist Illegitimate Authority." Writing in 1971, Michael Ferber and Staughton Lynd claimed that "a thousand statements bloomed" in the 1960s in support of draft resistance, which caused consternation among the people asked to sign them. "Everyone was confused, not least the resisters who were the intended beneficiaries of all the verbiage," according to Ferber and Lynd. In the end, "one emerged pre-eminent in scope, publicity, and political impact," Waskow and Raskin's "Call."[32] Interviewed not long after he coauthored the "Call," Raskin claimed that the inspiration to write the statement came from Bernard Fall, who had expressed dismay over Americans' indifference toward the atrocities being committed in Vietnam by the U.S. military: "His greatest anger was directed against the American left, their failure to become aroused over the torture of Vietnamese prisoners of war and the use of napalm. There seemed to be no one to speak out against it, as the French did on Algeria." Inspired by the example of the French protestors, Raskin sought to re-create, for an American audience, the French intellectuals' Manifesto of the 121.[33]

The "Call" denounced the Vietnam War from both a moral and legal standpoint, which belies the usual image of anti–Vietnam War protestors as primarily interested in only the former. Claiming that "moral issues felt so obvious that juridical justifications seemed superfluous," Barbara Keys has argued that the antiwar movement usually couched its opposition in moral rather than legal terms. Historians of the anti–Vietnam War movement tend to agree. One chronicler, Melvin Small, claims that the "vast majority" of opposition to the war stemmed from moral revulsion, while another scholar, Sandy Vogelgesang, has suggested that radical intellectuals' overbearing moralism led to "powerlessness" since it worked against their involvement in politics.[34] For IPS, however, legality and morality went hand in hand.

In the section on morality, the "Call" stated that America's youth "are finding that the American war in Vietnam so outrages their deepest moral and religious sense that they cannot contribute to it in any way." "We share their moral outrage," the "Call" proclaimed. Regarding the legality and constitutionality of the Vietnam War, the "Call" castigated the president and Congress for leading the nation into an unconstitutional war that rejected the principles enshrined in the UN Charter. The Charter "requires member states to exhaust every peaceful means of settling disputes" independently or with the assistance of the United Nations. Moreover, the United States "systematically violated" the UN Charter. U.S. military action in Vietnam mirrored the "crimes against humanity for which individuals were to be held personally responsible . . . and for which Germans were sentenced at Nuremberg to long prison terms and death." After stating the legal and constitutional arguments against the Vietnam War, the "Call" declared its intentions: "Therefore, we believe on all these grounds that every free man has a legal right and a moral duty to exert every effort to end this war, to avoid collusion with it, and encourage others to do the same." Why use resistance to the draft to oppose the Vietnam War? The "Call" claimed that such "open resistance" would "strengthen the moral resolve" of antiwar activists to end the draft and eventually the war.[35]

Blending legalism and moralism, the "Call" found support from a wide swath of the American public. At least two thousand academics, professionals, clergy, and ordinary Americans signed the "Call" as it spread through informal channels and appeared in magazines.[36] By mid-1967, a who's who of antiwar activists had added their names to the "Call," including Howard Zinn, Richard Flacks, Gar Alperovitz, Paul Goodman, Benjamin Spock, Al Haber, Staughton Lynd, Sidney Lens, Allen Ginsberg, Dwight Macdonald, Gabriel Kolko, Susan Sontag, William Sloane Coffin, Herbert Marcuse, Noam Chomsky, Linus Pauling, and Carl Oglesby. Some prominent intellectuals, though, refused to sign. Speaking for himself and his University of Michigan colleague Arnold Kaufman, the author of *The Radical Liberal*, Donald Michael, one of the original fellows at IPS, criticized the statement because in addition to supporting draft resisters "it gives the impression that signers want to incite youths to stay out [of Vietnam]." This seemed to Kaufman and Michael a questionable legal position for the signers to agree with. Furthermore, seeing the statement as one "of moral commitment rather than a political statement," Kaufman and Michael suggested making the latter point clearer.[37] Michael's prediction about the legal repercussions proved prescient, but Raskin and Waskow thought that intellectuals had to stick their heads out and not depend entirely on the bravery of America's young.

The methods proposed in the "Call" received the most criticism. Historian Merle Curti disagreed with Waskow's contention that American actions in Vietnam constituted an illegal act. Curti reminded his former student that by approving funds for the war, Congress, "which is the duly elected representative of the majority of voters," put its stamp of approval on Johnson's Vietnam policies. Moreover, Curti thought that most Americans would "react unfavorably to what might be regarded as civil disobedience or even to this kind of education," which dissuaded him from signing the "Call." While expressing "emotional sympathy" for draft resistance and the antiwar movement in general, Curti argued that ending the war required "mass resistance," something he thought unlikely to occur in the United States.[38] Perhaps the most prominent peace researcher in America, Kenneth Boulding, also expressed misgivings about the "Call," especially its targeting of the Selective Service. He preferred an electoral approach since "responsibility for the war in Vietnam lies . . . squarely at the door of the President." Additionally, he could not publicly support draft resistance because Americans, in his opinion, "ha[d] been indoctrinated for so long in the myth of national greatness established by military might that I am very much afraid a frontal attack on the draft would be unsuccessful." With these prospects in mind, Boulding suggested campaigning for antiwar Democrats in the 1968 elections.[39] IPS intellectuals, however, had already given up on reforming the Democratic Party, so Boulding's suggestion fell on deaf ears.

On October 21, 1967, tens of thousands of protestors marched from the Lincoln Memorial to the Pentagon as part of Stop the Draft Week.[40] Raskin, Waskow, Benjamin Spock, William Sloane Coffin, and several other draft resisters took a briefcase filled with draft cards to the Justice Department for Assistant Attorney General John McDonough, who ultimately refused to take it. Both Raskin and Waskow added their cards to the collection. Though only eight months away from his thirty-fifth birthday, and thus no longer eligible for the draft, Waskow claimed that he could really "empathize" with draft resisters who had taken part in the protest. Therefore, Waskow could not ask the students to do what he himself refused to do. "My feeling had been that it was a bad scene for 'safe' people to be encouraging resistance . . . and returning the card was thus an attempt to step outside the charmed circle."[41]

The government responded on January 5, 1968, when the U.S. District Court in Massachusetts issued indictments to pediatrician and author of a best-selling child-rearing book Dr. Benjamin Spock, Yale University chaplain William Sloane Coffin, writer and teacher Mitchell Goodman, Harvard University graduate student Michael Ferber, and Raskin. Inexplicably, Waskow, who personally handed the assistant attorney general the case with the draft cards at the Pentagon protest and whose name clearly appeared as one of the coauthors of the "Call," dodged prosecution. The fact that Waskow escaped punishment is even stranger considering that in the section of the indictment dealing with the "overt acts" committed by the defendants, overt act number one stated that Coffin and Spock "distributed and caused to be distributed" the "Call." The district court based its indictment on a series of charges against the defendants accusing them of conspiring to encourage, as well as aid and abet, draft resistance among America's draft-age youth.[42] In the end, Raskin avoided prosecution—the only defendant out of the five to do so—because of his minor role in the whole affair.

Though an active participant in these events, Raskin held an unfavorable view of the draft card turn-in at the Pentagon. He described the protest as "silly" and reported that he "squirmed" when the protestors handed the assistant attorney general the briefcase containing the draft cards. Nonetheless, Raskin joined Waskow and the others in order to speak directly to officials from the Justice Department about investigating American atrocities in Vietnam. Raskin explained during the conspiracy trial that his concern was with "the illegality of the war and the problem of war crimes" in Vietnam, not so much the draft. During the brief exchange with the assistant attorney general, Raskin brought up the issue of war crimes in Vietnam and asked McDonough to speak to the attorney general about creating a "special committee" to investigate U.S. conduct in Vietnam.[43]

Despite IPS's best efforts to eliminate the divide between theory and activism, the actual ideas found within the "Call" did not always resonate with the young draft resisters. Antiwar activists looked to the Nuremberg Principles primarily to defend their decision to avoid serving in Vietnam.[44] Meanwhile, veterans, most notably the Vietnam Veterans Against the War (VVAW), sought to publicize war crimes to end the conflict. For instance, the VVAW hearings held in Detroit in 1971 uncovered U.S. misdeeds in Vietnam, leaving no doubt that immoral and criminal acts occurred, but the organizers remained silent on the issue of accountability. Like the earlier Russell International War Crimes Tribunal, organized by British philosopher Bertrand Russell and French philosopher Jean-Paul Sartre in 1967, the war crimes hearings initiated by VVAW lacked the legal mechanisms to bring war criminals to justice and thus served more as a show trial to increase public knowledge of U.S. war crimes to end the war. In the case of the Russell Tribunal, Russell admitted as much when he wrote just prior to the event, "It claims no other than a moral authority."[45] Yet, as IPS intellectuals understood, without the threat of legal prosecution, officials could ignore the stories offered by returning veterans. As the next chapter shows, IPS intellectuals' interest in war crimes extended beyond self-interest and ending the Vietnam War.

*   *   *

The desire for self-determination in Southeast Asia undergirded IPS's opposition to the Vietnam War far more than pro-communist sympathies. While U.S. officials looked at events in Southeast Asia through the prism of the Cold War, IPS intellectuals viewed the conflict as a colonial struggle for independence. Ho Chi Minh was not Hitler. By refusing to advocate open negotiations, U.S. officials exhibited a lack of pragmatism and let ideology blur reality. In the end, Eisenhower's domino theory continued to stand in the way of ideological pluralism. As it became clear that the United States would not condone indigenous development that failed to conform to Western-style political and economic blueprints, IPS turned to "the people." The thousands of signatures obtained in support of the "Call" demonstrate IPS's ability to influence and educate America's youth about the immoral and illegal aspects of the war. Yet, indicative of the difficulties faced by intellectuals seeking an audience among activists, the draft resisters focused on the narrow issue of conscription instead of American militarism and empire.

In the debates within the Left over whether to support or criticize the Socialist Republic of Vietnam government's postwar reconciliation program, IPS chose to downplay the human rights abuses committed by the new regime. The pragmatic minds at the institute realized that a categorical rejection of armed intervention required a recognition that the United States could not choose the sort of world it inhabited. To think otherwise led to military action abroad, which threatened the peace. This led the peace intellectuals at IPS to argue that the United States had to live with illiberal and undemocratic governments, letting the dominoes fall where they may. More importantly from IPS's perspective, the United States pursued its goals with reckless abandon and no concern for morality or legal restraint. The United States could not always solve the problems facing other nations, human rights or otherwise, but it could put its own house in order. Why did the United States repeatedly commit such horrific acts against foreign populations? IPS intellectuals argued that the personnel involved in making these decisions were to blame. These "national security managers," as Barnet and others at IPS designated them, are the focus of the next chapter.

CHAPTER 4

The National Security State and the Men Behind It

Writing nearly a decade after serving in John F. Kennedy's State Department, and as the last American troops left Vietnam, Richard Barnet bemoaned the "bureaucratization of homicide" among a group of officials he labeled the "national security managers." These bureaucrats developed strategies that involved massive bombing campaigns, defoliation missions, and assassinations without setting foot on the battlefield. Barnet went so far as to compare the planners to Nazi leaders. Like Reinhard Heydrich and Adolf Eichmann, "the bureaucratic killer looks at an assigned homicidal task as a technical operation much like any other. He does not question its moral purpose," he wrote. Thus, to restrain U.S. militarism, bureaucrats needed to be held responsible for their immoral acts. In 1971, Marcus Raskin offered a solution. He argued that "there is precedent from the Nuremberg and Tokyo tribunals for the criminal conviction of civilians both on the basis of atrocities against noncombatants which, as part of the chain of command, they had a duty to prevent, and on the basis of the 'aggressive war' policies the civilian leaders helped to develop."[1]

In comparison to Barnet and Raskin's punitive approach, Arthur Schlesinger Jr., a fellow New Frontiersman who had held a position far closer to the seat of power as Kennedy's special assistant, offered an apologia of sorts for the planners of the Vietnam War and urged caution when doling out punishment. Writing in 1966, Schlesinger described U.S. involvement in the Vietnam War as "a triumph of the politics of inadvertence." He blamed a "series of small decisions," not calculated planning, for America's growing involvement in the war. "It is not only idle but unfair to seek out guilty men," he declared.[2] Critics like Schlesinger viewed the Vietnam War as a one-time blunder caused by incompetent leaders and poor decision making on the part of the president's advisors. Peace intellectuals at IPS disagreed. They pointed to institutional mechanisms that privileged a technocratic outlook unencumbered by moral, ethical, or legal restraints, resulting in the militarization of U.S. society and the ebbing of democracy.

Since the nineteenth century, peace activists, academics, and politicians offered various proposals to either make war illegal or bring it under the jurisdiction of a world court tasked with arbitrating disputes. With the success of the outlawry of war movement and the passage of the Kellogg-Briand Pact of 1928, which renounced war as an instrument used in international relations, it appeared as if humankind had crossed an important threshold.[3] Then came World War II and the Cold War, and with each the inevitable bloodshed.

IPS sought to explain the reasons behind the continued violence, both visible and covert, and develop an alternative to the existing ineffectual international laws. To explain the incessant wars, IPS developed two unique theoretical constructs, the "national security manager" and the "national security state." The institute sought to transform the American legal system into a tool to strike at the heart of U.S. militarism and restore democracy. IPS wanted to bring the Nuremberg trials to America. IPS intellectuals blamed a legal system that lacked personal responsibility laws to restrict the malicious actions of unaccountable officials in bureaucracies, which guaranteed a reoccurrence of Vietnam-like conflicts. IPS intellectuals understood the resistance to the enforcement of international laws within the borders of nation-states, which led to their proposal to domesticate Nuremberg's legal statutes. Besides bringing accountability to U.S. foreign policy, IPS aimed to rein in Barnet's homicidal bureaucrats through a much-expanded role for the citizenry in foreign policy decisions. In short, making the world safe for diversity and constructing a post–Cold War order required a concomitant campaign carried out within the belly of the beast, that is, the United States, to strengthen democracy through personal accountability laws and the democratization of U.S. foreign policy.

National Security Managers, the National Security State, and American Democracy

America's transformation from isolationist to global policeman after World War II had important implications for U.S. society. Even before the conclusion of the war, political scientist Harold Lasswell, writing in 1941, referred to America as a "garrison state" because of the perpetual threat of war. "With the socialization of danger as a permanent characteristic of modern violence the nation becomes one unified technical enterprise" run by a small group, he argued. Who controlled the "garrison state"? Writing in 1956, C. Wright Mills introduced readers to the "power elite," a group that included military leaders, corporate heads, and politicians. Forming an "interlocking directorate," the power elite manipulated the American people into accepting the dictates of the military, corporate, and political leaders.[4] Led by Mills's "directorate," the United States became a "warfare state" and a "national security state." The warfare state received its closest examination in Fred Cook's 1962 book of the same title. For Cook, "propaganda" and "fear" drove Americans to accept the creation of a warfare state, which resulted in vast discrepancies between military and domestic spending. Thus, when Franklin Roosevelt's "Dr. Win-the-War" replaced "Dr. New Deal" in late 1943, the latter never practiced again as a bipartisan foreign policy consensus preserved the warfare state.[5] IPS devised its own terminology—the "national security manager" and the "national security state"—to reveal how undemocratic structures within the United States led to the development of a foreign policy indifferent to democracy abroad.

The national security state thrived due to the efforts of a collection of foreign policy officials Barnet labeled "national security managers." Barnet and other IPS intellectuals blamed these bureaucrats for Vietnam and America's other imperial ventures. As the American state grew and became more centralized, the administration of government, or bureaucracy, garnered much attention from intellectuals. IPS's critique of national security managers mirrored the growing anti-bureaucratic feeling of the 1960s in response to "managerial liberalism" and its reliance on technocrats.[6]

Barnet offered his harshest appraisal of national security managers in his 1972 book *Roots of War: The Men and Institutions Behind U.S. Foreign Policy*. As technocrats flocked to Washington, they brought with them a unique skill set as efficient administrators and experts in quantitative and statistical analysis. These ultrarational technocrats had no moral qualms about employing overwhelming force to defeat America's enemies. Barnet lamented this "militarization of the civilian leadership" as bureaucrats outdid even the military brass in their preference for military solutions over diplomatic ones. According to Barnet, the national security mangers lacked the vocabulary necessary for negotiations: "Factors which can be fed into computers such as 'kill ratio' sound more persuasive than political analysis, which is hard to prepare and hard to comprehend." Preferring the certainty of mathematical calculations, U.S. officials avoided entering into unpredictable negotiations in Vietnam and elsewhere. Discussing the run-up to the Vietnam War, Barnet lamented, "No staff work of any consequence was devoted to the kind of peace settlement" that might have precluded a military response. In fact, the national security managers offered just two options: victory or surrender. With its outright rejection of negotiations, the national security bureaucracy "reduced a complex political reality to a test of the American will" in its fight against communism.[7]

Barnet's national security managers thrived within a culture of unaccountability and elite decision making. Despite the numerous opportunities for peace in Vietnam—UN Secretary-General U Thant, Hanoi, and Moscow offered several proposals early on—the national security managers could not overcome the allure of an overpowering military victory. Barnet suggested that "rewards and incentives" tended "to absolve men from personal responsibility for bureaucratic homicide," which encouraged technocrats to use excessive force to end conflicts quickly, with no concern for the collateral damage caused by their war plans. Moreover, national security managers did not have to deal with public scrutiny, according to Barnet. He claimed that they inhabited a "separate government" that was "insulated from the people of the United States" and not particularly responsive to citizens' demands.[8] A lack of personal responsibility and undemocratic tendencies, therefore, allowed national security managers to run amok, leaving a trail of destruction in their path.

Given the unelected status of the national security managers, IPS warned that these technocrats owed no allegiance to the citizenry and therefore rarely kept the public interest in mind when formulating U.S. foreign policy. "We have built into our system a set of incentives for continuing the arms race by recruiting the National Security Managers from the weapons industry. The taxpayers have been paying for biased judgment," Barnet complained. In the process, America had become weaker. As "the National Security Managers have been piling up useless and obscene hardware . . . the cities rot and Americans turn on each other in frustration," he lamented. For this reason, Barnet called the national security managers "America's number one problem." Given free rein to carry out a militaristic foreign policy, bureaucrats, hidden from the public's view, endorsed profligate spending on weapons systems. The constant revolving door in presidential administrations, furthermore, encouraged short-term thinking by bureaucrats seeking immediate successes in hopes of improving their chances of obtaining a job once they left government. "The canny bureaucrat is sustained by the faith that when the policy collapses he will be somewhere else," Barnet explained. In such a system, the bureaucrat could promote military measures without considering the long-term likelihood of success or failure.[9] Meanwhile, a penchant for military displays of power led the United States into one disaster after another for which the American people were left to face the consequences.

Since the national security managers remained hidden from most Americans, IPS aimed to expose their tight grip on foreign policy. According to Barnet's "bureaucratic model of reality," information made its way through the bureaucracy before reaching the president's desk in a much-altered state. Far from offering impartial advice, the bureaucrat recommended policies developed with the interests of the bureaucracy in mind. Only loosely connected to reality and the wishes of the American people, these proposals led America down a catastrophic path in Vietnam and elsewhere. As Barnet argued, "The roots of the Vietnam failure lie more in the structure and organization of the national security bureaucracy than in the personality of the President or the idiosyncrasies" of his advisors. "The President may decide, but the bureaucracy structures the decisions by setting out the choices." And given their connections to arms producers and corporations, national security managers rarely presented the president with diplomatic alternatives.[10]

Raskin agreed, arguing that technocrats like National Security Advisor McGeorge Bundy and Deputy National Security Advisor Walt Rostow deserved far more blame for the disastrous policies in Vietnam. "Thus, if the President is to be faulted, it is that he allowed himself for a period of time to be sold a bill of goods by people who have no diplomatic or political abilities, no touch with our society or anyone else's, and no sense of the rhythm of history and practical ideals of our nation," Raskin explained. He advised the president to fire his foreign policy advisors in 1964 and replace them with people like civil rights activists Martin Luther King and James Farmer; diplomat George Kennan; former undersecretary of labor Arthur Larson; Benjamin V. Cohen, an advisor to President Franklin Roosevelt; and Telford Taylor, U.S. counsel at the Nuremberg Trials.[11]

By endorsing an unusual cast of characters to replace the national security managers, IPS hoped to draw attention to how the decisions made by unelected, faceless bureaucrats produced hardship at home as well as abroad. Following in the steps of Raskin, Barnet offered his own set of recommendations for the National Security Council (NSC). Concerned that the NSC lacked perspectives from outside the Pentagon, he suggested expanding the advisory body to welcome non-military voices into the policymaking process. Barnet wanted the NSC to include secretaries from Transportation, Housing and Urban Development, Health, Education, and Welfare, as well as "other spokesmen for domestic interests." With a greater array of viewpoints, the military and its supporters would have to defend taking funds

away from "such domestic threats as poverty, disease, ignorance, and the poi-
soning of the environment," Barnet explained. Making a similar argument
almost twenty years later, he added that an enlarged NSC could "develop
a long-range national planning process which integrates economic, social,
environmental, and military considerations" when creating proposals for
the president.[12] Americans could not escape the consequences of militarism,
which threatened the well-being of the United States as well as other nations.
From IPS's perspective, "the people" deserved to know who controlled the
levers of power behind the scenes so that they could replace the national security managers with individuals who spoke for the interests of all Americans.

While identifying the consequences of depending too heavily on national
security managers, Barnet also hoped to expose a deficiency in Marxist analyses of foreign affairs. He criticized Marxists for "not explain[ing] the peculiar
dynamics of American imperialism" at those moments when non-economic
factors drove U.S. foreign policy. For instance, America fought in Vietnam
despite it being "an economic loser," in the words of Barnet. He also took Marxists to task for ignoring the national security managers. These men did not
conform to Marxist theory since they "do not *think* they are acting solely or
primarily to protect private corporate interests." In the end, bureaucrats did
not always act "rationally" and to think that they did so solely in pursuit of
financial gain seemed to Barnet "overly optimistic" and oversimplified. "They
often trade economic gain for such irrational intangibles as the thrill of domination and the mastery of paranoid fears," Barnet wrote.[13] Therefore, ending
U.S. imperialism required more than the demise of America's capitalist system.

Not everyone found Barnet's portrait of the national security managers
convincing. Critics accused Barnet of overstating their clout while ignoring
obvious examples of bureaucrats speaking out against militarism. One reader
challenged Barnet's fixation on the national security managers, which made
it seem as though the American people, Congress, and the North Vietnamese
bore no responsibility for the Vietnam War. Referring to the revelation in
the Pentagon Papers that Secretary of Defense Robert McNamara attempted
to disengage the United States from Southeast Asia, the reader also chided
Barnet for ignoring evidence that contradicted his overarching claim that the
national security managers only understood violence.[14]

Meanwhile, during a conference on Vietnam in 1968, defense intellectual
Albert Wohlstetter questioned the veracity of Barnet's indictments against
the national security managers and charged the IPS cofounder with misunderstanding recent history. As an example, he pointed to those times when
military officials "greatly overestimated enemy forces and as a result did not

intervene," while Barnet claimed the opposite always occurred. Wohlstetter also disputed Barnet's assertion that the missile gap argument used by then-senator John F. Kennedy against President Dwight Eisenhower originated within the national security bureaucracy. Describing the missile gap myth as "a political gambit of the 'outs'—the Democrats," Wohlstetter claimed that Barnet too readily accepted "a very popular misunderstanding."[15] Politicians, not bureaucrats, advanced the missile gap myth for political gain, according to Wohlstetter.

At the same conference, Schlesinger, relying on his experiences as a witness to the major policy discussions within the Kennedy administration, painted a different portrait than Barnet of the inner workings of government. Schlesinger took Barnet to task for exaggerating the power of the national security managers. He found "a certain amount of insight mingled with a great deal of extravagance and error" in Barnet's paper. Schlesinger claimed that Barnet's national security managers "made no important decisions on anything" during Kennedy's presidency. While Barnet saw Vietnam "as the model for every decision in foreign policy made since World War II," Schlesinger considered the war a "culmination of error" specific to a unique set of circumstances. In fact, Schlesinger claimed, "the important things" achieved by the United States since World War II had been "political and economic rather than military in nature." Nor did Schlesinger agree with Barnet's depiction of the national security bureaucracy as a "unified monolith," which did not stand up to historical scrutiny. For instance, during the Cuban Missile Crisis, the national security managers frequently disagreed. In terms of influence, Schlesinger highlighted the difference between the bureaucrats "who give the advice" and "those who take the advice" and use it to make the actual decisions. Barnet, Schlesinger claimed, focused far too much on the former, which explained why he did not ask "why anyone listens to what they have to say."[16]

The ill-defined character of Barnet's national security managers made his theoretical construct susceptible to contestation. Yet Barnet purposely kept it abstract to highlight the faceless quality of bureaucratic power holders. In response to Wohlstetter's and Schlesinger's critical assessment of his work, Barnet held firm to his claim that upon entering the bureaucracy America's "top civilian leadership" became militarized. To explain this shocking transformation, Barnet pointed to "institutional structures which generate pressures that influence men toward militarist analysis and militarist solutions." At the same time, Barnet refused to blame Americans' pronounced affinity for war on any innate biological tendency toward violence. "If human beings . . . have biological urges to slaughter their own species at regular intervals there is nothing to be done," Barnet exclaimed. By locating the "roots of war" in social institutions, activists could use domestic reform to limit war.[17] There is an unacknowledged tension between Barnet's and Raskin's understanding of U.S. militarism, with the former placing the blame on structures and the latter on individuals.

Raskin's national security state also held a central place in IPS doctrine. Upon learning that the institute intended to expand its program on domestic issues, Howard Romaine of the Institute for Southern Studies urged Raskin to reconsider: "The central notion of the National Security State as the chief obstacle to a more democratic and decent society at home, and the major threat to a more peaceful and economically equitable world, is what the Institute stands for in my eyes." Raskin's interest in the national security state predated IPS. Seeing the post–World War II era as unique, he argued in a research proposal from early 1963 that the new weaponry developed for World War I did not result in "new institutions and lobbies to nurture and protect them," which precluded the development of a "National Security State." Following World War II, however, a more "organizationally committed (managerial and administrative)" mind-set took hold of society, making it difficult "to 'unpeel' national security machinery." Why did such "machinery" matter? Beyond the ramifications for domestic society, Raskin worried that these structures complicated disarmament. He sought to determine whether the existence of such institutions prevented "adjust[ing] the meaning of national security to disarmament as the major security measure of the United States."[18] In other words, wars ended, but militarism endured.

The existence of the national security state allowed the United States to maintain its empire without having to worry about opposition from the public. Americans would not tolerate war without end, as U.S. leaders discovered during the Vietnam War. Yet, despite having as its purpose the "continuous preparation for war, the distortion of the economy, [and] the development of capitalists whose livelihood depends on the arms race and continuous covert and military engagement," the national security state survived. According to Raskin, Nixon deserved much of the credit because "he realized that to save the principles and the apparatus of imperialism he had to stop the involvement of the military in a war-fighting role."[19] Consequently, the national security state thrived in the shadows, which had important ramifications for democracy in America.

In 1979, Raskin devoted an entire book, *The Politics of National Security*, to the subject of the national security state. Global instability caused by the threat of wars and revolutions erupting, frailties in the capitalist system, and technological advances in warfare gave birth to the national security state, according to IPS's cofounder. Characterized by a lack of democracy, the national security state allowed "ruling elites to implement their imperial schemes and misplaced ideals" without interference from the public. A growing bureaucracy and an all-powerful president who acted "as a broker and legitimating instrument of national security activity" aided in the creation of the national security state, Raskin argued.[20]

According to IPS doctrine, the transformation began in 1947 with passage of the National Security Act. Saul Landau claimed that the new law created a "bifurcated state," which he described as one part "open and accessible to the U.S. public" and another "a secret, suprastate entity whose agenda and inner workings had to be kept not only from the enemy, but from the state's own citizens as well." The secrecy inherent in the law led to the creation of what Raskin called "para-law." In the national security state, para-law replaced older forms of law. Para-law did "not emerge from either legal decision, public debate, or congressional decision," though the courts and legislature often approved it after the fact. Instead, it was "forged in private, outside the public forum, without public debate although it is made by public officials or executive proclamation." According to Raskin, para-law sustained the national security state by providing legal cover for acts traditionally considered illicit. In addition to para-laws, NSC-68, which Raskin called the "magna carta of the national security bureaucracy," provided a rationale for the national security state. It served as a sort of organizational glue for the 1947 law, coordinating agencies, corporations, police and military forces, technicians, and labor leaders to carry out "empire making and preparing for war, and transforming nature into material processes for domination," Raskin argued.[21]

For IPS intellectuals the national security state posed a special dilemma because its existence severely limited public debate, which in turn ensured its survival. In 1970, Barnet and Raskin argued that constant preparation for war turned the United States into a "War Machine." In control of America's economic, political, and military institutions, the War Machine created a state of "permanent war" even in times of peace. "It *cannot* respond to popular pressure for peace or for a different set of priorities because it cannot stop itself," Barnet and Raskin declared. Moreover, Barnet argued, when a state failed "in maintaining social peace," it often used "national security" to discourage continued citizen protest. Raskin still held out hope that a crack, or a "contradiction," as he called it, in the foundation of the national security state might provide an opening. He anticipated that profligate military spending and continued intervention abroad would spark a citizen uprising against the national security state, along with the demand that it "not be contained as a self-enclosed bureaucratic process."[22] IPS refused to wait for such a rupture to occur naturally. Instead, the institute crafted blueprints to bring law and order to the national security state and reinvigorate American democracy.

Bringing the Nuremberg Trials to America:
IPS's Case for War Crimes Trials

Seymour Hersh's dispatches in 1969 about the innocent Vietnamese peasants slaughtered by U.S. soldiers in My Lai forced Americans to reckon with the carnage wrought by the U.S. presence in Vietnam. Two years later, Neil Shee-han jump-started discussions about how to punish the individuals respon-sible for committing war crimes with an article titled "Should We Have War Crimes Trials?" in the *New York Times*. While reviewing recent books written on the atrocities committed by U.S. soldiers in Vietnam, Sheehan concluded, "If you credit as factual only a fraction of the information assembled . . . and if you apply the laws of war to American conduct there," U.S. officials, up to and including President Nixon, "may well be guilty of war crimes." Sheehan wondered whether "a moral and legal distinction [could] be drawn between those killings in World War II, for which General Yamashita paid with his life," and the thousands of civilians killed as a result of the American bomb-ings in Vietnam.[23]

Years before Sheehan's provocative review appeared in the *New York Times*, IPS had taken up the issue of war crimes, offering documentation of the horrendous and illegal acts committed by U.S. troops in Vietnam. In an unpublished 1966 "legal memorandum," Barnet argued that the nature of the war in Vietnam made it impossible for the United States to protect the rights of citizens established during previous war crimes trials. For instance, international law protected Vietnamese peasants who refused to leave their homes, but U.S. officials viewed their defiance as evidence of support for the guerrillas. In reaching such a conclusion, "the U.S. is claiming the right to remove the status of 'protected persons' from a civilian population if they resist evacuation," Barnet wrote. To ensure that the United States abided by international laws meant to protect innocent civilians, Barnet proposed bringing U.S. officials before a judge in the United States to rule on the legal-ity of their actions. Time was of the essence for Barnet, who wanted to pre-vent laws from becoming the "servant of the victor," so he demanded that the war crimes trials begin immediately, while the United States still waged war in Vietnam. To do otherwise would support the notion that "might makes right." Moreover, war crimes trials conducted at the end of a war usually allowed the victorious country to escape prosecution. Accordingly, Barnet warned, "only the officials of weak states are likely to pay much attention to their jeopardy under international law, and it is rather the officials of powerful states who most need the guidelines and restraints of law."[24] The stronger nation, after all, expecting to win the war, had no reason to abide by the rules of international law.

Besides prosecuting war criminals, IPS felt that the trials would serve an educative purpose. Even if the courts rendered an innocent verdict, Barnet believed that the process itself "could have an important long-term educational effect on the country." The proceedings would force Americans to look more closely at the actions of their chosen leaders and at least consider the possibility that wrongs had been committed. "Conversely, if no serious moral opposition, rooted in law, develops against the Viet-Nam war, and the public is left with the view that the only ones who raise these issues are Viet Cong sympathizers and the most radical critics of United States foreign policy," Barnet predicted, "the next intervention will become that much easier to accept."[25] Focusing on war crimes allowed Barnet to target war itself rather than a particular conflict. In doing so, he and IPS sought the outlawry of all wars.

In 1967, Barnet and Richard Falk, a professor of international law at Princeton University, wrote a legal brief for U.S. Army Captain Howard B. Levy, who was on trial for refusing to train Green Berets. Barnet and Falk depicted U.S. actions in Vietnam as "illegal" and "in flagrant violation" of the 1949 Geneva Conventions, especially in relation to the treatment of prisoners of war and protection of civilians. In all, Barnet and Falk found at least "3,000 incidents in which it appears that the laws of war have been violated." For example, U.S. troops put prisoners of war under the watch of South Vietnamese soldiers who committed acts of torture, often with weapons supplied by the United States. As for Vietnamese civilians, Barnet and Falk alleged that U.S. soldiers took part in the "removal of civilian villagers on the theory that in a guerilla war the 'people' are indistinguishable from the 'enemy,'" which represented an "inherently illegal" act. Claiming that the Vietnamese refused to be relocated because of historical ties to an area or to protect their crops, Barnet and Falk accused the United States of making "a unilateral determination that residents of Vietnamese villages who do not submit to Government demands for relocation cease to have any protection against loss of life and property." Based on these facts, Barnet and Falk disagreed with the court-martial of Captain Levy.[26] Despite the efforts of Barnet and Falk, Levy was court-martialed and served two years in prison.

Though Barnet joined in the campaign to defend Levy, IPS focused less on supporting individual acts of resistance than on constructing a new legal edifice to bring to justice the individuals who devised the plans that led to war crimes. In the late 1960s and early 1970s, IPS considered setting up a "War Crimes Task Force" to study the atrocities committed during the Vietnam War. Leonard Rodberg, the director of IPS's PhD program, opposed the idea, seeing in it "an attempt to find scapegoats." He argued that the blame for the Vietnam War extended far beyond the president, the military, and even Congress. Rodberg maintained that a large percentage of the public supported the tactics used in Vietnam. Consequently, he criticized war crimes trials for targeting only certain "guilty" officials while leaving countless others untouched. Making a distinction between "individual guilt" and "structural defects," Rodberg feared that too many proponents of war crimes trials ignored the difference, which would "lead to a reign of terror, fascism, or a civil war." He accused the American Left of embracing the trials to "discredit the liberal establishment" rather than trying to gain a better understanding of why U.S. officials knowingly ordered soldiers to commit war crimes and developing mechanisms to put an end to atrocities on the battlefield. Rodberg doubted whether trials could carry out such a task. In the end, he lambasted his colleagues for foolishly thinking that "we can use the laws of the State to undermine the State."[27] Despite Rodberg's concerns, Raskin did not cease naming names when it came to U.S. officials he considered "guilty" of committing war crimes. In a 1972 interview, for instance, he listed Robert McNamara, Dean Rusk, Walt Rostow, and William and McGeorge Bundy as war criminals.[28]

Those within IPS who supported war crimes trials tended to ignore the strong public approval for the Vietnam War. Though not as visible as the antiwar movement, a large contingent of conservative, pro-war Americans demanded either escalation or, at the very least, support for U.S. troops fighting in Southeast Asia.[29] Aware of the public's continued backing of the war effort, IPS trustee David Riesman cautioned IPS against isolating public officials from the people whom they represented. He told Barnet that an undue emphasis on "the political leadership tends to hide from view the mammoth support they had or could have had from the public at large." Riesman pointed to public opinion polls in 1967 and 1968 that showed support for not only the war but also escalation.[30] Neither Raskin nor Barnet ever considered the possibility that Congress acted as it did in response to the wishes of the

American people. A tendency that reemerges in much of the work coming out of IPS is an unwavering belief in "the people." IPS looked to participatory democracy as the panacea for all of America's ills. Yet sometimes, as Riesman recognized, Americans supported ideas inimical to IPS's worldview.

Understanding IPS's campaign to bring U.S. officials under the jurisdiction of personal responsibility laws requires a brief foray into the seminal event that influenced IPS's thinking on the subject. Following World War II, the Allies organized war crimes trials in Nuremburg and Tokyo.[31] Prior to the trials, the Allies agreed on the Nuremberg Charter in August 1945. Article VI of the Charter included three "crimes" for which individuals could be brought to trial: "crimes against peace," when officials planned for or fought a "war of aggression"; "war crimes," generally meaning "violations of the laws or customs of war," or more specifically mistreatment of prisoners of war or a blatant disregard for citizens and their property; and "crimes against humanity," which involved acts of mass murder of civilians.[32] IPS intellectuals focused especially on "crimes against peace" and "war crimes," which corresponded with the initial concerns of the Allies.[33]

IPS intellectuals repeatedly referenced the trials that took place in Germany and Japan following World War II. Raskin called for greater personal responsibility for American officials directly involved in planning the Vietnam War. Embedding the ideal of personal responsibility into policymaking required following the steps taken in Germany and Japan after World War II. He recommended making the 1946 Law for the Liberation from National Socialism and Militarism, which created categories of responsibility and sentences ranging from death to the loss of employment, part of the U.S. legal code. Raskin looked at personal responsibility laws as necessary to avert a revolution and allow for peaceful "democratic reconstruction" instead.[34] Far from extreme, Raskin viewed his blueprint for war crimes trials as a middle-of-the-road approach that responded to the concerns of the disenchanted citizenry and precluded the need for a violent uprising.

Raskin laid out his most detailed blueprint for dealing with war crimes during a conference held in Washington, D.C., in mid-1971. His plan involved the formation of a new "legal office of the president" responsible for determining the legality of national security policies using the standards found in the Uniform Code of Military Justice and at the trials held in Nuremberg and Tokyo following World War II. He also proposed setting up "a court of international law and security" to hear cases brought by citizens against U.S. officials accused of committing illegal acts abroad. At the legislative level, Raskin suggested having a "national security legal advisor" work with Congress to ensure that all bills conformed to international law and the UN Charter. To guarantee implementation of all of these measures, Raskin suggested using a "jury system" composed of citizens to oversee the process. If the government and its armed forces continued to commit war crimes, Americans could refuse taxation or induction into the armed forces. Raskin described his proposal as "a triple level of involvement." Following passage of personal responsibility laws, Raskin anticipated the creation of a new legal system allowing for more scrutiny over U.S. foreign policy and to hold U.S. officials accountable. As a fail-safe measure, Raskin's "third level" would empower "the people themselves" to review court decisions to ensure compliance and determine whether they, as U.S. citizens, should partake in tax refusal or "redirect their taxes away from the federal government."[35]

Even if the plan were implemented, Raskin anticipated that government and military leaders would try to evade the new legal structures, but he argued that the very survival of the United States required some sort of response to curb war crimes. Describing his blueprint as a "middle course," he argued that should government officials prove incapable of following his proposed "code," the only recourse left was revolution. He believed that his code made possible "a value change in society, as, for example, did the civil rights laws." Did Raskin fear that hunting war criminals could lead to the revival of McCarthyism? Unlike those punished for "losing" China, Raskin argued that officials involved with Vietnam were "being challenged not for their opinions but for the initiation of policies which had clearly been branded by American leaders some fifteen years earlier as criminal."[36] In fact, while initially in favor of holding war crimes trials for the architects of the Vietnam War, Raskin altered his views, fearing that the passions of the era might ignite a second round of McCarthyism. Writing in 1971, he made it clear that he did not support "purge tactics," including prosecuting administration officials involved in the planning process for U.S. policy in Vietnam. "New standards must be found to deal not so much with what has happened, as with what will happen in the *future*," Raskin explained.[37] By restricting war crimes trials to future conflicts, Raskin distinguished himself from other antiwar critics who used the issue of war crimes merely to end the Vietnam War. IPS had a larger goal in mind: ending militarism.

In 1972, Raskin finalized the blueprint he had presented the year before at the conference in Washington, D.C., and sent it to several senators as a proposed amendment to the 1947 National Security Act. Included was a provision making anyone on the White House staff, in the Executive Office, and policymakers at or above the rank of deputy assistant secretary "directly accountable as offenders for any and all plans and policies" that, among other things, advocated assassinations, planned "mass bombing in an undeclared or aggressive war," annihilated the land and resources of another nation, aided in regime change, used nuclear, chemical, biological, or radioactive weapons, or forced migration. Individuals found guilty of "ordering" any of the above policies would face "confiscation of property beyond the amount necessary to guarantee a reasonable living standard for the accused and his family" and "custodial imprisonment for 7 years at socially useful work as aides in the helping professions." Another provision established a Legal Office for National Security Affairs in the Executive Office tasked with providing "advisory opinions to the President and the Congress on the legality of any contemplated military or national security action, program or weapons acquisition." The Legal Office would make judgments based on existing domestic, international, and military laws found in the U.S. Constitution, the UN Charter, treaties, U.S. military codes and manuals, "and directives of the United States in Japan and Germany which defined and developed standards for the dismantling of militarism and ultranationalism." The proposed amendment required officials—excluding the president, his cabinet, vice president, and federal judges—to go before a newly created nine-judge court of National Security and International Law, which possessed powers comparable to the U.S. Court of Appeals. Should any of the above measures fail to bring the perpetrators to justice, Raskin proposed allowing citizens the right to sue U.S. officials and demand an immediate cessation of the unlawful act.[38]

IPS considered Congress an important bulwark against the national security state, but the institute struggled to find support for its ideas in the legislative chamber. Senator J. William Fulbright, chair of the Committee on Foreign Relations and a vocal critic of the Vietnam War, responded to Raskin's amendments by calling the plan "a most unusual concept," and then explained that "congressional approval will be difficult to obtain," particularly given the nature of the Vietnam War and Congress's reluctance to act.[39] The idea of personal accountability for public officials eventually found support from an old ally of IPS. In 1973, Congressman Robert Kastenmeier— who had held hearings on the Vietnam War in his congressional district of Madison in 1965—introduced a war crimes bill. According to Kastenmeier, the post–World War II trials in Nuremberg and Tokyo and the UN Charter "all reflected the basic notion that a nation's political leaders should be held personally accountable for criminal acts committed at their command." Prevention of another My Lai and the bombing of neutral nations like Cambodia required "embedding the fundamental principles of Nuremberg in our own national law." Kastenmeier proposed inserting the language of "international laws and customs of war" into the Federal Criminal Code and creating an "institutional mechanism" to investigate and prosecute the laws."[40] Not surprisingly, Kastenmeier's legislation faced a slow death in committee.

Nonetheless, Kastenmeier reintroduced the bill on several different occasions, including in July 1975. In this latest attempt, he stressed the need to rein in the activities of civilian policymakers. While the Uniform Code of Military Justice restricted the actions of military officials, Kastenmeier noted that "civilian officials remain legally unaccountable." He lamented the "imbalance" of the current statutes that allowed for "the conviction of an enlisted man for implementing an illegal plan devised by an unaccountable civilian official." Despite the destruction caused in Vietnam by U.S. bombs and napalm and the relocation of Vietnamese peasants from their homes to hamlets, U.S. officials not only avoided criminal charges but received praise and career advancement. Thus, according to Kastenmeier, "crime does pay," except for those Vietnamese who died as a result of such planning or who lived and struggled to bring their nation back to life.[41]

Interestingly, IPS intellectuals never referred to the most notable war crimes trial of the Vietnam era, that of Lieutenant William Calley, which might have raised questions about the feasibility of holding U.S. officials accountable for war crimes. Following his conviction for killing twenty-two Vietnamese civilians at My Lai, Lieutenant Calley received much public adulation. Governors, state legislators, and even Nixon endorsed a lenient sentence for Calley. One scholar has suggested that "a certain skepticism about the whole concept of war crimes" existed in the minds of most Americans that worked to Calley's advantage. Moreover, many Americans blamed higher-up officials in the military.[42] Given the difficulties of holding the military accountable for war crimes, IPS's campaign to bring non-military planners to justice likely faced an uphill battle.

Beyond the challenges associated with trying to garner support for bringing U.S. officials to trial for war crimes, IPS intellectuals ignored the limitations of international law. A closer look at the discussions during the early stages of the Nuremberg and Tokyo trials illustrates that international law is far from impartial and rarely prevented a nation from carrying out the military component of its foreign policy. Part of the problem stemmed from a decision made regarding who should be brought before the Nuremberg Tribunal. During these debates, Clement Attlee, Winston Churchill's deputy prime minister, argued for including top-ranking military officers. Attlee's suggestion, however, faced opposition since it ensnared Allied military officials in its prosecutorial web. To preclude such an event from occurring, the Allies tore up the indictments related to German bombing of civilians.[43] Similar problems plague international law more generally. Laws of war tend to forgive the use of violence during times of war even when it results in the loss of human life. These statutes protect the perpetrators of violence far more than the victims.[44] Thus the aversion to punishing military officials at Nuremberg, to say nothing of bureaucrats and politicians, combined with international laws lacking protections for noncombatants made IPS's task that much more difficult.

The People Versus the National Security State

In addition to designing new legal and political mechanisms to end U.S. militarism, IPS, as it did in so many matters, turned to the American people. When discussing Barnet's national security managers, Wohlstetter claimed that the IPS cofounder's views on bureaucracy "lead us so directly to genocide, nothing remains except a prayer that the world can be broken up into very small self-subsistent units in which contacts are face to face." Even then, fighting still broke out between the Greek city-states, which led Wohlstetter to conclude that Barnet's argument "cannot be taken literally."[45] In reality, IPS proposed something far simpler than creating small, autonomous city-states. IPS intellectuals suggested that a reformed Congress offered the key to dismantling the national security state.

Threatened by an "imperial presidency," Congress sought new authority and institutional fixes to empower the legislative branch and prevent a repetition of the debacle in Vietnam and the Watergate scandal. Reformers set their sights on committee chairs in an attempt to disperse power and make Congress function in a more democratic fashion. Led by the Watergate Babies, who ran in 1974 promising to end corruption and scandal in Washington, legislators sought to unseat long-time committee chairs and weaken filibuster rules. In terms of foreign policy, Congress passed the War Powers Act in November 1973. This legislation restricted the president's ability to send American troops abroad without congressional approval. Congress also instituted new procedures for appointing an independent counsel to investigate wrongdoing in the executive branch; passed legislation to weaken the president's ability to redirect federal funds; and developed new campaign finance laws.[46] IPS had more in mind than congressional empowerment or institutional reform. While in agreement regarding the need to shift the balance of power away from the executive to the legislative branch, IPS went one step further in calling for Congress to strengthen its ties to "the people."

IPS intellectuals acknowledged that Congress's foreign policy record did not exactly offer hope. "The inability or unwillingness of Congress to act as a co-equal branch of government," which allowed Nixon to prolong the Vietnam War, irked Raskin. Moreover, even when Congress conveyed its disapproval, the president used the support of the American people during elections to downplay the congressional response. "It will be put to the American people as a question for ratification much in the manner of plebiscites," which, Raskin noted, "are used as ratificatory devices to support decisions the 'commander leader' has already made." Still, Raskin refused to indict Congress for providing additional funding for the Vietnam War. He argued "that such appropriations were [not] to be construed as support for the war" but rather to protect the troops already serving.[47]

From IPS's perspective, the legislative branch's inability to thwart previous foreign policy missteps stemmed from the disconnect between the citizenry and members of Congress. Raskin called on America's legislative body to look elsewhere for its "legitimacy." He argued that members of Congress "must find their legitimacy in the people, who will act as citizens to determine their interests and purposes in confrontation with the present corporate structures." With "its roots in the people," Raskin suggested at another time, Congress represented the most adept instrument to crush the national security state. Ending the national security state's "mythicizing [of] people," which involved deceiving Americans into thinking they had a genuine role in making foreign policy decisions, required dialogue between members of Congress and their constituents. According to Raskin, the social movements of the 1960s and 1970s already "demythiciz[ed] people and forc[ed] dialogue among those who refused to see one another except as abstract entities" and thus made democracy real.[48] In other words, Raskin wanted "We the People" to serve as something more than patriotic propaganda.

Strengthening the relationship between Congress and the citizenry required a return to a custom of the eighteenth century. Looking at the implementation of the grand jury in the United States at that time, Raskin explained that it "was used to find out the problems of government and to institutionalize citizen control and participation." Reinstituting grand juries would "open the way to the emergence of a participatory nation in which citizenship would become the linchpin of a modern American democracy," he maintained. Raskin wanted to empower them to "investigate the major public institutions" and "address the content and direction of governing in the districts" to remove the "barriers" that existed between Congress and the people. Each member of Congress would be responsible to several juries in his or her district. Raskin proposed having one jury for every fifty thousand citizens, with each jury composed of twenty-four citizens serving two-year terms. Members of Congress, as required by law, would have to meet with their jury for at least one week at the end of each legislative session.[49] As envisioned by Raskin, grand juries made possible greater collaboration between Congress and its constituents on all matters, not just foreign policy.

Once again, Raskin's romanticized view of the citizenry led him to ignore the possibility that even if implemented, a grand jury system might not lead to a drastically different outcome in terms of U.S. foreign policy. In challenging Reinhold Niebuhr's "children of darkness," whom the theologian described as "moral cynics," who "are evil because they know no law beyond the self. . . . [and] are wise, though evil, because they understand the power of self-interest," Raskin went too far in the other direction, equating citizens with Niebuhr's "children of light."[50] Beyond the issue of whether individual citizens would aspire to Raskin's "common good," there is the more prosaic problem of time and desire. As public intellectuals, IPS thinkers could live the life of the mind, but the average citizen working a nine-to-five job and raising a family did not have such a luxury. One of IPS's closest allies recognized as much and explained how it worked against Raskin's blueprint. After reading *Notes on the Old System*, George McGovern wrote to Raskin to say that he found the grand jury system one of the more interesting aspects of the book. He did, however, have certain "practical questions," including how to provide "jurors the time and resources to be able to make informed judgements on legislative solutions."[51] The problem highlighted by McGovern did not seem insurmountable, but altering the innate self-interest of humankind represented a major hurdle for IPS.

That is not to say that Raskin never had his doubts about Congress. For instance, he denounced legislators in 1969 for cowering before the national security state, which succeeded in turning Congress into "a permanent talk group which arrives at no decisions and effects no changes in terms of the actual direction of the society." Moreover, the legislative chamber willfully submitted to the executive branch, which sought a rubber stamp from the legislature after having already ensnared America in a war. Raskin claimed that by reasserting its constitutional right on matters related to war, Congress risked making the executive branch look like "a band of thieves who up to that point had engaged in a criminal enterprise" by not seeking legislative approval. However, refusing to authorize the president's war plans had its own dangers. If the public thought the commander in chief acted unconstitutionally, they might demand impeachment. Thus, "members of Congress will comply rather than risk internal revolution to stop a war abroad," Raskin predicted.[52]

A strengthened system of checks and balances required a closer relationship between the citizenry and Congress, which partially depended on greater transparency. For Raskin, governmental secrecy represented nothing less than an attack on American democracy and the right of the people to know how their government functioned. "What we see happening through secrecy and executive privilege is an attempt to interrupt the relationship between Congress and the people by withholding information from Congress," Raskin said in testimony before a Senate subcommittee in 1976. As a solution, Raskin encouraged members of Congress to read secret documents on the House floor so that the public had access to the information, thereby empowering them to make informed decisions. The previous year, during an event to honor Congressman Michael Harrington, Raskin implored his congressional audience to serve as a conduit of information. He went on to argue that "it is only within the context of making such information public that the citizenry can participate and therefore be expected to see themselves as feeling that the government is *their* government rather than one controlled by secret boards, hidden advisory groups and floating juntos which operate against the people." Barnet had made a similar claim in 1969 when he called for greater transparency to counter the dictum "'The President knows best.'" "The 'If you only know what I know' mystique undermines the very principle of democratic government," Barnet concluded.[53] Making government more open, accountable, and responsive to citizens required a commitment by Congress to maintain an honest dialogue with the American people.

*   *   *

Beginning with the national security managers and then turning their attention to the more extensive national security state, IPS intellectuals found in these two concepts an explanation for America's frequent intervention abroad to suppress ideological pluralism and to suffocate democracy on the home front. Though cognizant of the dangers inherent in a too powerful executive, the institute paid little attention to the so-called "imperial presidency." Instead, the peace intellectuals at IPS blamed technocratic liberalism for giving birth to the national security managers who worked behind the scenes managing America's empire. Elitist by nature, their very existence precluded the involvement of the American public in decisions of national import. They existed, furthermore, as part of a much larger and more encompassing national security state, which worked to nullify public worries over the activities of the national security managers by embedding within the American psyche a constant fear of attack from the enemy. Out of the national security state grew secrecy.

Despite the alarming conditions uncovered by the peace intellectuals at IPS, they never advocated revolution. Instead, the institute looked for ways to work within the system to restrain the elite and enhance the powers of "the people." As a first step toward the restoration of democracy and making the world safe for diversity, IPS encouraged the passage of personal responsibility laws to put an end to the immoral and illegal activities of the national security managers. Yet, even as Congress targeted foreign dictators for committing human rights abuses, Raskin's domestic legislation found few supporters. As IPS discovered continuously during the Cold War, U.S. politicians tended to ignore the immoral and criminal behavior carried out by Americans, whether public officials or private corporations. The battle against communism left no room for self-examination. As another option, IPS sought the revival of republicanism. Peace intellectuals at the institute looked to the American people as a savior, albeit this time speaking through a Congress brought closer to the citizenry through holding grand juries and sharing information. In endorsing a greater role for "the people" in foreign affairs, the institute took inspiration from anti-militarists of the Progressive Era, who offered several mechanisms, most notably referendums, to stop U.S. foreign intervention.

The same national security managers who thwarted democracy in the United States and stood in the way of self-determination in Vietnam also prevented Third World nations from constructing their own development model when such schemes strayed too far from the liberal democratic capitalist prototype. They did not work alone, however. Private banks and corporations, with the acquiescence of Jimmy Carter, the only other Democrat besides Lyndon Johnson to occupy the White House since IPS opened its doors, put guns and money in the hands of undemocratic rulers who opposed communism and revered free-market capitalism.

CHAPTER 5

Pocketbooks, Morality, and Human Rights

"A review of our files on the Letelier assassination has provided what we regard as convincing evidence that President [Augusto] Pinochet personally ordered his intelligence chief to carry out the murder," the CIA concluded in 1987.[1] With this admission, the CIA substantiated the claim made by IPS immediately after the explosion that rocked Sheridan Circle in Washington, D.C. and killed Orlando Letelier and Ronni Karpen Moffitt. Despite the protestations of IPS, the U.S. government refused to isolate Pinochet, much less accuse him of committing a terrorist act on American soil that resulted in the death of a U.S. citizen. Denied justice, IPS set out to investigate and publicize the role played by the U.S. government and private banks and corporations in strengthening Pinochet's military junta, which allowed the strongman to continue to rule Chile with an iron fist, much to the detriment of Chileans' human rights.

The rise of Augusto Pinochet in Chile in 1973 provided IPS intellectuals with a clear-cut example of how the abrogation of economic rights led directly to the torture given so much attention by mainstream human rights organizations. Furthermore, in targeting Chile, IPS hoped to expose the complicity of U.S. officials, banks, and corporations in propping up a ruthless dictator. IPS intellectuals repeatedly pointed to the support given to Pinochet by these institutions, which provided political cover for the dictator and bankrolled his presidency. Thus, curtailing human rights abuses around the world began at home for IPS. Until America's elected and unelected leaders promoted a more ethical approach to international relations, human rights abuses would never abate. Focusing on atrocities committed abroad shielded U.S. actors from censure. IPS engaged in a campaign to exorcise America's own demons.

Letelier's activism while at IPS inspired the institute to look more deeply into the myriad links between the U.S. government, corporations, and banks and foreign dictators committing torture and other brutal acts. In telling the story of how the institute came to embrace a broad conception of human rights, this chapter aims to complicate the human rights narrative of the 1970s. During his brief sojourn at IPS, Letelier exposed for the world to see how U.S.-based economists transformed Chile's economy and paved the way for Pinochet's reign of terror. Letelier's assassination shattered any chance IPS might have had to serve as the brain trust of Jimmy Carter's administration. IPS intellectuals resented Carter for not, in their opinion, doing enough to bring Pinochet to justice for his role in the death of Letelier. Nor did the president consider how private banks, corporations, and U.S. arms sales contributed to human rights abuses. Instead of using human rights to search abroad for monsters to destroy, IPS looked at the ways in which neoliberal economics and an anti-communist foreign policy coalesced around support for brutal dictators. In the process, the United States implicated itself in the global campaign to weaken ideological pluralism and democracy.

The Chilean Coup, the Downfall of Democracy, and Economic Rights

IPS intellectuals tended to mark off certain regions of the world as more important than others when it came to demanding protection of human rights. As David P. Forsythe has shown, "ideological and partisan considerations" determined how members of Congress voted on human rights legislation. Conservative Republicans supported bills intended to punish leftist regimes and liberal Democrats favored laws directed toward right-wing dictators.[2] Like the latter group, IPS intellectuals mainly targeted autocrats in Latin America. Writing in the introduction to the 1979 book *Workers Against the Gulag: The New Opposition in the Soviet Union*, which included firsthand accounts of Soviet workers who had been mistreated by their government, Richard Barnet distinguished between the abuses depicted in the book and other forms of human rights violations. While not denying "the moral weakness of the Soviet regime" for its dismal treatment of workers and emigrants, Barnet claimed these abuses did not compare to "the wholesale slaughter" of innocents in South America's Southern Cone, especially Argentina and Chile, or in Stalin's Soviet Union. He made a similar statement during a 1977 conference on the future of détente. Barnet did not dismiss the "horror stories" coming out of the Soviet Union regarding its human rights record, but he refused to focus disproportionate attention on a single country. Taking aim at Carter, Barnet declared, "If we want to have some kind of moral force and make the kinds of initiatives that the President is commendably doing, we must do it from a stance of some kind of single standard" applied to friend and foe alike.[3] IPS took issue with U.S. politicians giving greater weight to Soviet atrocities because of the Cold War, even though human rights abuses in Latin America greatly exceeded, in both scale and degree, those committed by the Soviet Union.

Addressing Latin America's dismal human rights record afforded IPS the opportunity to show the hidden role played by U.S. interests in the region. Unlike IPS, human rights activists of the 1970s tended to direct attention away from the United States. In focusing on the physical act of torture, these individuals and organizations ignored the underlying issues that explained why such violence occurred in the first place. Consequently, the enemies of humankind remained external to the United States. IPS, in contrast, pointed a finger squarely at the United States—not at the American people but at its leaders, both corporate and political. IPS trustee Peter Weiss's response to Carter's dismissal of Brady Tyson, a low-level State Department official who gave a controversial speech at the UN Human Rights Commission meeting in 1977, provides a glimpse into IPS's thinking on human rights. Tyson offered what IPS intellectual Peter Kornbluh described as an "official apology" for U.S. assistance to the plotters of the coup against Allende. The president immediately recalled Tyson and disavowed his statement. In a letter to Carter following the incident, Weiss criticized the White House's brash response. Weiss explained that he "believ[ed] that no real progress will be made in the work of the United Nations' Human Rights Commission until some country has the courage to abolish the rule that the speaker's finger must always be pointed away from himself."[4] Since the United States refused to indict itself, IPS did by exposing the machinations of economists, politicians, banks, and U.S. corporations that made possible the torture in Chile and elsewhere.

In 1970, Salvador Allende, a socialist and Marxist associated with the Unidad Popular coalition, sent shockwaves through the world with his victory in Chile's presidential election. His ascension to power garnered global attention as watchful eyes looked to see how the socialist leader handled domestic and international affairs. During Allende's presidency, however, internal and external forces prevented him from carrying out his political program. The end of this socialist experiment came on September 11, 1973, when the Chilean military staged a coup. With the presidential palace surrounded by troops, Allende defiantly proclaimed in a radio speech that he intended to remain in power. In the end, however, Allende took his own life rather than face capture. Allies of the former Chilean president blamed counterrevolutionaries within Chile but also pointed to interference from outside forces, including corporations based in the United States and Richard Nixon's administration.[5] Following the ouster of Allende, General Pinochet took over as president, granted himself dictatorial powers, and brought in economic advisors from the United States to transform Chile's economy into a citadel for free-market ideals.

Initially, IPS's concern over events in Chile had less to do with human rights than the crushing of ideological pluralism in Latin America. In February 1974, IPS's sister institute, the Transnational Institute (TNI), held a conference at its offices in Amsterdam to discuss the coup. Besides intellectuals from IPS and TNI, participants included members of Allende's Unidad Popular coalition and Chile's Revolutionary Left Movement (MIR), a leftist guerrilla organization. Former senator Eugene McCarthy also attended. The discussions focused less on the coup itself than on what it meant for the future of socialism, especially whether the reformist and constitutionalist route chosen by Allende remained feasible.[6] IPS's attention, however, shifted when Saul Landau invited one of the leaders of the worldwide solidarity movement, Orlando Letelier, to join IPS.[7] Under Allende, Letelier served as ambassador to the United States before moving through the ranks as minister of foreign affairs, interior, and finally defense. After the coup he spent most of the next year imprisoned. Settling in Caracas, Venezuela, following his release in mid-1974, Letelier and his family left for Washington, D.C., in late 1974 after IPS offered him a position.[8] More than anyone else at IPS, Letelier sought to explain how particular economic systems produced an environment conducive to torture and other forms of abuse.

The example of Chile is notable, according to Juan Gabriel Valdés, because "the state literally dismantled itself" to implement neoliberal economic programs. Whereas many Latin American countries adopted neoliberal policies at the behest of the International Monetary Fund, Chilean politicians voluntarily and enthusiastically worked with economists to transform their nation. A group of University of Chicago economists, known collectively as the "Chicago Boys," directed the efforts in Chile. Trained between 1957 and 1970 at Chile's Catholic University and at the University of Chicago, the Chicago Boys had few followers in Chile until Pinochet came to power in 1973. Concerned about Allende's policies, moderate businessmen and entrepreneurs became more accepting of the measures advocated by far-right conservatives. Unintentionally, therefore, Allende's policies brought neoliberal economic ideas beyond the ivory tower. The "shock treatment," as the Chicago Boys labeled their policies, led to devastating cuts to social services.

Aid for health services fell by 17.6 percent from 1970 to 1980, while aid for education declined 11.3 percent during the same period. By 1980, the average salary of a Chilean worker decreased by 16.7 percent compared to 1970. Economic stratification continued to grow as Pinochet's government sold 197 companies between 1974 and 1978.[9]

Shortly before his death, Letelier wrote an article for the *Nation* titled "The 'Chicago Boys' in Chile: Economic 'Freedom's' Awful Toll." Letelier aimed to identify the source of Chile's horrendous human rights abuses in its economic policies. He complained of the wall separating human rights abuses and government repression from "the classical unrestrained 'free market' policies that have been enforced by the military junta." Chile's subterfuge allowed the World Bank to issue a loan to Pinochet without an iota of shame.[10] Moreover, such a distinction allowed prominent economists in the United States to celebrate the economic miracle of Pinochet's Chile without acknowledging the related decline in civil liberties.

Besides laying bare the links between economic policies and human rights abuses, Letelier set out to show how U.S. actors helped perpetuate the indignities carried out in Chile. The Chicago Boys, flush with CIA funds, offered the junta their "intellectual assets" to help institute a free-market economy through "shock treatment," as economist Milton Friedman called it. Indifferent to the fact that such policies did not conform to the economic reality in Chile, the Chicago Boys and their hosts brought neoliberalism to the Southern Cone. In doing so, they created massive levels of inequality, which led to a growing resistance to Pinochet's economic policies. The regime responded by increasing repression. In Letelier's view, the strong political showing by Allende's Popular Unity government in the 1973 congressional elections "convinced the national bourgeoisie and its foreign supporters that they would be unable to recoup their privileges through the democratic process." When, in the aftermath of the coup, the new leaders could not "destroy the consciousness of the Chilean people," repression ensued. As Letelier explained, "The economic plan has had to be enforced, and in the Chilean context that could be done only by the killing of thousands, the establishment of concentration camps all over the country, the jailing of more than 100,000 persons in three years, the closing of trade unions and neighborhood organizations, and the prohibition of all political activities and all forms of free expression."[11]

Letelier's *Nation* article represented only the latest effort by the exiled Chilean to publicize the horrors inflicted on Chileans under Pinochet. Landau described Letelier as "a major leader and unifier of the forces seeking the restoration of democracy in Chile." Letelier, according to Landau, "assumed the responsibilities of political leadership in exile," which involved speaking at venues around the world, writing for various outlets, and meeting with governments. In 1976, Letelier convinced Holland to renege on a $6.3 million credit to Chile. That same year he organized a small congressional delegation to Chile. He also helped write and secure passage of the Kennedy-Harkin bill. In response to Chile's poor human rights record, the amendment prohibited military aid and limited economic assistance to $27.5 million for Chile. Michael Moffitt, whose wife also died in the explosion, "believed that Orlando would be a high officer in the next Government of Chile, if not a candidate for president." Pinochet took notice of Letelier's rising stature and viewed him as a direct threat. During a meeting with Secretary of State Henry Kissinger in Chile on June 8, 1976, Pinochet complained of the "strong voice in Washington" of Letelier and other exiles. He specifically mentioned Letelier because of his "access to Congress."[12] Then came the explosion near Sheridan Circle on September 21, 1976, that killed Letelier and Moffitt. Though IPS intellectuals had taken notice of the dictatorship in Chile prior to Letelier's death, Pinochet became the prime target of IPS following the assassination.

A Victim of the (Inter)National Security State

The investigation into who killed Letelier and Moffitt ran into problems almost immediately due to IPS's contentious relationship with the Federal Bureau of Investigation (FBI). When the bomb went off in Sheridan Circle, IPS was locked in a legal struggle with the FBI over its use of illegal phone taps, surveillance, and mail tampering during an investigation into the institute. As a result, IPS demanded a special prosecutor for the Letelier investigation, which the FBI refused to provide. Besides questions about the impartiality of the FBI, IPS had to contend with widespread disbelief that a foreign government would orchestrate a brazen attack on U.S. soil. The *New York Times*, for instance, while calling for a comprehensive investigation into the murders, nonetheless concluded, "It is hard to believe that even as ham-handed a regime as Chile's junta would order the murder of so eminent an opponent as Mr. Letelier in the capital of the United States, where it has worked hard recently to improve its image and on whose largesse it so heavily depends." Nor did the FBI agents involved in the investigation initially consider the possibility of Chile's involvement. When IPS intellectuals told agents to look at DINA, Chile's secret police force, as a likely culprit, FBI officials looked confused and asked, "Who is Deena? What is her last name?"[13]

IPS also accused the FBI of ignoring the role of U.S. actors in the killing of their colleagues. The institute, as it turned out, had reason to suspect CIA involvement in the bombing. Jack Anderson, the intrepid columnist who exposed the partnership between the CIA and International Telephone and Telegraph (ITT) to prevent Allende's election in 1970, obtained a copy of a Senate Foreign Relations Committee report on Operation Condor in 1979. In addition to serving as a clearinghouse for intelligence obtained by the Southern Cone nations involved in the operation, Condor also had a "Mafia-like enforcement arm," according to Anderson. "Phase Three," as it was known, involved sending operatives to foreign nations to find exiled leftist critics and former military and political officials who opposed the anti-communist totalitarian regimes of the region. Once located, assassins moved in on their targets. Nearly a quarter century after the bombing in Sheridan Circle, new information came to light showing that the CIA knew about Operation Condor's "Phase Three" prior to the assassination, though not Condor's intent to target Letelier. Rather than demand that the Southern Cone nations involved in Operation Condor cease their violent and bloody campaign, the United States allowed national security interests to override human rights concerns.[14]

Even before the grand jury handed down the indictments, and lacking access to the secret documents, IPS saw the fingerprints of DINA and the CIA on the bomb placed under Letelier's car. IPS assumed from the start that Chilean secret police, working in concert with the CIA, had played a part in the assassination. Not surprisingly, IPS had long decried the machinations of the CIA, seeing it as emblematic of the national security state. Shortly after the Senate voted overwhelmingly in 1975 to create a bipartisan panel, subsequently known as the Church Committee after its chairman, Democrat Frank Church of Idaho, Barnet warned that illegal methods used by the CIA abroad would not stop at the water's edge. "It is not possible to maintain a bureaucracy of hired killers, thieves, and con men for use against foreigners who get in our way without soon feeling the effects at home," he exclaimed.[15] Barnet proved prescient, as shown by events in Sheridan Circle a little more than a year later.

IPS's skepticism of the FBI and CIA led it to turn to its allies in Congress for assistance. On September 21, 1976, Democrats Edward Kennedy, James Abourezk, and Hubert Humphrey cosponsored Senate Resolution 561, which stated that the U.S. Senate "condemns the brutal and senseless murders" and demanded a proper investigation.[16] The IPS codirectors labeled DINA the "prime suspect" and demanded that the chairman of the Senate Committee on Intelligence Activities investigate the group's "relationship" with the

CIA. Since Letelier and the other ex-Chilean officials murdered in Buenos Aires and Rome "were the most prominent and visible symbols of hope for a decent alternative to the military dictatorship" that existed in Chile, Barnet and Raskin had no doubt that DINA and Pinochet were involved in Letelier's death. At the same time, given the nature of the attack, Raskin and Barnet argued, "it is unlikely that such a bomb could have been developed without techniques available only to professional demolition experts." They called on the chairman of the intelligence committee, Democrat Daniel Inouye, to look into the relationship between the CIA and pro-Pinochet forces before and during Allende's rule in Chile and to "investigate the CIA's 'penetrations' of DINA," which the codirectors claimed existed.[17] There is no proof that the CIA had foreknowledge of the plans for the assassination of Letelier, but the recently unearthed Operation Condor documents leave little doubt that the United States looked the other way when it learned about the sinister activities being carried out by Chile and other Southern Cone countries. No inquiry into CIA involvement in the assassination ever took place.

Nearly two years after the murders, on August 1, 1978, the U.S. Grand Jury indicted several persons associated with DINA and exiled Cubans. DINA agent Michael Vernon Townley, an American citizen who moved to Chile and joined the agency, agreed to a plea that made him eligible for parole in as little as forty months. His wife, a Chilean national working with DINA, also testified and escaped prosecution. The following month, on September 18, 1978, the FBI named bomb makers Jose Dionisio Suarez Esquivel and Virgilio Paz Romero as suspects in the case, offering a $25,000 reward for their capture. Authorities arrested Alvin Ross Diaz and Guillermo Novo and charged them with conspiracy to commit murder. Ignacio Novo paid a $25,000 bond after being charged with perjury. Around the same time, George Landau, U.S. ambassador to Chile, asked Pinochet to extradite General Manuel Contreras Sepulveda, the former head of DINA; Colonel Pedro Espinoza Bravo, Sepulveda's chief of operations; and DINA captain Armando Fernandez Larios. The indictments fell short of IPS's expectations. The absence of charges against Pinochet and silence regarding the role of the United States in the assassination disheartened IPS.[18]

Though the indictment of Manuel Contreras Sepulveda satisfied IPS, many intellectuals at the think tank believed that the investigation into Letelier's and Moffitt's deaths did not go far enough. Referring to a passage in the indictment that started, "With others unknown to the Grand Jury," IPS director Robert Borosage argued that absolute justice required the arrest of Pinochet, who, Borosage alleged, "took personal command of DINA, and used it virtually as his own personal police force." "It is inconceivable that the order to assassinate Orlando Letelier on the streets of Washington, D.C. came from anyone but Pinochet himself," Borosage continued. He demanded investigations of Pinochet, the U.S. government, the CIA, multinational corporations, and private banks to determine the role each played in Letelier's murder. As Nixon and Kissinger helped Pinochet rise to power, the CIA "recruited and supplied Cuban refugees for a campaign of terror, disruption and murder aimed against Fidel Castro" and then set these mercenaries loose when no longer needed, Borosage reported. "In American law," he explained, "one who sets a 'dangerous instrumentality' in motion is culpable for the damage it wreaks, even if no longer in control over it." Despite the pleas of IPS intellectuals, both in public and during private meetings with Attorney General Edward Levi, who headed the Letelier investigation, Congress and the government did not investigate the relationship between the CIA and DINA.[19]

IPS intellectuals also speculated on why it took so long for the indictments to be handed down. In their 1980 account of the assassination and the subsequent manhunt for the perpetrators of the crime, John Dinges and Landau attributed the drawn-out investigation to the stalling tactics of the U.S. government. Landau and Dinges found a glaring problem in the FBI's handling of information related to Townley's unsuccessful attempt to obtain false passports in Paraguay, which the United States found out about and derailed. "No bureaucratic explanation can account for the detours and obstacles the investigators encountered in solving the case. It was not DINA's cover-ups nor the secretiveness of the Cuban Nationalist Movement that stymied the investigation for almost a year, but rather the actions consciously taken or willfully omitted by officials and agencies of the United States government," Dinges and Landau wrote.[20] In the eyes of IPS intellectuals, the national security state had thwarted justice.

A Liberal Defends an Assassin: IPS Versus Jimmy Carter

Perhaps it is surprising that IPS intellectuals excoriated Carter, who devoted so much attention to the issue of human rights both rhetorically and in policymaking decisions. Carter referred to human rights in his inaugural address and he touched on the issue again when he spoke before the United Nations. During a 1977 commencement address at Notre Dame, Carter announced a new direction for U.S. foreign policy based on a greater respect for human rights. To this end, Carter strengthened the Human Rights Bureau of the

State Department by staffing it with well-regarded officials. Carter also challenged foreign ambassadors and world leaders he met with to improve their poor human rights records.[21] Despite Carter's attempt to refashion America's foreign policy by making it more humane and less concerned with communism, IPS remained convinced that underneath it all stood an unabashed Cold War liberal.

Just days before Ronald Reagan's first inaugural, Isabel Letelier, who joined IPS following the death of her husband, blasted Carter's timidity. She described the departing president's human rights policies as a "bold step" that made possible "the only opening provided to the Cold War since the 1940s" but argued that Carter failed to take advantage of the crack in the Cold War consensus. She described Carter's policies as "a yellow light of caution to many Latin American dictators" but nothing more. She blamed Carter's misguided actions in the region on "very little understanding of Latin American reality, and why it is *that* reality which creates liberation movements and not the Soviet Union." By this, she meant the poor economic conditions and violence exacted upon the people living in Latin America. "To close one's eyes to this reality is to become a part of a system of denial of basic human rights and to become an ally of those who practice violence against the majority," Letelier explained.[22] Even out of the White House Carter did not escape the institute's barbs. IPS intellectuals claimed that America's reluctance to support revolutions greatly impeded efforts to solve the world's real problems. With the Vietnam War over and superpower détente in full swing, Carter's early years in the White House represented a period of relative calm. IPS intellectuals, however, criticized the president for failing to take advantage of the situation. A 1984 report written in part by IPS intellectuals described Carter as being "locked in ambiguity" as he attempted to balance his desire for ending human rights abuses with the need to prevent revolutions.[23] From IPS's perspective, Carter remained too wedded to the liberal capitalist international order and thus did not embody a truly post–Cold War president.

The president's indifference to the Letelier assassination colored IPS's perception of Carter's human rights policies in Latin America. Isabel Letelier and Moffitt sent a letter to Carter requesting time to talk with him about Orlando's death and what it meant for human rights. Brzezinski recommended against such a meeting and proposed First Lady Rosalynn Carter as an alternative before settling on Robert Lipshutz, the president's counsel. Letelier met with Lipshutz on March 1, 1978. During the encounter, he admitted that "this case may not be resolved to everyone's total satisfaction."[24] IPS's response to the investigation proved Lipshutz correct. After reviewing his colleagues' *Assassination on Embassy Row*, Barnet could not help but wonder why Carter did not take a tougher stance against Pinochet. He ascribed Carter's reluctance to force Pinochet to extradite Contreras to an instance whereby "geopolitics has triumphed over justice." "Despite the thousands of murders to his credit," Barnet continued, "Pinochet has brought a good investment climate to Chile and he is clearly preferred in the Carter White House to the uncertainties that would follow his collapse. Such is standard *realpolitik*." Thus, despite rhetorical flourishes alluding to a new direction for U.S. foreign policy, IPS intellectuals viewed Carter as no different from earlier presidents bent on preserving the liberal order.[25]

Even after Carter took action against the Chilean government, IPS intellectuals considered the response weak, particularly given that Pinochet orchestrated an attack on American soil. Moffitt and Letelier used Carter's inaction to criticize his human rights record. In a letter to members of Congress written in mid-1977, Moffitt and Letelier claimed that to give loans to known dictators "would bury in hypocrisy any future for human rights in Latin America." IPS intellectuals continued to press the administration to punish Pinochet. In a letter to Hodding Carter, the assistant secretary of public affairs, Kornbluh expressed astonishment over the lack of sanctions against Pinochet. Asking for evidence of a stronger U.S. response, Kornbluh belittled the administration for "its cowardice in the face of a handful of cut-throat generals and a handful of foreign investors."[26] Simply put, Carter did not move fast enough for IPS intellectuals.

Despite IPS's repeated entreaties, the Carter administration refused to hold Pinochet accountable for his actions. Summarizing an "unfortunate confrontation" he had with Robert Pastor, a member of Carter's National Security Council, Kornbluh reached the conclusion that the Carter administration, believing that it had responded accordingly to the Letelier murder, would do no more. While Kornbluh argued that Carter's decision to cut off military aid to Chile represented a "token response," Pastor believed just the opposite. According to Kornbluh, Pastor thought "that Carter had really done a great deal in response to the assassination." Pastor claimed that "diplomatic limitations" prevented Carter from blaming Pinochet's government for the crime and, furthermore, "no hard evidence" existed to prove Pinochet's role in the assassination. At this point in the conversation, "I was told pretty bluntly that the U.S. had done all it was going to do in this case," Kornbluh reported. Admitting that the "conversation had turned quite sour," Kornbluh "suggested to Mr. Pastor that the Carter administration had let Pinochet, a petty military dictator, pull the wool over its eyes," at which point Pastor accused

Kornbluh of using Reagan's argument against Carter. From his brief meeting with Pastor, Kornbluh concluded, "The Carter Administration doesn't feel the assassination was of sufficient importance to warrant any further steps than the ones they have taken." With respect to the Letelier investigation, Kornbluh added, "The case is dead as far as they are concerned." "They think they did a strong job of demonstrating their dissatisfaction to the junta," he recounted.[27] As for suggestions that the United States should recall Ambassador George W. Landau indefinitely, limit or prohibit private bank loans, or sever ties completely with Chile, Secretary of State Cyrus Vance explained that such measures "would not serve our interests in Chile or elsewhere."[28]

In fact, from the start, high-ranking officials in the Carter administration played down the importance of the Letelier assassination. A State Department official at the Chile Desk later remarked, "I do not believe myself that there was that much interest in the highest levels of the U.S. government over Chile." Thus, while the Carter administration "expressed its regrets" about human rights in Chile when confronted by Congress or reporters, it "was busy with much more important things in other parts of the world and didn't put that much effort into Chile." This explains why IPS, especially Isabel Letelier, looked elsewhere, to low- and mid-level officials, FBI agents, Department of Justice prosecutors, and members of Congress, who pushed back against "executive caution," as one historian has described it, in the Carter and Reagan administrations.[29]

As Carter equivocated, IPS turned to Congress. Senator Kennedy and Representative Tom Harkin gave speeches critical of Carter's close ties to Pinochet—accentuated by a recent invitation from Carter to the Chilean president to visit the United States—during an IPS Congressional Conference on U.S.-Latin American (Southern Cone) Policy and Human Rights in September 1977. IPS also organized the Conference on the Future of U.S.-Chile Relations, which took place in the Dirksen Senate Office Building in July 1978. In addition to Harkin, Democratic senators Frank Church, Alan Cranston, and James Abourezk and Republican Mark Hatfield attended, as did Representative Donald Fraser, among others. Harkin and thirty-seven other members of Congress hand-delivered a letter to President Carter on August 1, 1979, regarding the continued intransigence of the Pinochet government. Like IPS, Harkin and his cosigners linked the Letelier-Moffitt murders to the larger issue of human rights. He implored the president to take "the strongest measures necessary" to force Contreras and other participants in the assassination to stand trial in America. Otherwise he predicted that "our government's passivity can only be perceived as a signal that the United States will compromise on our residents' and citizens' most basic human right—the right to live." Harkin continued to press Carter to take a stronger stand against Chile for its role in the Letelier assassination.[30]

On one such occasion, Harkin, along with his fellow Democratic congressmen Toby Moffett and George Miller, wrote to President Carter to inform him of a congressional resolution demanding sanctions against Chile for its unwillingness to extradite the persons charged with planning or carrying out the Letelier-Moffitt murders. They forcefully argued that "the Pinochet regime has literally gotten away with murder." The resolution, cosponsored by sixty members of Congress, noted that while Carter undertook "the strongest possible measures" to punish other governments involved in either carrying out terrorist acts or protecting terrorists, the administration refused to do the same with Chile. Supporters of the resolution wanted the United States to remove the U.S. ambassador from Chile; end all bilateral and multilateral aid to Chile; stop sending military aid, both equipment and advisors, to Chile; prohibit Export-Import Banks and private banks from offering loans to Chile; and demand that Pinochet restore civil rights in Chile.[31] On November 30, 1979, Carter removed some U.S. personnel from Chile and ended all weapons sales to the country. The Carter administration also restricted Export-Import Bank activities in Chile. These administration responses fell far short in the eyes of Harkin and Kennedy.[32] Both remained loyal IPS allies. As late as 1987, they introduced the Democracy in Chile Act, which, among other things, required "concrete progress in bringing to justice those responsible for the murders of Rodrigo Rojas, Orlando Letelier, and Ronni Moffitt."[33]

While Allende's overthrow in 1973 and Orlando's assassination in 1976 energized human rights activists, their attention eventually turned to other hot spots. Orlando's wife, Isabel, however, remained steadfast in her determination to maintain the pressure on Pinochet and the U.S. government. She did so through the Chile Committee for Human Rights, which she started in 1976. The organization publicized events in Chile to "raise awareness about the need to safeguard human rights and democracy as primary universal concerns" in the human rights campaign. Additionally, the committee carried out fund-raising for Pinochet's victims in Chile. Conducting research represented another priority of the committee. It investigated the practice of "exile, relegation, expulsion, and the right to return," which the Pinochet regime employed regularly to encourage compliance among Chileans. The committee also strove to act "as a vehicle for the preservation and promotion of Chile's cultural traditions, now besieged by the military government's imposition of an economic model heavily emphasizing materialistic values

and which promotes a commercially oriented culture." Letelier's Chile Committee for Human Rights remained a thorn in the side of the U.S. and Chilean
governments. "Simply by remaining active," one scholar has written, "Letelier
served as a constant reminder that the Chilean government challenged the
integrity of the American legal order" when it carried out an assassination on
the streets of Washington, D.C. Through her various activities at IPS, Isabel
served as a mouthpiece for Chileans silenced by Pinochet. As a Human Rights
Project report detailed, "Ms. Letelier is often the first contacted by those in
Chile with news that requires quick distribution and immediate response."[34]

Carrying on Orlando's Spirit:
U.S. Capitalism and Human Rights

Even in death, Letelier's work on Chile influenced IPS. In a letter from Barnet and his colleagues at IPS to the editors of the *Wall Street Journal*, they
chastised the newspaper for ignoring Chile's blatant disregard for human
rights while celebrating Pinochet's economic policies. They bemoaned the
paper's "casual attitude toward oppression in Chile," which reminded them
"of those who used to celebrate Mussolini's ability to make the trains run on
time and Hitler's success in reducing unemployment through war production."[35] Despite the best efforts of Pinochet's boosters in the United States, IPS
refused to let Chile's economic miracle conceal the regime's brutal methods.

The peace intellectuals at the institute remained committed to tearing
down the imaginary wall separating economics and human rights in the popular imagination, as well as exposing the involvement of U.S. actors. IPS's
1977 *The Southern Connection* report specifically referred to Chile's dismal
human rights record, which it linked to "U.S. policy decisions that encourage
certain kinds of development" that favored the "elites" at the expense of the
masses. The report went on to declare, "Vast disparities in socio-economic
opportunities obstruct the creation of a climate in which human rights can
be fully respected. Practical steps to reduce these inequities are thus also
steps toward the mitigation of the broader human rights crisis of our times."
Meanwhile, in a speech observing the ten-year anniversary of Allende's
death, Isabel Letelier laid bare the connection between the United States and
Chile. She did so by comparing the events in Chile after Allende's overthrow
to the actions of conquistadores of centuries before. The present-day con-
querors, like their predecessors, had European origins, though they were not
actually from the continent. Instead, "the greedy conquistadors that smashed

our economy studied in Chicago, and the armed forces that wanted us to disappear in the name of national security studied abroad as well," in U.S. military schools.[36] The ties binding the United States to Chile, and vice versa, ran deep, which did not escape the notice of IPS intellectuals.

In 1977, IPS announced the creation of the Letelier-Moffitt Human Rights Award, which honored the lives of Orlando Letelier and Ronni Karpen Moffitt. Over the years it went to individuals or organizations fighting to advance the cause of social justice. Weiss, the chairman of IPS's board of trustees, spoke at the event about the connection between neoliberal economic policies and human rights abuses. "The use of psychiatric institutions to harbor political dissidents is a perversion of professional responsibility; so is the failure of hospitals to care for the sick. Arbitrary arrest and detention violate the integrity of the person; so does the impersonal system of triage which, under a regime of enforced scarcity, decides who is to live and who is to die," Weiss explained to the audience. He went on to argue that Letelier died because "Pinochet could not afford . . . to have the outside world translate human rights policies into financial and economic action."[37] Weiss's remarks leave no doubt that IPS kept Letelier's vision of human rights alive.

The spread of free-market ideology to more countries coincided with a decline in the personal and economic welfare of citizens, a fact that did not escape the notice of IPS. To fix the problem, Landau suggested replacing national security ideology with a new approach based on the promotion of human rights. He lamented how Westerners limited human rights to political and civil freedoms while ignoring economic security. For instance, the U.S. government and certain human rights organizations overlooked the "endemic poverty" found throughout Central America. Such an "oversight," Landau claimed, "covers up the responsibility of U.S. policy for causing these disastrous conditions through U.S. support for military dictators and local oligarchies." The reconceptualization of human rights required a new outlook among Americans. "To become a moral guideline for policy, human rights, not welfare, must be internalized in the public mind," he wrote.[38] Thus, as the 1980 Brandt Commission report, among others, called for redistribution to deal with global inequality, Landau encouraged a semantic shift away from "welfare" to "human rights." By doing so, he hoped to lessen the stigma attached to providing food and shelter to the poor and heighten the importance of economic human rights.

Despite the efforts of IPS intellectuals to link the two, Pinochet succeeded in keeping human rights separate from economics. Protesting the "economic private bank bailout" of Chile after foreign governments cut off aid to Pinochet's government, Isabel Letelier and Moffitt declared that "an enormous influx of *private* bank loans since 1976 has enabled the junta to thumb its nose at the international human rights campaign." Letelier and Moffitt calculated that loans from private firms totaled approximately $1 billion by the end of 1978, with about $927 million of this coming from American banks. Absorbed with "maximizing global profits and minimizing risks," private banks evinced little concern for the human rights records of the countries receiving the loans. That is how Letelier and Moffitt explained the massive private loans to Chile, which amounted to 90 percent of that nation's foreign capital. In the mid- to late 1970s, six multinational banks with headquarters in the United States loaned Chile over $800 million.[39]

The IPS report caused a stir in congressional circles and sparked an immediate response on Capitol Hill. On April 11, with Letelier and Moffitt by his side at a press conference, Representative Harkin announced his intention to sponsor legislation forcing private banks to keep Congress informed about loans to countries accused of human rights violations. "Banks should not be allowed to undermine our efforts to reestablish basic human rights in these countries and at the same time pretend they are aiding our endeavors," he stated. The following day, Democratic representative Henry Reuss, the chairman of the House Banking Committee, sent a letter to six of the banks named in the IPS report. He excoriated them for acting contrary to U.S. interests. "Your lending actions are not helpful to the U.S. policy of restricting loans to countries found to be in violation of human rights," Reuss exclaimed. Moffitt worked closely with Senator Kennedy and his staff during the subsequent congressional hearings on the matter. Despite the attention given to the issue, without Carter's support the legislation proposed by Harkin and Kennedy to rein in the activities of private banks went nowhere.[40]

Outside of Congress, IPS organized boycotts against banks that offered loans to Chile. As part of its D.C. Bank Campaign in 1979, IPS closed its account at Riggs National Bank. Such banks, Moffitt and a coauthor wrote, were "among those whose redlining policies are hastening the deterioration of our major cities while they loan and/or invest in morally bankrupt regimes whose economic policies warrant force to impose them on the majority of the population." Prior to the large-scale divestment movement of the mid-1980s in opposition to apartheid in South Africa, IPS sought to "make it unprofitable" for banks to do business with nations that committed human rights abuses. IPS director Borosage and Landau wrote to the chairman of the board at Riggs and compared the bank's willingness to make loans to Chile and South Africa to lending money to the Nazis. While IPS recognized that banks had "a duty to seek profitable investments," financial institutions also had to abide by "moral limits."[41]

IPS's Response to America as the World's Arms Market

In uncovering the massive amounts of armaments sold by the U.S. government and corporations to foreign nations, IPS exposed the complicity of the United States in torture and repression. As head of IPS's Militarism and Disarmament Project, Michael Klare led the effort. One scholar has described Klare as having "been virtually alone in describing and critiquing the illegal arms trade."[42] Noting that Third World countries spent $100 billion in 1980 on military-related goods, with Iran alone accounting for $30 billion of the total, Klare declared that "Third World militarism is reaching epidemic proportions." Yet he did not place the blame entirely on the countries receiving these tools of torture and repression. Klare rejected the argument that militarism represented "some sort of inherent consequence of Third World 'backwardness'—as if authoritarianism and repression were somehow intrinsic to underdevelopment and poverty." Instead, he described militarism as "a communicable disease," one "not indigenous but exported to them by the industrial powers for their own profit and gain." How did the United States and other developed nations aid in the process? By supporting "friendly military elites" in the Third World who promised to maintain order in their countries and protect U.S. interests, according to Klare.[43] As Americans sought to limit U.S. foreign intervention, selling arms to regional despots offered an alternative means to promote U.S. interests.

A series of actions undertaken by the Nixon administration in the summer of 1973—including the overriding of congressional limits on arms sales to Latin America and the sale of $10 billion worth of new weapons to Iran prior to making them available to NATO—represented a new direction in U.S. foreign policy, according to IPS's Militarism and Disarmament Project. "The cumulative impact of these decisions was to nullify *in toto* the policies which had governed U.S. arms sales abroad since World War II," a funding proposal declared. No longer would the United States "prevent needless expenditures on non-developmental programs" by Third World nations. Citing Pentagon statistics, the proposal showed that military sales to underdeveloped nations in the 1950s and 1960s averaged $230 million per year, while arms sales in the mid-1970s reached $6.7 billion each year. Though Carter made much of his rejection of 614 weapons requests totaling $1 billion, arms sales actually increased during his presidency because of loopholes in the provisions. Thus, besides allowing for "more orderly processes," Carter's arms sales policy, his biographer has written, "was oversold."[44] With their narrow focus on torture, most human rights activists ignored how dictators obtained the weapons used against their own people. IPS, however, more attuned to U.S. involvement in the international arms trade, sought to expose America's role in making torture possible. In the process, IPS further sullied Carter's human rights policies.

Despite Carter's claims to the contrary, IPS discovered massive arms sales by the U.S. government. An investigation by Klare and Max Holland found that under Carter limits on foreign arms sales did not pertain to America's allies in NATO or Japan, Australia, and New Zealand, which from 1976 to 1978 had purchased 25 percent of all U.S. arms on the market. Klare and Holland also noted that the president could override the limits at his discretion, which Carter did when he sold radar planes to Iran. Overall, Klare and Holland concluded that "when all is said and done, Carter's new guidelines will not make a significant dent in the outflow of U.S. arms, equipment, and services." What, then, was needed to close the loopholes and limit the president's ability to override restrictions on arms sales? Klare and Holland recommended an $8 billion cap on military exports, with a 10 percent reduction in the ceiling each subsequent year. They also called for an end to arms sales to nations experiencing internal turmoil.[45]

Such an approach appealed to IPS intellectuals because previous legislation restricting arms sales had failed. Klare, writing with Cynthia Arnson, lamented that even with the passage of Section 406 of the Arms Export Control Act of 1976, which prohibited the sale of arms to Chile, the Carter administration allowed weapons in the "pipeline," meaning arms purchased prior to the restriction, to arrive in Chile as late as 1978. Arnson and Klare argued that the Carter administration, though adhering to the 1976 legislation, should have invalidated the sales with Chile, as it did in the case of Ethiopia. Arnson and Klare concluded that, by choosing not to, the "administration places greater emphasis on maintaining close relations with the Chilean military than it does on carrying out any of its promises to dissociate the United States from countries that are guilty of trampling on human rights."[46] The rhetoric of Carter aside, IPS intellectuals viewed the president's refusal to stop arms sales to dictators like Pinochet as indicative of his Cold War mentality, which meant continued support for anti-communist allies regardless of their human rights record. Thus, even Carter, purportedly the first post–Cold War president, placed preservation of the liberal order above all else. In the process, the United States remained the handmaiden of torturous regimes.

IPS's documentation of U.S. arms sales showed how heavily foreign nations relied on the United States not only for defense-related goods but also for the tools used by dictators to suppress internal opposition.[47] In an updated edition of *Supplying Repression*, Klare and Arnson criticized the U.S. government for "stand[ing] at the supply end of a pipeline of repressive technology that extends to many of the world's most authoritarian regimes." Though Carter trumpeted human rights, the authors provided evidence showing that the ten most repressive countries received one-third of all military aid, or $2.3 billion, and these nations bought an additional $13.7 billion worth of American arms during Carter's term. Much of this aid, in the form of armored cars, tear gas, riot clubs, and instruments for "internal political warfare" against dissidents, went directly to the local police forces in these countries.[48]

Divulging America's role in the global arms market led to Klare's involvement in campaigns both inside and outside of politics to end U.S. arms sales. In addition to *Supplying Repression*, newspaper and magazine articles, op-eds, and media appearances, Klare's findings on the arms trade reached politicians and activists through the publication of several editions of *Arms Trade Data*. Klare's statistics and data were "used extensively," in the words of one Ford Foundation official, by groups like the Center for Defense Information, the Center for National Security Studies, the Coalition for a New Foreign and Military Policy (CNFMP), SANE, and the American Friends Service Committee, among others. Klare served on the CNFMP's Arms Sales Subcommittee and the Mobilization for Survival's Arms Sale Task Force. The former appeared following IPS's Conference on the International Arms Trade: Components, Consequences, and Control held in April 1978. CNFMP also published a newsletter, *Up Against the Arms Trade*, and organized protests in front of the "arms bazaars" held by weapons manufacturers in cities across the country, both of which relied on information uncovered by Klare. His research also found its way into legislation. Language in a foreign aid bill borrowed directly from the recommendations put forth in Klare's report. Most notably, the amendment prohibited transfers of "crime control and detection instruments" for foreign police forces unless the Departments of State and Commerce approved an export license, which could occur only under "extraordinary circumstances" anyway.[49]

The Carter administration's silence regarding the role of private banks in propping up dictators forced IPS to contend with the question of how

America's economic system worked against the very rights the institute hoped to protect. Certain IPS intellectuals reached the conclusion that stopping human rights abuses required changes to the capitalist system and the rules regulating the international economic order. While giving a speech on the role of banks in keeping South African and Chilean dictators in power, Moffitt boiled the human rights issue down to capitalism. "It is impossible to understand the importance of international banks, the importance of Chile or South Africa without going to the root of the problem, the international expansion of the capitalist system," he told the crowd. How a president who championed human rights more forcefully than any previous occupant in the White House could also oppose blocking private loans to South Africa and Chile puzzled Moffitt. "The large private banks have given the governments a green light to go on violating human rights. Freed from international pressure, they act with impunity attempting to solidify and enhance their rule," Moffitt explained.[50] As a result, international banks and loans took on added importance in the writings of IPS intellectuals as the globalization of both finance and industry took off in the 1970s.

Shattered Dreams: Democracy's False Start in Chile

Having amassed "strong evidence" that Pinochet ordered Letelier's assassination, Secretary of State George Shultz encouraged Ronald Reagan in 1987 to distance the United States from the dictator: "What we know about Pinochet's role in these assassinations is of the greatest seriousness and adds further impetus to the need to work toward complete democratization of Chile." For myriad reasons, Reagan listened to Shultz, though the administration's promotion of democracy in Chile and elsewhere proved far more circumscribed than the president and his advisors claimed in public, essentially denying leftist groups an opportunity to participate in the elections. U.S. national interest always took precedence over the implementation of democratic reforms in Chile. The administration also went along with the protections accorded to Pinochet in Chile's 1980 constitution, which guaranteed lifetime immunity.[51] Therefore, even as the Reagan administration changed course in Chile, the United States did not absolve itself of its past sins, at least from IPS's perspective. Pinochet escaped punishment and democracy remained elusive in Chile.

Ten years after the coup that brought Pinochet to power, IPS fellows Landau and Kornbluh blamed the United States for thwarting an experiment in democratic governance by a popularly elected socialist politician. "Had Allende been allowed to serve out his full term in office, the lesson in Chile might have been that socialists and communists *can* play by the electoral rules of democracy and that profound changes *can* be accomplished peacefully rather than violently," the two critics wrote.[52] Reagan's efforts to promote democracy did little to change the calculus that guided U.S. foreign policy for much of the Cold War. It certainly did not allow for ideological pluralism.

*   *   *

From the perspective of IPS intellectuals, the United States could not duck responsibility for furthering the pain and suffering of Third World peoples living under ruthless dictators. The U.S. government, corporations, and even economists provided the ammunition, both actual and theoretical, for these despots. Given that Orlando Letelier spent his brief final years at the institute, it should come as no surprise that IPS focused on Chile. Just as important, Letelier's interest in the relationship between economics and human rights abuses led IPS to use a wide lens when investigating torture and other abuses. By fixating on the bodily harm done to individuals, most human rights activists ignored the underlying systemic reasons behind these physical acts as well as the much larger class of people suffering in other ways. In doing so, they failed to tackle the root of the problem, which required looking at regimes' economic policies and their foreign supporters both in and out of government. IPS, on the other hand, made these connections visible, compelling the think tank to turn inward and look at how entities within the United States aided human rights abusers.

While Carter put human rights at the forefront of U.S. foreign policy, serious limitations inherent in his policies prevented the president from getting at the root of human rights abuses abroad. Carter's unwillingness to pursue Pinochet following Letelier's assassination served as proof for IPS that the president, along with liberals more generally, would avoid at all costs the weakening of a stalwart anti-communist ally. Thus, even in Carter's post–Cold War order, ideological pluralism had no place. This ensured the survival of the liberal capitalist order but also inhibited democracy in Chile and elsewhere. More than any other organization, IPS laid out for the world to see how Carter turned a blind eye to private loans and arms making their way into the hands of dictators. In other words, IPS endeavored to blur the lines separating the "good guys" and "bad guys." The idea of the United States as exceptional and on the right side of history did not stand up to the institute's scrutiny. Less beholden to the Cold War paradigm, IPS intellectuals targeted America's anti-communist allies and focused on the myriad ways the United States propped up foreign dictators. It soon became clear, however, that each of the players targeted by IPS acted within the constraints of the capitalist system. With this realization, IPS intellectuals entered the debate over the New International Economic Order, sometimes working in concert with the Third World and other times going beyond the demands of the G-77 nations.

CHAPTER 6

A War for the World's Resources

"Like all the other poor countries of the world, we have been exploited for years. We ask our workers to break their backs under sugar estates to make sugar. And then we have to send sugar abroad. And the money we get for the sugar is what helped to bring the tractor into Jamaica. Every year the tractor costs more, but we can't make it. Every year the machinery costs more, but we can't make it. So we have to bring it from abroad. And that system that has us there, giving up ourselves for the sugar, is a system known as imperialism." Saul Landau captured this speech by Jamaican prime minister Michael Manley while producing a campaign film for the candidate in the 1976 election, a task he would repeat in 1980. Other scenes in the documentary capture Manley being flocked by Jamaicans as he visits sugarcane fields, new access roads to help farmers get their produce to market, and an aluminum mine recently purchased by the government from a foreign-owned corporation.[1] Manley served as the lodestar for IPS intellectuals, who saw in the defiant Jamaican politician someone who could lead the fight to free the Third World from the oppressive bonds of capitalist imperialism.

Despite the growing recognition that the challenges facing the United States in the 1970s required greater interdependence, industrialized countries, multinational corporations, and international trade precluded the development of a truly ideologically diverse world, either politically or economically. As a result, even as détente led to the tearing down of some of the barriers that divided East and West, an unjust and unfair international economic system reinforced the boundary separating North and South. Looking to make the world safe for diversity, IPS entered the debate over the New International Economic Order (NIEO).[2] IPS found itself in agreement with many of the NIEO demands. Yet the institute remained skeptical about the underlying capitalist principles found in the NIEO program. Whereas IPS sought to topple the liberal international capitalist order, most Third

World nations preferred less substantive changes. From IPS's perspective, in seeking to re-create the powerful liberal state in the Third World and join the liberal capitalist order, these nations replicated the same undemocratic political, economic, and social structures found in industrialized nations, including the United States. IPS blamed top-down, expert-led modernization theory, which owed its existence to Cold War liberals like Walt Rostow, for creating the inequitable economic conditions in the Third World that led to global famine. IPS refused to look at world hunger as a health issue caused by unforeseen circumstances. Rather, the institute dusted off the 1948 Universal Declaration of Human Rights to argue that human rights abuses took many forms, including denying people nourishment. Cognizant of the links between economic and human rights abuses as a result of Orlando Letelier's writings on Chile, IPS blamed hunger on another liberal creation, the multinational corporation.[3]

IPS's inability to shift public opinion in the United States in favor of a more equitable international economic order forced it to look abroad for allies. In its search for a Third Way between liberal capitalism and socialism, the institute turned to the Third World, seeking out nations that shared IPS's affinity for decentralization and participatory democracy. In the process, IPS embraced democratic socialists like Manley in Jamaica and Julius Nyerere in Tanzania. Though not averse to replacing capitalism with socialism, IPS preferred an entirely new "post-capitalist" order composed of both capitalist and non-capitalist economic systems.[4] To that end, it created a sister organization, the Transnational Institute, and increased its efforts to deprive the International Monetary Fund (IMF) of support in the United States, primarily by exposing the links between the IMF's austerity programs and human rights abuses. Even as most critics of capitalism had retreated from the utopian dream of a post-capitalist order, IPS's participation in the South-North Conference on the International Monetary System and the New International Order in 1980 represented the best last-ditch effort to avert the global turn to neoliberalism.

Modernization, the NIEO, or Something Else?

Existing development models left much to be desired, which led IPS intellectuals to pursue their own novel path to modernization. In a letter to members of the North-South Food Roundtable, an organization to which she belonged and that included NGO leaders and UN officials, IPS fellow

Susan George outlined three development "paradigms." One, "the 'growth/trickle-down' model," embodied in the thinking behind the Green Revolution of the 1960s, held "that greater national production will automatically benefit hungry people living in the same national space." Hoping to replicate the economic growth experienced by Western nations, Third World leaders sought additional technological inputs from the West and an increased presence of corporations. The second model borrowed from dependency theory and served as a "corrective" to end the abuse of the periphery by the center nations. It also, George argued, "rests on an assumption of global interdependence, but stresses that serious adjustments will have to be made in the world system" to allow for greater fairness. The G-77 nations pursued this development strategy because the "model concerns States, and States alone," according to George.[5] She found neither of these strategies appropriate for the Third World.

Grounded in liberal capitalist values, modernization theory lacked the means to solve the Third World's economic dilemma. Nor could the NIEO, with its tepid embrace of socialism, reduce the massive levels of poverty that existed across the Global South. Therefore, George proposed a more vigorous approach that "does not deny the need for a NIEO" but also understood the importance of "class" issues. George's model took the well-known premise of a "rich" North and "poor" South and applied it to the internal dynamics of Third World nations. "It holds that the NIEO is an incomplete solution to hunger and underdevelopment because nothing guarantees that increased national revenues or food production will benefit the poorest classes more than marginally," George explained.[6]

The horrendous economic conditions present in the Third World confirmed the bankruptcy of modernization theory. As George wrote in 1979, "The ranks of poor and landless peasants have swelled while cities have become unlivable for all but the privileged minority. 'Development' has resulted in roughly 300 million totally or partially unemployed people in the Third World (not to mention an estimated 15 million in the OECD countries). In spite of the most bountiful harvests in the world's history, 'development' has led to ever more widespread malnutrition and famine."[7] Clearly, the American-led modernization project had gone off the rails. At the same time, the NIEO framework had its own inadequacies.

IPS intellectuals considered both communism and capitalism antiquated and unlikely to meet the real needs of the world's citizens. Writing in 1980, Barnet accused the Soviet Union of being "subject to the same kind of imperial fantasies" as the United States, which led him to call for the "development of a serious, *genuinely* non-aligned movement" to "take the initiative on issues of global concern—the resources access issue, the environment, and the reconstruction of the world monetary system—which the industrialist countries have tried to settle for themselves and have totally failed to do."[8] In short, Barnet sought a Third Way. That said, IPS's critique centered on liberal capitalism as the primary impediment to a more democratic and equitable international economic order. As an internal 1975 report for the newly created International Economic Order (IEO) project headed by Orlando Letelier and Barnet noted, the program's "fundamental objective" was "to contribute to a more just relationship between the large capitalist nations and the emerging countries of the Third World" while also "encourag[ing] a real participation of the vast majorities in the economic process and in the distribution of its economic benefits."[9]

It quickly became clear to IPS intellectuals that building "a more just relationship" between the industrialized and developing countries required a wholesale transformation of the global economy. As Michael Moffitt, who took over the IEO following Letelier's assassination, wrote in 1978, "we begin from the perspective that the current economic, political and social situation in the Third World countries is a product of the historical development of the international capitalist system." Referring to Barnet's book on multinational corporations, Moffitt explained, "One of the lessons that I have retained from the criticisms of *Global Reach* is that it is necessary to talk about the capitalistic system not just multinationals."[10] IPS intellectuals soon targeted what one IEO report in the 1980s described as the "three pillars of the postwar international economy." These included private banks and the IMF in "finance," corporate trading practices and the General Agreement on Trade and Tariffs as aspects of "trade," and the "production" activities of transnational corporations and the World Bank. The proposal charged that "these institutions now are failing to generate the economic activity necessary to meet the demands of the majorities in both the developing and developed world."[11] Accordingly, modernization theory, multinational corporations, and the IMF came under intense scrutiny from IPS.

Though IPS accepted many of the ideas found in the NIEO and related proposals, the issue of national sovereignty prevented complete agreement. As Nils Gilman has noted, as much as "the NIEO represented a call for *socialism among states*, its devotion to national sovereignty meant that it also was "quite amenable to *capitalism within states*" and the inequality that came with the latter economic system.[12] Thus it is important to keep in mind the vast differences that existed within the Group of 77 nations touting the NIEO. IPS sided with the socialist nations, especially Jamaica and Tanzania, that sought equity not just between countries of the North and South but also within their own nations.

Intent on bolstering the sovereign powers of the state so long denied to them as colonial possessions, advocates of the NIEO ignored questions about the distribution of power in their own countries, which allowed unjust economic and social relations to flourish. As a result, IPS offered only qualified support. Writing in the fall of 1977, Moffitt declared that "a real NIEO is socialism," though this did not mean that IPS could not ally with the G-77 nations seeking more limited reforms. In answering his own question about "whether or not [the] NIEO constitutes an advance or a retreat within the framework of the worldwide anti-imperialist struggle," Moffitt wrote that "it most certainly is." Nonetheless, he did not trust the "national bourgeoisies in the Third World [who] are interested in doing nothing more than solidifying underdeveloped capitalism" in their countries. From the perspective of Moffitt and others at the institute, even if the NIEO freed the Global South from its status as an economic colony of the North, which many at IPS doubted unless combined with the complete dismantling of capitalism, conditions would not improve for most Third World peasants. Writing in 1982, George stated that "any development formulas lacking a class analysis, for both North *and* South, are doomed to failure." She expressed astonishment at how even sympathetic commentators continued to believe that "all Third World governments are indeed interested in the welfare of their own people and given more resources would do something about it."[13] In reality, without a socialist transformation within Third World nations, as occurred in Tanzania and Jamaica, the NIEO would prove inadequate.

More than any other figure at IPS, George disagreed with the central tenets of the NIEO ideology, most notably the priority given to commodity pricing. Even before the announcement of the NIEO, the United Nations Conference on Trade and Development (UNCTAD) put a tremendous amount of time and energy into formalizing agreements with industrialized nations to stabilize raw material and crop exports from the Third World. These efforts expanded and became more focused in the 1970s as the NIEO, working with UNCTAD, sought the creation of a Common Fund, which would use buffer stocks to help with erratic pricing.[14] In 1979, IPS's IEO project published George's *Feeding the Few*, where she questioned the prominence accorded to commodities within the NIEO framework. She argued for the necessity of including other reforms because "*of themselves* such [price] adjustments would certainly not erase the problems of poverty and underdevelopment."

As evidence, George pointed to the "class structure" of Third World nations, where a small percentage of the population received most of the income derived from exporting commodities. In Brazil, for instance, 27 percent of the profit went to the top 5 percent of the population, whereas only 5 percent reached the poorest 20 percent. These statistics led George to conclude that "upper classes do not cheerfully share their privileges," nor did they use the money to create jobs.[15]

According to IPS doctrine, improving the lives of Third World peasants required a greater reliance on locally derived development models and internal political changes. In 1977, Jimmy Carter's special assistant, Peter G. Bourne, contacted Moffitt for insight on how to deal with world hunger. Moffitt told him that "we will make little progress in alleviating world hunger without alleviating some of the more destructive symptoms of economic under-development." He explained that "in many countries of the Third World the poor majorities, which include perhaps 60 to 80% of total populations, have not shared the benefits of economic growth, and in some cases the poor are even worse off today." Moffitt encouraged the president to support the Common Fund, but he also advocated more far-reaching policies. For instance, he wanted the administration to support "inward-looking development" in the Global South so "the poor majorities would not see foreign assistance generating exports for affluent consumers in the developed world while their children have no milk to drink or no schools to attend." Yet, for such an approach to succeed, U.S. leaders needed to overcome their distrust of ideological pluralism. Moffitt argued that "U.S. development policies must be based less on 'national security' considerations than on how the poor majorities in those countries fare," which required an end to U.S. meddling in other countries' affairs. In other words, it could not repeat what it had done in Chile to weaken Salvador Allende.[16]

World Hunger: The Hidden Holocaust

"Malnutrition is the hidden holocaust of our day," Barnet declared in 1980. "It is avoidable," he continued, "and because it is avoidable, it is as much an indictment of this generation of bystanders as Hitler's Holocaust stands as an indictment of the last."[17] Barnet made this controversial statement in response to a similarly contentious idea offered in 1974 by biologist and author of "The Tragedy of the Commons," Garrett Hardin. Advocating "lifeboat ethics," he asked, "does everyone on earth have an equal right to an equal share of its resources?" In posing this combative question, Hardin compared the United States, as well as other wealthy nations, to a lifeboat stranded at sea with castaways, that is, poorer countries, "begging for admission to our boat or for handouts." Hardin encouraged his readers to remain in the lifeboat and brush the needy aside.[18] Shocked by Hardin's callous attitude toward the poor and hungry, Barnet issued a clarion call for making access to food the *first* human right. "It takes only a small intellectual leap to conclude that the surplus population must be controlled or eliminated for the benefit of the productive citizens," he wrote in response to Hardin's lifeboat ethic. "Thus, hunger lies at the very heart of the global human rights problem."[19]

Inspired by the 1948 Universal Declaration of Human Rights, IPS demanded more than the preservation of civil and political rights. Social, economic, and cultural rights also deserved safeguarding. Article 25 of the Declaration professed, "Everyone has the right to a standard of living adequate for the health and well-being of himself and of his family, including food, clothing, housing and medical care and necessary social services," along with other protections related to employment status, age, and disease.[20] Yet existing international economic structures, multinational corporations, and local elites in the Third World all acted with impunity to undermine these rights. To add to the indignity, human rights activists remained indifferent to the plight of the impoverished masses. IPS, on the other hand, exhibited no such historical amnesia about the 1948 Universal Declaration.

Perhaps the most novel aspect of IPS's critique of modernization theory and other development models was its attempt to make access to food a human right. In the 1970s, "basic needs," viewed as an alternative to large-scale, high-technology, and top-down modernization projects, became the new, much ballyhooed, approach to development. Increasingly, the World Bank directed foreign aid and funding from international financial institutions toward meeting the "basic needs" of people. Focused on improving health, education, food and water supply, and sanitation in the Third World, the World Bank's efforts failed to solve the problem of inequality, especially income disparity. Such conditions persisted because of defects in the Bank's strategies to reach the Third World poor. Commercial landowners, and to a lesser extent small farmers, received the majority of aid, leaving landless peasants impoverished.[21] Consequently, "basic needs" offered no guarantees for the world's most vulnerable citizens but rather "sufficiency," or the notion that each individual's needs are met just enough to stay above an agreed-upon "bottom line," pushing aside any hopes for "full-fledged redistributive justice" and leading to massive inequality, as Samuel Moyn has argued.[22] IPS intellectuals offered a more expansive vision, going beyond weak appeals for "basic needs" to guarantees of economic and social rights.

Given the historical amnesia surrounding the 1948 Universal Declaration of Human Rights, IPS intellectuals struggled to bridge the gap between social and economic rights on the one hand and political and civil rights on the other. Writing in the early months of the Carter presidency, Barnet criticized the targeting of specific dictators for human rights abuses. "Understanding the causes of systematic violations of human rights and trying to remove them is a far more promising way to raise the minimum standards of treatment of human beings around the world than selective hectoring," he wrote. Furthermore, human rights activists tended to focus on physical torture and disappearances while ignoring the many indignities faced by the impoverished. Barnet sought to shed light on these more common forms of human rights abuses. "Without establishing the notion of minimum substantive rights for every citizen of the globe," among which he included access to food, health care, housing, and employment, "the procedural rights which Americans cherish and which are increasingly violated around the world—freedom of speech, assembly, press, religion, and thought—will remain irrelevant for a majority of mankind and utterly unattainable." In short, Barnet discovered a disconnect that existed between human rights activists and the victims they purported to help. Rescuing the latter meant a restoration of their basic needs before moving on to the more commonly acknowledged political rights. Later in the same year, during a news conference announcing the inaugural Letelier-Moffitt Human Rights Award, the chairman of IPS's board of trustees, Peter Weiss, made a similar point when he spoke of the need "to erase the dividing line between first and second class human rights." To illustrate his point, he noted that "the electrode to the nipple is an affront to human dignity; so is the nipple that has no milk for the suckling infant."[23]

Before IPS could embark on a campaign to extend the umbrella of human rights protections to basic needs, including access to food, it first had to debunk the myth that world hunger stemmed from overpopulation, poor farming techniques, or natural disasters. Several books in the late 1960s and early 1970s alerted Americans to the coming Armageddon induced by massive population growth. Most notably Paul Ehrlich, in his 1968 best seller, *The Population Bomb*, concluded that "the battle to feed all of humanity is over" and predicted massive food shortages "where hundreds of millions of people are going to starve to death" over the following decade. A more subdued analysis came four years later with the Club of Rome's *The Limits to Growth*, but this report also lambasted "the present world system" for continuing to stubbornly cling to the belief that it was possible "to produce more people with more (food, material goods, clean air and water) for each person." In response to these alarming forecasts, international organizations and individual nations undertook population control measures that often targeted the weakest and most vulnerable of humankind.[24]

Fears about a global food crisis led the United Nations to hold a World Food Conference in 1974. At the meeting, UN Secretary-General Kurt Waldheim, like many other participants, spoke of the need for expanding food production through "massive transfers of capital and technology." During his keynote address, Secretary of State Henry Kissinger repeated these calls for higher productivity as he blamed the food crisis on overpopulation. Agricultural economist and former official of the UN World Food Programme John Shaw has concluded that "with its focus on 'the world food problem' and the need to increase production and stability of supplies, it failed to address adequately 'the world food security problem,' including measures to ensure access of the poor to the food they needed." The resolutions adopted at the conference point to the primary concerns of its participants. These included resolutions on development, fertilizers, additional "agricultural research, extension, and training," pesticides, seeds, and food aid.[25]

Representatives from IPS's sister institute, the Transnational Institute (TNI), also attended the Rome meeting but offered a far different take on world hunger. Prior to the event, an internal progress report explained that in undertaking a study of its own, TNI aimed to "challenge the conventional analysis presented by [Gerald] Ford, Kissinger, and agribusiness-dominated FAO [Food and Agriculture Organization]" in addition to "the Green Revolution and population control strategies and show why the problem is not fundamentally one of increased production but of more equitable distribution." Upon completion, TNI distributed seven hundred copies to conference attendees. Members of TNI also held a meeting that attracted the press and some four hundred agricultural experts, government officials, and the president of the G-77, Edmundo Flores. Afterward, Flores thanked TNI for its "outstanding contribution" and encouraged the institute to "redouble its efforts" in support of the NIEO.[26]

The TNI report submitted to the main conference strongly denounced population control. TNI and IPS intellectuals refused to "blame the victim," preferring instead to call attention to how elites, both domestic and foreign, worked in unison to preserve the status quo. "Development without an effective distribution system reaching the neediest sectors of the population is not enough, for if the benefits of the development are not widespread, the minority will continue for many years to live in luxury while the great masses of the people live in misery," with Brazil a recent example of such an outcome.[27] IPS, along with TNI, implored officials in governments and international bodies to recognize that humans caused famine, and solving the crisis required fundamental changes to the world's economic and social structures.

Goodbye to the Nation-State?
Multinational Corporations and World Hunger

On March 21, 1972 *Washington Post* syndicated columnist Jack Anderson turned the spotlight on multinational corporations with his disclosure that International Telephone and Telegraph (ITT) had organized a campaign against Chilean socialist Salvador Allende. When these efforts failed to prevent his victory in the 1970 presidential election, ITT continued to look for ways to impede the democratically elected leader of Chile, frequently turning to top U.S. officials in the White House and CIA. "These documents portray ITT as a virtual corporate nation in itself with vast international holdings, access to Washington's highest officials, its own intelligence apparatus and even its own classification system," Anderson remarked.[28] The exposure of ITT's nefarious plans to create "economic chaos" in Chile led the chairman of the Senate Foreign Relations Committee, Democrat William Fulbright, to create a special Subcommittee on Multinational Corporations, headed by Frank Church of Idaho. Church's committee produced various reports related to corporate activities in the oil industry and corporate trade and investment in Eastern Europe but produced little in terms of actual legislation, except for the Foreign Corrupt Practices Act of 1977. Internationally, in 1975, delegates from forty-eight countries met to discuss a Code of Conduct on Transnational Corporations. Divisions between less developed countries and members of the Organization for Economic Cooperation and Development (OECD) over whether to make the code binding and issues of sovereignty, especially regarding expropriation and the compensation of multinational corporations, stalled progress. The OECD created Guidelines on Multinational Enterprises in 1976, but a Code of Conduct never materialized.[29]

Besides meddling in Chile's internal affairs, corporations came under increased scrutiny for soaring energy costs, questionable contributions to the reelection campaign of Richard Nixon in 1972, and general malfeasance. Howard Brick and Christopher Phelps have suggested that anger toward corporations matched, and in some cases surpassed, the antigovernment feelings of the era. In fact, the two often went together, with corporate critics claiming that a few wealthy business leaders had hijacked government for their own benefit and at the expense of the American people.[30] Though more widespread in the 1970s, anti-corporate harangues long occupied an important place in Marxist theory. In a 1966 article, Paul Baran and Paul Sweezy argued that the corporation had replaced the industrialist and banker as the primary beneficiary of U.S. imperialism. The U.S. government, they argued, needed "to make a world safe for Standard Oil," among others. Journalist Robert Scheer echoed this sentiment in a book published the following decade, where he applauded Baran and Sweezy's attempt to link the rise of multinational corporations to monopoly capitalism. He also sought to prove Vladimir Lenin's prescience, claiming that the theorist "anticipated not only the further economic penetration of the Third World," which Karl Marx, too, had predicted, "but also the rise of newer capitalist institutions" to further U.S. imperialist aims.[31] Due to questionable domestic and foreign activities, the corporation became the scourge of the world by the 1970s.

IPS entered the conversation with the publication of *Global Reach: The Power of the Multinational Corporations* in 1974 by Richard Barnet and Ronald Müller. Barnet and his cohorts at IPS wanted to reveal how these powerful firms redirected U.S. foreign policy. While most critics viewed corporations as an appendage to the U.S. government, with the former seeking to advance the strategic and economic interests of the latter, IPS intellectuals argued that a rupture had occurred by the 1970s. In the early years of the Cold War, corporations and the U.S. government worked side by side, or as Barnet and Müller put it, "capital and ideological purity were preserved together." As a result, the CIA could rid itself of a radical leftist government in Guatemala while also preserving the business interests of United Fruit. Economic and military setbacks in the 1960s and 1970s, however, made this partnership less appealing to corporate executives. As Barnet and Müller noted, "Broken windows and bomb threats from militant groups opposed to the U.S. intervention in Indochina helped convince some American companies in Europe that they should get rid of their American label."[32]

Untethered from the United States, the corporation began pursuing its own self-interest with reckless abandon, regardless of the ramifications for the United States, or any other nation-state for that matter. Shortly after publication of *Global Reach*, Barnet described corporations as "disturbers of the peace" and pointed out that "in the pursuit of private profit they have helped bring about a transformation in the world economy in which, increasingly, the pursuit of their own interests conflicts with the interests of local communities," both in America and around the world. As their power increased, corporations replaced the nation-state as the primary force in the international economy. Barnet claimed that "corporations see government very much as a servant of their interests," relegated to "playing the back-up role for the development of a transnational world economy which the corporations basically control."[33] The fact that the multinational corporation supplanted the nation-state is not what bothered IPS intellectuals, however. Unlike critics from the Global South, who tended to focus on issues of state sovereignty, the institute concentrated on how these global firms harmed the most vulnerable.[34]

From the vantage point of IPS intellectuals, modernization, ostensibly meant to improve the lives of the world's impoverished peoples, became, in the hands of corporate executives, a means to secure greater profits and create a global supermarket. Firms cared about only one group, the consumer. Barnet decried global society's "wide acceptance" of the "value system" of multinational corporations, where "happiness is directly tied to an ever greater profusion of consumer goods—that consumption is happiness, that technology has a life of its own and that what can be developed should be developed." This "consumptive ethic," as Barnet called it, allowed the multinational corporation to enhance its power and continue to promote its development model.[35] What did this mean for poor nations on the periphery? Using the seafood company Star-Kist as an example, George showed how the needs of foreign consumers in America led to food shortages in the Third World. For example, Ghana, struggling to feeds its own people, did not benefit from Star-Kist's transfer of a refrigeration plant and processing center to the African nation. Instead of providing nourishment to the people of Ghana, Star-Kist produced 67,000 cartons of tuna cat food. As a result, George argued that "there is every reason [to believe] that American cats take precedence over West African people, since the former can pay and the latter frequently cannot."[36] The consumerist ethic dominated the development strategies favored by corporations and thus made it acceptable for firms to ignore the hunger and poverty that continued unabated in underdeveloped nations.

IPS intellectuals pointed to corporate practices in developing nations as one of the leading causes of food shortages. Refusing to blame population or nature for the lack of available sustenance for certain people, Barnet claimed that "eliminating hunger is a matter of political choice" that required corporations conducting business in the Third World to take specific actions to ensure that the host nation's population received adequate compensation for their work. For instance, Barnet demanded that agribusiness corporations pay fair wages to "farmers turned employees" so that their workers could purchase imported food and maintain a healthy diet. Lamenting the increasing role played by multinational firms in "the production and marketing of food," he called for making access to food a human right. "If food power is not to become a threat or a weapon to be used against people on the edge of starvation, then the notion of secure access to food must be vigorously reasserted as a right that attaches to all men and women at birth," Barnet wrote. Returning to his earlier demand for corporations to pay displaced workers a livable wage, he declared, "A corporation that is not willing to pay on such a scale is committing a clear violation of human rights." He claimed that corporations could end hunger. "All it needs to do is to forgo the profit margins afforded by exploitation just as it had to forgo them in the industrial world with the rise of the labor movement, the social democratic ethic and social legislation," he argued.[37] In short, Barnet demanded a New Deal for the world.

The fact that neither the U.S. Congress nor the United Nations could garner enough support in the 1970s for binding legislation or codes illustrated the difficulties associated with reining in corporate activities. Even before these missteps, Barnet and Müller had their doubts as to whether the U.S. government possessed the "knowledge" to regulate multinational corporations that had become adept at evading national laws. "The U.S. government is a little like the orchestra conductor who discovers midway through the symphony that the principal players have left," the authors remarked dourly. Meanwhile, "space-age alchemists," in the words of Barnet and Müller, found ways to skirt government regulations by "turn[ing] banks into nonbanks, dividends into interest, and profits into losses." All the while, the federal government lacked the money and skills necessary to stop such accounting practices.[38]

Just as the United States faced limits in its ability to carry out its foreign policy vision after Vietnam, it found itself powerless to control multinational corporations. Nonetheless, Barnet still urged presidential candidate Carter to use the full force of the government to bring corporations to heel. In a policy paper for Carter, Barnet claimed that multinational corporations "represent the United States more powerfully than any other American institution in many areas of the world," which made it both "legitimate and necessary" for the U.S. government to set rules and standards for these firms. To preclude businesses from operating abroad in a manner detrimental to U.S. interests, Barnet argued for an immediate end to the U.S. government's "indiscriminate subsidization of foreign investment" for multinational corporations. He also advised Carter to work with other industrialized nations to force multinational corporations to pay 2 percent of their "global profits" to a "U.N. development fund" for use by host countries.[39]

In many ways, IPS's emphasis on the human rights of the individual presaged later efforts in the United Nations to restrain multinational corporations. Beginning in the late 1980s, discussions at various global forums took up the issue of whether international human rights laws applied to the activities of corporations. Years later, a working group created under the auspices of the UN Human Rights Commission, known as the Working Group on the Working Methods and Activities of Transnational Corporations, produced a set of Draft Norms on Responsibilities of TNCs, which went up for a vote before the commission in the spring of 2004. After several years of debate, the commission, by this time known as the Human Rights Council, voted for an alternative set of Guiding Principles. The rejection of the earlier Draft Norms stemmed from the notion that human rights laws applied only to states, not private actors. Though defeated, the Draft Norms produced in the late 1990s and early 2000s offer evidence of a changed perspective within the United Nations concerning corporations, the state, and human rights. Whereas the Draft Code of Conduct on TNCs, which was debated between 1975 and 1992, looked at how to keep corporations from infringing on a country's "national sovereignty," the later Draft Norms focused on the rights of individuals.[40] Since neither the nation-state nor corporations worked in the interest of humankind, IPS sought to bypass both by empowering the people.

Bringing Jefferson's Yeoman Farmer to the Third World

National sovereignty frustrated efforts to make food a human right. The strong nationalism inherent in the NIEO platform did not allow the sort of development advocated by George and others at the institute. Rather than rely on the state to achieve redistributive justice, IPS appealed directly to "the people." Admonishing the United Nations for not considering "the problem of the State," George suggested that eradicating hunger required the empowerment of "popular organizations like cooperatives, women's groups, etc., which the State may often (correctly) see as directly opposed to its major priorities." Lacking faith in the ability of multilateral institutions and national governments to feed the poor, George had earlier advocated sending foreign aid to "local or regional, community-based associations and popular organizations." "We should be concentrating on enhancing local capacity to use aid money constructively," she wrote, "*outside* the dominant (State) system if need be."[41]

IPS intellectuals differed substantially from other radical critics of foreign aid in that they favored redirecting it to the people rather than curtailing it.[42] When asked about U.S. foreign aid priorities by Representative Bradford Morse and other Republican members of Congress, IPS's cofounders encouraged the United States to begin "identifying its interests with the poor, the wretched and the dispossessed: not the bureaucracy, the elites or the rich landowners." The outlay of foreign aid, Barnet and Marcus Raskin suggested, required the "maximum involvement of the poor" in the creation and enactment of the programs. Furthermore, the codirectors questioned whether "we [are] so sure of our political science that we can export it, or should," to nations struggling to develop their economies. In fact, Raskin and Barnet "urg[ed] that we see what can be taken from other societies which we, in our arrogant way[,] think of as underdeveloped" and apply it to America's own struggling cities.[43] These three key components—decentralization, participatory democracy, and ideological pluralism—voiced by IPS's cofounders early in the institute's existence remained a constant of IPS's development program.

Besides changing how foreign aid was distributed, IPS intellectuals realized that eradicating hunger required a fundamental transformation in the way Third World nations interacted with industrialized countries. Since Western-oriented development models proved so disastrous for the Global South, IPS intellectuals encouraged nations to develop indigenous food systems. Barnet, for instance, promoted the idea of "maximum feasible self-reliance of nations and regions" to achieve food security. "The injunction to feed the hungry cannot be accomplished with food aid, the modern missionary basket, or with the ethic of the zoo in which 'basic needs' are periodically dumped into a cage," he declared. When Barnet and his cohorts at IPS advocated food self-sufficiency, they expected Third World nations to maintain a minimal level of trade. George, however, embraced autarky. In a study completed for the research arm of the Ministry of Agriculture in Nicaragua in March 1981, she advised the country to "make absolutely sure that it is self-sufficient in basic food grains." In addition to a diminished U.S. grain stock, George pointed to the possibility of the Reagan administration using food as a "weapon" against its enemies and strategically unimportant nations. To prepare for such an eventuality, George implored Nicaragua to "direct every necessary resource" to achieve agricultural self-sufficiency rather than continuing to focus on export crops. Once Nicaragua grew enough to feed its people, George recommended looking for trading partners in Latin America for its surplus crops.[44]

IPS intellectuals understood that they proposed a risky venture. Even as George touted "authentic food systems"—meaning "environment enhancing" production that protected the land while also providing affordable and nutritious sustenance to everyone "to ensure national food self-sufficiency, as a guarantee against outside political manipulation through food or exports"— she acknowledged the difficulties associated with such an undertaking. While confident in the ability of Third World nations to achieve "authenticity," she could not guarantee it due to "the permeable nature of their food system and their vulnerability to outside pressures."[45] The precarious situation facing Nicaragua in the early 1980s served as a case in point, but even more than other states, corporations threatened self-reliance and hampered the extension of human rights protections to food and other basic needs.

In search of a solution for Third World underdevelopment, IPS joined with other critics in targeting modernization theory's fixation on technology as the key to progress. As Stephen Macekura has shown, both U.S. and Third World officials possessed "a deep faith in the power of large-scale technologies to increase productivity, generate wealth, and overcome persistent material scarcity—in short, to remake societies for the better." By the late 1960s, however, opposing views rose to the surface as intellectuals such as Herbert Marcuse and Theodore Roszak questioned the benefits of new technologies. The most well-known diatribe against technology transfers to the Third World came from Ernst Friedrich Schumacher, who authored the 1973 tract *Small Is Beautiful*. In his book and in correspondence with the world's leaders, Schumacher encouraged officials to seek the input of local peasants. These criticisms gave rise to the "appropriate technology" movement, which sought to replace expensive, labor-reducing machines with equipment more suited to local conditions in terms of scale and workforce requirements.[46]

In her 1977 book, *How the Other Half Dies*, George blamed world hunger on a Western-style model of development dependent on technology that was ill-suited for the Third World. George implored underdeveloped nations to avoid purchasing farming machinery and fertilizer from multinational corporations and developed societies. Instead, she encouraged them to look to "local artisans" for these supplies. While locally produced farm tools and fertilizers lacked the appeal of the latest products marketed by foreign companies, the former promoted higher levels of development. "What may appear to be the most advanced techniques—and those that may thus most appeal to development planners who want 'only the best' for their countries—may actually *increase and perpetuate underdevelopment*; because of their initial and maintenance costs, the relationships of dependency they establish, their effects on local society and their long-term setting of wrong national priorities," she explained.[47]

George held self-serving local elites responsible for the enduring craze for Western technology. George believed that government officials needed "to listen to one's own peasants" to understand how technology affected their livelihood. She had her doubts as to whether local officials would seek out the advice of average citizens. Therefore, she admitted that true self-reliance might require "retrain[ing] higher echelon personnel" who belittled the voices and experiences of the lowly peasants. Even appropriate technology did not guarantee a more egalitarian and democratic society. "No technology of *itself* will alter social relations," she explained, "and many technologies, even when small-scale, have the effect of reinforcing the power of the rich," as evidenced by events in India, where the wealthy employed such appropriate technology as biogas converters and bamboo tube wells, but the peasants did not.[48] Thus, changing the tools of development had to go hand in hand with alterations to the power dynamics of Third World nations.

Unless coupled with the restructuring of Third World nations themselves, self-sufficiency would not end world hunger. As the "basic needs" approach became fashionable in the early 1970s, the World Bank funded a study, *Redistribution with Growth*. The report acknowledged that "more than a decade of rapid growth in underdeveloped countries has been of little or no benefit to perhaps a third of their population." In spite of this fact, the Bank still hailed "growth" as the cure-all for Third World underdevelopment, combined with the minimal use of more "direct measures" such as land reform, greater educational opportunities, and expanded public programs.[49] IPS brushed aside economic indicators, preferring instead to look at how the power dynamics within most underdeveloped countries perpetuated inequality. As George explained in a 1979 report for the United Nations University, she much preferred "redistribution of power over resources" than simple "income redistribution" since the latter required overall "prosperity" as a prerequisite and did little to transform societal and economic relations.[50] Without changes to the political, economic, and social systems within Third World nations, hunger and poverty would endure.

For George, "power," more than any other variable, explained hunger. Wealthy landowners, usually from foreign nations, controlled most of the fertile land. Additionally, "water, fertilizer, bank credit, and other vital inputs not to mention political power" tended to benefit these same individuals. Left without land, peasants had to rely on the powerful landlords for employment, but modern technology and seeds required less manual labor. "There is already enough food to provide for us all, plus enough land, water, and know-how to keep producing food for as long as anyone can see. If chronic

hunger continues, one logical conclusion is that its causes lie beyond science, technology, and management, and in the realm of power relationships,
locally, nationally, and internationally," George stressed.[51] Therefore, if the
United States truly desired an end to global inequality, it needed to overcome
its hostility to socialism and other political and economic systems.

The Internationalization of IPS: The Transnational Institute

Writing in 1978, IPS fellow Mark Hertsgaard reflected on the institute's efforts
to persuade the human rights movement to tackle the issue of economic injustice. He claimed that the IEO already had completed "some of the best work
in this field." Underlining "the importance of working around the issue of economic human rights," he encouraged further research aimed at "explaining
the dynamics by which modern capitalism denies the right to employment,
nutrition, health care, etc. to many people throughout the world." Still, Hertsgaard worried that the information from these reports and studies failed to
reach the masses. "In the past," he wrote, "IPS and TNI have concentrated on
and done well with, 'elite politics,'" by which he meant "political work that con-
centrates on actual policy makers, international officials, and so forth." While
not denigrating this work, which connected IPS to the Manley government in
Jamaica and the Non-Aligned Movement, Hertsgaard wanted equal emphasis
on "mass political education." If IPS failed in its outreach efforts, he warned,
"we cannot hope to mount a truly effective, powerful human rights campaign
in this country, much less question the established capitalist order."[52]

To reach non-elites, Hertsgaard proposed publishing a newsletter to help
enlarge the scope of human rights in the public mind. "The next step in the
human rights campaign must be to legitimize the notion of economic human
rights," which, Hertsgaard claimed, had faltered due to conservatives' ability
"to limit the public debate to traditional concepts of civil liberties by pointing
at the suppression of rights in the U.S.S.R. and the Eastern European states."
To counter such thinking, he proposed using the newsletter to show "how
the capitalist world system degrades our fellow humans all over the world by
denying them such simple rights as adequate food to stay healthy."[53] Not long
after Hertsgaard composed his letter, IPS chose to go in the opposite direction, focusing its energies on two major conferences outside of the United
States in Jamaica and Tanzania.

Even before Hertsgaard raised concerns about IPS's ability to reach domestic constituencies, the institute had made the decision to expand internationally.

Only a decade after Barnet and Raskin established IPS in Washington, D.C., the cofounders and their chief benefactor, Samuel Rubin, realized that America's global ambitions and capitalism's carnivorous appetite required the building of a new think tank with a transnational focus. More immediately, the combined pressures of the FBI investigation of IPS and the tense atmosphere in Washington during the Nixon administration motivated Barnet and Raskin to look for a location outside the United States as a possible safe haven.[54] Planning for the Transnational Institute (TNI) began in late 1972.

The process commenced when Barnet and Raskin asked French American author and activist George to organize a dinner between the codirectors, philanthropist Rubin, and antiwar activists and writers in Paris. More than twenty individuals, including Jean-Paul Sartre, Simone de Beauvoir, Michel Foucault, and Roland Barthes, met at La Closerie des Lilas in Paris to debate the merits of a new institute. The following year, 1973, Eqbal Ahmad, a Pakistani political scientist, spent five weeks in Europe talking with hundreds of people about the proposed institute.[55] In May 1973, the IPS Executive Committee approved a plan to lease a building in Amsterdam from the Janss Foundation for $3,000 a year for five years to serve as TNI's headquarters. Ahmad became the institute's first director when TNI opened its doors on November 9, 1973.[56]

What motivated IPS to create an additional institute? TNI's statement of purpose described the institute as "a community of scholars from different countries who are committed to the search for alternatives to imperialism." As its "central areas of concern" the statement listed "the transnational political economy and those exploited by it, development, militarism, and forms of resistance to imperialism." A 1987 trustees meeting report noted that TNI launched in order "to address the fundamental disparity between the rich and poor peoples and nations of the world." During the same meeting, Weiss provided a brief history of TNI. He mentioned that IPS had intended to create institutes on every continent and chose Europe for TNI because of the "need to spread the discussion of 'social invention' across the Atlantic" to deal with myriad issues. Along similar lines, future IPS director John Cavanagh suggested that TNI saw itself as "a transmission belt" between nations. It connected "social movements in the Third World to power structures in Europe" and sought "to link the poorer majorities of the Third World to the movements of the First World" to expose the terrible conditions of countries in Asia and Latin America.[57]

Other intellectuals at IPS looked to TNI to bring diversity to discussions about international affairs and move beyond an elitist white perspective.

Writing shortly after its founding, Barnet saw TNI as a counterweight to the ideas promulgated by David Rockefeller, Henry Kissinger, the Trilateral Commission, and others who sought "a new status quo consensus based on corporate and military power." More than a decade after its formation, Robert Borosage envisioned TNI playing a similar role. In developing "a new set of assumptions" to replace outdated thinking, TNI would work "in conjunction with and reflecting the values of those who were not present at Dean Acheson's creation—the workers, women, minorities, bearers of new culture in Europe and the U.S., and the majorities of the Third World."[58] In other words, TNI worked toward the democratization of foreign policymaking, opening the process up to non-elites and non-Western voices.

Almost immediately TNI's leadership clashed with IPS's cofounders. Ahmad praised IPS as "a valuable meeting place and servicing institution" that held conferences, provided funding for unorthodox studies, and disseminated information gleaned from events and research, but he saw TNI playing a far more important role. TNI, along with other similar institutions, could act as "schools of fresh analyses and havens for displaced intellectuals and social thinkers." As was the case in the 1930s, Ahmad explained, "large numbers of creative persons are being driven out of their homes and jobs by fascist or proto-fascist takeover of their countries," but the present generation of exiles could not escape to America or Europe for protection. Thus, Ahmad envisioned TNI serving as a refuge for dissidents from Chile, Brazil, South Africa, Uruguay, Greece, and Indonesia.[59]

Ahmad, as it turned out, had reason to worry about TNI coming under the control of IPS. As early as 1974, only a year after TNI's founding, a grant proposal to the Samuel Rubin Foundation concluded that the "excitement" surrounding TNI was due to the institute being "a project of Americans whose ideas are viewed as progressive and whose connections and influence in the U.S. can be a powerful asset."[60] The codirectors basically said as much in a letter to Ahmad in mid-1974. Though in favor of "a truly transnational program in which non-Americans play an increasingly important role," with TNI serving as the first of several "autonomous centers" located abroad, Barnet and Raskin advised Ahmad against severing all ties with IPS. Close affiliation allowed "anti-imperialist Americans to work out relations of trust and support with Third World people," something Barnet and Raskin thought unlikely without an IPS-TNI partnership. The codirectors wanted to strengthen the dialogue between Americans and citizens of "the colonial and neo-colonial world," which required a strong relationship between the two institutes. According to Barnet and Raskin, TNI helped diminish the

otherwise "appalling ignorance and unconcern" for the Third World prev-
alent among Americans by exposing them to the problems caused by U.S.
meddling in the region. TNI's Caroline Heikens thought that Raskin's position on the IPS-TNI relationship resembled that of a "husband and wife
with TNI as the wife."[61] In the end, the institutional independence favored by
Ahmad never came to be.

By 1976, tensions diminished when Orlando Letelier became the director of TNI. Signaling a victory for Barnet and Raskin, Letelier remained in
Washington, while Basker Vashee, who was a member of the socialist Zimba-
bwe African People's Union and had recently earned his Ph.D. in economics
from the University of Sussex, took over as "resident director" in Amsterdam. Following Letelier's murder in 1976, TNI more and more took on the
form envisioned by IPS's codirectors. Landau, who succeeded Letelier as the
director of TNI, sided with Raskin and Barnet on the question of the institute's relationship to TNI. In a letter to TNI's benefactor, Landau proclaimed
that he "would state categorically that I believe that an institute dedicated
to addressing the fundamental disparity between the rich and poor peoples
and nations of the world, and to investigating its causes and developing alternatives for its remedy, should have its center at the center of the problem—
the center of the empire." While not discounting the need to bring in people
from the Third World and create "centers of gravity" in other nations, Landau
argued that such practices "should not be taken to conceal the basic thrust
of TNI investigation: the world-wide empire managed and dominated from
the United States."[62] Considering the role played by the United States in creating the conditions in the Third World and beyond, the push to embed TNI
within IPS made sense. Why not attack imperialism from the belly of the
beast rather than from thousands of miles away?

"Capitalism's New Policeman":
The IMF and the Post-Capitalist Economic Order

Given the fundamental precepts that guided modernization theorists, IPS's
opposition is not surprising. In fact, the institute joined a chorus of critics
who all shared misgivings about developmentalism as carried out in the
1960s and 1970s. Disapproval of modernization theory could be heard from
across the ideological spectrum. On the conservative end, political scientist
Samuel Huntington voiced concern over the propensity of modernization
schemes to cause chaos in underdeveloped countries, which communists

might exploit. Opposite Huntington on the Left, sociologist Andre Gunder Frank and other dependency theorists claimed that far from helping underdeveloped countries, exporting capitalism to the Third World actually slowed economic growth. Forced into an export-led model of development, these nations had to forgo industrialization. Other critics, belonging to neither the Left nor the Right, also lambasted modernization theory. Groups like the Club of Rome complained that in pursuit of growth, Western development schemes threatened the global environment. Still others wanted to celebrate the traditional cultures of underdeveloped nations for their uniqueness.[63] IPS intellectuals based their criticism of modernization theory on Frank's dependency theory.

Strewn throughout the works of IPS intellectuals is the terminology made famous by Frank in his classic *Capitalism and Underdevelopment in Latin America: Historical Studies of Chile and Brazil*. Though influenced by Argentine economist Raúl Prebisch, especially his notion of "center" and "periphery," Frank offered a far more devastating critique of capitalism. In Frank's theory, the "capitalist metropolis" exploited the "colonial satellite" through, among other ways, the expropriation of surplus wealth away from these outlying regions. Nor did Frank believe that capitalism offered the satellite nations "any way out of underdevelopment." Since national capitalism mirrored the structure of the world capitalist system, ending social and economic inequality within nations required a new global economy because "the central world metropolis" had a firm grasp on the domestic economies of the satellites.[64] This argument influenced IPS and other critics of modernization theory because it pointed to the need for structural changes to the world economy. Thus, while IPS intellectuals continued to search for solutions to the Third World's economic quandary, they soon realized that any such changes had to occur in tandem with major alterations to the international economic order.

Frank's broadsides against his former Ph.D. advisor, University of Chicago economist Milton Friedman, only increased the affinity IPS intellectuals felt for Frank and his ideas. While writing his 1976 *Nation* article on the "Chicago Boys," Orlando Letelier relied heavily on Frank's "letter" to Friedman and Arnold Harberger. In fact, Frank's "letter" appeared in the journal *Review of Radical Political Economics* due largely to the "instrumental" efforts of Orlando's wife, Isabel, who personally worked with Frank on revising and editing the article prior to publication. In 1976, Orlando Letelier and Moffitt collaborated on an essay chronicling the history of the international economic order and its relationship to the Third World. They continued writing late into the night on September 20, 1976, the day before Letelier and Moffitt's wife died from injuries sustained from the car bombing in Sheridan Circle. Their essay, published the following year as a TNI pamphlet, offered an argument familiar to readers of Frank's dependency theory. Letelier and Moffitt asserted that "the heart of the problem is unequal international specialization" as a result of the center-periphery dynamic, which led to a "growing gap between export possibilities and import needs."[65] Unwilling to live in a world divided between haves and have-nots, IPS set out to demolish the capitalist system.

Though dependency theory inspired both the G-77 nations and IPS intellectuals, the latter found the former's proposals inadequate. Therefore, even as Frank's paradigm served as a sort of intellectual glue, encouraging Third World nations to unite in defense of their sovereignty, as one scholar has argued, the program developed by these countries fell short of being truly revolutionary. As a later critic charged, the NIEO, despite recognizing the unfairness of the existing economic order that kept Third World countries dependent on the center, did not proffer an alternative system. Instead, the NIEO demanded preferential treatment in certain areas to make capitalism work better for more countries.[66] With the NIEO nearly moribund by the 1980s, George remained skeptical of its goals. She implored her IPS colleagues to "ask ourselves to what degree the implementation of NIEO measures would serve to integrate totally the Third World in a world capitalist market economy structure and lock it into a slightly modified pattern of dependency with no hope of escape."[67] Clearly, from the perspective of IPS intellectuals, the rigidity of global capitalism required more extreme measures. With this in mind, the institute took aim at the IMF.

Events in the Middle East led to IPS's initial interest in the IMF. By mid-1977, attuned to the growing unrest in Egypt after protests broke out in the country as a result of an IMF austerity program, IPS's IEO project turned its attention to this central edifice of the capitalist economy. Economist Howard Wachtel, who with Moffitt headed the IEO project, initiated the campaign with his pamphlet *The New Gnomes*. Echoing Frank's dependency theory, Wachtel described how the Third World's export-led model of growth created a massive debt crisis for the region. Discouraged from developing domestic industry, underdeveloped nations had to import finished goods. When the worldwide recession of the 1970s led to lower prices being paid for raw materials from the Third World, debt skyrocketed as the prices of imports remained the same or increased. Denied loans or aid from the IMF and World Bank, underdeveloped nations had no choice but to turn to private banks. Only after these countries struggled to repay the high-interest loans from private banks did the IMF step in, and then often at a great cost to the people living in the debtor nations. Moreover, as this process unfolded, the industrialized countries tended to "see the problems as internal to the LDCs, echoing the position of 'blaming the victim,'" according to Wachtel.[68]

Published five years before the debt crisis became front-page news with Mexico's loan default in 1982, *The New Gnomes* sparked much debate over the IMF. The Department of Treasury called the report "irresponsible," while the State Department contracted with the Brookings Institution to conduct its own study. A major labor union in Sweden "made it a centerpiece of their efforts at the OECD" as it adapted it for its home audience.[69] Recent events had also helped bring attention to Wachtel's pamphlet. In 1977, IMF managing director Johan Witteveen proposed a Supplementary Financing Facility, the so-called Witteveen Facility, which earmarked $10 billion for the most debt-ridden developing nations. As part of its battle to dismantle the IMF, IPS geared up for its campaign against the Witteveen facility.

Strongly opposed to the $1.7 billion slated to come from the United States, IPS turned to its allies in Congress to stop the authorization of the funds. Since debtor nations receiving IMF loans primarily used the money to repay private banks, Moffitt and Wachtel considered the facility an "indirect subsidy" to these financial institutions. Moreover, in a letter to Democratic congressman Michael Harrington in early 1977, they claimed that by helping contribute to the facility, the U.S. government would signal its approval of the austerity measures forced on underdeveloped countries by multinational banks: "In return for this nasty political task [imposing austerity programs], the International Monetary Fund and the World Bank will be rewarded with more money, authorized by Congress, to make loans."[70]

Though the IMF's economic policies seemed harmless, Moffitt and Wachtel sought to expose how they often had deadly consequences. During a press conference to introduce *The New Gnomes*, Moffitt and Wachtel made clear that the "belt tightening" required by the IMF had deleterious effects on Third World peoples. "Austerity as an economic policy tends to develop a symbiotic relationship with conservative regimes," Wachtel told the assembled crowd, which included a reporter from the *Washington Post*. "Austerity measures can lead to political repression," he concluded. As Wachtel pointed out the following year, the Fund had a clear preference for helping governments led by "conservative political forces that wanted to reestablish a regime favorable to the international financial and corporate communities." Thus, the IMF did not assist Bolivia until a coup brought the dictatorial Hugo Banzer to power. A similar response awaited Peru after its leftist leader was toppled. Consequently, austerity programs imposed by international banks on Third World nations "led to the diminished ability of LDCs to meet the basic needs of their people and, at times, has forced them into political postures that constitute gross violations of human rights."[71] By disclosing how the IMF's austerity programs led to the curtailment of economic and political rights, IPS intellectuals chose to focus on the plight of individuals rather than the implications of IMF intervention on state sovereignty.

In the end, IPS intellectuals struggled to convince Harrington and others in Congress that the United States should reject the plea by Witteveen for additional IMF funds. Part of the failure stemmed from the general popularity of the Fund in the United States. While many Third World nations balked at the stringent conditions the IMF placed on loan recipients, Americans tended to look more favorably at the Fund. Though usually opposed to large-scale intervention in the economy, the United States continued to strongly support the IMF. U.S. officials admired the Fund because it achieved what the U.S. government could not, at least without criticism: a major restructuring of foreign economies.[72]

IPS intellectuals found Representative Tom Harkin, a close ally of the institute, most responsive to their pleas. The congressman contacted IPS prior to the vote on the Witteveen facility seeking information on the Fund. According to Moffitt, a "long meeting" between himself, Wachtel, and Harkin took place, the first of several, including one prior to Harkin's discussion with C. Fred Bergsten and Anthony Solomon from the Treasury Department. These sessions with the congressman resulted in disappointment for IPS since Harkin agreed to back the facility. However, Harkin also attached an amendment to the bill requiring the U.S. representative to the IMF to oppose loans to countries with a record of human rights abuses. The amendment passed in the House, but a similar measure proposed by Democrat James Abourezk in the Senate went down to defeat. In the end, the IMF received additional funding from the United States without any strings attached.[73]

With congressional authorization of the Witteveen facility, IPS's efforts to weaken, and possibly replace, the IMF through legislative channels took a major blow. Nor were the G-77 nations finding much success in their fight for the NIEO. Every administration since Nixon paid lip service to the demands of the Third World, but never seriously committed the United States to enacting any reforms.[74] Faced with an unfavorable domestic climate, IPS looked abroad for allies that shared the institute's desire for a post-capitalist world order. In June 1978, Moffitt brought up the idea of organizing a conference "on the world capitalist financial system and its relationship to the crisis which has beset the Third World." Participants would "explore the general hypothesis that the IMF is capitalism's new policeman in the Third World, which is used by the developed countries to keep the Third World in line." Norman Girvan, director of Jamaica's National Planning Agency, offered encouragement, extending an invitation to hold the event in Jamaica.[75] With the backing of Manley's government, IPS began exploring the possibility of an international conference on the IMF and capitalism in the Third World.

Throughout the planning stages for the meeting, IPS worked closely with officials from the Jamaican government, including Prime Minister Manley. He belonged to a group of Third World leaders involved in a process Adom Getachew has labeled "worldmaking." Rather than looking at colonialism as the domination of one nation by another, Manley understood that empire endured due to the existence of international structures, whether legal, economic, or political, that ensured unequal relations between industrialized and developing nations. After World War II, Manley attended the London School of Economics, where, under the tutelage of Harold Laski, he learned about British Fabian socialism. Years later, Manley coupled his support for the NIEO with appeals for socialism. He recognized that once freed from the grip of external control, newly independent Third World nations needed to decolonize their own governments to ensure economic security for all their citizens, something he thought possible only under socialism. While IPS shared Manley's dissatisfaction with the capitalist international economic system, the prime minister's devotion to *democratic* socialism is just as important in understanding the alliance between the American intellectuals and the Jamaican prime minister. Though Manley embraced certain Marxist concepts associated with dependency theory, he spoke less about socialism than about bringing participatory democracy and radical egalitarianism to Jamaica, all in an effort to end the foreign domination of his country and empower "the people."[76]

The struggles faced by the island nation since Manley's reelection in 1976 epitomized for IPS intellectuals the dangers posed by the IMF to ideological pluralism. As Moffitt organized the conference, he published an article depicting the IMF's terms for a recent $220 million loan to Jamaica as part of a plan to weaken Manley. Moffitt predicted that "the harsh conditions which the Fund attached to the stand-by agreement with Jamaica may well reverse the process of democratic social change set in motion by the government." Manley's "experiment in building democratic socialism in Jamaica" made him a pariah in the eyes of the United States and other developed countries. Moreover, Moffitt continued, the prime minister was "genuinely committed to self-reliant development and meeting basic human needs." According to

Moffitt, developed nations understood that en route to such goals, Jamaica would "dis-engage itself from the international capitalist system."[77] To prevent this from happening, Moffitt argued, the IMF stepped in to redirect the course of Jamaica's development along a capitalist path.

Unlike the U.S. government, IPS did not view Manley as a threat. Landau, who knew the Jamaican prime minister better than anyone else at IPS, praised the leader in 1980 because he "refused to define the world in an East-West context. The issue, he says, is the creation of a just international economic order." Landau considered Manley a modern-day Franklin Roosevelt or Lyndon Johnson and suggested that his economic program represented "a kind of New Deal for the Third World" that both former presidents would have welcomed. As Manley struggled to revive Jamaica's economy, IPS intellectuals came to the defense of the embattled prime minister in the run-up to the October 1980 election, which he ultimately lost to the U.S.-backed Edward Seaga. Moffitt, for example, commended Manley's decision to refuse further IMF funding, claiming that "the three I.M.F. 'stabilization' programs, which Jamaica undertook between July 1977 and December 1979, failed miserably." Inflation and unemployment rose, while real wages and consumption rates dipped. Moreover, the "political sacrifices" made by Manley's government did little to improve the country's standing with private banks. The promised loan rescheduling and lines of new credit never materialized. "Politics seems to have been instrumental in the banks' decisions," Moffitt concluded.[78] Other nations, of course, likely took Manley's troubles as a warning not to confront the IMF, but in the eyes of IPS intellectuals, such defiance made him even more attractive.

Jamaica remained a key partner in IPS's efforts to organize a conference on the IMF and Third World development. In a letter to Wachtel, Manley described the proposed meeting as "extremely timely." Besides allowing Jamaica to "exchange experiences with other developing countries facing similar problems to ours," the gathering promised to strengthen North-South solidarity and amplify calls for a new international economic order. Before the main conference in Arusha, Tanzania, in 1980, a preliminary meeting occurred in October 1979 in Kingston, Jamaica, where participants presented country reports to better understand the effect of the IMF on underdeveloped nations. Moffitt used the occasion to ridicule the Fund's policies vis-à-vis Jamaica. He denied that Manley's socialist policies caused the most recent economic downturn. Instead, by forcing Jamaica to follow an outdated and rigid export-led development strategy, the IMF contributed to the poor economic conditions in the late 1970s. Lacking the industrial capacity necessary for such an approach to be successful, Jamaica had no chance of economic growth. "If exports cannot grow rapidly, then export-led growth is impossible," Moffitt stated matter-of-factly. More generally, Moffitt balked at the notion that Jamaica could experience growth if it just "adopt[ed] the correct policies," which ignored the "structural" reasons for underdevelopment. "These are not 'problems' that can be 'solved' by monetary adjustments. They are part and parcel of a peripheral capitalist economy," Moffitt concluded.[79] Thus, all signs seemed to point to the need for ideological pluralism, not prefabricated economic models developed for industrialized Western nations.

IPS intellectuals and other participants at the Terra Nova Hotel in Kingston understood all too well that the IMF's origins precluded the international body from accepting a non-capitalist development model. The working group that took part in the proceedings included Moffitt as the IPS representative; officials from the Jamaican government; academics from Cuba, Peru, Ghana, and Portugal; and Tanzania's ambassador to the United Kingdom. Those assembled at Kingston viewed the IMF as a creation of the industrialized countries and thus incapable of understanding Third World economics. "The Fund's basic orientation does not equip it to deal with 'development' deficits and 'cyclical deficits,' which are structural features of the balance of payments of Third World countries, but rather with temporary deficits of industrialized capitalist countries which may be amenable to treatment by class exchange rate and monetary and fiscal policy measures," the Terra Nova Statement concluded. Despite the advantages accorded to industrialized nations, they could, as the United States did when it ended convertibility of the dollar to gold, sidestep the IMF. Meanwhile, the Third World remained firmly within its grip. While the statement composed at the Kingston meeting offered preliminary suggestions about how "to replace the now obsolete Bretton Woods arrangements," the real work remained on hold until the Arusha meeting the following year.[80]

In between the initial meeting in Kingston in October 1979 and the conference in Arusha the following summer, Moffitt and other IPS intellectuals committed to the idea of replacing the Bretton Woods institutions with truly global economic bodies that welcomed ideological pluralism. Moffitt and Borosage, for instance, informed their colleagues at IPS that the conference sought the creation of "a new Bretton Woods, a formal constitution of a new international monetary system for development, reflecting the changed economic conditions and power relations in the world, and grounded on the premise of equity, participation and even efficiency." In sum, they promised "a new international monetary system with a new World Central Bank and a new international currency."[81] IPS wanted to make the economy truly global, and in the process discard artificial divisions such as North and South, which underscored the unequal power dynamics present in the existing economic order. IPS intellectuals hoped that the financial downturn of the 1970s impressed upon industrialized countries the need for a complete over-haul of the international economy. As Moffitt explained to Henry Ruiz, the minister of planning in Nicaragua, the conference sought "to associate Third World dissatisfaction with, and criticism of, the present monetary (non) sys-tem with industrial country concerns about inflation and growing monetary disorder." Such discussions, Moffitt predicted, would make possible a form of "global development" to replace "the North-South frontier" of prior eco-nomic models.[82]

Though the Global North and South came together to construct a new international economic order, IPS intellectuals and others involved with the Arusha Initiative made it clear that the they aimed to cast aside prevailing power norms. Thus, in choosing a title for the conference, the organizers selected "South-North Conference on the International Monetary System and the New International Order," inverting North and South as a symbolic representation of the new power dynamic sought by the participants. Besides IPS, other organizations involved included the Dag Hammarskjöld Founda-tion, the International Foundation for Development Alternatives, the Latin American Institute for Transnational Studies, and the Third World Forum. As expected, due to decolonization and other changes to the global environ-ment, IPS intellectuals and the others called for a new international order that recognized the diversity of nations. The world needed "a new mone-tary system that would reflect the employment and development needs of the people living in different material conditions, social systems and cultural environments." The Bretton Woods system, a product of the United States and other industrialized nations, only "provid[ed] a stable basis for economic relations within the capitalist world."[83]

In no uncertain terms, the Arusha Initiative laid out its criticisms of the IMF: "Alternative development patterns that reduce or control the space for private market logic are labelled as inefficient in economic terms and con-sidered inadequate in political terms." The IMF's "orientation" was "funda-mentally incompatible with an equitable conception of structural change, self-reliance and endogenous development." When Third World nations pur-suing a non-capitalist route to development turned to the IMF for assistance, the Fund forced them to undertake austerity programs meant to preserve the status quo. Jamaica and Tanzania, of course, offered direct evidence of such discriminatory lending policies. Accordingly, the Arusha Initiative made clear its support for Manley and Tanzanian prime minister Julius Nyerere in their respective battles against the IMF. "We call upon progressive forces, groups and institutions, in both industrialized and Third World countries, to express in practical terms their support for the right to determine autonomously national development objectives."[84]

In the case of Manley, the participants at Arusha went a step further, agreeing to a separate resolution to express their solidarity with Jamaica. The declaration accused the IMF of "clear political motivation and calculation" when it refused loans to Jamaica and expressed "concern" over what the action meant for Third World nations pursuing alternative development models. Like Jamaica, many of these countries were "either on the verge of a breakdown in relation with the IMF or forced to change progressive policies to fit the immutable, unattainable and doubtful technical criteria of the IMF and its entrenched power structure, and their politically motivated multiple standards of treatment." In defending Jamaica's economic experiment, the participants hoped to protect the entire Global South from the heavy hand of the IMF.[85]

Though ignored by the U.S. press, the Arusha Initiative found a more receptive audience abroad. Paul Fabra of the French newspaper *Le Monde* observed that the report "perfectly achieved its goal, which was to orchestrate a vast movement, political, diplomatic, and intellectual, which aims at nothing less than to modify profoundly the functioning of the international financial institutions where the Western influence, and more particularly the American, is omnipresent." UNCTAD and a UN special session on development, both of which met in late 1980, also received copies of the Arusha Initiative. On the heels of the South-North Conference, Tanzania obtained a $200 million IMF loan. In exchange for the funds, Nyerere promised to decrease government expenditures. Still, according to the *New York Times*, Tanzania received "far more lenient terms" than the IMF traditionally granted to nations. For instance, the two sides agreed to delay a decision on the devaluation of Tanzania's currency, which had stalled negotiations in the past. Though Moffitt rejected the notion that the country's prominent role in the South-North Conference led to the more generous IMF package, others, including the *New York Times*, thought otherwise.[86]

The release of the Arusha Initiative in 1980 underscored the diversity of views and ideologies of Third World nations. For instance, statements made by the G-24, composed of the better-off countries in the G-77, focused primarily on enlarging the scale and scope of the IMF's special drawing rights to deal with unequal balance of payments and to further development. The G-24 nations also demanded greater participation in the World Bank and IMF. As one commentator noted in the early 1980s, the G-24 offered proposals meant to "function within the framework of the Bretton Woods institutions, and do not raise the basic questions about the system raised by the Arusha Initiative." By the time of the Non-Aligned Movement (NAM) Summit Conference held in New Delhi in 1983, the G-24 became ascendant. According to Vijay Prashad, these nations "welcomed IMF-driven globalization," and in the process, NAM became an advocate for "globalization with a human face," which meant that the G-7 nations would remain in control of the world economy, while offering "some bargains" to a select few countries.[87]

*   *   *

By standing in solidarity with Jamaica and Tanzania, among other smaller Third World nations, IPS evinced enthusiasm for a revolutionary reconfiguration of the global economy. Skeptical of the ability of top-down, elite-led, and technologically driven modernization schemes to improve the economic circumstances of the Global South, IPS turned to the ideal of self-reliance and localism as a means to export participatory democracy to the Third World. As part of their critique of modernization theory, IPS intellectuals articulated an expansive vision of human rights that included the right to food, which put them in direct conflict with many Third World nations that equated the NIEO with greater state sovereignty and better terms within the liberal capitalist international order. Thus, IPS targeted multinational corporations not because they threatened territorial sovereignty but because they were responsible for world hunger.

Besides Third World nationalists, IPS had to contend with the structures of capitalism. As IPS developed a blueprint for a truly global and diverse post-capitalist world order, it took aim at the IMF. Here too, IPS used a novel approach. Rather than denounce the IMF for impinging on state sovereignty, the institute sought to expose how austerity measures led directly to human rights abuses. In doing so, IPS remained committed to Orlando Letelier's argument regarding the relationship between economic policies and torture. Unable to sway domestic leaders, IPS made common cause with Third World socialists. Just as IPS encouraged populism within the United Nations, it had a similar goal in mind with regard to the IMF. The international economy had undergone tremendous changes since the birth of the IMF in 1945. As globalization swept across the planet, genuine interdependence required

new, updated international organizations. Rather than renovate these institutions in such a way that underdeveloped nations might achieve better economic growth within the capitalist system, IPS intellectuals wanted to tear
them down and construct new edifices to support ideological pluralism. Yet,
in the end, as evidenced by what happened in Jamaica and Tanzania, this
post-capitalist vision underestimated the power of capitalism and could not
withstand the onslaught of neoliberalism.[88]

It became increasingly clear to IPS intellectuals that building a new global
economy required the destruction of not only the liberal international economic order but all "four pillars that have undergirded postwar United States
foreign policy," in the words of Barnet. The other pillars were nuclear deterrence, the alliance system, and anti-Communist interventionism.[89] Only after
the collapse of every one of these pillars could a new world order rise up from
the ashes of the old. To this end, IPS sought to educate Americans about how
to achieve "real security" while also downplaying the Soviet threat and aiding anti-nuclear activists in their campaign to demilitarize the United States.
According to IPS doctrine, an educated citizenry would bring the Cold Warriors to their knees, paving the way for a post–Cold War order at home and
abroad.

CHAPTER 7

A Citizen's Army for a Post–Cold War Order

While testifying before a Senate investigating committee in *The Spike*, a surprising 1980 fiction best seller written by Arnaud de Borchgrave and Robert Moss, Viktor Borisov, a Soviet KGB defector, highlights the activities of the Institute for Progressive Reform. "Now, if you asked me to specify the single most important operation—in terms of both deception and penetration—in which I was personally involved during the time I was stationed in the United States, I would have to nominate the work of the Institute for Progressive Reform, here in Washington. Through this institute, Directorate A [the KGB] has been able to influence media and congressional reflexes to Soviet policy moves. It has also served as our most important recruitment base for agents of influence in Washington under the last three administrations." On the surface, the Institute for Progressive Reform (IPR) might seem like a meaningless backdrop in a fictional spy thriller, but commentators immediately picked up on its significance. Though Borchgrave and Moss denied it, reviewers noticed similarities between the fictional think tank and the Institute for Policy Studies. In *The Spike*, IPR had infiltrated the White House, occupied by President Billy Connor, the stand-in for Jimmy Carter, and IPR-affiliated staffers had the ears of powerful members of Congress.[1]

By advocating so forcefully for a post–Cold War foreign policy, IPS became a favorite target of conservatives. Though often outlandish, critiques of IPS's pro-Soviet views had some merit. At the same time, IPS generally saw the Soviet Union—and America's fascination with it—as a hindrance to the institute's desire for a post–Cold War world. Thus, rather than focus on IPS's purported pro-Soviet views, it is important to understand the institute's true ideological lodestar was not Karl Marx but Thomas Jefferson. Since its auspicious beginning in 1963, IPS saw itself as democracy's think tank. In the end, it served "the people" more than the Soviet Union.

IPS sought a more pragmatic and less ideological U.S. foreign policy pre-mised on what it called a "new realism." The institute warned that groups like the Committee on the Present Danger (CPD) hampered efforts to end the Cold War with their alarmist rhetoric. Whereas defense intellectuals thrived under the military-industrial complex, providing the rationale for the cor-nucopia of weapons it produced, the peace intellectuals at the institute bemoaned its existence and effect on democracy. Therefore, IPS turned to "the people" to build a citizen's army to dismantle the military-industrial complex and deprive defense intellectuals of their lifeblood. To this end, IPS developed a Real Security Education Project. Though short-lived, the program helped educate the public to recognize the folly of high defense spending. IPS also served the anti-nuclear movement, most notably as the brain trust for the GWEN Project, which sought to prevent the spread of communication towers used during the outbreak of a nuclear conflict. IPS's partnership with the GWEN Project allowed it to bring attention to a largely unknown element of Raskin's vast national security state. The Real Security Education Project and the GWEN Project represented the true embodiment of IPS's ideals. Whereas defense intellectuals thrived in the halls of power, peace intellectuals at IPS did some of their best work at the grassroots. For all the difficulties that it faced, particularly during the conservative epoch of the Reagan era, IPS thrived when it carried out its role as I. F. Stone's "insti-tute for the rest of us."

IPS and Cold War Revisionism

In 1959, William Appleman Williams shook the foundations of the historical profession with the publication of *The Tragedy of American Diplomacy*. In it, he spoke of "the firm conviction, even dogmatic belief, that America's *domestic* well-being depends upon such sustained, ever-increasing overseas economic expansion." Guided by this mentality, William McKinley's secre-tary of state John Hay issued the Open Door Notes of 1899 and 1900, which demanded U.S. access to Asian markets, setting the United States on the path to expansionism. Williams's economic interpretation of U.S. foreign policy found a growing audience among "revisionist" historians in the 1960s, many of whom sympathized with the New Left and blamed the United States for the Cold War. This perspective contrasted sharply with the "orthodox" his-torians of the 1940s and 1950s who published studies highly critical of the

Soviet Union's role in provoking the Cold War.[2] Influenced by Williams, IPS subscribed to the "revisionist" school of thought. Gar Alperovitz, who graduated with a degree in history from the University of Wisconsin in 1959 and served as a founding fellow of IPS, offered one of the best-known "revisionist" histories in his 1965 book, *Atomic Diplomacy: Hiroshima and Potsdam*. Alperovitz argued that America's use of the atomic bomb had no military basis. Rather, the United States used the device to strengthen its economic and political position in Eastern Europe.[3] Alperovitz's fellow peace intellectuals at IPS presented similar arguments against the United States and the Cold War.

From IPS's vantage point, the United States was as culpable as the Soviet Union for the Cold War. Richard Barnet made this point abundantly clear in a 1971 *Foreign Policy* article in which he argued:

> Indeed, the naive visitor might well have concluded that the problem of military aggression in the postwar period had its source in the United States. Soviet armies stopped at the point of their farthest advance in World War II and withdrew from adjacent areas such as Czechoslovakia only to return when political domination threatened to fail. The United States retained the major bases it had acquired in World War II and acquired more. Within a few years the Soviet Union was surrounded by air and later missile bases from which devastating nuclear attacks could be launched—all at a time when the Soviet Union lacked a similar capacity to attack the United States. It has been the United States and not the Soviet Union that has stationed its military forces on every continent and spread nuclear weapons in the tens of thousands on the continents of Asia and Europe and on the high seas. It is the United States and not the Soviet Union that has intervened with its military and paramilitary forces almost every year since 1945 on the territory of other countries either to prevent local insurgent forces from taking power or displacing them from power.[4]

Only after Stalin's death did the Soviet Union begin supporting liberation movements in the Third World. Barnet blamed this reversal on "the strategy chosen by the U.S. to deal with the limited Soviet challenge to American supremacy," which forced a Soviet response.[5]

Such views made IPS circumspect in the eyes of conservatives. A longstanding IPS critic, Rael Jean Isaac, published "The Institute for Policy Studies:

Empire on the Left" in 1980, from which multiple excerpts appeared in other conservative publications. Her diatribe against the think tank began with a mix of truth and hyperbole. Isaac asserted that "the Institute represents an unprecedented success story: the achievement of the New Left, after its supposed demise, in shaping United States policy." Next, Isaac set out to highlight IPS's anti-American position in an effort to strengthen her claim that the institute wanted to bring the United States to its knees. After scouring through IPS's prolific paper trail, Isaac concluded, "What IPS Fellows never concede is that the Soviet Union poses any threat to the United States. Soviet behavior is invariably defined as 'defensive' in nature." Not to be outdone, another detractor of IPS accused the institute of possessing a "worldview" that tended "to be shaped by the embrace of versions of Marxism-Leninism" and "animated by the belief that the United States is the most evil society in history and certainly in the contemporary world."[6] These critiques of IPS found traction among conservative writers and politicians, particularly in the 1980s.

While not apologists for the Soviet Union, IPS intellectuals refused to let anti-communism blind them to the aggressive actions committed by the United States during the Cold War. Barnet explained that he came to a "revisionist" view of history in the late 1950s while conducting research for *Who Wants Disarmament?* At the start of the project, Barnet's acquaintances predicted that the study "would be a very good way of documenting how the Russians used the disarmament issue for political maneuvering," but the future IPS cofounder reached a different conclusion. He discovered that both U.S. and Soviet officials had a hand in derailing the disarmament negotiations. Barnet's time in the John F. Kennedy administration only hardened his conviction that the United States had no interest in reaching an agreement with the Soviet Union to end the Cold War. He noticed a tendency among officials to use "tremendous abstractions" and show "very little concrete thinking about international interests or what the Russians were really up to." Though classifying his work as "revisionist," Barnet did not particularly agree with the label. When a reporter described IPS as "a center of revisionists," Barnet noted, "In a way, it's a misnomer to call us revisionists because there hasn't been any history of the Cold War to revise. What is called 'history' have been books that were written without consulting the primary documents in the field. The authors wrote them knowing their ideas would be popular and wouldn't be challenged for lack of proof."[7] Instead of erudite thinking on American-Soviet relations, in other words, U.S. officials, as well as the early chroniclers of the conflict, allowed ideology to color their view of the Soviet Union.

What Soviet Threat? IPS's Efforts to End
the Ideological Cold War

IPS blamed U.S. officials for allowing ideology to drive foreign policy. IPS intellectual Alan Wolfe documented several instances in which "ideology" spurred petulant "action" on the part of the United States. The first "ideological offensive" occurred immediately after World War II, culminating in NSC-68, which gave currency to the idea that the Soviet Union sought global domination. During this time, U.S. officials "emphasized the most negative features of Soviet activities in an ambiguous context," providing cover for the United States to expand militarily across Europe. To the dismay of Barnet, even the Vietnam War failed to temper the anti-Soviet passions of the Cold Warriors. Reviewing Charles Bohlen's late 1960s account of the Cold War, Barnet expressed astonishment over how the former ambassador to the Soviet Union repeatedly referred to the contest between the superpowers as an "ideological war," signaling that the Soviets could not be reasoned with. "A Soviet Government which can be dealt with only through ever increasing military power rather than diplomacy is the perfect adversary for an American Government whose primary activity is war preparation," Barnet lamented.[8]

IPS's campaign to end the ideological Cold War became more difficult in 1976. Eugene Rostow, who served as Lyndon Johnson's undersecretary for political affairs, reorganized the CPD after it had lain fallow for years—former undersecretary of the army Tracey Vorhees had created the first CPD in 1950 to promote NSC-68. The most recent incarnation emerged shortly after conservative foreign policy intellectuals set up Team B to contest CIA estimates of the Soviet threat.[9] Indicative of his later hostility toward the CPD, Raskin strongly opposed the creation of Team B. He took issue with the group's fixation on "estimates" of Soviet nuclear strength. Even more disconcerting for Raskin was that Team B members ignored Soviet "intentions," which "can only be learned through a far deeper analysis than the type that is usually given in 'estimates.'" In a letter to Theodore Sorensen, whom Carter had just nominated to head the CIA, Raskin conveyed his doubts about the validity of the Team B report. He encouraged Sorensen to press Carter to bring together a third group, consisting of private citizens, to investigate Soviet capabilities. Among others, Raskin recommended former diplomat George Kennan, historian William Appleman Williams, and arms control expert Paul Warnke to lead the study.[10] Raskin's dream of a "Team C," if you will, never materialized, leaving U.S. officials with alarmist reports of the Soviet Union's capabilities.

IPS took it upon itself to blunt the effects of the CPD's sinister warnings. Writing in the *Libertarian Review*, Barnet criticized Team B leader Richard Pipes and the CPD for zeroing in on "bloodcurdling Soviet military maxims" to buttress its call for higher defense spending. Barnet clarified that the Soviet Union used ostentatious language to make its nuclear deterrent seem more sincere to discourage an attack by the United States. He explained that "the deterrence system is sustained by huge bureaucracies which are paid a substantial share of the national treasure to think about winning nuclear war, planning for it, making it credible by pretending that it is a real political option." In other words, the CPD needed to take the Soviet threats of nuclear annihilation in context and stop using them as a pretext for increased defense spending. IPS, of course, fundamentally disagreed with the CPD's campaign to initiate a huge military buildup. Beyond the ability of nuclear weapons to "inspire feelings and convey intentions," Barnet questioned the logic of adding to the arms race. "The national insecurity that can be so easily fanned by a 'Committee on the Present Danger' cannot be cured by 9,000 more bombs," Barnet wrote. Mocking the CPD for trying to fulfill the role of "the Paul Reveres of their generation," Barnet cautioned against inciting "war hysteria" in the present moment. The Soviet Union's growing nuclear arsenal, military technological advances, and the rising expectations of hundreds of smaller nations in a world with finite resources made the antagonistic remarks by CPD members extremely dangerous, according to Barnet.[11] The second incarnation of the CPD, in other words, acted as if it were 1947 instead of 1977.

On May 14 and 15, 1979, IPS held a conference titled "The Myths and Realities of the 'Soviet Threat.'" Cosponsors included the Coalition for a New Foreign and Military Policy, Americans for Democratic Action, Democratic congressman Ted Weiss, and Senator George McGovern. That same year, Wolfe published *The Rise and Fall of the "Soviet Threat": Domestic Sources of the Cold War Consensus*, where he accused domestic pressure groups like the CPD of exacerbating tensions between the superpowers at pivotal junctures in the Cold War. These "constellations of political forces" stoked fears about Soviet expansionism that often did not correlate with the facts on the ground.[12] Faced with the threat of a "new Cold War" in the 1980s, IPS refused to let the CPD and other groups in its orbit lead the nation down the path to nuclear Armageddon.

IPS intellectuals sought to end the ideological Cold War by injecting a dose of realism into foreign policy discussions. Raskin championed a "new realism" that required "changing our relationship with the Soviet Union to one in keeping with our national interest rather than ideological pretension."[13] Allowing the latter to take precedence over the former led to a massive increase in America's nuclear arsenal and its infrastructure, which posed a far greater danger than the Soviet Union. Barnet, meanwhile, turned to his faith for a solution. Christian Realism, which is normally associated with Cold War liberals like Reinhold Niebuhr, assumes all persons are selfish and untrustworthy and blames these qualities for the rise of totalitarianism and aggressive tendencies. Yet there also existed a more progressive strain. Groups critical of U.S. foreign policy, like the World Council of Churches, also belonged to the Christian Realist tradition.[14] Barnet, a member of the Church of the Saviour in Washington, D.C., came out strongly against Niebuhr's brand of Christian Realism. "Peacemaking is a spiritual struggle," he wrote in 1981 for *Sojourners*, one of the leading periodicals of the evangelical Left. In America, he claimed, there existed a "faith system" that involved "believ[ing] that our security is to be derived from intimidating others" using nuclear threats. Another "faith system," which Barnet subscribed to, was guided by "a faith in God, a faith that is inseparable from a faith in human beings, because the two faiths are one. The possibilities of peace . . . stem from a fundamental belief that human beings can love one another."[15]

Barnet's involvement with the Church of the Saviour and *Sojourners*, where he also served as contributing editor, points to the IPS cofounder's true ideological predisposition. Jim Wallis, the founder of *Sojourners* and a well-known figure in the evangelical Left, worked closely with Barnet and his colleagues at the institute. Wallis came to Barnet's defense when his detractors labeled him a communist. As he explained in a 1981 editorial, "Barnet is simply part of a growing body of Christians in this country who refuse to accept the propaganda of either the Soviet Union or the United States, who sees both superpowers as threats to peace, and who believes the greatest danger in the world today to be neither from communism nor capitalism but from the nuclear arsenals that both sides now possess. It is not any ideological loyalty that puts us at odds with the policies of both superpowers, but a faith rooted in the Bible which judges the present arms race as nothing but idolatry."[16] Not all IPS intellectuals shared Barnet's religious perspective, but they agreed with the IPS cofounder that the Cold War between the United States and the Soviet Union threatened humankind. Therefore, IPS downplayed the Soviet threat and contested the alarmist rhetoric of groups like the CPD to diminish nuclear fears.

With the CPD and Ronald Reagan on the ascent, anti-communist rhetoric and ideological warfare reached a fever pitch reminiscent of the early days of the Cold War. It is not surprising, therefore, that the Soviet invasion

of Afghanistan in late 1979 reignited debates over the Soviet Union's expansionist tendencies. During a foreign policy meeting held at IPS in early 1980,
Barnet disagreed with the widespread view, which he called the "Master Plan
model," that the Soviet Union had invaded Afghanistan as part of a scheme to
control uncontested regions of the world. Using a "defensive model," Barnet
argued that the Soviet Union did not seek world domination but rather the
protection of its borders. As the summary of the meeting explained, "While
not a justification for Soviet behavior, this model, Barnet suggested, may contribute to understanding what motivated the Soviets." When Earl Ravenal
inquired about why the group spent so much time on the Soviets' "motiva-
tions," Barnet claimed that "if the conception of the USSR as a power hungry
aggressor, a Hitlerian type, was allowed to go unchallenged the hawks will be
able to successfully argue that the Russians are a nation that can't be negotiated with, that they only understand the meaning of armed force."[17]

Some at IPS even suggested that increasing Soviet involvement in the
Third World had its benefits. IPS intellectual Fred Halliday told Borosage
in late 1981 that "the USSR has a duty—to help liberation movements fight
for victory," as it did in Spain during the civil war in the late 1930s and later
in Cuba, Vietnam, and Angola. Halliday disagreed with the "tendency to
portray all Soviet military action abroad as negative, imperialistic, etc." He
blamed such thinking on conservatives and "naïve liberal[s]," who somehow
thought that the poor peoples of the Third World could achieve their aims
without assistance from either of the superpowers. Halliday went so far as
to criticize the Soviet Union's "cowardly behavior in southern Africa," which
opened the door to interference by South Africa. He did not hide his reasons for supporting the Soviet Union in Afghanistan. "I abominate Islamic
fundamentalism and tribesmen, in all forms I know of. Better imperialism
than Islam, however popular the latter is. I think too many people are wooly
or indulgent about [Supreme Leader of Iran Ruhollah] Khomeini and ditto
about the Afghanistan resistance and as secular, rational, progressive people
we have to take a clear stand."[18] The United States, of course, recognized the
dangers of radical Islam but allowed immediate concerns, mainly defeating
the Soviet Union in Afghanistan, to transcend long-term interests. IPS excoriated such shortsighted policymaking devoid of pragmatic analysis.

While critical of the U.S. response to the situation in Afghanistan, IPS
defended Soviet actions. According to Halliday, the Soviets "tried their best
to avoid going into Afghanistan," doing so only after communist leader Hafi-
zullah Amin angered Afghan peasants and assured a future rebellion. In fact,
Halliday argued that the Soviets "consistently resisted" pleas by both Amin

and President Nur Muhammad Taraki to enter Afghanistan in early 1979. He portrayed the Soviet invasion as an action of last resort to protect a nation on its border from coming under the control of a hostile enemy. Citing the aid provided by Pakistan, China, and other Arab nations to Afghan rebels, Halliday claimed that without such outside interference "it is much less likely that the Russians would have gone into Afghanistan directly." With the Soviets still bogged down in Afghanistan in 1988, Barnet and Eqbal Ahmad wrote in the *New Yorker* that "it seems clear that the Soviet goals in Afghanistan have always been limited." They based their argument on the fact that the Soviets never "claimed sovereignty over Afghanistan" and sent only a limited number of soldiers into the country. The Soviets, moreover, "agreed in principle" early on to remove their troops, "a promise they had never made with respect to Eastern Europe."[19] In short, Afghanistan was not Poland. For the CPD, however, the "new Cold War" looked eerily like the Cold War of the 1940s, which unnerved the pragmatic minds at IPS who recognized the important differences between the two eras.

According to IPS doctrine, frequent interventions by the United States did far more to upset the global order than did Soviet activities abroad. It is another thing entirely, however, to label IPS pro-Soviet. Laying the blame for the U.S.-Soviet rivalry at the door of the United States allowed IPS intellectuals to retain the belief that the institute could end the Cold War by speaking truth to power. To achieve its goal, however, IPS would need a people's army. With this in mind, the institute developed two projects in the 1980s aimed at educating and empowering the people to wage a struggle against the military-industrial complex and the hidden national security state.

Real Security for and by the People

Opposed to the ideological dimension of the Cold War, IPS challenged the Cassandras in the CPD and tried to downplay the Soviet threat so that the United States could finally confront the litany of domestic problems plaguing the nation. In tackling the issue of economic conversion, IPS entered a crowded field. Seymour Melman, a leading expert on the topic, alone published numerous books in the 1960s and 1970s. In *Our Depleted Society* (1965), he warned of a "depletion process" caused by excessive spending on war production, which prevented the updating of machines used in domestic manufacturing. Then, in *Pentagon Capitalism* (1970), he charged the Department of Defense with controlling the American economy and in the process redirecting resources toward the military. Finally, with *The Permanent War Economy* (1974), Melman detailed the growth of an entirely new economy, a form of state capitalism, but with the Department of Defense in the driver's seat.[20] Many of the same arguments came out of IPS, but in searching for a way out, the institute turned to "the people." Operating on the principle that "human beings can love one another," Barnet and IPS looked outside the beltway to end the nation's love affair with military spending.

IPS intellectuals argued that for too long the real needs of the American people escaped the attention of officials in Washington. Powerful advocacy groups like the CPD promoted the idea that military blunders and insufficient defense spending led to America's decline in the 1970s. Barnet offered an alternative perspective. He contended that U.S. officials misunderstood the meaning of power at the twilight of the American century. According to Barnet, instead of worrying about the "Finlandization" of America and calling for massive arms increases, as the CPD did, the United States needed to learn from France's fall to Hitler in 1940. "The greatest army in Europe surrendered because the society it was defending had rotted," he claimed. To guard against internal decay, the United States needed to redirect its limited resources to social programs and preserve the "values for which the nation was founded—justice, opportunity, and the liberation of the human spirit."[21]

Barnet did not believe that America's waning global influence had anything to do with the nation's military strength. He set out to convince Americans that a skyrocketing defense budget actually had the opposite effect. By the 1980s, Barnet asserted, "the traditional relationship between the capacity to make war and the ability to exercise political power" evaporated. Military supremacy did not guarantee success in other areas. According to Barnet, the thriving economies of West Germany and Japan hinted at an "uncoupling of economic power and military power" and sounded the death knell for military Keynesianism, the notion that massive defense spending stimulated the economy. In fact, Barnet argued that "excessive military spending now produces some of the same consequences as military defeat; that is, it gives foreign governments greater control over the life of the country."[22] Consequently, as the United States continued pouring money into its military, it fell further behind Germany and Japan, both of which enhanced their domestic industrial capabilities to adapt to the new international economy.

Just as federal assistance went to private corporations to research and develop advanced weaponry, IPS intellectuals argued, transitioning to a post–Cold War economy required government funding for infrastructure and other non-military projects. Barnet realized that without the government to soften the economic consequences of disarmament, conversion would not occur. "Only when making high-speed transport systems is as profitable as making missiles will the weapons-makers voluntarily move out of the death business," Barnet claimed. He further added that the federal government needed to "subsidize the technology of peace as it has subsidized the technology of war" by requiring high wages for non-military production and offering funds for general research. Barnet recommended a new National Conversion Commission to aid in the transition from a war to peace economy. The commission would provide funding for scientists and engineers as they shifted from making technology for wars to consumer goods and infrastructure. As for the towns devastated by the loss of military production facilities, Barnet proposed "special assistance" since "they are 'disaster areas' and should be eligible for the sort of extraordinary relief that is given to communities stricken by flood or tornado."[23]

Though his program for economic conversion required a high degree of "planning," Barnet remained committed to democratic decision making. He recognized that "to replace the Pentagon bureaucracy with a pollution-control bureaucracy of similar size and character would increase the chances of survival but not the prospects for freedom." In search of the latter, Barnet proposed giving local bodies, such as town halls and city councils, the power to reject, approve, or amend decisions reached by the National Conversion Commission.[24] Such pleas, however, as had those of other critics of the military-industrial complex, went unnoticed by the government.

Getting nowhere in Washington, IPS turned to the grassroots. In 1986, the institute initiated its Real Security Education Project. As project director Barbara Wien explained, "We were trying to shift [toward] the constituents outside the beltway. We were trying to shift the public's understanding." The change in strategy represented a realization that Washington was "this huge vortex that you could get sucked into" while competing against powerful and influential military contractors and lobbyists. The American people, untainted by Washington politics, offered IPS a more promising alternative. "The most underutilized resource in our country is the untapped wisdom of the people," a funding proposal stated. "By exposure to new information and perspectives over a sustained period of time," the proposal continued, "citizens begin to create a new 'public judgment' on significant social questions" and demand a new approach to foreign policy.[25] Armed with this knowledge, the people could confront the networks that maintained the military-industrial complex.

Though in existence for less than three years, the Real Security Education Project spread IPS's concept of real security to a diverse group of activists.

The first real security education conference took place over several days in early March 1987 at Placid Harbor, an educational facility for the International Association of Machinists and Aerospace Workers (IAM). As Wien later remembered, the president of IAM, William Winpisinger, "put his full support behind the project," which is not surprising given that his union had been at the forefront of the movement for economic conversion, working closely with groups like the Committee for a Sane Nuclear Policy (SANE). In fact, most of the participants at the real security conferences had ties to labor unions, including the Hospital Workers Union, the United Farm Workers, and the United Auto Workers. More than five hundred labor union leaders and members attended the project's first thirteen training sessions, far surpassing the totals for other representative groups, which included students and social movement activists.[26] This alone made the Real Security Education Project a success. Never in its history had IPS been able to reach the labor unions to such an extent.

Participants at the real security education conferences heard an occasional speech from an IPS intellectual, but "worker education" filled up most of their schedules. As Wien later remarked, "Our motto was based on the British trade union method of worker education—it was all done in circles, small group discussion. I would have, maybe, fifteen small groups of five people in each study group, and they would debate and discuss. I did not try to control the discussion in every small group. It was all meant to be democratic, the dialogue in small groups." Educational sessions began with attendees being "asked to evaluate major social, economic, and military trends in the U.S. by answering a series of questions and studying charts and data in small groups." Following this exercise, the participants looked at "world trends and institutions" to determine the connections between domestic and international issues. At the end of the session, smaller groups designed alternative policies.[27]

The attendees had positive things to say about their experiences. State chapters of the Women's Action for Nuclear Disarmament (WAND), an antinuclear organization begun in the early 1980s by the Australian physician and activist Helen Caldicott, attended a session in 1988 and wrote that they "gained knowledge, insights, and new ways of viewing disparate relationships." This early involvement by WAND led to "ongoing work" between it and the Real Security Education Project. Andrew Douglas, president of Local 14 of the Graphic Communications International Union in Philadelphia, also praised the project after attending a seminar in February 1988: "The manner in which the participants were involved was excellent and I personally learned from the program." Describing it as not "the usual run of the mill type of program union officials normally attend," Douglas explained that "most of us have heard enough of negotiation, grievance and organizing etc., it certainly was refreshing."[28]

The Missing "Peace Dividend"

IPS and other peace activists hoped that the cessation of the Cold War meant an accompanying reduction in defense expenditures. In the end, however, the collapse of the Berlin Wall failed to produce the "peace dividend" many predicted would come after the Cold War. Even before the events of the late 1980s, IPS intellectuals demanded substantial cuts to the defense budget. Most anti-nuclear activists, on the other hand, tended to target specific weapons, including the B-1 bomber and MX and Trident missiles, rarely speaking out against militarism. Organizers feared that doing so would tear their fragile coalitions apart.[29]

This strategy bewildered IPS intellectuals. A funding proposal for the institute's real security program in the early 1980s lambasted activists who "focus their opposition on waste, on single weapons systems or on efficiency" without considering the overall nuclear posture that remained in place, even after cuts to specific weapons. Raskin also looked skeptically at liberal campaigns to either stall or stop production of new weapons systems, most notably the MX missile. He preferred "a practical vision of future policies and actions" to excite the American public and convince them to support disarmament. Focusing on the minutiae of the nuclear arms race distracted opponents of nuclear war from the larger goal of general and complete disarmament. Pushing stopgap measures, furthermore, only encouraged politicians to accept less ambitious policies. Raskin predicted that even if the Democrats reclaimed control of the White House in 1985, they "would keep in place the war system as well as the programs which Reagan initiated and add to conventional forces."[30]

Rather than support these piecemeal efforts, IPS intellectuals looked for more far-reaching initiatives. Raskin found this in a budget proposal from California congressman Ronald Dellums and the Congressional Black Caucus. Dellums wrote to Raskin in early 1986 to thank him for supporting his "alternative military budget." The congressman, who served with Raskin on SANE's board, reminded the IPS cofounder that "we have both known for a long time that it is not enough to advocate a nuclear freeze, or to oppose individual weapons systems." During debates over the 1987 budget, the congressman proposed an amendment to reduce Reagan's military expenditures by $64.8 billion and increase domestic spending on social programs by $24 billion. The House defeated the measure by a vote of 356 to 59.[31]

Besides supporting congressional efforts to trim the defense budget, Raskin joined Melman, whom he had known for decades, in creating a new organizational vehicle to demand economic conversion. Along with the economist Lloyd J. Dumas and Melman, Raskin founded the National Commission for Economic Conversion and Disarmament in October 1988. Other notable "commissioners" included Heather Booth of the activist group Citizen Action, Representative Dellums, economist John Kenneth Galbraith, former senator McGovern, IAM president Winpisinger, and Atlanta's mayor Andrew Young. Though not as central to the commission as Melman, whose two students Jonathan Feldman and Robert Krinsky took on much of the organizational work, Raskin's disarmament treaty, discussed in greater detail in the next chapter, served as a central plank in its platform for economic conversion. Claiming that "the United States is poorly equipped to address the problems of formulating, negotiating, and implementing a disarmament process," the commission recommended using Raskin's proposal as a blueprint for such discussions.[32]

Raskin and Melman hoped their organization would play a leading role in drafting a post–Cold War budget that considered America's real security needs, but they and other proponents of a peace dividend faced only disappointment in the immediate aftermath of the Cold War. Writing nearly a year before the 1992 election, and one day after the dissolution of the Soviet Union, Melman and Raskin criticized the presidential candidates for avoiding any talk of "depression, demilitarization and democracy." They bemoaned the fact that as America's cities, schools, and hospitals deteriorated, the Pentagon was still flush with dollars. Solving this dilemma required a combined program of demilitarization and economic conversion with "planning" undertaken by the federal government to prepare for the transition from war to peace production. At the same time, Melman and Raskin sought a decentralized process. "Local authority for organizing conversion of each facility, to avoid ineffectual bureaucratic control from distant Washington," needed to exist as part of any conversion plan, they argued. While the presidential candidates remained silent on the issue, Melman and Raskin commended Representative Ted Weiss for introducing House Resolution 441. The New York Democrat had offered similar resolutions dating back to 1987. His most recent Defense Economic Adjustment Act called for an Office of Economic

Adjustment to develop federally funded public works projects to further the process of economic conversion, especially in communities hit hardest by the move from a defense to a peace economy.[33]

Knowledge Is Power: The GWEN Project and IPS

Secrecy was the lifeblood of the Cold War. Nuclear weapons research, covert campaigns abroad, and countless other activities remained unknown to most Americans. Unaware of the extensive national security state encircling them, citizens generally accepted the continuation of the Cold War. Periodically, however, this acquiescence gave way to outrage. Not surprisingly, IPS sided with individuals and groups seeking to penetrate the national security state and bring its secrets out into the open. To this end, IPS helped grassroots activists uncover undisclosed information for use in their campaigns. A very successful, if lesser-known, example of this assistance involved IPS's work with the GWEN Project, an organization that sought to prevent the Air Force from building Ground Wave Emergency Network (GWEN) towers across America.

The Cold War altered the American landscape in countless ways. Most notably, the dawn of the missile age in the late 1950s and 1960s required hundreds of underground silos, many of them in Middle America, especially North and South Dakota. Protests arose over the selection of these sites, but local activists could not counter the national security arguments offered by the Air Force or convince their neighbors to forego the financial benefits that came with military facilities. Later critics of the MX missile stationing scheme in Utah and Nevada also had difficulty moving beyond discussions about "land use" to debates over "nuclear strategy." Speaking on the latter issue required a more nuanced form of knowledge these groups did not possess and a willingness to criticize the U.S. national defense strategy, which would have threatened the already fragile coalitions protesting the MX.[34]

Besides sidestepping the issues of national security and nuclear strategy, these early disputes rarely involved questions about how the sites chosen by the military served to enhance secrecy. This changed in the late 1980s when Samuel Day Jr. and Nukewatch began publicizing the locations of missile silos scattered across the United States. Gretchen Heefner has argued that Day "hoped to force a national reckoning with the hidden geography of Armageddon." Besides bringing publicity to America's invisible infrastructure, Day wanted to link local activists, who carried out much of the research that led to the discovery of the silos in and around their communities, with the national anti-nuclear movement. In 1988, Nukewatch printed *Nuclear Heartland: A Guide to the 1,000 Missile Silos of the United States.*[35]

IPS recognized the importance of making information about America's nuclear infrastructure available to the citizenry. Since its beginnings in 1981, the Arms Race and Nuclear Weapons Research Project had uncovered a massive trove of information on America's nuclear arsenal and its related components. This alone represented a striking blow against the cult of secrecy underlying the Cold War, but IPS had higher aspirations. William Arkin and his staff used this data to expose the Reagan administration's plans for fighting and prevailing in a nuclear war against the Soviet Union. The project aimed to help ordinary Americans understand how seemingly innocuous items in America's vast nuclear infrastructure signaled a dramatic departure from the nation's past nuclear strategy. By looking at the policy implications of the quantitative data it compiled, IPS offered a more comprehensive critique than did its contemporaries, which proved attractive to grassroots activists.

Even before arriving at IPS in the early 1980s, Arkin had developed a modus operandi that would serve him well at the institute. From 1974 to 1978, Arkin served as a military intelligence analyst for the U.S. Army in West Berlin. After a stint as special assistant to the deputy chief of staff of intelligence, he worked briefly at the Center for Defense Information, determining the locations of U.S. nuclear arsenals. His work gained the attention of peace researchers in West Germany, who connected Arkin to *Stern*, a weekly news magazine. *Stern* published an article in February 1981 based on Arkin's findings, which subsequently aroused anti-nuclear activists in West Germany. While at IPS, Arkin continued to view secrecy as a tool used by governments to keep its citizens docile. He saw it as his duty, therefore, to remove the veil of secrecy not only to aid anti-nuclear activists but to preserve democracy. "Information is of utmost importance to U.S. national security, and therefore the public should possess the means to evaluate the government's sources," he concluded. Traditionally, news reporters and "experts" assessed this material before releasing it to the public in a much-altered form. Arkin favored giving the public greater access to unfiltered information. "The more that the public finds out about the way the system works, the less cynical and manipulated it will be, and the more the system will be a working democracy," Arkin proclaimed.[36] Though critical of IPS for myriad reasons, Arkin shared with the institute a fundamental faith in democracy and the ability of an informed citizenry to choose the best course of action.

The Arms Race and Nuclear Weapons Research Project's tireless efforts to promote transparency in the name of democracy and citizenship solidifies the institute's standing as I. F. Stone's "institute for the rest of us" and puts to rest the idea of IPS as a Soviet front. Arkin later remembered how many of his critics were shocked when one of the volumes of *Nuclear Weapons Databook* (published by the Natural Resources Defense Council [NRDC]), which he played a major part in preparing while at IPS, dealt with Soviet arsenals. "And the reason we did was everyone involved in this enterprise was firm in their belief that the enemy was nuclear weapons, not the U.S. or Russia. Our focus was putting as much of a spotlight on nuclear weapons as we could. That was our focus." Arkin categorically rejected the idea that "anti-American" views led him to carry out the work he did while at IPS. Instead, he demanded of himself and those working with him a "focus on nuclear weapons as the bad thing, as opposed to focusing on the United States as the bad thing. But I had no patience for that. Nobody worked for me who wasn't interested in breaking the veil of secrecy. That was our goal. That was our objective. And it made it very difficult for anyone to ignore us."[37] IPS's critics, however, did just that, neglecting Arkin's work because it did not conform to their image of IPS as a hotbed of communism.

Though by no means pro-Soviet, most IPS intellectuals avoided strong denunciations of the Soviet Union and did not hesitate to blame the United States for prolonging and militarizing the Cold War. Arkin and his staff in the Arms Race and Nuclear Weapons Research Project rejected such equivocations. "So, I do have an ideology. My ideology is I believe in democracy. I don't want ideology to be appropriated by one party. I would say very strongly that we had a very clear ideology. And there was nobody who worked for me, nobody, who didn't believe the same," Arkin asserted years later. One of his researchers, Kathleen Clark, even described herself as "pretty anti-Soviet—I wouldn't say that I was anti-communist—but I was anti-Soviet because I had lived in the Soviet Union." During her time in the Soviet Union, where she had spent a semester in college studying Russian, she found the country "corrupt." In this, Clark felt like she shared a similar perspective with Arkin, whom she described as working at "building up the capacity of democracy to deal with this policy issue [of nuclear proliferation]. It didn't come from the point of view of 'Let's trust the Soviets.' He wasn't deluded about the Soviet Union by any means." Conversely, Clark explained, "I don't know that outside of the nuclear weapons project there were any other anti-Soviet people" at IPS.[38]

Research from Arkin's project reached the citizenry in a multitude of ways. As he later admitted, IPS acted "as a little bit of a constraint on my ability to work with more mainstream organizations, which were often reluctant or hesitant to work with us because of the IPS moniker. But too bad, we were so good at what we did that that transcended that." Regardless of these concerns, the information and analysis put together by Arkin and his staff reached various news outlets and activist organizations. The project provided materials to all the major television networks, including ABC, NBC, CBS, and the BBC; national newspapers, such as the *New York Times*, the *Washington Post*, and the *Chicago Tribune*; and "scores of local and foreign media outlets." The project's greatest success came in 1985 when Arkin and Richard Fieldhouse published *The Nuclear Battlefields: Global Links in the Arms Race*. The book brought attention to what Arkin called "the unexplored nuclear infrastructure" constructed by the United States. Because the study looked at more than just the number and location of warheads and missiles, it attracted the attention of newspapers across the country shocked to learn about local ties to America's vast nuclear complex.[39]

Through Arkin's personal involvement with other organizations and news outlets publishing its findings, the project's research came to the attention of activists. In addition to the *Nuclear Weapons Databook* volumes at the NRDC, Arkin also helped Greenpeace develop its anti-nuclear weapons program. Mobilization for Survival (MfS), a prominent anti-nuclear organization, which collected more than 110,000 signatures in 1985 in support of a referendum to prevent a base on Staten Island from allowing nuclear-armed naval ships at its docks, relied on Arkin's research.[40] Other groups also used materials from the Arms Race and Nuclear Weapons Research Project.

Ignored by national anti-nuclear organizations interested only in targeting the most visible manifestation of the Cold War struggle, the nation's nuclear stockpiles, local activists turned to IPS. The Arms Race and Nuclear Weapons Research Project's interest in "expos[ing] the links between programs and activities of the national security state and the local community" appealed to ordinary Americans intent on resisting such encroachment. Arkin and Fieldhouse described their research for *Nuclear Battlefields* as part of the "new activism," which, unlike the "old," not "only considered the physical presence of warheads" but rather "focuses increasingly on the overall infrastructure that supports the weapons." This involved investigating "a complex made up of thousands of obscure research, testing, electronic, and command facilities."[41] As Arkin took up this issue in articles and in *Nuclear Battlefields*, he inspired an art teacher and a psychiatrist to speak out against a GWEN tower proposed by the Air Force for Amherst, Massachusetts.

Talk of strengthening America's command, control, and communication network appeared in a presidential directive issued by Carter in 1980. Reagan put his predecessor's plan into motion, which led to the decision to build GWEN towers. Since the electromagnetic waves produced by an aboveground nuclear explosion would purportedly disable electronic communications systems, the Air Force needed an emergency network to order a retaliatory nuclear strike. The three-hundred-foot-tall GWEN towers, which used low-frequency radio signals, offered a solution.[42] The No-GWEN Alliance, which later became the GWEN Project when it moved beyond Amherst, issued a shot across the bow in January 1985 when Nancy Foster wrote an anti-GWEN editorial in the *Amherst Bulletin*. Like critics of missile silos, Foster pointed to the increased likelihood of the town becoming a nuclear target if the tower became a reality. She explained that "if GWEN is really important for credible deterrence it is hard to understand why the Soviets would not spare a few of their more than 8,000 strategic nuclear weapons" to destroy the fifty-seven towers the Air Force planned to construct.[43] On the surface, this appears similar to the "not in my backyard" response frequently uttered when the U.S. government attempted to extend the national security state into a local town or city during the Cold War. Yet Foster insisted that the No-GWEN Alliance wanted to prevent the building of *all* fifty-seven towers, not just the one slated for Amherst.

Foster's editorial laid out for Amherst residents how a seemingly provincial issue concerning the construction of a few nonthreatening towers had important life-and-death consequences for people the world over. To make this argument, Foster relied on Arkin's research on command, control, and communication, designated C-cubed by the military. She warned her neighbors that the ability of the GWEN towers to withstand a first-strike nuclear attack heightened the possibility of a protracted nuclear war, resulting in countless deaths well beyond Amherst's borders. Rejecting the Air Force's proposal lessened the likelihood of such an outcome and sent a message to Washington that the residents of Amherst supported arms control.[44]

Associating the towers with protracted nuclear war, and the deaths of millions of Americans, became a centerpiece of the anti-GWEN campaign. Shortly after Foster pleaded with Amherst residents to oppose the massive structure, Arkin published an article provocatively titled "Preparing for World War IV." He argued that the realization of GWEN represented "a radical new goal of nuclear planning: maintenance of command during 'general nuclear war.'" In other words, the U.S. military moved beyond wanting to preserve America's nuclear arsenal and infrastructure for "an initial retaliatory response" to keeping them functional during protracted nuclear warfare, or World War IV.[45] Arkin made the same argument when he traveled to Amherst to speak on behalf of the No-GWEN Alliance. Alerted to the possibility of a

GWEN tower near their town by Foster's editorial, Amherst residents held a public hearing before the Hampshire County Commissioners in Northampton, Massachusetts, in Hampshire County on February 12, 1985.

Arkin's presence at the county meeting caused quite a stir. Paul Hollander, a frequent critic of IPS, contributed an article to the local newspaper alerting residents of the institute's, and by association Arkin's, radical credentials. Yet, while describing IPS as "a fiercely partisan organization" that offered "radical critiques of the United States," not once did Hollander refer to Arkin. Meanwhile, the Air Force reversed its decision to send a representative to defend the towers. The local newspaper reported that "the Air Force feels Arkin's presence shifts the forum's focus from local issues to global ones, and that Arkin may present sensitive information that should not become public knowledge." A statement from the Air Force referred negatively to the inclusion of "people from outside the communities involved" and worried about the "tone" of the meeting due to the presence of such persons. Arkin was the only outside voice scheduled to appear. More importantly, his efforts to link the "local" and "global" threatened the interests of the Air Force.[46]

By the next morning, the Air Force's reasons for not wanting to share the stage with Arkin became clearer. In a front-page story for the *New York Times*, Leslie Gelb wrote about "contingency plans" prepared by the United States to station nuclear weapons in Canada, Iceland, Bermuda, and Puerto Rico. Officials from these countries had no knowledge of the possible deployments until told of the plans by Arkin. Prior to publishing the story, Arkin provided the *New York Times* with the same 1975 document he had given to the foreign leaders. According to Gelb, "The [U.S.] officials expressed strong displeasure about Mr. Arkin's activities and raised the question of whether he may have violated laws prohibiting disclosure of such information."[47] Given this explosive discovery, it is not surprising that the Air Force joined in the protests against Arkin's involvement at the Hampshire County hearings.

While Hollander and the Air Force maligned Arkin, most Amherst residents shared his anti-GWEN sentiments. The five-member Amherst Select Board voted against the tower proposal. Subsequently, an Amherst Town Meeting, which had 250 elected members, "overwhelmingly" opposed the measure as well. The Air Force fared no better in neighboring Hampshire County, which forced it to look thirty-five miles east of Amherst, in Barre, Massachusetts, where residents also mobilized against the tower. Referring to the extension of the anti-GWEN campaign into neighboring countries, No-GWEN Alliance cofounder Lois Barber later remarked that "we specifically did that because it wasn't just 'Not in my backyard.' We realized that the whole concept of building a nuclear warfighting plan with communication systems, etc., would allow generals to think that they could fight and prevail in a protracted nuclear war that was dangerous to everybody in the United States and the world. It wasn't just a matter of having a tower in your town. It was a matter of the whole system possibly leading us into nuclear conflict because the generals would think that they might actually be able to win such a thing. So that was an important element for us—to oppose the whole system." By the spring of 1987, eleven other towns besides Amherst—from Maine to California and Wisconsin to North Carolina—held public hearings about proposed towers, each relying on information, and sometimes testimony, from the GWEN Project and IPS. As a result, the Air Force chose either "to reject or reconsider" placing towers in Barre, Massachusetts, Sherman and Castine, Maine, and Eugene, Oregon.[48]

The duplicity of U.S. officials is what seemed to anger the GWEN Project and IPS intellectuals most. Reports and analyses released by the Air Force, for instance, touched on the technical aspects of the towers but hid their relationship to nuclear warfighting. Arkin worried that "some town councilman in Oregon or Wisconsin who receives that document and the site surveys . . . would think this is just a communications tower; he wouldn't think twice" about approving the structure. In her remarks at a hearing to consider a tower in Gettysburg, Clark deplored the secrecy and bullying of the Air Force and the federal government. She claimed that "the Air Force has systematically gone into communities, quietly leased land for GWEN relay stations, planning to build the towers in the requisite 30 days, and leave town, providing minimal information to state and local authorities on the nature of the communications system." When confronted by local officials about the illegality of the towers due to zoning or land-use laws, the Air Force "invokes 'national security' and 'federal supremacy' as ways to undermine the concerns of local communities," she said. Thus, to the uninformed, the GWEN towers appeared as an "innocuous radio system" when in fact they served "as part of the infrastructure for fighting a protracted nuclear war."[49]

To rectify the situation, the Arms Race and Nuclear Weapons Research Project unearthed a trove of documents that detailed the true purpose of the GWEN towers. Both Arkin and Clark felt strongly that simply making the information obtained through Freedom of Information Act (FOIA) requests and the parsing of other unclassified materials, especially information conveniently left out of Air Force statements and reports, available to the public would convince Americans to oppose the GWEN towers. For instance, when Clark spoke at a hearing about the towers in Elmira, New York, she promised that she would not "talk about my own views on the subject." Rather, she implored the local residents to "judge for yourself whether GWEN's nuclear role was adequately explained to this community before the tower was built."[50]

The Arms Race and Nuclear Weapons Research Project's work with the GWEN Project exemplified Barnet and Raskin's earliest vision of IPS intellectuals as "public scholars" arming citizen activists with the knowledge to speak truth to power. As Barber and Foster explained in a letter, "We believe we complement each other's work on this issue. The IPS Project has provided its resources, its expertise and its credibility as a research organization. Our grassroots organizing has been crucial in inducing elected officials to call public hearings at tower sites, the media to recognize GWEN as a live controversy, Congressmen to pay heed to criticism of GWEN, and the Air Force to prepare an Environmental Impact Statement." Noting the GWEN Project's "frustrating confrontations with Pentagon double-talk," Barber and Foster praised Arkin's project for "bring[ing] into the open the vast network of nuclear weapons facilities and infrastructure the military is constructing in our midst and the often delusional purposes it is intended to serve." Arkin helped the GWEN Project in numerous ways. For example, Foster turned to him after a congressional aide had asked her to explain the strategic purpose of GWEN and its relationship to accidental nuclear war. Foster also discussed nuclear literature with Arkin. Moreover, Arkin opened the "IPS files" to Foster whenever she visited Washington. The GWEN Project, as Barber explained in a letter to her IPS allies, also "sent many copies of both of your writings to individuals, groups and the press at scores of GWEN sites across the country, as well as to many national peace organizations."[51] Barber and Foster repeatedly pointed to the involvement of IPS in the GWEN Project as a key reason for the campaign's success.

Besides providing information and analysis on the GWEN towers and U.S. nuclear strategy, Arkin and Clark connected the GWEN Project to sympathetic legislators and their aides. As the GWEN Project called attention to the GWEN towers, Congress took notice. For instance, Ed Long, who served as an aide to Senator Tom Harkin, contacted Clark to learn more about the structures and their purpose. Clark also connected Foster and Barber with aides in the offices of Senators Gary Hart and Carl Levin. Thomas Longstreth of Senator Edward Kennedy's office worked closely with the GWEN Project. On several occasions, Clark provided him with questions to ask the Air Force about GWEN. She also reached out directly to members of Congress. For example, in a letter to Representative Silvio Conte, a Republican ally of anti-nuclear activists, including the GWEN Project, Clark informed the congressman that recent testimony by the assistant secretary of defense papered over the more sinister aims of the towers: "The evidence from internal documents and Congressional testimony leaves little doubt that GWEN is intended for a protracted nuclear war. Yet on several occasions during the Subcommittee's recent hearings, Defense Department officials attempted to deny that GWEN is 'survivable' or that it could be used during a protracted nuclear war. This attempt to deflect attention from GWEN's nuclear warfighting capabilities interfere[s] with Congress's right to examine exactly what our defense strategy and capabilities are."[52]

Due to the GWEN Project's public campaign and congressional lobbying against the GWEN towers, support for the structures dwindled. Congress cut funding for the towers in the fall of 1987. In May 1988, Arkin encouraged the GWEN Project to "declare victory!" According to Foster, Arkin said that the campaign "stopped GWEN as a protracted war system. Now it's just a 'back-up for a back-up.' Mission requirements have changed." Though it would be a slow death, Arkin correctly predicted the demise of the GWEN towers. Construction on the original fifty-six "thin line" towers continued, though it took until early 1990 to finish the structures. The final blow came on November 11, 1993, when Congress passed its annual defense appropriations bill with an amendment offered by Democratic congressman Martin Sabo that banned further construction of the GWEN towers.[53]

* * *

Though willing to apportion blame to the United States for instigating and at times intensifying the Cold War, it is inaccurate to say that IPS sought victory for the Soviet Union and communism. Despite what its critics believed, the institute's radicalism had indigenous roots, preferring the decentralization and republican virtues of Thomas Jefferson over the class-based, centralization inherent in Marxism. IPS did not speak out against the Cold War to further any foreign ideology but rather to preserve humankind. According to IPS doctrine, peace, and with it the reemergence of democracy from its decades-long exile, necessitated an end to the ideological Cold War that propagated fears of the Soviet Union. Ideology, after all, was inimical to the institute's pragmatic mind-set. IPS believed in ideas, not ideologies. Too often the latter led to conflict, most notably the Civil War and the Cold War.

When IPS failed to influence the power brokers in Washington, it turned to "the people." IPS mobilized a citizen's army to wage war against the national security state and deny its foot soldiers, the defense intellectuals, the tools used to carry out their war games. Despite the best efforts of the Real Security Education Project, the military-industrial complex withstood the onslaught of IPS and its allies, as evidenced by the lack of a peace dividend in the years after the Cold War. The institute, working with the GWEN Project, found much greater success in halting the expansion of the GWEN towers. Regardless of the outcomes of the two campaigns initiated by the institute in the 1980s, each of them embodied *the* guiding spirit of IPS. The institute did not serve the masters of war; it represented "the people," and therefore is deserving of the moniker "democracy's think tank." IPS provided grassroots activists with the ammunition they needed to confront political and military defenders of the national security state.

Yet democracy could not flourish if the nuclear-tipped "sword of Damocles" continued to hang over the United States and the world. Moreover, America's nuclear arsenal gave strength to the targets of the grassroots campaigns described in this chapter, which made them less susceptible to democratic pressure. Since arms control failed to crush Damocles' sword, IPS intellectuals demanded the elimination of all nuclear weapons.

CHAPTER 8

Arms Control Is Not Disarmament

From May 24 to May 29, 1983, Minneapolis hosted the U.S.-U.S.S.R. Bilateral Exchange Conference, a meeting between U.S. and Soviet activists, academics, and ordinary citizens organized by IPS and the Institute for the Study of the U.S.A. and Canada, a Soviet think tank. Not surprisingly, the event caught the attention of conservatives. Arch-IPS critic John Rees informed his readers that the conference included several past and present members of the Soviet Union's secret police force, the KGB. Most troublesome for Rees was the participation of Mikhail A. Milshteyn, who had previously—though Rees questioned whether he had ever left the position—served in the Soviet intelligence directorate. Rees referred to early morning meetings between Milshteyn, "a handful of Russians," "experienced intelligence officer" Gennady I. Gerasimov, and a couple Institute of the U.S.A. delegates in the middle of the hotel pool, ostensibly, Rees claimed, "to prevent electronic interception of the conversations." At some point, IPS cofounder Raskin and IPS director Borosage joined the Soviets in the pool to discuss "how various members of the American delegation were reacting to certain Soviet lines offered during the previous sessions."[1]

IPS experimented with several different approaches to stop the nuclear arms race. Most of them centered around empowering the citizenry to participate in nuclear decision making. As a first step, IPS attempted to show the absurd efforts undertaken by defense intellectuals to rationalize nuclear warfare. Meanwhile, IPS's long-standing opposition to arms control put it at odds with the larger anti-nuclear movement. Unlike most liberal activists, IPS remained circumspect of arms control, seeing it as a tactic used by elites to assuage public concerns about nuclear weapons without taking the necessary steps toward disarmament. The outlook of the defense intellectuals remained dominant in Washington, as did the continued reliance on arms control. To move the nation in a different direction, IPS turned to "the people." In doing so, the institute approached two distinct sets of actors. At the grassroots, IPS worked closely with one of the leading anti-nuclear organizations, the Committee for a Sane Nuclear Policy (SANE). IPS also tried its hand at citizen diplomacy, organizing a series of conferences between U.S. and Soviet officials, academics, and activists. Much of IPS's work at both levels involved educating activists and moving them in the direction of supporting general and complete disarmament.

Despite IPS's calls for general and complete disarmament being branded utopian by politicians and activists alike, pragmatism undergirded the institute's pleas. IPS intellectuals looked at the proposals offered by both the United States and the Soviet Union prior to the 1963 Limited Test Ban Treaty, especially the 1961 McCloy-Zorin Accords, which created a road map for general and complete disarmament. In the aftermath of the 1963 agreement, however, neither superpower carried out experiments in nuclear disarmament. Thus, IPS aimed to educate the citizenry, both in the United States and the Soviet Union, about these prior efforts in the hope that the experiments might finally see the light of day. Once IPS succeeded in doing away with the historical amnesia regarding general and complete disarmament, "the people" on both sides of the iron curtain would seize the initiative and demand something more than arms control. IPS's efforts to rekindle support for general and complete disarmament clashed with the more limited aims of perhaps the largest anti-nuclear campaign in history, the nuclear freeze movement, as well as Soviet citizen diplomats. IPS confused the past with the present. The Cold War had dampened hopes for the eradication of nuclear weapons. Consequently, intellectuals at the institute transformed from pragmatists into dreamers due to their failure to recognize the lack of public support for general and complete disarmament. IPS had become generals without a citizen's army.

Megadeath Intellectuals, Arms Control, and the Unending Arms Race

The arms race began with the Soviet Union's first nuclear test in 1949. U.S. officials turned to defense intellectuals for strategic advice on how to deal with a nuclear-armed Soviet Union. Out of this milieu came deterrence theory, which held that the possession of nuclear weapons would protect the United States against aggression. By the late 1950s, nuclear strategists had modified the theory of deterrence in such a way that encouraged the acceleration of the arms race. As Alex Abella has argued in his study of RAND, Albert Wohlstetter's 1959 *Foreign Affairs* article "The Delicate Balance of Terror" succeeded in "laying the groundwork for the constant escalation of the nuclear arms race" that led to each superpower building massive arsenals. Wohlstetter stressed that the types of nuclear weapons mattered more than the size of the arsenal since securing a second-strike capability required more than a numerical advantage. Guided by such thinking, the United States diversified its nuclear stockpiles to include a "triad" of bombers and land- and sea-based delivery systems. The arrival of intercontinental ballistic missiles (ICBMs) in the late 1950s also encouraged a shift in strategy from a first-strike, counterforce strike, which relied on bombers and intermediate-range ballistic missiles (IRBMs), to a second-strike retaliatory attack.[2] By the 1960s, guided by a strategy of deterrence that promised protection against a Soviet nuclear attack, the United States initiated an arms buildup unprecedented in scale and variety. Ironically, these same weapons caused Americans to live under a cloud of fear, aware that at any moment nuclear missiles might fall from the sky.

For IPS, the solution was obvious: remove the threat by ridding the world of nuclear weapons through general and complete disarmament. U.S. and Soviet officials, however, more interested in preserving their respective deterrent capabilities, preferred arms control. Therefore, IPS sought to undermine arms control by discrediting deterrence theory, which was anathema to the institute because it countenanced the slaughter of millions of innocent civilians. Lamenting the "moral costs" of the strategy, Barnet compared it to the Holocaust. He claimed that deterrence involved "the overthrow of the most basic principles at the heart of our religious faiths, our professed ideas of civilization, and our national purpose."[3]

IPS's campaign against deterrence forced it to confront Raskin's "megadeath intellectuals," whom the institute accused of deceiving the American people by rationalizing the irrational: nuclear Armageddon. These strategists often justified nuclear war by arguing that it could be controlled, which astonished Waskow. He described such scenarios as "non-scientific strategies" and questioned whether believers of controlled nuclear wars were "real scientists" or just "science-fiction writers." Analysts at think tanks like RAND, he continued, "have responded [to the absence of a thermonuclear war] by spinning out of their own brains, with the help of their computers, the quasilogical fantasies of controlled thermonuclear war: fantasies that have nothing to do with science" since no historical precedent existed.[4] Most Americans, however, bewildered by the technical jargon employed by defense strategists, accepted the conclusions of prominent voices like that of Wohlstetter. Raskin

once referred to the "special language" used by defense intellectuals, strategists, and government officials that served to "ease their moral qualms, make
the extraordinary ordinary, the emotional abstract, seemingly rational and
quasi-comfortable." Because of such "verbal camouflage," Raskin claimed
that citizens no longer participated in politics as equally informed parties.[5]
Just like the national security managers who led America into war in Vietnam, defense strategists used rational and technical language to hide the fact
that their planning would lead to the deaths of millions of innocents.

Interestingly, IPS also found itself in conflict with the Arms Control and
Disarmament Agency (ACDA). As a former official at the agency, Barnet had
an up-close view of the ACDA's work. Several years after cofounding IPS,
Barnet offered his perspective on the agency. He found it unimaginative when
considering possible paths toward disarmament and too concerned with preserving American military supremacy. Looking at the origins of the ACDA,
Barnet distinguished between "two quite different constituencies" involved
in the early discussions. One group "stressed the need for 'new ideas,' but
what they had in mind were techniques for implementing established policy,
primarily in the area of inspection, rather than radical new concepts which
could be the basis of alternative policies," Barnet explained. Government officials, arms control experts, and individuals with ties to the military dominated this group. Others involved in the debate preferred a more dramatic
break from existing policies. They sought an agency devoted not only to
disarmament, as opposed to arms control, but also to the "investigation of
the causes of war and the consideration of various alternatives for establishing and maintaining peace." Congressman Robert Kastenmeier, who along
with twenty-six other members of the House of Representatives introduced
a bill in 1961 for a National Peace Agency, joined with those individuals who
favored an agency intent on transforming U.S. foreign policy.[6]

The studies carried out by the ACDA pointed to the success of the first
group. For the most part, Barnet reported, the ACDA concentrated on inspection and the effect disarmament would have on America's military strength.
Indicative of this trend, the ACDA's budget for fiscal year 1965 earmarked
almost $10.5 million, out of a total budget of $11 million, for "inspection studies" and "inspection field reports." Barnet argued that the ACDA's reluctance
to develop innovative approaches to disarmament prevented the agency from
looking beyond the Cold War calculus. "Far too much has been made of the
'lack of specifics' in disarmament proposals," Barnet complained as he criticized the ACDA's preoccupation with finding real-world solutions to the

arms race. He suggested that officials spent too much time obsessing over numbers—how many inspections and observers to permit and the quantity and types of missiles to allow each side—without offering a vision of a nuclear-free world. Consequently, U.S. and Soviet officials "had only a partial view of where they wanted to go and where they thought their own proposals would lead them," he wrote.[7] Unable to imagine a disarmed future, the two superpowers preferred to stay with the known rather than take a leap of faith into the unknown. "Lack of understanding of the way in which disarmament would work causes uneasiness," Barnet concluded, ultimately leading to rejection of anything but arms control proposals. Since the ACDA refused to produce a "theory of peace," Barnet considered the agency a failure.[8] In many ways, IPS played the role that Barnet originally envisioned for the ACDA.

Events in the early 1960s ensured that general and complete disarmament remained out of the realm of reality for most U.S. officials. To begin with, the 1961 publication *Strategy and Arms Control* by Thomas Schelling and Morton Halperin signified the liberal acceptance of arms control.[9] With the backing of these same liberals, John F. Kennedy secured passage of the Limited Test Ban Treaty of 1963, which banned all nuclear testing in the atmosphere, space, and underwater. Neither it nor the 1968 Nuclear Non-Proliferation Treaty, which sought to prevent the spread of nuclear weapons to other nations, did anything to slow the nuclear arms race between the superpowers.[10] By the time Kennedy affixed his signature to the test ban treaty in 1963, the American public lost interest in nuclear matters, leaving experts free to hammer out the details of subsequent arms control agreements.

A shifting geopolitical climate also discouraged planning for a nuclear-free world. Barnet described "a sudden surge of interest in disarmament" following the Cuban Missile Crisis, but this proved short-lived as commentators linked success in Cuba to U.S. nuclear superiority. Additionally, the Kennedy administration "turned their eyes anxiously to Europe and found that the Soviets did not dare to move, that a real truce has been achieved in Europe without arms control or disarmament." Moreover, problems within NATO— particularly French leader Charles De Gaulle's efforts to create a European-led alliance and the European-wide campaign to improve East-West relations— made the United States reticent to carry out disarmament. U.S. officials had a "deep-seated fear that the whole structure of U.S.-continental relations is shaky and that nothing must be done to disturb it further," Barnet wrote. Confronted with these conditions, U.S. officials pursued "détente in Europe to maintain the status quo rather than move towards arms control," Barnet claimed. Support for disarmament ebbed even further as U.S. involvement in Vietnam deepened.[11]

Despite the steady march toward détente, which opened the door for the first Strategic Arms Limitation Treaty (SALT) in 1972, IPS intellectuals argued that improved relations between the superpowers had only a minimal effect on the nuclear stockpiles amassed by each country. The fact that SALT originated in the Department of Defense, rather than the ACDA, helps explain its shortcomings. From early on, defense officials looked at how to use arms control to strengthen America's position vis-à-vis the Soviet Union, never once mentioning disarmament.[12] Nixon and his national security advisor, Kissinger, pursued arms control limitations for geopolitical reasons that had little to do with reducing the nuclear threat. In fact, both men touted the benefits of possessing such weapons and downplayed the dangers. Under the influence of advisors who warned of a growing Soviet nuclear threat, Nixon initiated a new counterforce strategy that involved the selective targeting of military sites. As part of the policy shift, the number of nuclear targets increased to upwards of twenty-five thousand. Though "rhetorically qualified" by every president except Ronald Reagan, each administration since Johnson's followed the tenets of counterforce strategy. Even Jimmy Carter, who spoke of a nuclear-free world, accepted Nixon's NSDM-242, which called for a strategy of flexible response including the use of nuclear strikes against the Soviet Union in the event of a ground invasion.[13] Given the policies enacted by U.S. officials as they pressed for arms control, it is little wonder that IPS intellectuals remained cynics.

The SALT I agreement set the stage for Nixon's visit to Moscow in 1972 and earned the president many accolades for his statesmanship, but IPS withheld praise. The aspect of arms control subject to most frequent attack by IPS was the focus on numerical limits. SALT I set the precedent for later arms control talks by using launchers, instead of missiles or nuclear warheads, as the key "currency," in the words of Strobe Talbott.[14] At IPS, Fred Kaplan disagreed with the excessive emphasis negotiators placed on "static indicators," like the number of missile launchers, which made verification easier but did little to stem the growing nuclear threat. Kaplan preferred "indirect ways of controlling the spiraling escalation of arms," such as setting limits on nuclear missile tests to delay the production of new weapons.[15] Lacking the restrictions suggested by Kaplan, SALT I and subsequent arms control proposals failed to slow the arms race. The Vladivostok agreement, which served as the blueprint for SALT II, restricted the United States to 1,320 multiple independently targetable reentry vehicles (MIRV), meaning missiles that included several warheads. Officials in the United States had planned on MIRVing 1,046 missiles but felt that they had, in the words of Barnet, an "obligation" to build more MIRVed missiles. Even more disconcerting for Barnet was the fact that the Soviets had no MIRVed missiles. Therefore, Barnet claimed that the "agreement was a cap for an empty tube that is only now being filled."[16] The deficiencies of arms control catalogued by IPS intellectuals explained why Nixon could sign the SALT I agreement while simultaneously increasing the number of targets in a nuclear war. Most Americans, however, not up to date on the various weapons systems and acronyms, took the word of commentators and politicians that the agreement limited nuclear weapons.

According to IPS doctrine, arms control effectively neutralized the public by allowing experts to dominate the process and denying citizens the ability to participate in life-and-death decisions. During a speech at Columbia University in 1985, Raskin warned the audience not to confuse arms control with disarmament. The former offered much promise, but the negotiations usually served as little more than political theater and failed to end the arms race. "The Reagan administration sees negotiating on arms as a sacrament to buy off one's own population," Raskin argued. These discussions provided "a way of cooling out opposition in both countries and getting people off the streets." Raskin implored his audience to see through Reagan's subterfuge and demand real disarmament.[17] Raskin also worried about the lack of citizen involvement in arms control negotiations. He described how so-called experts convinced Americans "that there is an inherently rational process to the arms race system and that those involved in it as experts and managers know what they are doing." Raskin disagreed, arguing that "we have a system of arming which is predicated on the most soggy of assumptions" and usually based on whether a particular weapons system was "vulnerable or invulnerable." Nonetheless, he feared that uninspiring and tedious arms control negotiations discouraged the public from becoming involved in the process. "The discussions of strategy and arms control, which accept the given—and the present imposed future given—as true can only fail to excite large numbers of people," Raskin wrote.[18] This alone, combined with the inability of arms control to curtail nuclear weapons, led IPS to seek an alternative approach to disarmament.

IPS intellectuals also blamed liberal support for arms control for misleading the public. Writing in 1986, Arkin argued, "It is with the liberal establishment and their allies in the arms control community that we have our biggest fight," not necessarily conservatives and Reagan. He referred to "non-disarmament groups," such as the Committee for National Security, the Union of Concerned Scientists, and the Center for Defense Information, "which fool their public supporters into believing that they are working on an *end* to the arms race, when in fact they are only trying to make it safer." He scoffed at peace activists for being into "fads" and depending on "capricious funders" and holding generally "partisan" views, all of which led to support for measures that fell short of general and complete disarmament. Arkin thought that activists needed to actively oppose Reagan's Strategic Defense Initiative (SDI) because it threatened disarmament. As he explained, "The only way to defeat SDI . . . is to obviate the justification for it (particularly as an augmentation of offensive deterrence) by eliminating nuclear weapons."[19]

Preparing the American Mind for Unilateral Disarmament

Addressing the radical pacifist War Resisters International in 1966, Waskow boldly predicted a nuclear-free world within twenty years. After all, Waskow explained, America's nuclear arsenal failed to stop the spread of communism in Korea, Cuba, or Vietnam. Therefore, Waskow concluded, U.S. policymakers needed to rethink America's war-fighting strategy. Unable to achieve a clear-cut victory in the Cold War hotspots, and under increasing pressure from American citizens, Waskow claimed that nuclear weapons no longer served a purpose.[20] U.S. officials, of course, did not agree. The arms race continued unabated. Given this reality, IPS intellectuals looked for ways to transform the American psyche and build a groundswell of support for nuclear disarmament.

Though nuclear weapons possessed no intrinsic military value, IPS intellectuals understood that they had been deeply ingrained in the American psyche for so long that they needed to mentally prepare the nation for disarmament. Even the threat of nuclear annihilation during the Cuban Missile Crisis did not diminish the allure of nuclear weapons. Referring to Kennedy's reluctance to remove Jupiter missiles from Turkey in exchange for the dismantling of Soviet missiles in Cuba, Barnet argued that the goal had become "victory itself, the vindication of the American will." The nuclear weapons in Turkey served no strategic purposes, but Kennedy still wavered over whether to remove them and end the crisis in Cuba. Barnet blamed Kennedy's recalcitrance on a new ethos guiding U.S. nuclear policy. "When a nation defines its interests as winning irrespective of the concrete economic and political objectives for which it fights, then the 'weapons culture' has overwhelmed the art of statecraft," he concluded. Therefore, the United States continued to build up its nuclear arsenal and construct new weapons systems, which offered "transcendent symbolic and abstract goals" but little else for America. According to Barnet, even the U.S. military realized that nuclear weapons were of little use in the current environment, where revolutions occurred more frequently than wars. Thus, the U.S. military had "to justify a bad bargain" using "mystical or heroic terms" since the inflated "defense budget would not stand the test of practical social or political accounting."[21]

IPS faced a similar problem abroad as foreign nations, following the lead of the superpowers, fetishized nuclear weapons. U.S. officials waxed lyrical about disarmament, but by "affirming through our military policy and diplomacy the importance of nuclear weapons for great power status we have whetted the appetite of other countries for them," Barnet argued. Accordingly, if the United States made "it clear that nuclear weapons are to play a diminished role in their day to day diplomacy, other nations would probably lose some of their interest in them."[22] Barnet admitted that "exhortations by the great powers on the advantages of nuclear abstinence will not be enough" without certain "guarantees" related to safety in the post-nuclear world. Even then, he expected resistance from nations unwilling to give up their nuclear deterrent in exchange for promises of protection. Moreover, nuclear weapons offered a nation more than just security. They served "as symbols of independence and national sovereignty," Barnet claimed. Beyond their capacity to destroy the enemy, nuclear weapons became "status symbols" and acted as a sort of "currency of international bargaining." These intangible factors meant that extending the U.S. nuclear umbrella to other nations did not guarantee a reduction in these deadly weapons globally. Barnet claimed that "for a nation to accept a nuclear protectorate is to admit that it is less than fully sovereign."[23] Therefore, IPS had to find a way to reduce the "incentive" to build nuclear weapons in the first place. Such an approach, however, required the United States to take the initial step toward a nuclear-free world.

According to IPS doctrine, diminishing the importance of nuclear weapons and moving beyond inadequate arms control measures required a greater willingness on the part of U.S. officials to initiate unilateral disarmament. Prior to the 1960s, before arms control dominated nuclear policy discussions, *Liberation* magazine and the historian H. Stuart Hughes, among others, supported unilateral disarmament.[24] Although the idea fell out of favor in the United States, IPS intellectuals remained committed to it. Writing in the late 1970s, Barnet encouraged the United States to end production of cruise missiles, the Trident, the MX, the neutron bomb, and various other weapons systems. Noting the "superfluity of nuclear destructive power in American hands," he argued that the United States possessed "ample room for experiments that could lead the world back from the edge of madness."[25]

U.S. officials and politicians did not share IPS's enthusiasm for unilateral disarmament. During a congressional seminar held at IPS in 1965, Democratic congressman John Conyers, one of IPS's closest allies, called out the institute for being so naïve as to believe that popular support existed for unilateral disarmament. "We couldn't go out tomorrow morning to our respective jobs and even roll out to quorum talking like this," he explained. Gaining public approval for such a proposal required "a big education task," Conyers argued. The congressman's advice proved prescient, as supporters of a nuclear freeze proposal discovered nearly twenty years later when opponents tarred the measure by linking it to unilateral disarmament.[26] Despite Conyers's warning, IPS's public scholars accepted the challenge, never wavering in their belief that "the people" possessed the capacity to build a nuclear-free world. In doing so, the institute risked straying from the pragmatic course it set for itself.

Unilateral disarmament retained a prominent place in nearly every IPS proposal. For instance, the first part of a three-step plan developed by Raskin in the mid-1970s required the United States to unilaterally halt production of missiles, uranium, and plutonium. Next, U.S. officials needed to engage in a "process of 'agonizing reappraisal' and reconsideration" to prevent disarmament measures from being "sabotaged." Then, during the final stage, the United States could begin pursuing "regional disarmament agreements" that, among other things, prohibited stationing conventional armies, nuclear weapons, and missiles in certain regions of the world. Raskin tasked the United Nations with overseeing compliance. His proposal also included "'confidence building' measures" to encourage "national leaders to move to the abolition of weapons and armed forces except for purposes of internal order."[27] Dissatisfied with the expert-led process and limited achievements of arms control, IPS broke with other liberals in favoring its own more far-reaching disarmament proposal. Before it could be implemented, however, the institute needed to build a groundswell of public support.

Disarmament for and by the American People

Though IPS stayed on top of developments in nuclear strategy and technology in the 1970s, most activists, to say nothing of average Americans, turned to other issues. To counteract this trend, IPS worked closely with anti-nuclear organizations to prepare the citizenry for disarmament. In 1977, for example, Klare encouraged his colleagues to attend the Mobilization for Survival's (MfS) first national conference. He thought it would be "a historical event and I think IPS should be at the center of this new movement." Klare also took part in MfS teach-ins and allied with MfS "to promote [an] international movement against [the] arms race, nuclear weapons, and nuclear power." This partnership led to IPS holding a "cram session" for MfS organizers to discuss issues related to the weapons industry, employment, and economic conversion. The meeting "provid[ed] up-to-date information and perspectives on critical issues" for use at the upcoming MfS teach-ins and offered a way to "build links between various groups working on disarmament and nuclear energy."[28]

Held at the Carnegie Endowment for International Peace in Washington, D.C., over one hundred people attended the "cram session," coming from as far away as Pittsburgh, Pennsylvania. Panel topics included "SALT and the nuclear arms race," "nuclear energy and nuclear proliferation," "long-range perspectives for disarmament and energy alternatives," and "organizing strategies for a non-nuclear future." A report on the "cram session" described the panels as "high quality with good rapport between the panelists and a high degree of interest from the audience." Besides IPS, other organizations represented at the event included the Center for Defense Information, Critical Mass, Friends of the Earth, Coalition for a New Foreign and Military Policy, and Women's International League for Peace and Freedom. Aside from educating activists, the "main accomplishment" of the "cram session" was the strengthening of the anti-nuclear alliance. "These groups have not been all that cooperative in the past, despite their common interests," the report explained, "and thus it was quite significant that they cooperated in putting together the cram session, and more important, were able to draw links to each other's concerns during the panels themselves."[29]

IPS also worked closely with SANE, especially after David Cortright became the latter's executive director. While still in the Army, Cortright received an invitation from activists to speak at an antiwar event in Washington, D.C., in the early 1970s. Prior to the rally, he stayed at Raskin's house. As he ate breakfast with Raskin and a few other visitors from IPS the morning of the demonstration, Cortright spoke about his experiences in the GI antiwar movement. Later in the conversation, Raskin encouraged Cortright to enroll in IPS's new Ph.D. program. Cortright accepted the offer and chose Raskin as his advisor. Cortright wrote his dissertation on GI resistance to the Vietnam War, which became his first book, *Soldiers in Revolt.* After earning his Ph.D. in 1975, he worked briefly with future IPS director Borosage at the Center for National Security Studies. Then, in 1978, he became the executive director of SANE. Unbeknownst to Cortright, Raskin had personally recommended him to Seymour Melman, a long-time friend of the IPS cofounder and a leader within SANE. The two would stay in touch over the next several years—Cortright urged Raskin to join SANE's board in 1978, but he refused—with Raskin serving as a mentor to Cortright, providing organizational and political insight. When IPS struggled to keep afloat financially during the conservative 1980s, SANE loaned the institute $12,000 in 1983.[30]

The ties between the two organizations deepened when Raskin joined SANE's board in 1985, serving as cochairman with the head of the International Association of Machinist and Aerospace Workers union, William Winpisinger. In early 1986, Raskin presented his strategic vision for the organization to the SANE board. According to the minutes of the meeting, he "intended [the paper] to chart an alternative direction for SANE away from 'arms control' as 'managing the arms race' and toward a serious effort to move from a war system to a peace system." In response, "the Board commended the Chair on his paper and expressed support for the vision it articulated." With the backing of the board, Raskin produced a formal statement, titled "The Cutting Edge or Alternatives with Hope (A Peace System by 2000)," for the SANE membership. After explaining his desire to position SANE as "a trustee for future generations" by working toward a "peace system" that involved "transform[ing] the present precarious system of instability and war preparations to one of trust, security and general disarmament," Raskin turned to what SANE needed to avoid. SANE had to distance itself from measures that viewed "the present system of arming" as "a stable system" or a means to "better managing the arms race," both of which prevented a "peace system" from taking root. Raskin also dismissed "incremental steps which are pyrrhic victories and which tend to defuse public support for moving to a peace system," warning SANE not to support such measures or the politicians who backed these sorts of policies. With the approval of its membership, Raskin's "Alternatives with Hope" became "the operating, officially-approved statement of goals" for SANE.[31]

Discouraged by the slow pace of arms control as carried out by elite experts, IPS turned to MfS and SANE in the hope that grassroots anti-nuclear activists might finally steer the United States toward general and complete disarmament. For years, in fact, IPS had urged the arms control community to open its doors to diverse groups. In 1972, Leonard Rodberg demanded the introduction of new blood into the arms control talks. He blamed the deficiencies of the SALT I agreement on the Nixon administration's "heavy curtail[ment] of secrecy," which "cut off those voices outside the government which could have supported a more progressive, forthcoming negotiating posture." Consequently, the military dominated the deliberations, resulting in an inadequate agreement. Moreover, the drawn-out debate over how many anti-ballistic missiles to allow each nation seemed farcical since the proposals left untouched the thousands of nuclear weapons possessed by each superpower. "Thus," Rodberg concluded, "there seems to be no appreciation within the bureaucracy of the excessive level of nuclear armaments which is so apparent to those of us who live outside that system, in the cities which are under the gun." To avoid the same mistake in future agreements, Rodberg advocated having "knowledgeable, 'responsible' voices in the public and the Congress," as well as "women, minorities, [and] 'ordinary' Americans," involved in future talks to allow for "voices and perspectives that are outside of the national security bureaucracies."[32]

The constitutional crises of the 1970s only strengthened IPS's conviction that future arms control negotiations required greater public input. Speaking at a convocation held at Riverside Church in the late 1970s, Barnet argued that ceding control to nuclear experts on matters of life and death put Americans "in the same position as the people of Jonestown." Raskin shared Barnet's concerns. Seen by some as "a system of tacit and explicit agreements between the superpowers to arm together and to assure that the mandarins on both sides of the Atlantic pursued similar goals, methods and acceptable 'codes' of arming behavior," arms control faced new demands from the American people, Raskin argued. Disenchanted with their leaders following the Vietnam War and the Watergate scandal, "the people" wanted to have their voices heard. The surge in anti-nuclear activism showed that Americans refused to accede to Raskin's "mandarins" any longer.[33] IPS hoped to tap into this new energy to finally bring foreign policy under the control of ordinary citizens. Given the horrendous track record of U.S. officials, IPS argued that the United States stood to benefit from opening up the foreign policy process to "the people." Leaving disarmament to "the Joint Chiefs of Staff, national security bureaucracies, and defense corporations is a little like expecting corporations to self-regulate," Raskin argued.[34] Once given the opportunity to enter the discussions on nuclear policies, IPS intellectuals predicted that the citizenry would choose peace.

The arms race, however, had two competitors. IPS also had to convince the Soviet Union to join the campaign for general and complete disarmament. To achieve this goal, the institute relied on citizen diplomacy. In May 1983, IPS and the Institute for the Study of the U.S.A. and Canada of the Soviet Academy of Sciences organized a meeting in Minneapolis involving representatives from the United States and the Soviet Union. Follow-up conferences took place in the Soviet Union in 1984 and in San Francisco in 1985. Participants at the inaugural conference included Patricia Derian, former assistant secretary of state for human rights, and Donald McHenry, former U.S. ambassador to the United Nations. McHenry cochaired the conference with Minneapolis mayor and former congressman Donald Fraser. Paul Warnke, who had served as director of the ACDA and a negotiator at the SALT II talks, provided a paper for the conference, though he did not attend due to illness. Other well-known activists involved included Randall Forsberg, Cora and Peter Weiss, Reverend William Sloane Coffin, editor of the *Bulletin of the Atomic Scientists* Ruth Adams, Jerome Grossman of the Council for a Livable World, and SANE cochairman Melman.[35]

The bilateral exchanges had a dual purpose: to encourage transnational debate between scholars and activists and to spur U.S. and Soviet officials to accept a new Weltanschauung and discard old shibboleths. To lead this herculean effort, IPS turned to ordinary Americans and Russians. Explaining the rationale behind the event in a fundraising letter, Raskin wrote, "There is great fear in the nation on the question of the drift towards war and nuclear war. It can only be interrupted by citizens setting the framework for politicians who have to act against this inertial drift." Similarly, a funding proposal for one of the later meetings stated that discussion between Soviet and American scholars and activists "develop[ed] an educated community able to challenge conservative scholars in discussion on what is possible with the Soviet Union."[36]

Disillusioned with the glacial pace of arms control, IPS hoped to reawaken dormant calls for general and complete disarmament among officials in Washington and Moscow. An IPS report described how the planners intended to use the meeting to move beyond the freeze proposal currently in vogue in policymaking circles. Participants would explore "radical proposals to *reverse* the arms race." Meanwhile, the report suggested that meetings at the "unofficial level" would eventually "begin to influence the official negotiating agenda." Raskin predicted "that by 1988 our work could be presented to all nations in many different forums." To publicize the agreement, Raskin suggested that "joint U.S.-Soviet teams should travel together to discuss these matters with nations of military significance."[37] The gatherings, in other words, aimed to end the isolation of government officials and bring alternative viewpoints into foreign policy debates.

Conservative politicians and commentators, however, did not have such an open mind when it came to reaching agreement with the Soviets. Republican congressman Larry McDonald, along with several of his colleagues, claimed in a letter to Secretary of State George Shultz, "All available evidence indicates that the 'exchanges' and 'dialogue' advertised for the Minneapolis conference are a fraud." Offering no proof, the letter charged that the Soviet delegation would be "salted with professional KGB officers to have full access to American decision-makers and those who influence U.S. public opinion." Therefore, McDonald wanted to withhold visas from some Soviet participants.[38] John Rees also warned of Soviet espionage at the meeting. "Among the Soviets were known 'active measures' specialists," Rees alleged, "and they played the conference as a classical political influence operation." As for the U.S.S.R.-U.S.A. Friendship Society and the Institute of the U.S.A. and Canada, he claimed that these organizations took orders from "a shadowy and supreme Soviet espionage service," the International Department of the Soviet Communist Party Central Committee, formerly the Comintern, that also controlled the KGB.[39] IPS's conferences received more attention from the conservative press and anti-communist politicians than from more respectable media venues and political leaders in the United States.[40] In the highly charged atmosphere of Cold War politics, even citizen diplomats with the best of intentions faced a difficult time reaching the decision makers in Washington.

Back to the Future: General and Complete Disarmament

Whether working with MfS and SANE or organizing conferences with Soviet citizens, the peace intellectuals at IPS touted the benefits of general and complete disarmament. In pursuing such a goal, IPS sought the revival of a "peace race" to replace the arms race.[41] "The search for general and complete disarmament is not an exercise in utopianism," Raskin declared in the early 1980s. Both Kennedy and Soviet leader Nikita Khrushchev, men not known for their "soft headedness," supported disarmament and viewed arms control as a means toward that end rather than an end in itself. According to Raskin, Kennedy felt that "arms control by itself would be nothing more than a Sisyphean task in which each torturous step forward for arms limitations would be accompanied by several quick steps backward into the arms race."

Following Kennedy's death, however, disarmament was abandoned. According to Raskin, arms control aimed to "fit within standards and assumptions of security that are reflected in the military arms race," which allowed nuclear proliferation to accelerate.[42] Therefore, halting the arms race required a return to the days when general and complete disarmament did not seem fanciful.

IPS hoped to use the bilateral exchanges to broaden support for general and complete disarmament and move "beyond the freeze proposal." Randall Forsberg, a founding director of the Institute for Defense and Disarmament Studies in Cambridge, Massachusetts, grabbed the attention of the American public and politicians when she issued a "Call to Halt the Arms Race" in 1980. The "Call" became popular due to its simplicity. It demanded an immediate stoppage of all weapons testing, production, and deployment. Various individuals had put forward similar demands for a freeze, including the lead U.S. negotiator for the SALT I talks, Gerard Smith, but Forsberg's appeal found the largest audience and led to the formation of the nuclear weapons freeze campaign.[43]

Unlike most liberals, IPS expressed strong reservations about the freeze, especially its silence on disarmament. Before Forsberg popularized the idea of a freeze in 1980, Barnet wrote an article for *Foreign Affairs* in early 1979 in which he called for "a mutually agreed-upon three-year moratorium on the procurement, testing and deployment of all bombers, missiles and warheads." Barnet supported a freeze because it kept arms control agreements from becoming obsolete due to technological advances. Moreover, and along the same lines, a freeze, unlike arms control measures, made the "question of ultimate intentions" null and void, according to Barnet. He claimed a freeze would disarm critics of arms control by denying the Soviet Union the ability to build new technologically advanced weapons on the heels of an agreement.[44] For Barnet, the freeze served to reinforce arms control treaties, allowing the superpowers to move on to the next stage of the process: general and complete disarmament.

The absence of unilateral measures in Forsberg's proposals also caused IPS to qualify its support for the freeze. In a 1982 letter to peace activist Cora Weiss—daughter of IPS's major funder, Samuel Rubin, and wife of Peter Weiss, who served as IPS's first chairman of the board of directors—Raskin expressed his reservations about the nuclear freeze movement. He feared that politicians would either water down the proposal or use it to forestall disarmament talks. He warned that the Democrats had already co-opted the issue and, in the process, took the initiative away from the American people. As politicians and the general public gravitated toward a nuclear freeze, the principles underlying the original proposal disappeared and were replaced by a "shared rhetoric" vaguely supporting an end to the arms race. For Raskin, the fact that so many officials who had previously supported massive spending on arms suddenly changed course and advocated a nuclear freeze made it "hard to distinguish the victims from the executioners" of a nuclear war.[45] Raskin's fears became a reality as a weakened version of the freeze found bipartisan support on Capitol Hill.[46]

Raskin's unfavorable view of the nuclear freeze put him at odds with his protégé at SANE, Cortright, who, despite his own misgivings about Forsberg's "Call," threw his organization's support behind the campaign. On the other hand, Cortright offered a blunt assessment of Raskin's alternative vision of general and complete disarmament. "While I fully share the judgement of you, Seymour [Melman], and others on the Board that we should have a comprehensive program for reversal of the arms race which goes beyond the freeze," Cortright deemed Raskin's approach "unrealistic and unworkable." He ultimately decided against SANE "mak[ing] a major organizational commitment to it." Though in full agreement with the overarching goal of the proposal—ending militarism—Cortright claimed that Raskin's sweeping plan lacked support in the current political climate. "But I hope you also know," he explained, "from my long experience as an organizer, that I am keenly sensitive to the need for practical, workable initiatives which can be realistically supported by large numbers of people. It will do us no good, indeed it might hurt us, to propose grandiose plans which will be perceived widely as hopeless and naïve. Unfortunately, I think that many of the provisions in the proposed Program have these qualities." Cortright specifically highlighted the call for a nuclear-free world by 2000. "There is simply no way in the world that such a process could occur in fifteen short years, and no amount of legal documents or treaties, no matter how solemnly entered into, can alter this," he wrote.[47]

Raskin and Cortright also held divergent views on the proper game plan for the anti-nuclear movement. Whether offering support for a nuclear freeze or targeting specific weapons like the MX missile, Cortright had to contend with Raskin, initially from outside SANE, and long-time SANE board member Melman. As Cortright remembered years later, "There was a tension, and it continued through the whole period that I was the director of SANE. Marc and I would talk about this a lot. They [Raskin and SANE's board] never forbid me from organizing the MX campaign or being a supporter of the freeze campaign. To me these folks were intellectuals, and not organizers. Marc was able to organize and build the institute, but that was a different kind of process. I was interested in building a massive grassroots campaign for disarmament and peace." This "tension" remained after Raskin joined SANE's board, where he, Melman, and others continued to call for general and complete disarmament. Cortright noted a "kind of curious parallel development, with the SANE board wanting total nuclear disarmament, but SANE working on the freeze, stopping the MX and the neutron bomb, and other specific weapons."[48] Thus, in the end, Raskin was unable to redirect the energies of SANE toward his vision of general and complete disarmament.

Transcending the freeze would require herculean efforts by IPS. While the peace intellectuals at the institute implored the U.S. government to undertake unilateral disarmament, Soviet delegates at the 1983 bilateral exchange rejected outright any suggestions that the Soviet Union follow suit. After Forsberg and Anne Cahn, an academic and former government official, pleaded with the Soviet Union to take "courageous historic, action," in the words of the latter, by dismantling some of its SS-20s, Soviet delegates replied, "Concessions can't be made on one side. The U.S. considers such initiatives as a sign of weakness." Later, when delegates from each country appeared on television, Borosage, in recognition of Reagan's strong opposition to disarmament, stated, with the European peace movement in mind, "Now is the moment for supporting that movement with unilateral action. The U.S. is not going to take the initiative to change course in Europe. The Soviets should." The Soviet delegates strongly disagreed. Soviet Academy of Sciences member Boris Khalosha said that reaching an agreement required the "principle of equality and equal security."[49]

Besides refusing to remove its intermediate-range missiles in Europe as a show of good faith, the Soviet delegates also brushed aside Raskin's call for general and complete disarmament. Genrikh Trofimenko of the United States and Canada Studies Institute remarked, "Of course, it sounds very good to make this drastic approach, but in reality, it wouldn't work." "The U.S. government doesn't want to make a treaty because some commas in a draft look like they favor the Soviet Union. So it would be impossible to make agreements with the United States if we take this drastic approach," he argued. According to Nodari Simoniya, a member of the U.S.S.R. Academy of Sciences, Reagan's massive defense budget discouraged the Soviet Union from undertaking unilateral measures. Moreover, he doubted whether taking such steps, even if combined with pressure from the anti-nuclear movement, would alter Reagan's views of the Soviet Union. Simoniya pointed to congressional support for the arms race as a further reason to question the approach favored by the American delegates. He predicted that if the Soviet

Union carried out the unilateral steps proposed by the U.S. participants, Reagan would claim that expanding America's nuclear arsenals led the Soviets to disarm, resulting in calls for further increases.[50] Thus, despite IPS intellectuals' hope that the bilateral exchanges might serve as a catalyst for greater trust between the two superpowers, the first meeting pointed to the difficulties involved with such a task.

The Soviet delegates also had strong reservations about discarding arms control talks in favor of disarmament. When U.S. delegates (including Ruth Adams, editor of the *Bulletin of the Atomic Scientists*; W. H. Ferry, European Nuclear Disarmament Representative; Melman, chairman of SANE; George Rathjens of MIT; and Raskin) proposed using the McCloy-Zorin principles as a blueprint for disarmament, the Soviet delegates demurred. General Mikhail Milshteyn, for example, "suggested that abandonment of arms control would throw out ten years of detailed work on definitions and negotiation concepts." According to IPS's post-conference report, the Soviet participants sought to revive détente, which reduced the likelihood of a nuclear holocaust but allowed for the continuation of the arms race. "In this view," the report went on to state, "they agreed with the American arms control community which argues that it is impossible to change the framework of international relations and therefore one has to learn to live with the bomb and the arming process." The Soviets apparently "were surprised" by the U.S. delegates' opposition to arms control. "They had not previously met thoughtful Americans who believed that the arms race was no longer manageable in terms of arms control." The U.S. approach to disarmament did gain some adherents on the Soviet side. While professor Nodari Simoniya considered the "radicals" among the U.S. delegates "naïve," another academic, Fyodor Burlatsky, supposedly "one of the higher-ranking Soviet delegates," offered "a ringing statement in favor of the disarmament approach." Meanwhile, professor Genrikh Trofimenko went "from very negative to expressing interest in pursuing the questions."[51]

The Soviet delegates' reluctance to move away from official policies remained a roadblock in future meetings. Describing his disappointment with the 1984 exchange, Raskin wrote, "One purpose of the discussions was to try and break through the rigidity of governments which hug old frameworks often believing that talk in and of itself is sufficient." To his surprise, Raskin discovered a similar tendency among the Soviet delegates. The fact that they "felt so comfortable with their official positions" prevented the delegates from "working out new schemes with those in the American group who wanted to go beyond both U.S. and Soviet official positions." Raskin and his fellow delegates, on the other hand, endorsed ideas "that are more popular in progressive and Democratic party circles," he explained. He also noted that the "internal political situation" facing the Soviet delegates led to more "cautious" proposals. In reference to the Soviet participants, Raskin concluded, "They reminded me of arguing with representatives of a doctrinal church which attempts to justify new directions in terms of old dogma." Other participants, including former presidential candidate and senator George McGovern, recognized these same tendencies among the Soviet delegates.[52]

While the stubbornness of the Soviet delegates annoyed the American participants, Patricia Derian, Carter's assistant secretary of state for human rights, felt that the meetings needed to occur. "We must meet because our diversity seems mad to them and their singular intolerance of diversity seems mad to us," she explained. Finding some sort of common cause between the superpowers, Derian continued, "comes with meeting the same people over and over again, getting past opening statements and host/guest rituals to whatever else is there."[53] Although the Soviet and American participants of the first bilateral exchange rarely agreed, further annual meetings lessened the distrust between the delegates.

Continued interactions between the U.S. and Soviet delegates seemed to finally bear fruit in 1986. Raskin referred to "a major shift in Soviet attitudes," particularly during the bilateral exchange held in San Francisco the previous year. Mikhail Gorbachev's embrace of disarmament further convinced him that the Soviet Union had undergone a transformation in its thinking about nuclear weapons. In January, Gorbachev issued his plan for the elimination of all nuclear weapons across the globe, which, along with similar proposals that he presented to Reagan at Reykjavik in October 1986, resembled Raskin's thinking. "In important ways the Soviet proposal runs on a parallel and intersecting course to the plans and programs of the IPS project," Raskin declared. He hinted at the role played by Georgi Arbatov, who headed the Institute for the Study of the U.S.A. and Canada and served as cochair of the bilateral meetings with IPS, for the turnaround in Soviet attitudes toward disarmament. The founder of IPS concluded that the exchanges were "beginning to show public results of substantial significance."[54]

While not wanting to claim sole responsibility for Moscow's acceptance of disarmament, Raskin later admitted, "I'm persuaded that our efforts began to affect their position, which since the early 1970s had been merely a limited arms control approach. By the mid- and late 1980s their positions began to change. Ours was not the only influence, of course, but their interest in our ideas was genuine." As Matthew Evangelista has shown, the "structure" of

Soviet society and government, though hierarchical and seemingly imper-
vious to outside influence, proved more receptive to transnational activists'
concerns. America's democratic structures offered non-state actors direct
access to the power brokers, but the cacophony of voices often meant that
their pleas were garbled. In the Soviet Union, on the other hand, once ideas
breached the fortress walls, strong leaders usually acted quickly to initiate
them. Gorbachev's ascension to power only enhanced this feature of the
Soviet political system. Raskin claimed that his Treaty on Common Security
and General Disarmament also had "major support from many non-aligned
countries, including China and India." SANE's board, members of Congress,
and former presidential candidate Jesse Jackson also praised Raskin's proposal. Democratic senator Paul Simon even held a press breakfast in January
1987 to publicize the treaty.[55]

Raskin's Treaty on Common Security and General Disarmament took
as its launching point the McCloy-Zorin Agreement of 1961. In a paper for
a Militarism and Disarmament Project study group held in 1977, Raskin
criticized arms control officials for seeking short-term agreements, that is,
SALT I and SALT II, without providing a path to disarmament in the future.
Whereas the McCloy-Zorin plan prescribed a date at which nuclear weapons production would end, later agreements offered no specific timetable.
Raskin described subsequent talks and proposals as being "chopped up into
pieces all of which did not appear to relate to each other and none of which
had an interlinked time boundary to them." Therefore, despite limitations on
individual weapons systems, nuclear stockpiles continued to multiply. The
history of arms control led Raskin to argue that "any serious comprehensive
agreement must be *time* bound" and offer signposts to direct future actions
to prevent against reversals, technological or otherwise.[56]

Not surprisingly, deadlines held a place of prominence in Raskin's proposal. Relying on a newly created International Disarmament Organization
within the United Nations to monitor compliance, Raskin's plan, like the
McCloy-Zorin agreement, involved three stages—a 30 percent reduction in
the first stage, followed by another 40 percent cut, and then the dismantling
of the remaining 30 percent—with complete disarmament by 2008. Raskin
had a specific reason for carrying out disarmament in this manner: "So long
as the disarming process is continuous and cumulative, temporary advantage
by one nation over another because of disparity between particular weapon
systems will not be fatal."[57]

To underscore that his thinking did not represent a dramatic break
from past protocol, Raskin repeatedly acknowledged his debt to the 1961

proposal. While "serious people thought general and complete disarmament was a public relations stunt," Raskin claimed that Kennedy's disarmament advisors, John McCloy and Arthur Dean, genuinely wanted to end the arms race. In regard to their efforts, he wrote that "it is hard to believe that, if it were a stunt, these senior members of the Establishment, both Republicans, would have spent so much time negotiating with the Soviet Union, setting up an Arms Control and Disarmament Agency, and negotiating within the U.S. government for an American commitment to try comprehensive disarmament as an alternative national security policy." Raskin also referred to another group within the administration, composed primarily of scientists, including the chairman of Kennedy's Science Advisory Committee, Jerome Wiesner, who sought an accord. Yet the advice of Wiesner and his cohorts was "not necessarily heeded," he admitted.[58]

Raskin claimed that certain officials in the Kennedy administration, who cared less about reaching agreement than gaining a propaganda advantage over the Soviet Union, sabotaged the campaign to rid the world of nuclear weapons: "The military Machiavellis of the Administration agreed to the goal because they believed that it would be possible to control the speed of disarmament and *pause* between the various stages." These same officials advocated "proportional cuts," which benefited the United States because of its numerical advantage. According to Raskin, the Soviet Union worried that the reductions, combined with the interlude between stages of disarmament, would give the United States a first-strike capability. Despite strong opposition to the treaty from his own advisors, Kennedy supported Dean and McCloy, so negotiations continued, which, in the words of Raskin, "produced only the framework" for a future agreement. Yet Raskin argued that the framework created by Dean, McCloy, and their Soviet counterparts offered an alternative to the "limited measures [that] have been successful in a less than limited way," specifically the Partial Test Ban Treaty of 1963 and the various arms control agreements reached in the 1970s.[59]

Still, Raskin found himself having to defend his disarmament blueprint against detractors who considered it unrealistic. He described his treaty to his former boss, Representative Kastenmeier, as "neither utopian nor impracticable." He contrasted his own plan with the "technically utopian" strategies devised by arms control experts and bureaucrats that did not look "beyond the narrow confines of individual and piecemeal arms control topics and critiques of particular weapon systems." Expecting pushback, Raskin noted that "at least six arms control treaties and UN resolutions," all of which had the support of the United States, advocated general disarmament, while also acknowledging that none appeared after 1962.[60]

Not surprisingly, IPS intellectuals did not find the 1987 Intermediate-Range Nuclear Forces Treaty to their liking. Though obviously pleased that a treaty seemed imminent, Raskin explained to Senator Paul Simon that "it does not begin to scratch the surface of the problems of the arms race."[61] Moreover, the agreement seemed to place greater weight on inspections than actual disarmament. Besides approving "an intrusive and otherwise formidable verification system," John Newhouse has shown that the treaty reduced each superpower's nuclear arsenals by just 4 percent, or 50,000 weapons. Both short-range and long-range weapons still threatened the world. Thus, the criticisms by IPS intellectuals that inspection often received more attention than disarmament proved true in the case of the 1987 treaty.[62] In the end, as illustrated by the 1991 Strategic Arms Reduction Treaty (START), which required the elimination of just one-third of each superpower's nuclear warheads and bombs, Raskin's call for general and complete disarmament faced the same fate as the original 1961 McCloy-Zorin Accords.

* * *

In the interest of human survival, IPS confronted "megadeath" defense intellectuals and experts on arms control. IPS hoped to usher in a new era in which an enlightened citizenry led the way toward a world without nuclear weapons. IPS intellectuals disdained the bipartisan consensus surrounding the arms race and arms control. Liberals, as much as conservatives, they thought, had given up on general and complete disarmament. As an elixir, the institute turned to the nation's republican principles. Exhibiting a populist disdain for elites, IPS looked to "the people" of the United States and the Soviet Union to chart a new path forward to a disarmed world. IPS failed to break the grip that arms control had on Washington, but more surprising is that the institute also faced difficulties in other circles. Dismayed by the lack of imagination within the government, IPS stepped in and produced its own blueprint for a nuclear-free world. Yet no one used it to set up an experiment to show the feasibility of general and complete disarmament.

For IPS, peace and the reawakening of democracy required the absence of war, which necessitated the abolition of nuclear weapons. Every day that the nuclear threat lingered, democracy suffered, and the fate of humankind hung in the balance. According to IPS doctrine, U.S. nuclear strategy had

undergone a retrograde movement by disavowing general and complete disarmament. This seemed irrational to the pragmatic minds at IPS. Turning
back the hands of time, however, proved difficult for IPS. In arguing for general and complete disarmament, IPS pushed too far ahead of its foot soldiers,
"the people." IPS's inability to revive nuclear disarmament in the 1980s illustrates the utopian element of the pragmatist dreamers at the institute. The
end of the Cold War in 1991 raised the hopes of many activists and commentators that the nuclear arsenals might disappear, but IPS intellectuals, always
cognizant of the deep roots of the national security state, remained skeptical.

Reviving Democracy in Post–Cold War America

Nearly thirty years after the Cold War, IPS stubbornly persists. Possessing nowhere near the funding or star power of other think tanks, the institute is still recognized by leading figures on the Left. As the *Nation* wrote in celebration of IPS's fiftieth anniversary in 2013, "Today, Heritage [Foundation] provides a multimillion-dollar home for the New Right; the American Enterprise Institute is a center for the Fortune 500; the Brookings Institution, for executive branch managers; and the Center for American Progress, for the Wall Street wing of the Democratic Party. On a much smaller budget, IPS remains, in the words of I. F. Stone, the 'institute for the rest of us.'"[1]

Though born out of the Cold War, the post–Cold War era exhibited the same set of problems that led Marcus Raskin and Richard Barnet to establish IPS more than a quarter century earlier. Both liberalism and democracy underwent significant transformations during the Cold War and looked considerably different post-1989 compared to pre-1947. Thus, as most of the nation celebrated America's triumph over the Soviet Union, IPS looked at the landscape and feared for the future of liberalism and democracy in America.

IPS intellectuals quickly realized that even without the Soviet Union as an enemy, the "pillars" undergirding the Cold War, most notably NATO and the IMF, remained as strong as ever. Barnet wrote in June 1989 that "as the Cold War is pronounced over, the institutions that have provided the energy for this struggle are still intact." He warned of the "danger that U.S. political leaders will miss opportunities for peace" because they remained stuck in the old framework. Though a "real event," the culmination of the Cold War did not mean the end of Raskin's national security state because "the structures of the Cold War: large military forces, police, espionage, secrecy, and military production," remained. And unless "the domestic institutions of the nation conform to the new political, economic, and ecological realities of contemporary life," the end of the Cold War meant little, according to Barnet. For the IPS cofounder, any sort of "transformation" hinged on "the participation of masses of people" since "elites cannot—and will not—steer complex societies along these new paths." Noting a global "movement for the renewal of democracy," Barnet believed that the real battle for "political participation and economic justice" could finally commence with the Cold War relegated to the dustbin of history.[2] Yet, next to the bodies strewn across the Cold War battlefields lay liberalism and democracy.

IPS found the Democratic Party under the control of the so-called New Democrats, a group bearing little resemblance to the progressives of earlier eras. The institute's involvement in the 1988 primary campaign brings this point home. Shortly after IPS opened its doors, senator and future vice president Hubert Humphrey thanked Raskin for sending him a copy of his recent *New York Review of Books* article. "I definitely want to keep in touch with you and your colleagues over at the Institute for Policy Studies," Humphrey wrote in the letter. "I know that you are going to be doing exciting work in the field of arms control and disarmament as well as on other aspects of foreign policy," he predicted.[3] Humphrey's championing of the Vietnam War, and his adherence to Cold War liberalism more generally, precluded a close relationship with IPS, but no mainstream candidate in 1988 reached out to IPS.

With the Cold War nearing its end, the future of the Democratic Party hung in the balance. Among the candidates vying for the Democratic nomination in 1988, Jesse Jackson and Michael Dukakis offered strikingly contrasting visions of liberalism in the post–Cold War era. A journalist described Jackson as "the leader of what might be called the fundamentalist wing of the Democratic Party, those who pledge eternal vigilance against any drift to the right." In terms of policy, Jackson participated in the anti-apartheid campaign that targeted South Africa and spoke positively of Cuba's Fidel Castro and Nicaragua's Daniel Ortega. His domestic proposals leaned toward "economic populism" with an overriding focus on helping unemployed farmers, industrial workers, and building tradesmen. Jackson distanced himself from and disavowed the Democratic Leadership Council (DLC). While not a member of the DLC, Massachusetts governor Michael Dukakis offered similarly centrist policies. Though he favored cutting U.S. aid to the anti-Sandinista contras in Nicaragua and ending production of the B-1 bomber and the MX missile, Dukakis also campaigned for higher defense spending on conventional forces. Moreover, the governor touted his state's economic success, which he attributed to private sector growth, primarily in high-tech, and pushed for welfare reform and a balanced budget.[4] In short, the voters had the option of choosing between a leftist or centrist to lead the Democratic Party in the post–Cold War era.

Whereas Democratic and liberal standard-bearer Humphrey could, however briefly, praise the institute, only the dark horse candidate looked to IPS for support in 1988. Borosage, who had replaced Barnet and Raskin as director of IPS in 1978, resigned from that position to serve as Jackson's advisor. Designated the "chief organizer of expert intelligence" by the *Washington Post*, Borosage provided a direct link between the candidate and IPS, which greatly concerned conservatives. In the same article, Raskin referenced Jackson's "natural gravitation to the institute" as an explanation for IPS's influence.[5] That Borosage worked for Jackson, as opposed to Dukakis, the eventual Democratic nominee, says a lot about the transformation of the Democratic Party from 1963 to 1988. IPS's ideas failed to gain traction among liberal power brokers in the 1980s not because they were inferior but because of the clamoring for centrist policy proposals. Though Dukakis lost in the general election, his New Democratic policies remained firmly in place within the Democratic Party.

Democracy fared little better in the post–Cold War period. Emboldened by the U.S. victory over the Soviet Union, neoliberal defenders of free-market capitalism and its international structures—the same ideas and institutions targeted by IPS during the Cold War—endeavored to extend their gains. With neoliberalism ascendant, the United States became "Corporate America." In such an environment, the marketplace replaced politics. Through such doctrines as "public choice," neoliberals sought to undermine government and the programs it implemented to provide for the general welfare. At the same time, equating neoliberalism with the erosion of state power is inaccurate. Rather, neoliberals sought changes to states, laws, and other institutions to preserve a free-market economy and protect it from public pressure. Consequently, the late twentieth century witnessed the deterioration of democracy as citizenship became detached from governing and self-interest and individualism replaced the search for the common good. To make matters worse, the Democrats and other left-leaning political parties around the globe acceded to the neoliberals.[6]

Regardless, the denouement of the Cold War inspired hope on the Left that after nearly a half century of war the United States could focus on reform. Moreover, the radicals demanding fundamental changes spoke the language of IPS. Whether protesting unequal economic policies or opposing wars in the Middle East, activists repeated the refrain, "This is what democracy looks like!" In its campaigns, the Left has sought an inclusive, decentralized, non-elitist movement to contend with the growing corporatization of America and to end racial and economic injustice.[7] IPS's long-standing critique of multinational

corporations made it a natural ally of these activists. As one scholar noted in
2005, the 1974 book *Global Reach* "foreshadow[ed] arguments of the current
protest against 'corporate globalization.'" Like Barnet and Ronald Müller, these
later critics focused on the transfer of power from nation-states to corporations
or corporate-controlled bodies like the IMF and the World Trade Organization
(WTO), which diminished democratic participation.[8]

Anti-globalization activists did not have to look to 1974 for inspiration.
Throughout the 1990s, IPS became a vocal opponent of the North American Free Trade Agreement (NAFTA). Global free trade, a hallmark of Cold
War liberalism, became a central focus during New Democrat Bill Clinton's
presidency. In the words of one historian, "Globalization had become the
new magic lamp" that allowed the United States to spread its vision of liberal democratic capitalism to a degree not seen before. In promoting U.S.-led
globalization, Clinton subscribed to the philosophy of the centrist DLC. Celebrating the fact that the president, not even six months into his presidency,
"returned to the Democratic Leadership Council agenda," the organization's
president, Al From, encouraged Clinton to "push hard for approval of the
North American Free Trade Agreement," despite disagreements within the
Democratic Party. Several months later, From continued to press for NAFTA's
approval, claiming that "the losers in the battle for the heart of the Democratic Party are joining ranks against NAFTA."[9]

Among the "losers" derided by From, IPS led the resistance. Not surprisingly, in addition to emphasizing the effect that the trade agreement had on
labor and the environment, IPS focused on its elitist and anti-democratic
aspects. For instance, in a report on NAFTA's first two years, Sarah Anderson and John Cavanagh decried "the process of negotiating NAFTA," which
they described as "closed, secretive, and cut off from citizen dialogue." They
warned that corporate domination of the discussions guaranteed a free trade
agreement lacking basic labor and environmental regulations. Protestors
during the infamous "Battle of Seattle" in 1999 voiced similar concerns over
the WTO. Encouraging activists to attend the WTO Ministerial Conference,
the Direct Action Network Against Corporate Globalization (DAN) put out
a call that declared, "The World Trade Organization has no right to make
undemocratic, unaccountable, destructive decisions about our lives, our
communities, and the earth." As for IPS, Cavanagh took part in a teach-in
that also included consumer advocate Ralph Nader, environmentalist Van-
dana Shiva, and corporate and political supporters of the WTO. At one point
during the debate, at least a thousand protestors sought refuge in Benaroya
Hall to escape the tear gas being used by the police to disperse the crowds.[10]

Besides fighting for economic justice and democracy as part of the anti-globalization movement, IPS helped found the antiwar group United for Peace and Justice (UPJ). As many prominent liberals, whom English historian Tony Judt acerbically labeled "Bush's useful idiots," supported America's march to war in the pages of *Dissent*, the *New Yorker*, and other liberal periodicals, IPS turned to "the people" to build its own antiwar coalition.[11] Formed during a meeting in October 2002 in Washington, D.C., and attended by representatives from at least seventy organizations, UPJ helped plan a massive antiwar protest on February 15, 2003. Across more than 600 cities worldwide, protestors spoke out against the planned war, including 400,000 in New York City and tens of thousands in San Francisco.[12]

Phyllis Bennis, head of IPS's New Internationalism Project, played a key role in the founding of UPJ. A month after the U.S. invasion of Iraq, Bennis and Cavanagh explained that the "issue is not simply war in Iraq today but the Bush Administration's reckless drive for empire and power." Ending the conflict required "claiming the UN as our own," Bennis and Cavanagh wrote, and in the process "empower the UN as the legitimate replacement for the United States empire we seek to disempower." Just over a year later, Bennis encouraged "an actual end to the occupation," which required a "full U.S. withdrawal" and "the dissolution of the U.S.-imposed 'Governing Council'" to allow for the entrance of a UN-led "international team" that included representatives from the Arab League and Organization of the Islamic Conference. Bennis assured Iraqis that the international and regional actors involved in the "international assistance mission" would not interfere with Iraq's political, economic, or territorial sovereignty, leaving it to the people of Iraq to build a new government free from foreign or corporate domination.[13] Bennis and Cavanagh, among others, used arguments nearly identical to those their predecessors espoused during the height of the superpower conflict, highlighting how many of the issues IPS confronted outlasted the Cold War.

A Foreign Policy for the Left: IPS's Post–Cold War Blueprint in the Age of Endless Wars

The institute only rarely receives recognition, political and otherwise, for its efforts, both past and present, to build a more democratic and peaceful world. IPS is partially to blame for its low profile. Amid its struggles to redirect U.S. foreign policy in the post–Cold War era, the institute underwent several leadership changes. Eventually, Michael Shuman assumed the role of director in 1992. The following year, for a story about IPS's thirtieth anniversary celebration, Shuman discussed his plans for the institute. "There have always been people within the institute who have talked to the mainstream," he told a reporter for the *Washington Post*, "and I am trying to encourage them to do even more of that." Shuman's strategy, no doubt, clashed with the vision of IPS's founders, who still had misgivings about working too closely with the government. Barnet, for example, cautioned against trying to make IPS into a "player" in Washington. "We never want to see the institute become a rest stop for people to go in and out of government—not a player in that sense," Barnet explained.[14] Despite Shuman's best efforts, IPS never entered the mainstream during the 1990s, not that it ever wanted to achieve such a status. The institute always felt most comfortable existing on the fringes, serving as I. F. Stone's "institute for the rest of us."

A disinclination toward becoming mainstream or a player in Washington has certain drawbacks. In 2018, the University of Pennsylvania ranked the top think tanks in the United States based on the public reception of their ideas and the degree to which they influenced public policy. The Brookings Institution stood at the top of the list. The RAND Corporation continued to exert influence with a ranking of sixth. The only left-leaning, though avowedly centrist, think tank listed among the top ten was the Center for American Progress (CAP). Among conservative think tanks, IPS's ideological rival, the Heritage Foundation, held the fourth position. Meanwhile, the list ranked the American Enterprise Institute (AEI) as the sixteenth most influential research center. Fifty-five years after its founding, IPS found itself ranked sixtieth.[15]

IPS never aspired to reach the heights of the Brookings Institution or the RAND Corporation, but the visibility of these think tanks, along with the Heritage Foundation and AEI, on the airwaves and within the respective political parties has bolstered the militaristic foreign policy consensus. During the late 1990s and early 2000s, neoconservatives associated with Heritage and AEI carried out letter-writing campaigns, appeared on news channels, wrote columns, and joined the staff of the George W. Bush administration. In their writings and advisory roles, they urged the United States to stand firm against external threats, initially Saddam Hussein and then foreign terrorists. Their efforts paid off. By February 2003, President Bush, delivering a televised address from the AEI offices, spoke of the need for a "liberated Iraq," a process begun the following month with the U.S. invasion of Iraq. Even a supposedly left-leaning think tank like CAP, which opened its doors in 2003 after the start of the Iraq war, offered proposals that mirrored those of conservatives. Initially, in a 2005 report, CAP called for a phased withdrawal of U.S. troops from Iraq between January 2006 and December 2007. By 2014, however, faced with the growing threat of the Islamic State of Iraq and al-Sham, CAP advocated a different approach, which included air strikes. In Afghanistan, too, CAP advised President Barack Obama in 2009 to send an additional 17,000 troops to the country. The same report accepted a U.S. presence in Afghanistan for ten years.[16] Thus, both liberals and conservatives have ensured the continuation of "endless wars" in Afghanistan and Iraq into the late 2010s. Meanwhile, a preference for serving as an "institute for the rest of us" has obscured IPS's efforts to construct a leftist foreign policy.

After a decade and a half of conflict in the Middle East, a growing chorus of voices began calling for a new direction in foreign policy. In April 2017, two historians, Daniel Bessner and Stephen Wertheim, wrote an article for *Foreign Affairs*, the premier foreign policy establishment journal published by the Council on Foreign Relations, in which they referred to the growing disenchantment with experts. The public had reason to question policy recommendations from foreign policy specialists in the aftermath of the U.S. invasion and occupation of Iraq, but Bessner and Wertheim argued a more fundamental point: "Confined to the coastal cities, experts have failed to engage citizens where they live and work." In making such a statement, the authors acknowledged their debt to Dewey.[17]

At the same time, they found experts during Dewey's lifetime far more interested in interacting with the citizenry. Research institutes like the Foreign Policy Association and the Council on Foreign Relations, Bessner and Wertheim argued, "often approached citizens with respect and a desire to help them think for themselves." This back-and-forth between expert and citizen disappeared with the onset of the Cold War, never to return, according to Bessner and Wertheim. In search of a revived "public," the authors offered several proposals, including having "expert institutions and networks" serve as "facilitators of democratic deliberation"; allowing Congress to reclaim its powers vis-à-vis foreign policy; and the development of a stronger "culture of accountability" to prevent grossly inept individuals from continuing to influence foreign policy debates. In an op-ed published in the *New York Times* in September 2018, Bessner appealed once again for having democracy serve as the centerpiece of a left-wing foreign policy. This required a strengthening of Congress and a reduced role for the National Security Council. In addition to "professional accountability," Bessner also advised the Left to support criminal prosecution of U.S. officials for breaking domestic and international laws. Finally, Bessner called for a less interventionist U.S. foreign policy. This entailed closing foreign bases and limiting special forces operations to allow for a greater focus on diplomacy and multilateralism.[18] The parallels between Bessner and Wertheim's vision for a left-wing foreign policy and IPS's post–Cold War blueprint are striking.

Yet, IPS is never mentioned in these discussions about a leftist foreign policy. As a persistent critic of militarism and guardian of democracy for over fifty years, IPS's history is especially instructive for contemporary observers seeking an alternative to American empire. During the Cold War, critics tarred the institute as Soviet sympathizers or utopian. In reality, IPS fought to preserve America's republican traditions. The peace intellectuals at IPS were native insurgents waging a struggle against Cold War liberals to end the colonization of the United States and the world. Moreover, as pragmatists, IPS's peace intellectuals offered realistic blueprints for a democratic world order composed of diverse economic and political systems. Such a reality, IPS understood, required a recognition by U.S. leaders that they could no longer mold other nations to ensure the primacy of the liberal world order. According to IPS doctrine, only by accepting these limits and following a foreign policy of restraint could the United States shed its imperialist garb. Most importantly, IPS recognized that bringing an end to American empire required a changing of the guard. The expansion of democracy abroad depended on the revival of democracy at home. In short, twenty-first-century voices seeking a different path forward do not have to start from scratch. IPS's unrealized experiments are just as relevant today as during the Cold War. The Soviet Union collapsed, but democracy's enemies endured. Contemporary critics of American empire would benefit from looking at the blueprints designed at democracy's think tank.

NOTES

Introduction

1. Saul Landau, *They Educated the Crows: An Institute Report on the Letelier-Moffitt Murders* (Washington, DC: Transnational Institute, 1978), 1–2.

2. Orlando Letelier, "A Testament," *New York Times* (hereafter *NYT*), September 27, 1976, 31.

3. Marcus Raskin, "Memorandum," September 25, 1962, Institute for Policy Studies Records, Wisconsin Historical Society, Madison (hereafter IPSR), Box 104, Folder 38.

4. Marcus Raskin to McGeorge Bundy, April 20, 1961, National Security Files, John F. Kennedy Library, Boston (hereafter NSF), Box 323.

5. Walter Lippmann, *Public Opinion* (New York: Harcourt, Brace, 1922), 16, 399–400. Dewey's quote regarding *Public Opinion* is found in Robert B. Westbrook, *John Dewey & American Democracy* (Ithaca, NY: Cornell University Press, 1993), 294.

6. John Dewey, *The Public and Its Problems* (New York: Henry Holt, 1927), 126–27, 218–19, 209.

7. Westbrook, *John Dewey and American Democracy*, 548–50.

8. On the narrow vision undergirding Wilsonian liberal internationalism, see Erez Manela, *The Wilsonian Moment: Self-Determination and the International Origins of Anticolonial Nationalism* (New York: Oxford University Press, 2007); Susan Pederson, *The Guardians: The League of Nations and the Crisis of Empire* (New York: Oxford University Press, 2015); Adam Tooze, *The Great Deluge: The Great War, America and the Remaking of the Global Order, 1916–1931* (New York: Viking, 2014).

9. Or Rosenboim, *The Emergence of Globalism: Visions of World Order in Britain and the United States, 1939–1950* (Princeton, NJ: Princeton University Press, 2017); Elizabeth Borgwardt, *A New Deal for the World: America's Vision for Human Rights* (Cambridge, MA: Belknap Press, 2005).

10. On the connections between Wilsonian idealism and postwar liberal internationalism, see David Steigerwald, *Wilsonian Idealism in America* (Ithaca, NY: Cornell University Press, 1994); Frank Nincovich, *The Wilsonian Century: U.S. Foreign Policy Since 1900* (Chicago: University of Chicago Press, 1999); Tony Smith, *Why Wilson Matters: The Origin of American Liberal Internationalism and Its Crisis Today* (Princeton, NJ: Princeton University Press, 2017); G. John Ikenberry, *Liberal Leviathan: The Origins, Crisis, and Transformation of the American World Order* (Princeton, NJ: Princeton University Press, 2011). For a generally positive assessment of internationalism, and its perseverance, in the long twentieth century, see Glenda Sluga, *Internationalism in the Age of Nationalism* (Philadelphia: University of Pennsylvania Press, 2013). On the origins of the Cold War, see Melvyn P. Leffler, *A Preponderance of Power: National Security, the Truman Administration, and the Cold War* (Stanford, CA: Stanford University Press,

1992); Elizabeth Edwards Spalding, *The First Cold Warrior: Harry Truman, Containment, and the Remaking of Liberal Internationalism* (Lexington: University Press of Kentucky, 2006); Robert Latham, *The Liberal Moment: Modernity, Security, and the Making of Postwar International Order* (New York: Columbia University Press, 1997). On the United Nations and NATO, see Paul Kennedy, *The Parliament of Man: The Past, Present, and Future of the United Nations* (New York: Random House, 2006); Timothy Andrews Sayle, *Enduring Alliance: A History of NATO and the Postwar Global Order* (Ithaca, NY: Cornell University Press, 2019). For the argument that popular protest led to détente, see Jeremi Suri, *Power and Protest: Global Revolution and the Rise of Détente* (Cambridge, MA: Harvard University Press, 2003). On the origins of NATO, see Marc Trachtenberg, *A Constructed Peace: The Making of the European Settlement, 1945–1963* (Princeton, NJ: Princeton University Press, 1999). On liberal internationalist and world federalist support for NATO, see E. Timothy Smith, *Opposition Beyond the Water's Edge: Liberal Internationalists, Pacifists, and Containment, 1945–1953* (Westport, CT: Greenwood Press, 1999); Andrew Johnstone, *Dilemmas of Internationalism: The American Association for the United Nations and U.S. Foreign Policy, 1941–1948* (Burlington, VT: Ashgate, 2009).

11. On the Cold War consensus in U.S. foreign policy, see Ole R. Holsti and James N. Rosenau, *American Leadership in World Affairs: Vietnam and the Breakdown of Consensus* (Boston: Allen & Unwin, 1984), 222; Eugene R. Wittkopf, *Faces of Internationalism: Public Opinion and American Foreign Policy* (Durham, NC: Duke University Press, 1990); Richard A. Melanson, *American Foreign Policy Since the Vietnam War: The Search for Consensus from Nixon to Clinton* (Armonk, NY: M. E. Sharpe, 1996). On the fragility of the Cold War consensus prior to the Vietnam War, see Ronald R. Krebs, "How Dominant Narratives Rise and Fall: Military Conflicts, Politics, and the Cold War Consensus," *International Organization* 69, no. 4 (Fall 2015), 809–45. For the argument that the consensus survived the Vietnam War, see Campbell Craig and Fredrik Logevall, *America's Cold War: The Politics of Insecurity* (Cambridge, MA: Harvard University Press, 2009); Andrew Bacevich, introduction to *The Long War: A New History of U.S. National Security Since World War II*, ed. Andrew Bacevich (New York: Columbia University Press, 2007), ix.

12. Richard H. Pells, *The Liberal Mind in a Conservative Age: American Intellectuals in the 1940s and 1950s*, 2nd ed. (Middletown, CT: Wesleyan University Press, 1989), 145–46; Richard W. Fox, *Reinhold Niebuhr: A Biography* (New York: Pantheon, 1985); Marc Stears, *Demanding Democracy: American Radicals in Search of a New Politics* (Princeton, NJ: Princeton University Press, 2010), 121–44; Michael E. Latham, "What Price Victory? American Intellectuals and the Problem of Cold War Democracy," in *The Columbia History of Post–World War II America*, ed. Mark C. Carnes (New York: Columbia University Press, 2007), 402–24; Richard Aldous, *Schlesinger: The Imperial Historian* (New York: W. W. Norton, 2017). Representative works of democratic elitism include Reinhold Niebuhr, *The Children of Light and the Children of Darkness: A Vindication of Democracy and a Critique of Its Traditional Defense* (New York: Scribner, 1944); Arthur Schlesinger Jr., *Vital Center: The Politics of Freedom* (New York: Houghton Mifflin, 1949).

13. On the development of "managerial liberalism," see Brian Balogh, *The Associational State: American Governance in the Twentieth Century* (Philadelphia: University of Pennsylvania Press, 2015), especially 172–99; John A. Andrew III, *Lyndon Johnson and the Great Society* (Chicago: Ivan R. Dee, 1998). On its origins, see John M. Jordan, *Machine-Age Ideology: Social Engineering and American Liberalism, 1911–1939* (Chapel Hill: University of North Carolina Press, 1994). On the efforts to retain the democratic elements of technocracy in the years prior to the

Cold War, see Andrew Jewett, *Science, Democracy, and the American University: From the Civil War to the Cold War* (New York: Cambridge University Press, 2012).

14. On the influence of German émigrés on Cold War thought and strategy, see Jeremi Suri, *Henry Kissinger and the American Century* (Cambridge, MA: Belknap Press, 2007); Udi Greenberg, *The Weimar Century: German Émigrés and the Ideological Foundations of the Cold War* (Princeton, NJ: Princeton University Press, 2015); Daniel Bessner, *Democracy in Exile: Hans Speier and the Rise of the Defense Intellectual* (Ithaca, NY: Cornell University Press, 2018). On the role of social scientists during the Cold War, see Joy Rohde, *Armed with Expertise: The Militarization of American Social Research During the Cold War* (Ithaca, NY: Cornell University Press, 2013); Mark Solovey, *Shaky Foundations: The Politics-Patronage-Social Science Nexus in Cold War America* (New Brunswick, NJ: Rutgers University Press, 2015). On the "military-intellectual complex," see Stuart W. Leslie, *The Cold War and American Science: The Military-Industrial-Academic Complex at MIT and Stanford* (New York: Columbia University Press, 1993). For an account that downplays the influence of intellectuals on policymakers, see Bruce Kuklick, *Blind Oracles: Intellectuals and War from Kennan to Kissinger* (Princeton, NJ: Princeton University Press, 2006). On the National Security Council, see Andrew Preston, *The War Council: McGeorge Bundy, the NSC, and Vietnam* (Cambridge, MA: Harvard University Press, 2006); David Rothkopf, *Running the World: The Inside Story of the National Security Council and the Architects of American Power* (New York: PublicAffairs, 2005); John Gans, *White House Warriors: How the National Security Council Transformed the American Way of War* (New York: Liveright, 2019).

15. On the creation of the Cold War enemy, see Ron Robin, *The Making of the Cold War Enemy: Culture and Politics in the Military-Intellectual Complex* (Princeton, NJ: Princeton University Press, 2001); Ron Robin, *The Cold World They Made: The Strategic Legacy of Roberta and Albert Wohlstetter* (Cambridge, MA: Harvard University Press, 2016). For a contrasting view that sees intellectuals as more independent, see David C. Engerman, *Know Your Enemy: The Rise and Fall of America's Soviet Experts* (New York: Oxford University Press, 2009). On "wartime," see Mary L. Dudziak, *War Time: An Idea, Its History, Its Consequences* (New York: Oxford University Press, 2012). On the national security state and its ties to the growth of the New Deal state, see Michael J. Hogan, *A Cross of Iron: Harry S. Truman and the Origins of the National Security State, 1945–1954* (New York: Cambridge University Press, 1998); Douglas T. Stuart, *Creating the National Security State: A History of the Law That Transformed America* (Princeton, NJ: Princeton University Press, 2008); Anne M. Kornhauser, *Debating the American State: Liberal Anxieties and the New Leviathan, 1930–1970* (Philadelphia: University of Pennsylvania Press, 2015); James T. Sparrow, *Warfare State: World War II Americans and the Age of Big Government* (New York: Oxford University Press, 2011); Anna Kasten Nelson, "The Evolution of the National Security State: Ubiquitous and Endless," in *The Long War: A New History of U.S. National Security Policy Since World War II*, ed. Andrew J. Bacevich (New York: Columbia University Press, 2007), 265–301. For opposing views, see Aaron L. Friedberg, *In the Shadow of the Garrison State: America's Anti-Statism and Its Cold War Grand Strategy* (Princeton, NJ: Princeton University Press, 2000); David Ciepley, *Liberalism in the Shadow of Totalitarianism* (Cambridge, MA: Harvard University Press, 2007). The term "militarization" comes from Michael Sherry, *In the Shadow of War: The United States Since the 1930s* (New Haven, CT: Yale University Press, 1995). See also Laura McEnaney, *Civil Defense Begins at Home: Militarization Meets Everyday Life in the Fifties* (Princeton, NJ: Princeton University Press, 2000); Elaine Tyler May, *Homeward Bound: American Families in the Cold War Era* (New York: Basic Books, 1988). On the decline

of citizenship, see Elaine Tyler May, *Fortress America: How We Embraced Fear and Abandoned Democracy* (New York: Basic Books, 2017); Andrea Friedman, *Citizenship in Cold War America: The National Security State and the Possibilities of Dissent* (Amherst: University of Massachusetts Press, 2014).

16. On the "peace progressives," see Robert David Johnson, *The Peace Progressives and American Foreign Relations* (Cambridge, MA: Harvard University Press, 1995); Richard Drake, *The Education of an Anti-Imperialist: Robert La Follette and U.S. Expansion* (Madison: University of Wisconsin Press, 2013); Michael Kazin, *War Against War: The American Fight for Peace, 1914–1918* (New York: Simon and Schuster, 2017). On Dewey's involvement in peace campaigns and his foundational thinking on democracy, see Charles F. Howlett and Audrey Cohan, *John Dewey: America's Peace-Minded Educator* (Carbondale: Southern Illinois University Press, 2016).

17. Louis Menand, *The Metaphysical Club: A Story of Ideas in America* (New York: Farrar, Straus and Giroux, 2002), 439–41; William James, *Pragmatism: A New Name for Some Old Ways of Thinking* (New York: Longmans, 1908), 54; George Cotkin, *William James, Public Philosopher* (Baltimore: Johns Hopkins University Press, 1990), 84, 102–5, 121, 126, 136, 139, 142–45, 157.

18. Menand, *The Metaphysical Club*, 439–41; Robert W. Westbrook, *Democratic Hope: Pragmatism and the Politics of Truth* (Ithaca, NY: Cornell University Press, 2005), 9–10.

19. For the connections between Dewey and SDS, see James Miller, *Democracy Is in the Streets: From Port Huron to the Siege of Chicago*, 2nd ed. (Cambridge, MA: Harvard University Press, 2004), 94–98.

20. Max Elbaum, *Revolution in the Air: Sixties Radicals Turn to Lenin, Mao, and Che* (New York: Verso, 2002); Jeremy Varon, *Bringing the War Home: The Weather Underground, the Red Army Faction, and Revolutionary Violence in the Sixties and Seventies* (Berkeley: University of California Press, 2004); Aaron J. Leonard and Conor A. Gallagher, *Heavy Radicals: The FBI's Secret War on America's Maoists* (Alresford, UK: Zero Books, 2014). On native radicalism, see Timothy Messer-Kruse, *The Yankee International: Marxism and the American Reform Tradition, 1848–1876* (Chapel Hill: University of North Carolina Press, 1998); John L. Thomas, *Alternative America: Henry George, Edward Bellamy, Henry Demarest Lloyd and the Adversary Tradition* (Cambridge, MA: Belknap Press, 1983). By identifying IPS as a part of the New Left, this book aims to further weaken the "declension" narrative evident in early studies of the New Left. On the "New Left consensus," see John McMillian, "'You Didn't Have to Be There': Revisiting the New Left Consensus," in *The New Left Revisited*, ed. John McMillian and Paul Buhle (Philadelphia: Temple University Press, 2003), 1–10. See also Kirkpatrick Sale, *SDS* (New York: Vintage, 1973); Todd Gitlin, *The Sixties: Years of Hope, Days of Rage* (1987; reprint, New York: Bantam Books, 1993). On the ongoing debate over the life span of the New Left, see also Doug Rossinow, "Letting Go: Revisiting the New Left's Demise," in *The New Left Revisited*, ed. John McMillian and Paul Buhle (Philadelphia: Temple University Press, 2003), 241–56; Van Gosse, "A Movement of Movements: The Definition and Periodization of the New Left," in *A Companion to Post-1945 America*, ed. Jean-Christophe Agnew and Roy Rosenzweig (Malden, MA: Blackwell, 2002), 277–302. On post-1960s leftist activism, see Howard Brick and Christopher Phelps, *Radicals in America: The U.S. Left Since the Second World War* (New York: Cambridge University Press, 2015); Simon Hall, *American Patriotism, American Protest: Social Movements Since the Sixties* (Philadelphia: University of Pennsylvania Press, 2011). On the "left-liberal tradition," see Doug Rossinow, *Visions of Progress: The Left-Liberal Tradition in America* (Philadelphia: University of Pennsylvania Press, 2008). On struggles experienced by the New Left to form an alliance with liberals, see Daniel Geary, "The New Left and Liberalism Reconsidered: The Committee of

Correspondence and the Port Huron Statement," in *The Port Huron Statement: Sources and Legacies of the New Left's Founding Manifesto*, ed. Richard Flacks and Nelson Lichtenstein (Philadelphia: University of Pennsylvania Press, 2015), 83–94. On the Marxist rejection of liberal politics, see Andrew Hartman, "Against the Liberal Tradition: An Intellectual History of the American Left," in *American Labyrinth: Intellectual History for Complicated Times*, ed. Raymond Haberski Jr. and Andrew Hartman (Ithaca, NY: Cornell University Press, 2018), 132–45.

21. On the anti–Vietnam War movement, see Nancy Zaroulis and Gerald Sullivan, *Who Spoke Up? American Protest Against the War in Vietnam, 1963–1975* (New York: Holt, Reinhart, and Winston, 1984); Charles DeBenedetti with Charles Chatfield, *An American Ordeal: The Antiwar Movement of the Vietnam Era* (Syracuse, NY: Syracuse University Press, 1990); Terry H. Anderson, *The Movement and the Sixties* (New York: Oxford University Press, 1995); Tom Wells, *The War Within: America's Battle over Vietnam* (Berkeley: University of California Press, 1994); Simon Hall, *Rethinking the American Anti-War Movement* (New York: Routledge, 2012). On the anti-nuclear movement and its long respite after 1963, see Lawrence S. Wittner, *Resisting the Bomb: A History of the World Nuclear Disarmament Movement, 1954–1970* (Stanford, CA: Stanford University Press, 1997); Paul Boyer, *By the Bomb's Early Light* (New York: Pantheon, 1985).

22. Martin Klimke, *The Other Alliance: Student Protest in West Germany and the United States in the Global Sixties* (Princeton, NJ: Princeton University Press, 2010); Quinn Slobodian, *Foreign Front: Third World Politics in Sixties West Germany* (Durham, NC: Duke University Press, 2012).

23. On how Bourne's idea of a "transnational America" extended to international affairs, see Christopher McKnight Nichols, *Promise and Peril: America at the Dawn of a Global Age* (Cambridge, MA: Harvard University Press, 2011), 114–44.

24. On these debates and the changing international climate of the 1970s, see Natasha Zaretsky, *No Direction Home: The American Family and the Fear of National Decline, 1968–1980* (Chapel Hill: University of North Carolina Press, 2007); Niall Ferguson, Charles S. Maier, Erez Manela, and Daniel J. Sargent, eds., *The Shock of the Global: The 1970s in Perspective* (Cambridge, MA: Harvard University Press, 2010).

25. Akira Iriye, *Global Community: The Role of International Organizations in the Making of the Contemporary World* (Berkeley: University of California Press, 2002).

26. On the debate over Carter as a post–Cold War president, see David F. Schmitz and Vanessa Walker, "Jimmy Carter and the Foreign Policy of Human Rights: The Development of a Post–Cold War Foreign Policy," *Diplomatic History* 28, no. 1 (2004), 113–44; Nancy Mitchell, *Jimmy Carter in Africa: Race and the Cold War* (Stanford, CA: Stanford University Press, 2016).

27. Van Gosse, "Unpacking the Vietnam Syndrome: The Coup in Chile and the Rise of Popular Anti-Interventionism," in *The World the 60s Made: Politics and Culture in Recent America*, ed. Van Gosse and Richard Moser (Philadelphia: Temple University Press, 2003), 100–113. On the struggles Carter faced in implementing his human rights program, see William Michael Schmidli, *The Fate of Freedom Elsewhere: Human Rights and U.S. Cold War Policy Toward Argentina* (Ithaca, NY: Cornell University Press, 2013); Joe Renouard, *Human Rights in American Foreign Policy: From the 1960s to the Soviet Collapse* (Philadelphia: University of Pennsylvania Press, 2016), 125–66. For a positive assessment of Carter's human rights record, see Vanessa Walker, *Principles in Power: Latin America and the Politics of U.S. Human Rights Diplomacy* (Ithaca, NY: Cornell University Press, forthcoming).

28. On "maximalist" versus "minimalist" demands and the predominance of the latter by the 1970s, see Samuel Moyn, *The Last Utopia: Human Rights in History* (Cambridge, MA:

Harvard University Press, 2010); Patrick William Kelly, *Sovereign Emergencies: Latin America and the Making of Global Human Rights Politics* (New York: Cambridge University Press, 2018); Mark Philip Bradley, *The World Reimagined: Americans and Human Rights in the Twentieth Century* (New York: Cambridge University Press, 2016), 137. On Amnesty International's "minimalist" human rights discourse, see Ann Marie Clark, *Diplomacy of Conscience: Amnesty International and Changing Human Rights Norms* (Princeton, NJ: Princeton University Press, 2001).

29. On the "indivisibility" of human rights, see Daniel J. Whelan, *Indivisible Human Rights: A History* (Philadelphia: University of Pennsylvania Press, 2010). On the expansive collection of rights advocated by the writers of the Universal Declaration, see Johannes Morsink, *The Universal Declaration of Human Rights: Origins, Drafting, and Intent* (Philadelphia: University of Pennsylvania Press, 1999); Mary Ann Glendon, *A World Made New: Eleanor Roosevelt and the Universal Declaration of Human Rights* (New York: Random House, 2001).

30. On the significance of Vietnam to later human rights activism, see Barbara J. Keys, *Reclaiming American Virtue: The Human Rights Revolution of the 1970s* (Cambridge, MA: Harvard University Press, 2014). On the relationship between human rights activists and Congress, see Sarah B. Snyder, *From Selma to Moscow: How Human Rights Activists Transformed U.S. Foreign Policy* (New York: Columbia University Press, 2018).

31. On the Trilateral Commission, see Dino Knudsen, *The Trilateral Commission and Global Governance: Informal Elite Diplomacy, 1972–82* (New York: Routledge, 2016); Stephen Gill, *American Hegemony and the Trilateral Commission* (New York: Cambridge University Press, 1990); Holly Sklar, ed., *Trilateralism: The Trilateral Commission and Elite Planning for World Management* (Boston: South End Press, 1980). Another foreign policy organization that worked closely with the Trilateral Commission was the venerable Council on Foreign Relations (CFR), which had a history dating back to 1921. See Robert D. Schulzinger, *The Wise Men of Foreign Affairs: The History of the Council on Foreign Relations* (New York: Columbia University Press, 1984); Peter Grose, *Continuing the Inquiry: The Council on Foreign Relations from 1921 to 1996* (1996; reprint, New York: Council on Foreign Relations Press, 2006); Laurence H. Shoup and William Minter, *Imperial Brain Trust: The Council on Foreign Relations and United States Foreign Policy* (New York: Monthly Review Press, 1977). On U.S. foreign policy in the 1970s, see Daniel J. Sargent, *A Superpower Transformed: The Remaking of American Foreign Relations in the 1970s* (New York: Oxford University Press, 2015).

32. On transnational advocacy networks during the Cold War, see Margaret E. Keck and Kathryn Sikkink, *Activists Beyond Borders: Advocacy Networks in International Politics* (Ithaca, NY: Cornell University Press, 1998); Matthew Evangelista, *Unarmed Forces: The Transnational Movement to End the Cold War* (Ithaca, NY: Cornell University Press, 1999); Sarah B. Snyder, *Human Rights Activism and the End of the Cold War: A Transnational History of the Helsinki Network* (New York: Cambridge University Press, 2011). For a comparable transmission of ideas across borders, especially regarding race, ethnicity, and segregation, see Ruben Flores, *Backroads Pragmatists: Mexico's Melting Pot and Civil Rights in the United States* (Philadelphia: University of Pennsylvania Press, 2014).

33. See Sean L. Malloy, *Out of Oakland: Black Panther Party Internationalism During the Cold War* (Ithaca, NY: Cornell University Press, 2017); Keisha N. Blain, *Set the World on Fire: Black Nationalist Women and the Global Struggle for Freedom* (Philadelphia: University of Pennsylvania Press, 2018); Cynthia A. Young, *Soul Power: Culture, Radicalism, and the Making of a U.S. Third World Left* (Durham, NC: Duke University Press, 2006); Laura Pulido, *Black, Brown, Yellow, and Left: Radical Activism in Los Angeles* (Berkeley: University of California Press, 2006);

Teishan A. Latner, *Cuban Revolution in America: Havana and the Making of a United States Left, 1968–1992* (Chapel Hill: University of North Carolina Press, 2018).

34. According to Asef Bayat, "imagined solidarity" resulted from "different actors who come to consensus by imagining, subjectively constructing, common interests and shared values between themselves." See Asef Bayat, "Islamism and Social Movement Theory," *Third World Quarterly* 26, no. 6 (2005), 904.

35. Odd Arne Westad, *The Global Cold War: Third World Interventions and the Making of Our Times* (New York: Cambridge University Press, 2007).

36. On Rostow's modernization theory and his involvement in the development of Johnson's Vietnam policies, see David Milne, *America's Rasputin: Walt Rostow and the Vietnam War* (New York: Hill and Wang, 2008). On the links between technology, science, and modernity, see Michael Adas, *Dominance by Design: Technological Imperatives and America's Civilizing Mission* (Cambridge, MA: Belknap Press, 2006). On the development of modernization theory and its enactment abroad, see Nils Gilman, *Mandarins of the Future: Modernization Theory in Cold War America* (Baltimore: Johns Hopkins University Press, 2003); Michael E. Latham, *The Right Kind of Revolution: Modernization, Development, and U.S. Foreign Policy* (Ithaca, NY: Cornell University Press, 2011). For examples of the undemocratic nature of modernization theory in practice, see Jessica Elkind, *Aid Under Fire: Nation Building and the Vietnam War* (Lexington: University Press of Kentucky, 2016); Bradley R. Simpson, *Economists with Guns: Authoritarian Development and U.S.-Indonesian Relations, 1960–1968* (Stanford, CA: Stanford University Press, 2008); Thomas C. Field Jr., *From Development to Dictatorship: Bolivia and the Alliance for Progress in the Kennedy Era* (Ithaca, NY: Cornell University Press, 2014). On the role of international organizations in promoting a narrow development program, see Amy L. S. Staples, *The Birth of Development: How the World Bank, Food and Agriculture Organization, and World Health Organization Changed the World, 1945–1965* (Kent, OH: Kent State University Press, 2006). On experiments with alternative development models, see Daniel Immerwahr, *Thinking Small: The United States and the Lure of Community Development* (Cambridge, MA: Harvard University Press, 2015).

37. Odd Arne Westad, *The Cold War: A World History* (New York: Basic Books, 2017), especially 261–86.

38. Jennifer Bair, "From the Politics of Development to the Challenges of Globalization," *Globalizations* 4 (December 2007), 490–91.

39. On the "NGO International," see Paul Adler, "Creating 'The NGO International': The Rise of Advocacy for Alternative Development, 1974–1994," in *The Development Century: A Global History*, ed. Stephen J. Macekura and Erez Manela (New York: Cambridge University Press, 2018), 305–25.

40. Doug Rossinow, *The Reagan Era: A History of the 1980s* (New York: Columbia University Press, 2015); Natasha Zaretsky, *Radiation Nation: Three Mile Island and the Political Transformation of the 1970s* (New York: Columbia University Press, 2018), especially 144–90.

41. On the significance of conservatism and Reagan's presidency to this decade, see Sean Wilentz, *The Age of Reagan: A History, 1974–2008* (New York: Harper, 2008). On the opposition to Reagan's America, see Bradford Martin, *The Other Eighties: A Secret History of America in the Age of Reagan* (New York: Hill and Wang, 2011).

42. For the argument that arms limitations agreements were used by experts to sap public pressure for nuclear disarmament, see Matthew J. Ambrose, *The Control Agenda: A History of the Strategic Arms Limitation Talks* (Ithaca, NY: Cornell University Press, 2018).

43. On the moderation of the 1980s anti-nuclear movement, see Kyle Harvey, *American Anti-Nuclear Activism, 1975–1990: The Challenge of Peace* (New York: Palgrave Macmillan, 2014); Robert Surbrug Jr., *Beyond Vietnam: The Politics of Protest in Massachusetts, 1974–1990* (Amherst: University of Massachusetts Press, 2009), 136–70; Lawrence Wittner, *Toward Nuclear Abolition: A History of the World Nuclear Disarmament Movement, 1971 to the Present* (Stanford, CA: Stanford University Press, 2003), 322–25.

Chapter 1

1. Marcus Raskin, "A New Liberalism in the Democratic Party," April 1959, Marcus Raskin Papers, George Washington University, Washington, DC (hereafter MRP), Series 9, Box 28, Folder 6.

2. Schlesinger, *Vital Center*, 147.

3. "Tract for the Times," *Liberation* 1 (March 1956), 3–6.

4. Leilah Danielson, *American Gandhi: A. J. Muste and the History of Radicalism in the Twentieth Century* (Philadelphia: University of Pennsylvania Press, 2014), 272–73.

5. Kevin Mattson, *Intellectuals in Action: The Origins of the New Left and Radical Liberalism, 1945–1970* (University Park: Pennsylvania State University Press, 2002), 266–69, 102–4.

6. C. Wright Mills, *The Power Elite* (1956; reprint, New York: Oxford University Press, 2000), 6–9, 298–304; Daniel Geary, *Radical Ambition: C. Wright Mills, the Left, and American Social Thought* (Berkeley: University of California Press, 2009), 151–61; C. Wright Mills, "On Knowledge and Power," in *The Politics of Truth: Selected Writings of C. Wright Mills*, ed. John H. Summers (New York: Oxford University Press, 2008), 126–27, 132–33.

7. Mattson, *Intellectuals in Action*, 98–100.

8. Mattson, *Intellectuals in Action*, 113–18.

9. Paul Goodman, *Growing Up Absurd* (New York: Vintage, 1960), 217–18.

10. "We Are Facing a Danger Unlike Any Danger That Has Ever Existed," *NYT*, November 15, 1957, 15.

11. Marian Mollin, *Radical Pacifism in Modern America: Egalitarianism and Protest* (Philadelphia: University of Pennsylvania Press, 2006), 77–82; Petra Goedde, *The Politics of Peace: A Global Cold War History* (New York: Oxford University Press, 2019), 80–85, 91–93.

12. A. J. Muste, "Saints for This Age," in *The Essays of A. J. Muste*, ed. Nat Hentoff (New York: Bobbs-Merrill, 1967), 424. On Muste's pragmatism, see Danielson, *American Gandhi*, 41, 66.

13. Danielson, *American Gandhi*, 299–300; Milton S. Katz, *Ban the Bomb: A History of SANE, the Committee for a Sane Nuclear Policy, 1957–1985* (Westport, CT: Greenwood Press, 1986), 45–52.

14. Geary, *Radical Ambition*, 207–12.

15. Van Gosse, *Where the Boys Are: Cuba, Cold War America and the Making of a New Left* (New York: Verso, 1993), 235–37, 10, 138–41, 158–65.

16. C. Wright Mills, "Letter to the New Left," *New Left Review* 1 (September–October 1960), 18, 22.

17. Mollin, *Radical Pacifism in Modern America*, 108–10.

18. Sale, *SDS*, 30–31; Arnold S. Kaufman, "Human Nature and Participatory Democracy," in *The Bias of Pluralism*, ed. William E. Connolly (New York: Atherton Press, 1969), 184, 198.

19. Sale, *SDS*, 50.

20. The Port Huron Statement is published in its entirety in *The Port Huron Statement: Sources and Legacies of the New Left's Founding Manifesto*, ed. Richard Flacks and Nelson

Lichtenstein (Philadelphia: University of Pennsylvania Press, 2015), 239–83, here 242; Miller, *Democracy Is in the Streets*, 93–98, 141–50.

21. Rossinow, *Visions of Progress*, 240–47.

22. James Tracy, *Direct Action: Radical Pacifism from the Union Eight to the Chicago Seven* (Chicago: University of Chicago Press, 1996), 116–17.

23. J. David Hoeveler, *John Bascom and the Origins of the Wisconsin Idea* (Madison: University of Wisconsin Press, 2016), 3–4, 107–9, 189–92, 195; David P. Thelen, *The New Citizenship: Origins of Progressivism in Wisconsin, 1885–1900* (Columbia: University of Missouri Press, 1972), 288; Sally M. Miller, "Casting a Wide Net: The Milwaukee Movement to 1920," in *Socialism in the Heartland: The Midwestern Experience, 1900–1925*, ed. Donald T. Critchlow (Notre Dame, IN: University of Notre Dame Press, 1986), 23–24, 31–32, 38–39.

24. Matt Schudel, "Marcus Raskin, Think Tank Founder Who Helped Shape Liberal Ideas, Dies at 83," *Washington Post* (hereafter *WP*), December 26, 2017.

25. Arthur Waskow to David Riesman, August 8, 1961, Arthur Waskow Papers, Wisconsin Historical Society, Madison (hereafter AWP),Box 9, Folder 41.

26. Raskin, "A New Liberalism in the Democratic Party."

27. In addition to Kastenmeier, the Liberal Project included James Roosevelt (CA), George A. Kasem (CA), George P. Miller (CA), Charles O. Porter (OR), Frank Thompson (NJ), Byron Johnson (CO), Leonard G. Wolf (IA), William S. Moorhead (PA), James G. O'Hara (MI), William H. Meyer (VT), and Henry S. Reuss (WI). Five of these Democratic representatives lost their seats in the 1960 election. See *Congressional Record*, 87th Cong., 2nd Sess., 108, pt. 4, March 15, 1962, 3852.

28. Harris Dienstfrey, "'Fabianism' in Washington," *Commentary*, July 1, 1960, 23; Robert Kastenmeier to Pierre Hart, June 18, 1960, MRP, Series 9, Box 27, Folder 1.

29. Arthur Waskow, "Marc Raskin," *Social Policy* 30 (Winter 1999), 59–61; Russell Baker, "Republicans Mount a Drive to Link Liberal Democrats to 'Surrender' Policy," *NYT*, March 26, 1962, 18.

30. James Roosevelt, introduction to *The Liberal Papers*, ed. James Roosevelt (Chicago: Quadrangle Books, 1962), 5–6.

31. When questioned by the *New York Times* following the Republican attacks, the members listed by Kastenmeier in his 1960 press release asserted that the Wisconsin congressman "misrepresented" them by claiming their membership in the group. James G. O'Hara of Michigan, for instance, declared, "I never met this 'group' and discussed policy. Never. Never. Never. Never. Never." Baker, "Republicans Mount a Drive to Link Liberal Democrats to 'Surrender' Policy."

32. *Republican National Committee Newsletter*, June 26, 1964, AWP, Box 12, Folder 10.

33. Geary, "The New Left and Liberalism Reconsidered," 84–85, 89.

34. David Riesman to Clifford Durr, April 6, 1962; David Riesman to Cyril Dunn, February 28, 1962, both in Institute for Policy Studies Records, Wisconsin Historical Society, Madison (hereafter IPSR), Box 57, Folder 6; Michael Maccoby and David Riesman, "The American Crisis," *New Left Review* (September–October 1960), 25; "Unilateral Steps Toward Disarmament," *Harvard Crimson*, September 30, 1960.

35. Quoted in Marcus Raskin and Robert Spero, *The Four Freedoms Under Siege: The Clear and Present Danger from Our National Security State* (Westport, CT: Praeger, 2007), 273–75.

36. "The Liberal Papers," *Congressional Record*, 87th Cong., 2nd Sess., 108, pt. 5, April 16, 1962, 6708.

37. Raskin and Spero, *The Four Freedoms Under Siege*, 276; Marcus Raskin to McGeorge Bundy, May 23, 1961, National Security Files, John F. Kennedy Library, Boston (hereafter NSF), Box 323.

38. Marcus Raskin to McGeorge Bundy, April 20, 1961, NSF, Box 323.

39. Marcus Raskin Memorandum for McGeorge Bundy and Carl Kaysen, April 25, 1962, IPSR, Box 80, Folder 5; Marcus Raskin to McGeorge Bundy, October 10, 1961, NSF, Box 323.

40. Marcus Raskin Memorandum for McGeorge Bundy, "Student Onslaught, February 15," February 7, 1962, IPSR, Box 80, Folder 5.

41. McGeorge Bundy to President Kennedy, April 25, 1962, NSF, Box 323; McGeorge Bundy to James A. Perkins, November 26, 1962, NSF, Box 323.

42. Richard J. Barnet Biographical Information, undated, IPSR, Box 6, Folder 1.

43. Richard J. Barnet, *Who Wants Disarmament?* (Boston: Beacon Press, 1960), 17–22.

44. Barnet, *Who Wants Disarmament?* 30, 38–40.

45. Richard J. Barnet to Mr. Byroade, June 8, 1962, AWP, Box 9, Folder 10; Joe Holley, "Richard J. Barnet Dies; Founder of Institute for Policy Studies," *WP*, December 24, 2004, B06.

46. Arthur Waskow to Joy Matusky, September 1, 1966, AWP, Box 1, Folder 1.

47. Board Minutes Index, IPSR, Box 82, Folder 1; Minutes of Organization Meeting of Trustees of Institute for Policy Studies, February 6, 1963, IPSR, Box 82, Folder 2; Institute for Policy Studies Information Sheet, undated [1963], AWP, Box 6, Folder 50; Minutes of Annual Meeting of the Trustees of the Institute for Policy Studies, August 12, 1963, IPSR, Box 82, Folder 2.

48. "Formation of the National Institute for Policy Studies," enclosed in letter from Hugh Borton to Marcus Raskin, June 28, 1962, IPSR, Box 89, Folder 25.

49. "Formation of the National Institute for Policy Studies."

50. The RAND Corporation opened its doors in 1946 as a result of a partnership between the U.S. Army and Douglas Aircraft Company. Though independent of the military by 1948, the think tank continued contracted research for the various branches. On the history of RAND, see Alex Abella, *Soldiers of Reason: The RAND Corporation and the Rise of the American Empire* (Orlando, FL: Harcourt, 2008); Martin J. Collins, *Cold War Laboratory: RAND, the Air Force, and the American State, 1945–1950* (Washington, DC: Smithsonian Institution Scholarly Press, 2002); Bruce L. R. Smith, *The RAND Corporation: Case Study of a Nonprofit Advisory Corporation* (Cambridge, MA: Harvard University Press, 1966).

51. Paul Dickson, *Think Tanks* (New York: Atheneum, 1971), 158–59, 30–31. Beyond RAND, several philanthropical foundations, including Ford, Carnegie, and Rockefeller, existing in what Inderjeet Parmar has called "cooperative state-private elite networks," also advanced U.S. interests abroad. See Inderjeet Parmar, *Foundations of the American Century: The Ford, Carnegie, and Rockefeller Foundations in the Rise of American Power* (New York: Columbia University Press, 2012), 3–5, 15, 260.

52. Minutes from meeting on November 8, 1962, between Richard J. Barnet, Robert B. Livingston, and Robert Calkins, Field Haviland, and George Graham of the Brookings Institute, AWP, Box 6, Folder 49; Marcus Raskin to Hallock Hoffman, May 29, 1962, IPSR, Box 70, Folder 31. For a history of Brookings, see Donald T. Critchlow, *The Brookings Institution, 1946–1952: Expertise and the Public Interest in a Democratic Society* (De Kalb: Northern Illinois University Press, 1985), especially 110, 123–24, 129–35.

53. Arthur Waskow to Anatol Rapoport, November 29, 1962, AWP, Box 6, Folder 49.

54. Arthur Waskow to C. Vann Woodward, December 19, 1962, AWP, Box 6, Folder 49. Though his new job at Yale University prevented him from accepting Waskow's offer, Woodward

called IPS "one of the most promising and bold ventures in American academic life in several years." See C. Vann Woodward to Arthur Waskow, January 4, 1963, AWP, Box 6, Folder 50.

55. Marcus G. Raskin, "The Megadeath Intellectuals," *New York Review of Books*, November 14, 1963, 6–7.

56. Albert Wohlstetter, "Letters: Arms Debate," *New York Review of Books*, December 26, 1963, 18.

57. Cynthia Kerman, "Kenneth Boulding and the Peace Research Movement," *American Studies* 13 (1972), 149–65; Robert Scott, *Kenneth Boulding: A Voice Crying in the Wilderness* (New York: Palgrave Macmillan, 2015), 92–95. On PRI, see Brian S. Mueller, "Waging Peace in a Disarmed World: Arthur Waskow's Vision of a Nonlethal Cold War," *Peace & Change: A Journal of Peace Research* 40, no. 3 (July 2015), 339–67.

58. Martin Oppenheimer, "The Peace Research Game," *Dissent* 11 (Autumn 1964), 444–45, 447.

59. Arthur Waskow, "The Peace Research Reality," *Dissent* 11 (Autumn 1964), 449–50.

60. "Institute for Policy Studies Annual Report," undated, IPSR, Box 103, Folder 12; Arthur Waskow, "Looking Forward: 1999," *New University Thought* 6 (Spring 1968), 36.

61. Arthur Waskow, telephone interview by the author, October 16, 2014.

62. Richard Barnet to Howard Samuels, March 15, 1971, IPSR, Box 88, Folder 33; Waskow, "Looking Forward: 1999," 36–38; Richard Barnet to Richard Gunther, December 19, 1968, IPSR, Box 88, Folder 19.

63. "Remarks of Richard J. Barnet Before Senate Subcommittee on Constitutional Rights," September 29, 1971, IPSR, Box 2, Folder 44.

64. "Remarks of Richard J. Barnet Before Senate Subcommittee on Constitutional Rights."

65. Joshua Muravchik, "The Think Tank of the New Left," *NYT*, April 26, 1981, 40; Marcus Raskin and Richard Barnet to James Warburg, November 29, 1965, IPSR, Box 78, Folder 31; Arthur Waskow, "Draft of IPS Annual Report," April 20, 1966, AWP, Box 7, Folder 8.

66. "Easel Pad Notes from Needs Assessment Meeting," January 31–February 1, 1986, IPSR, Box 33, Folder 37; Michael Fortun and Kim Fortun, "Making Space, Speaking Truth: The Institute for Policy Studies, 1963–1995," in *Corporation Futures: The Diffusion of the Culturally Sensitive Corporate Form*, ed. George E. Marcus (Chicago: University of Chicago Press, 1998), 259.

67. Robb Burlage, "The State of the World," memo, undated [1969?], IPSR, Box 30, Folder 22; Don McKelvey to Arthur Waskow, Sue Thrasher, and Robb Burlage, June 26, 1966, AWP, Box 7, Folder 3.

68. "Report from IPS Program Council: Discussion Memo: Priorities for Growth," September 14, 1987, IPSR, Box 84, Folder 9. Hess quoted in "Institute for Policy Studies: 25th Anniversary Campaign for the Future," 1988, IPSR, Box 17, Folder 20.

69. On the debate over the definition of "liberalism," see the essays in Neil Jumonville and Kevin Mattson, ed., *Liberalism for a New Century* (Berkeley: University of California Press, 2007).

70. Arnold S. Kaufman, *The Radical Liberal: New Man in American Politics* (New York: Atherton Press, 1968), 6–7.

71. Kaufman, *The Radical Liberal*, 15.

72. Kaufman, *The Radical Liberal*, 47, 51.

73. On the significance of authenticity among New Left activists, see Doug Rossinow, *The Politics of Authenticity: Liberalism, Christianity and the New Left in America* (New York: Columbia University Press, 1998).

74. Daniel Geary, "Children of *The Lonely Crowd*: David Riesman, the Young Radicals, and the Splitting of Liberalism in the 1960s," *Modern Intellectual History* 10 (November 2013), 617–18. Though often critical of Raskin and Barnet's management of IPS, Riesman remained a trustee until 1972, when other responsibilities made it too difficult for him to remain an active part of the board of trustees. See Minutes of Meeting of Trustees of Institute for Policy Studies, January 30, 1970, IPSR, Box 82, Folder 5.

75. Arthur Waskow, telephone interview by the author, October 16, 2014.

76. David Riesman to James Warburg, September 29, 1965, IPSR, Box 89, Folder 25; Arthur Waskow to Liz Schneider, December 11, 1967, AWP, Box 1, Folder 4. Between the two codirectors, Raskin played a more active role in the antiwar movement of the 1960s. For instance, he spoke during the Vietnam Day Committee International Days of Protest at Berkeley in October 1967 and gave a speech, titled "Under What Conditions Can We Get out of Viet-Nam," at the October 1969 Moratorium to End the War in Vietnam War. See Vietnam Day Committee International Days of Protest Schedule for Berkeley Campus and Oakland Army Terminal, October 15 and 16, 1967, IPSR, Box 57, Folder 7; Moratorium Schedule—Marcus Raskin, October 15, 1969, IPSR, Box 88, Folder 26.

77. Jack Newfield, *A Prophetic Minority* (New York: New American Library, 1966), 179–80, 202–3. Representative of the New Left view of humanist liberals is Carl Oglesby, "Trapped in a System," in *The New Left*, ed. Massimo Teodori (New York: Bobbs-Merrill, 1969), 182.

78. Thomas Hayden to IPS, undated [likely 1964], AWP, Box 6, Folder 51; Todd Gitlin to Marcus Raskin, November 17, 1964, IPSR, Box 88, Folder 6; Todd Gitlin to Marcus Raskin, May 16, 1964, IPSR, Box 69, Folder 40; Paul Potter to Arthur Waskow, March 24, 1965, IPSR, Box 88, Folder 13; Lee Webb to Arthur Waskow, March 31, 1966, AWP, Box 7, Folder 2. Sue Thrasher, a civil rights activist and founder of the Southern Student Organizing Committee, joined IPS as a student in 1966. Sue Eanet, who worked in the SDS regional office in New York, became a student in September 1967. See Arthur Waskow to Sue Thrasher, July 18, 1966, AWP, Box 7, Folder 3; Minutes of Administrative Meeting, August 18, 1967, AWP, Box 1, Folder 2.

79. Marcus G. Raskin, *Being and Doing* (New York: Random House, 1971), 184.

80. "Being and Doing: An Inquiry into the Colonization, Decolonization, and Reconstruction of American Society and Its States," WBAI Broadcast, January 6, 1971, Pacifica Radio Archives, BC0021.28.

81. Raskin, *Being and Doing*, xiv–xvi.

82. On IPS's efforts to create the new knowledge necessary for social reconstruction, see Brian S. Mueller, "An Alternative to Revolution: Marcus Raskin's Theory of Social Reconstruction," *Journal for the Study of Radicalism* 13, no. 1 (2019), 43–74.

83. Raskin, *Being and Doing*, xxi–xxii; Marcus Raskin, "Soviet Dissent: In Search of Forgotten Men," *Ramparts* 12 (March 1974), 26, 56.

84. Marcus G. Raskin, "Sartre: A Life in History," *Nation*, June 7, 1980, 688; Raskin, *Being and Doing*, xxi–xxii.

85. George Cotkin, *Existential America* (Baltimore: Johns Hopkins University Press, 2003), 155–56, 232; Raskin, "Sartre: A Life in History," 689.

86. Raskin, *Being and Doing*, xvi, xxiii, 209–27; "Being and Doing," WBAI Broadcast, January 6, 1971.

87. Christopher Jencks, "A Revised (but still tentative) Proposal for a Five-Year 'Reconstruction Project,'" Field Foundation Archives, Part 1, Dolph Briscoe Center for American

History, University of Texas at Austin (hereafter FFA), Box 2T38, Folder Institute for Policy Studies, Spring 1969.

88. John Kenneth Galbraith, "No Dangerous Doctrines," attached to Minutes of Meeting of the Board of Trustees, Institute for Policy Studies, November 6, 1986, IPSR, Box 84, Folder 6; Peter Michelson, "Reconstruction or Revolution?" *New Republic*, July 10, 1971, 25–26.

89. Raskin, *Being and Doing*, 186–87, xxiii.

90. On the "Dump Johnson" movement, see William H. Chafe, *Never Stop Running: Allard Lowenstein and the Struggle to Save American Liberalism* (New York: Basic Books, 1993), 262–314.

91. Steven V. Roberts, "Dissident Democrats Organizing as a Permanent Power in Party," *NYT*, September 17, 1968, 38; Donald Janson, "Rebellious Democrats Establish Coalition to Seek Party Reform," *NYT*, October 7, 1968, 40.

92. The Editors, "The Decline and Fall of the Democratic Party: A History of One Week in Four Volumes," *Ramparts*, September 1968, 41.

93. Claudia Levy, "New Party Meets Here to Plan Election Strategy," *WP*, September 23, 1968, B1.

94. Marcus Raskin, "What's to Be Done? A Fourth Party?" *New Republic*, September 28, 1968, 17–18.

95. Steven V. Roberts, "Politics: New Party Leaders from 29 States Plan Organization and Strategy," *NYT*, September 23, 1968, 30; Raskin, *Being and Doing*, 300.

96. Arnold S. Kaufman, "Strategies for a New Politics: New Party or New Democratic Coalition," *Dissent* (January–February 1969), 13–14.

97. Kaufman, "Strategies for a New Politics," 15–16.

98. Raskin, *Being and Doing*, 291–94.

99. On McGovern, see Thomas J. Knock, *The Rise of a Prairie Statesman: The Life and Times of George McGovern* (Princeton, NJ: Princeton University Press, 2016).

100. Richard Barnet to George McGovern, January 26, 1971, IPSR, Box 88, Folder 32; Marcus Raskin to George McGovern, June 23, 1972, IPSR, Box 71, Folder 57.

101. Marcus Raskin to George McGovern, November 1, 1977, IPSR, Box 71, Folder 56; John Judis, "Turning Left, with Caution," *In These Times*, April 12–18, 1978, 2.

102. Marcus G. Raskin, "Progressive Liberalism for the '80s," *Nation*, May 17, 1980, front cover.

103. Raskin, "Progressive Liberalism for the '80s," 587–88.

104. Marcus Raskin, *Notes on the Old System: To Transform American Politics* (New York: David McKay, 1974), 124.

Chapter 2

1. Richard J. Barnet, "The Great Foreign Policy Debate We Ought to Be Having," *New Republic*, January 17, 1976, 17.

2. "The Port Huron Statement," in *The Port Huron Statement: Sources and Legacies of the New Left's Founding Manifesto*, ed. Richard Flacks and Nelson Lichtenstein (Philadelphia: University of Pennsylvania Press, 2015), 266–67; Michael Vester, "Port Huron and the New Left Movements in Federal Germany," in *The Port Huron Statement: Sources and Legacies of the New Left's Founding Manifesto*, ed. Richard Flacks and Nelson Lichtenstein (Philadelphia: University of Pennsylvania Press, 2015), 161–89; Klimke, *The Other Alliance*; Michael Vester, "The German

New Left and Participatory Democracy: The Impact of Social, Cultural, and Political Change," in *A New Insurgency: The Port Huron Statement and Its Times*, ed. Howard Brick and Gregory Parker (Ann Arbor, MI: Maize Books, 2015), 333–53.

3. Ronald Steel, *The End of Alliance: America and the Future of Europe* (New York: Viking, 1964); Henry A. Kissinger, *The Troubled Partnership: A Re-Appraisal of the Atlantic Alliance* (New York: McGraw-Hill, 1965).

4. Marcus Raskin to McGeorge Bundy, March 11, 1963, Institute for Policy Studies Records, Wisconsin Historical Society, Madison (hereafter IPSR), Box 88, Folder 1.

5. Richard J. Barnet and Marcus G. Raskin, *After 20 Years: Alternatives to the Cold War in Europe* (New York: Random House, 1965), 56–57.

6. Barnet and Raskin, *After 20 Years*, 70–72; Richard J. Barnet Statement to the Sub-Committee on International Organization, Committee on Foreign Relations, U.S. Senate, March 23, 1966, IPSR, Box 2, Folder 44.

7. Henry Kissinger, "Answers Aren't Easy," *New York Times Book Review*, June 27, 1966, B3, B7.

8. Barnet and Raskin, *After 20 Years*, 168–71.

9. Richard J. Barnet, "Why Would the Soviets Invade Europe?" *WP*, November 22, 1981, C1.

10. Committee on Foreign Affairs, Subcommittee on Europe, *The Cold War: Origins and Development*, 92nd Cong., 1st Sess., June 7, 11, 14, 18, 1971 (Washington, DC: US GPO, 1971), 115; Richard J. Barnet, "An Inquiry into a New Basis for the Atlantic Alliance," January 1968, IPSR, Box 1, Folder 4.

11. Gary B. Ostrower, *The United Nations and the United States* (New York: Twayne, 1998), 33.

12. Richard J. Barnet, "The United States, the United Nations, and a European Settlement," 1968, IPSR, Box 1, Folder 9.

13. Mark Mazower, *Governing the World: The History of an Idea* (New York: Penguin Press, 2012); G. John Ikenberry, *After Victory: Institutions, Strategic Restraint, and the Rebuilding of Order After Major Wars* (Princeton, NJ: Princeton University Press, 2001).

14. Arthur Waskow to Harlan Cleveland, May 24, 1965, Arthur Waskow Papers, Wisconsin Historical Society, Madison (hereafter AWP), Box 4, Folder 17.

15. Arthur Waskow (with Todd Gitlin), "Toward a Decent Manifest Destiny: An Exchange," *Correspondent* (Winter 1965), 89–92.

16. Arthur I. Waskow, "Populism and Peacekeeping at the UN," *War/Peace Report* 5 (May 1965), 8–9.

17. Richard J. Barnet, "The Illusion of Security," in *Peace and War*, ed. Charles R. Beitz and Theodore Herman (San Francisco: W. H. Freeman, 1973), 284–85.

18. Richard J. Barnet Statement to the Sub-Committee on International Organization, Committee on Foreign Relations, U.S. Senate, March 23, 1966.

19. "An Interview with Richard J. Barnet," *SAIS Review*, undated [likely 1974], IPSR, Box 12, Folder 36; Richard J. Barnet, "Farewell to the Nation-State," *NYT*, June 19, 1971, 27.

20. Richard J. Barnet, *A Time to Stop* (Washington, DC: World Peacemakers, 1978), 1–2.

21. Marcus Raskin to Ellsworth P. Carrington, December 19, 1983, IPSR, Box 59, Folder 21; Marcus Raskin and Joseph Duffey, "Toward a Modern National Security State: Convention Background Paper," *Democratic Review* (October/November 1975), IPSR, Box 60, Folder 45.

22. Marcus Raskin, "Transition and Change in National Security," undated [early 1980s], IPSR, Box 61, Folder 19.

23. Henry Steele Commager, "A Declaration of Interdependence," *Educational Forum* 40, no. 4 (1976), 393. On the various visions of interdependence in the 1970s, see Victor McFarland, "The New International Economic Order, Interdependence, and Globalization," *Humanity: An International Journal of Human Rights, Humanitarianism, and Development* 6 (Spring 2015), 217–33.

24. Lester R. Brown, *World Without Borders* (New York: Random House, 1972).

25. Robert O. Keohane and Joseph S. Nye, *Power and Interdependence: World Politics in Transition* (Boston: Little, Brown, 1977), 24–25, 30–36; Robert O. Keohane and Joseph S. Nye, "Power and Interdependence Revisited," *International Organization* 41 (Autumn 1987), 730, 733–34.

26. Earl Ravenal, "National Security and the New Internationalism," June 24, 1971, IPSR, Box 96, Folder 34.

27. Earl Ravenal, "Defense," in *A Foreign Policy Primer: A Guide to Foreign Policy Crisis Management*, ed. Linda Barnes and Saul Landau (Washington, DC: Institute for Policy Studies/Transnational Institute, 1975), 35.

28. Barnet, "The Great Foreign Policy Debate We Ought to Be Having," 17–18.

29. "Saul's Notes on Foreign Policy Discussion," March 29, 1976, IPSR, Box 37, Folder 56.

30. Patrick Anderson, *Electing Jimmy Carter: Campaign of 1976* (Baton Rouge: Louisiana State University Press, 1994), 36.

31. Memorandum, Zbigniew Brzezinski to Jimmy Carter, "A Critical Assessment of Your Foreign Policy," July 30, 1977, Jimmy Carter Library, Atlanta, Office of Staff Secretary, Presidential Files, Box 34, Folder 8/1/77; Richard J. Barnet, "Carter's Patchwork Doctrine," *Harper's* (August 1977), 29–31.

32. Richard J. Barnet and Richard A. Falk, "Cracking the Consensus: America's New Role in the World," *Working Papers for a New Society* (March/April 1978), 43–44, 48.

33. Sargent, *A Superpower Transformed*, 170–73.

34. Jerry W. Sanders, *Peddlers of Crisis: The Committee on the Present Danger and the Politics of Containment* (Cambridge, MA: South End Press, 1983), 172–78.

35. Zaretsky, *No Direction Home*, 172–75; Holly Sklar, "Trilateralism: Managing Dependence and Democracy," in *Trilateralism: The Trilateral Commission and Elite Planning for World Management*, ed. Holly Sklar (Boston: South End Press, 1980), 8; Michael Crozier, Samuel P. Huntington, and Joji Watanuki, ed., *The Crisis of Democracy: Report on the Governability of Democracies to the Trilateral Commission* (New York: New York University Press, 1975), 113.

36. Marcus G. Raskin, "The National Security State (Carter-Style)," *Inquiry*, April 3, 1978, 13–14; Richard Barnet, David Dellinger, and Richard Falk, "Symposium: U.S. Foreign Policy in the Middle East," *Journal of Palestine Studies* 10 (Autumn 1980), 5.

37. Earl Ravenal, "The Challenge of the Defense Budget," Testimony Before the National Security Task Force of the House Budget Committee, February 22, 1978, IPSR, Box 96, Folder 27.

38. On the evolving meaning of the term "national security," see Andrew Preston, "Monsters Everywhere: A Genealogy of National Security," *Diplomatic History* 38, no. 3 (2014), 477–500.

39. On the varied forms of "isolationism," see Brooke L. Blower, "From Isolationism to Neutrality: A New Framework for Understanding American Political Culture, 1919–1941," *Diplomatic History* 38, no. 2 (2014), 345–76; Christopher McKnight Nichols, "United States in the World: The Significance of an Isolationist Tradition," in *American Labyrinth: Intellectual History for Complicated Times*, ed. Raymond Haberski Jr. and Andrew Hartman (Ithaca, NY: Cornell University Press, 2018), 198–222.

40. Arthur Waskow, "Notes on a Trial Near Wall Street," *Liberation* (February 1966), 39; Barnet, "The Great Foreign Policy Debate We Ought to Be Having," 21.

41. Michael Klare and Franz Schurmann, "Rethinking Defense and National Security in an Increasingly Interdependent World," *Pacific News Service: Special Report* (May 1984), 11–12, IPSR, Box 96, Folder 31.

42. Karl Hess Jr., ed., *Mostly on the Edge: An Autobiography* (Amherst, NY: Prometheus Books, 1999), 183–84.

43. Rebecca E. Klatch, *A Generation Divided: The New Left, the New Right, and the 1960s* (Berkeley: University of California Press, 1999); Gregory L. Schneider, *Cadres for Conservatism: Young Americans for Freedom and the Rise of the Contemporary Right* (New York: New York University Press, 1998), 127–48.

44. Quoted in Jason Stahl, *Right Moves: The Conservative Think Tank in American Political Culture Since 1945* (Chapel Hill: University of North Carolina Press, 2016), 92; Marcus Raskin, "Notes on Trip to California, Dec. 7–12," IPSR, Box 65, Folder 7.

45. Anthony Harrigan, "Cato and the New Left," *Rappahannock Record*, December 21, 1978. Among other events, Ravenal, Michael Klare, and Steven Daggett helped organize a joint IPS-Cato seminar in 1978 titled "Consequences of Non-Intervention." See Discussion Paper for IPS/Cato Seminar, Consequences of Non-Intervention, April 6, 1978, IPSR, Box 38, Folder 11.

46. David Remnick, "The Lions of Libertarianism," *WP*, July 30, 1985, E4; Institute for Policy Studies Budget, IPSR, Box 83, Folder 4.

47. Sargent, *A Superpower Transformed*, 42–43, 55–58, 60–62. For an alternative view of the 1970s, which sees events in the decade as facilitating America's rise to unipolar power in the 1990s, see Hal Brands, *Making the Unipolar Moment: U.S. Foreign Policy and the Rise of the Post–Cold War Order* (Ithaca, NY: Cornell University Press, 2016).

48. Richard J. Barnet, "Is Kissinger Obsolete?—His Dove of Peace Has Flown the Coop," *Boston Globe*, April 27, 1975, B1, B4; "Saul's Notes on Foreign Policy Discussion," March 29, 1976. On Kissinger's tendency to equate nineteenth-century conditions to the Cold War, see Kuklick, *Blind Oracles*, 189–90, 193–95.

49. T. J. Jackson Lears, "Pragmatic Realism Versus the American Century," in *The Short American Century: A Postmortem*, ed. Andrew J. Bacevich (Cambridge, MA: Harvard University Press, 2012), 87.

50. Richard J. Barnet, "In Search of the National Interest," 1976, IPSR, Box 1, Folder 27.

51. Ellen Glaser Rafshoon, "A Realist's Moral Opposition to War: Hans J. Morgenthau and Vietnam," *Peace & Change* 26 (2001), 57–58, 63; John Bew, *Realpolitik: A History* (New York: Oxford University Press, 2016), 212. On the many facets of realism, see Joel H. Rosenthal, *Righteous Realists: Political Realism, Responsible Power, and American Culture in the Nuclear Age* (Baton Rouge: Louisiana State University Press, 1991).

52. Marcus Raskin, "Morgenthau: The Idealism of a Realist," in *Truth and Tragedy: A Tribute to Hans J. Morgenthau*, ed Kenneth Thompson and Robert J. Myers (New York: Routledge, 1984), 86–87; Richard Barnet, "In Search of the National Interest."

53. Barnet, "The Great Foreign Policy Debate We Ought to Be Having," 21; "Saul's Notes on Foreign Policy Discussion," March 29, 1976.

54. Ad Hoc Working Group on Latin America, *The Southern Connection: Recommendations for a New Approach to Inter-American Relations* (Washington, DC: Transnational Institute, 1977), ii, 4, 7, 10–11.

55. In 1985, the right-wing Council for Inter-American Security released a report titled *The Revolution Lobby*. In it, *The Southern Connection* came under intense scrutiny. Robert A. Pastor,

who had served as the executive director of the Linowitz Commission before joining President Carter's National Security Council, also served briefly on the Ad Hoc Working Group on Latin America at IPS. Critics of IPS accused Pastor of serving as "a respectable front man for the group." Speaking before the House Foreign Affairs subcommittee, General Gordon Summers Jr., who served as chairman for various conservative organizations, including the publisher of the study, claimed that IPS's *The Southern Connection* "reads like a blueprint for present Administration policies. Policies that have been or are being implemented often by individuals like Mr. Pastor and Mr. Schneider who first had a hand in formulating them." See Allan C. Brownfield and J. Michael Waller, *The Revolution Lobby* (Washington, DC: Council for Inter-American Security and Inter-American Security Educational Institute, 1985), 20, 22–23.

56. Latin American Unit to Saul Landau and Robert Borosage, January 5, 1978, IPSR, Box 24, Folder 32; Jeane J. Kirkpatrick, *Dictatorships and Double Standards: Rationalism and Reason in Politics* (New York: Simon and Schuster, 1982), 56–60.

57. Walker, *Principles in Power*, 100–101.

58. "Talking Paper: Transition Agenda for IPS," attached to Bob Borosage to Program Council Members, March 1987, IPSR, Box 86, Folder 6; Sidney Blumenthal, *Our Long National Daydream: A Political Pageant of the Reagan Era* (New York: Harper and Row, 1988), 289; Saul Landau to Stanley Weiss, November 3, 1977, IPSR, Box 36, Folder 16.

59. Saul Landau and Richard Barnet, "Draft Declaration on Central America," undated [early 1980s], IPSR, Box 40, Folder 8.

60. Richard J. Barnet, "Reflections: Rethinking National Security," *New Yorker*, March 21, 1988, 114; Richard J. Barnet, *The Economy of Death* (New York: Atheneum, 1969), 46; William A. Williams, *The Tragedy of American Diplomacy*, 2nd ed. (New York: Dell, 1962), 307.

61. Richard J. Barnet, *Intervention and Revolution: America's Confrontation with Insurgent Movements Around the World* (New York: World Publishing Company, 1968), 43; Richard J. Barnet, "Reflections: The Four Pillars," *New Yorker*, March 9, 1987, 84. On Fanon's support for revolutionary violence, see Frantz Fanon, *The Wretched of the Earth* (New York: Grove Press, 1966).

62. "Richard J. Barnet Interview with Public Agenda Foundation," transcript, April 27, 1976, IPSR, Box 2, Folder 41.

63. Earl C. Ravenal, "The Dialectic of Military Spending," in *The Federal Budget and Social Reconstruction*, ed. Marcus G. Raskin (Washington, DC: IPS, 1978), 151–52; Richard J. Barnet, introduction to *Atlantic Europe? The Radical View*, ed. Tom Nairn (Amsterdam: Transnational Institute, 1976), 6; "Santiago Carrillo Gives Seminar at Institute," *TNI Communications*, November–December 1977, Institute for Policy Studies, CDGA Collective Box, Swarthmore College Peace Collection, Swarthmore, PA.

64. "Report of Transnational Institute Conference: 'New Europe,' Amsterdam," April 1983, Institute for Policy Studies, 1980–1989 Papers, CDGA Collective Box, Swarthmore College Peace Collection, Swarthmore, PA; Robert Borosage to Philip Warburg, October 12, 1983, IPSR, Box 16, Folder 38; Barnet, introduction, 6.

65. Geir Lundestad, *The United States and Western Europe Since 1945: From "Empire" by Invitation to Transatlantic Drift* (New York: Oxford University Press, 2003).

Chapter 3

1. Henry Giniger, "Hanoi's Charges Denied by Lodge," *NYT*, November 25, 1969, 10.

2. "Raskin—Draft—November 10, 1964," Institute for Policy Studies Records, Wisconsin Historical Society, Madison (hereafter IPSR), Box 60, Folder 36.

3. William P. Bundy to Marcus Raskin, January 11, 1965, IPSR, Box 60, Folder 36; Marcus Raskin to William P. Bundy, January 25, 1965, IPSR, Box 56, Folder 46. Edward Beneš, as president of Czechoslovakia from 1935 to 1938 and 1940 to 1948, opposed German efforts to take over the Sudetenland and advocated expulsion of ethnic Sudeten Germans from Czechoslovakia. Following World War II, these expulsions continued, often resulting in massacres.

4. Richard J. Barnet, "Patterns of Intervention," in *The Vietnam War and International Law*, ed. Richard A. Falk (Princeton, NJ: Princeton University Press, 1969), 1168.

5. Arthur Waskow, "The New American Arrogance," rev. version, March 24, 1965, Arthur Waskow Papers, Wisconsin Historical Society, Madison (hereafter AWP), Box 2, Folder 30; Arthur Waskow to *War/Peace Report* Editors, October 7, 1966, AWP, Box 3, Folder 11.

6. Barnet, *Intervention and Revolution*, 12–18, 25–26.

7. John Simon to Marcus Raskin and Richard Barnet, November 30, 1966, IPSR, Box 74, Folder 25. According to Raskin, eleven publishers rejected *The Viet-Nam Reader* before Random House agreed to publish it in 1965. "They [publishers] said the war was a transitory episode that would soon be over, that the book would become irrelevant before it could be published," Raskin alleged. Quoted in Jessica Mitford, *The Trial of Dr. Spock* (New York: Knopf, 1969), 49. Fall was a leading commentator on the wars fought by France and the United States in Southeast Asia. An international relations expert, he traveled to Vietnam numerous times and wrote several books about the region. Though critical of U.S. policy in Vietnam, he supported U.S. efforts to create an independent South Vietnam. See Gary Hess and John McNay, "'The Expert': Bernard Fall and His Critique of American Involvement in Vietnam," in *The Human Tradition in the Vietnam Era*, ed. David L. Anderson (Wilmington, DE: Scholarly Resources, 2000), 63–80.

8. Marcus Raskin and Bernard Fall, "Introduction: The Issues at Stake," in *The Viet-Nam Reader: Articles and Documents on American Foreign Policy and the Viet-Nam Crisis*, ed. Marcus G. Raskin and Bernard B. Fall, 2nd ed. (New York: Random House, 1967), xix.

9. Ralph Stavins, "Washington Determines the Fate of Vietnam: 1954–1965," in *Washington Plans an Aggressive War*, ed. Ralph Stavins, Richard J. Barnet, and Marcus G. Raskin (New York: Random House, 1971), 153–59; Marcus G. Raskin, "A Citizen's White Paper on American Policy in Vietnam and Southeast Asia," *Congressional Record*, 89th Cong., 1st Sess., 111, pt. 7, 9587. Stavins's argument accords with what later historians have described as an almost fanatical concern among government officials over American "credibility." See, for instance, Craig and Logevall, *America's Cold War*, 276–77.

10. Marcus Raskin and Bernard Fall, "Diplomatic Alternatives to U.S. Policy: Editors' Proposals," in *The Viet-Nam Reader: Articles and Documents on American Foreign Policy and the Viet-Nam Crisis*, ed. Marcus G. Raskin and Bernard B. Fall (New York: Random House, 1965), 367–74. In the updated version of *The Viet-Nam Reader*, written eighteen months after the initial edition, Raskin and Fall admitted that their previous recommendations did not "constitute the 'best' solution to the problem" in Vietnam. Nonetheless, the authors argued that "they have the merit of being feasible since some of them can be implemented unilaterally up to a certain stage." See Bernard B. Fall and Marcus G. Raskin, "Diplomatic Alternatives to U.S. Policy," in *The Viet-Nam Reader: Articles and Documents on American Foreign Policy and the Viet-Nam Crisis*, ed. Marcus G. Raskin and Bernard B. Fall, 2nd ed. (New York: Random House, 1967), 465.

11. Mitford, *The Trial of Dr. Spock*, 49.

12. Robert D. Schulzinger, *A Time for War: The United States and Vietnam, 1941–1975* (New York: Oxford University Press, 1997), 202–3, 206–8.

13. Neil D. Rosenberg, "Military-Industrial Tie Assailed," *Baltimore Sun*, October 30, 1969; Marcus Raskin to Mark Hatfield, October 26, 1967, IPSR, Box 70, Folder 10; DeBenedetti and Chatfield, *An American Ordeal*, 171; Melvin Small, *Antiwarriors: The Vietnam War and the Battle for America's Hearts and Minds* (Wilmington, DE: Scholarly Resources, 2002), 65.

14. Marcus Raskin, untitled draft, February 16, 1966, IPSR, Box 60, Folder 36; Richard J. Barnet, "The Last Act in Vietnam," *NYT*, February 4, 1968, SM26.

15. Richard J. Barnet, "Vietnam: The Meaning of Negotiations," November 1967, IPSR, Box 1, Folder 1; Barnet sent his article to James P. Warburg, Senators McGovern, Eugene McCarthy, and Robert Kennedy, I. F. Stone, and Arthur Goldberg.

16. Richard J. Barnet, "The View from Hanoi II: How They View Themselves," 1969, IPSR, Box 1, Folder 11.

17. Staughton Lynd and Thomas Hayden, *The Other Side* (New York: New American Library, 1966), 63; Mary Hersberger, *Traveling to Vietnam: American Peace Activists and the War* (Syracuse, NY: Syracuse University Press, 1998), 45–46.

18. Richard Barnet, "Memorandum for Henry Kissinger," undated [likely 1969], IPSR, Box 12, Folder 51.

19. Richard J. Barnet, "The Conference Table and the Battlefield," September 1968, IPSR, Box 1, Folder 8; Barnet, "The Last Act in Vietnam."

20. Richard J. Barnet, "President Nixon's Choices: The Way out of Vietnam," *Congressional Record*, 91st Cong., 1st Sess., 115, pt. 5, March 19, 1969, 6889–90.

21. Richard J. Barnet to Nguyen Thi Binh, February 20, 1969, IPSR, Box 14, Folder 20.

22. Barnet, "Memorandum for Henry Kissinger."

23. Richard J. Barnet, "Hanoi's View," *Congressional Record*, 91st Cong., 1st Sess., 116, pt. 13, May 26, 1970, 7809; Richard J. Barnet, "How Hanoi Sees Nixon," *Congressional Record*, 91st Cong., 2nd Sess., 116, pt. 1, January 20, 1970, 381. Asking that Barnet's article "How Hanoi Sees Nixon," which originally appeared in the January 29 issue of the *New York Review of Books*, be added to the *Record*, J. William Fulbright called the article "a significant contribution to better informed public discussion of the prospect of the administration's policy."

24. Richard J. Barnet, "When the Americans Really Leave Vietnam," undated [likely 1973], IPSR, Box 1, Folder 51.

25. Barnet, "When the Americans Really Leave Vietnam."

26. See Andrew Wiest, *Vietnam's Forgotten Army: Heroism and Betrayal in the ARVN* (New York: New York University Press, 2008), 280–93. Several memoirs provide further details about the experiences of the South Vietnamese forced into these camps. See, among others, Edward P. Metzner et al., ed., *Reeducation in Postwar Vietnam: Personal Postscripts to Peace* (College Station: Texas A&M University Press, 2001); Nghia M. Vo, *The Bamboo Gulag: Political Imprisonment in Communist Vietnam* (Jefferson, NC: McFarland, 2004).

27. "To the American People, the Carter Administration and the Congress," *NYT*, January 30, 1977, E5.

28. Joan Baez, "Open Letter to the Socialist Republic of Vietnam," *NYT*, May 30, 1979, A15; Robert Lindsey, "Peace Activists Attack Vietnam on Rights," *NYT*, June 1, 1979, A8; "Intelligence and National Security," *After Hours*, WDYM-TV, Washington, DC, May 13, 1981, transcript, *Radio TV Reports*, 22–24.

29. For an overview of the Vietnam draft resistance movement, see Sherry Gershon Gottlieb, *Hell No, We Won't Go! Resisting the Draft During the Vietnam War* (New York: Viking, 1991).

30. Quoted in Mitford, *The Trial of Dr. Spock*, 47.

31. Arthur Waskow to John R. Seeley, April 20, 1967, and Arthur Waskow to Noam Chomsky, April 20, 1967, both in AWP, Box 14, Folder 49; Arthur Waskow and Marcus Raskin to Herbert Marcuse, May 9, 1967, AWP, Box 6, Folder 16.

32. Michael Ferber and Staughton Lynd, *The Resistance* (Boston: Beacon Press, 1971), 120–21.

33. Quoted in Mitford, *The Trial of Dr. Spock*, 49–50.

34. Keys, *Reclaiming American Virtue*, 55; Small, *Antiwarriors*, 4; Sandy Vogelgesang, *The Long Dark Night of the Soul: The American Intellectual Left and the Vietnam War* (New York: Harper and Row, 1974), 173–74.

35. Marcus Raskin and Arthur Waskow, "A Call to Resist Illegitimate Authority," RESIST pamphlet, 1967, AWP, Box 14, Folder 49. A copy of the "Call" is also in the appendix of Mitford, *The Trial of Dr. Spock*, 255–59.

36. Michael S. Foley, *Confronting the War Machine: Draft Resistance During the Vietnam War* (Chapel Hill: University of North Carolina Press, 2003), 94.

37. "Signers of 'Call to Resist Illegitimate Authority,'" July 9, 1967, and October 2, 1967; Donald Michael to Arthur Waskow and Marcus Raskin, June 13, 1967, all found in AWP, Box 14, Folder 49.

38. Merle Curti to Arthur Waskow, May 30, 1967, AWP, Box 14, Folder 49.

39. Kenneth E. Boulding to Marcus Raskin and Arthur Waskow, May 15, 1967, AWP, Box 14, Folder 49.

40. For a unique, though less than scholarly, treatment of the Pentagon protest, see Norman Mailer, *Armies of the Night* (New York: New American Library, 1968).

41. Arthur Waskow to David Riesman, February 19, 1968, AWP, Box 1, Folder 6. Waskow's actions at the Pentagon protest led to retribution by the Selective Service System, which changed his draft status from 4-F to 1-A. See Jared Stout, "Protestor: From 4-F to 1-A," *WP*, September 13, 1968, 1A; "Draft Board Rejects Protestor's Appeal," *WP*, September 15, 1968, C2.

42. The indictment is found in the appendix of Mitford, *The Trial of Dr. Spock*, 251–55.

43. Quoted in Mitford, *The Trial of Dr. Spock*, 159–60.

44. Luke J. Stewart, "'A New Kind of War': The Vietnam War and the Nuremberg Principles, 1964–1968" (PhD diss., University of Waterloo, 2014).

45. Elliott L. Meyrowitz and Kenneth J. Campbell, "Vietnam Veterans and War Crimes Hearings," in *Give Peace a Chance: Exploring the Vietnam Antiwar Movement*, ed. Melvin Small and William D. Hoover (Syracuse, NY: Syracuse University Press, 1992), 137–38; John Duffett, ed., *Against the Crime of Silence: Proceedings of the Russell International War Crimes Tribunal* (New York: Simon and Schuster, 1970); Andrew E. Hunt, *The Turning: A History of Vietnam Veterans Against the War* (New York: New York University Press, 1999), 72; Bertrand Russell, *War Crimes in Vietnam* (New York: Monthly Review, 1967), 125.

Chapter 4

1. Richard J. Barnet, *Roots of War: The Men and Institutions Behind U.S. Foreign Policy* (1972; reprint, New York: Atheneum, 1973), 14–15; Marcus G. Raskin, "Nuremberg and Vietnam: An American Tragedy, by Telford Taylor," *Yale Review of Law and Social Action* 1, no. 4 (1971), 4.

2. Arthur M. Schlesinger Jr., *The Bitter Heritage: Vietnam and American Democracy, 1941–1966* (Boston: Houghton Mifflin, 1966), 31.

3. For a positive assessment of these efforts to outlaw war, see Oona A. Hathaway and Scott J. Shapiro, *The Internationalists: How a Radical Plan to Outlaw War Remade the World* (New York: Simon and Schuster, 2017).

4. Harold D. Lasswell, "The Garrison State," *American Journal of Sociology* 46 (January 1941), 459. While pointing to the existence of a "garrison state," Laswell, unlike the intellectuals at IPS, did not demand its dismantling. In a later book, *National Security and Individual Freedom*, he wrote that "the main problem confronting the American people as a result of the continuing crisis of national defense is not *whether* to have an American garrison but how much to include within it and how to organize it." See Harold D. Lasswell, *National Security and Individual Freedom* (New York: McGraw-Hill, 1950), 127–28; C. Wright Mills, *The Power Elite* (1956; reprint, New York: Oxford University Press, 2000), 6–9.

5. Fred Cook, *The Warfare State* (New York: Collier, 1962), 100, 189. President Franklin Roosevelt referred to "Dr. Win-the-War" in a December 1943 press conference. See Franklin D. Roosevelt, Excerpts from the Press Conference, December 28, 1943, American Presidency Project, http://www.presidency.ucsb.edu/ws/?pid=16358.

6. Howard Brick, *Age of Contradiction: American Thought and Culture in the 1960s* (Ithaca, NY: Cornell University Press, 2000), 132. For earlier critiques, see Max Weber, "Bureaucracy," in *From Max Weber*, ed. H. H. Gerth and C. Wright Mills (New York: Oxford University Press, 1946), 196–266; James Burnham, *The Managerial Revolution: What Is Happening in the World* (New York: John Day Co., 1941). For contemporary critiques of technocracy, see David Halberstam, *The Best and the Brightest* (New York: Random House, 1972); John Kenneth Galbraith, *The New Industrial State* (1967; reprint, Boston: Houghton Mifflin, 1985).

7. Barnet, *The Economy of Death*, 82, 84–85; Richard M. Pfeffer, ed., *No More Vietnams? The War and the Future of American Foreign Policy* (New York: Harper & Row, 1968), 56–57.

8. Barnet, *The Economy of Death*, 90–91; Richard J. Barnet, "The National Security Managers," October 1968, Institute for Policy Studies Records, Wisconsin Historical Society, Madison (hereafter IPSR), Box 1, Folder 1.

9. Barnet, "The National Security Managers," 26–28, 30; Richard J. Barnet, "The National Security Bureaucracy and Military Intervention," in *The New Left: A Collection of Essays*, ed. Priscilla Long (Boston: Porter Sargent, 1969), 106–7.

10. Richard J. Barnet, "The Men Who Made War," in *Washington Plans an Aggressive War*, ed. Ralph Stavins, Richard J. Barnet, and Marcus G. Raskin (New York: Random House, 1971), 207; Barnet, "The National Security Bureaucracy and Military Intervention," 88.

11. Marcus Raskin, "Should Martin Luther King Be Secretary of State?" December 1964, IPSR, Box 60, Folder 36.

12. Barnet, *The Economy of Death*, 137; Richard Barnet, "Cobwebs and Catchwords: Rethinking National Security," in *Winning America: Ideas and Leadership for the 1990s*, ed. Marcus Raskin and Chester Hartman (Boston: South End Press, 1988), 264.

13. Richard J. Barnet, review of *Corporations & the Cold War*, edited by David Horowitz, *Commonweal*, June 26, 1970, 322–23.

14. Robert Pervidi to the editor of *Harper's Magazine*, November 3, 1971, IPSR, Box 1, Folder 14.

15. Pfeffer, *No More Vietnams?* 78–79.

16. Pfeffer, *No More Vietnams?* 83–86.

17. Pfeffer, *No More Vietnams?* 94; Barnet, *Roots of War*, 5–6.

18. Howard Romaine to Marcus Raskin, January 14, 1971, Arthur Waskow Papers, Wisconsin Historical Society, Madison (hereafter AWP), Box 7, Folder 27; Marcus Raskin, "National Security Institutions and Disarmament: Proposal," February 1963, National Security Files, John F. Kennedy Library, Boston (hereafter NSF), Box 323.

19. Marcus Raskin, *Notes on the Old System: To Transform American Politics* (New York: David McKay, 1974), 136–37.

20. Marcus G. Raskin, *The Politics of National Security* (New Brunswick, NJ: Transaction Books, 1979), 31, 33–34.

21. Saul Landau, *The Dangerous Doctrine: National Security and U.S. Foreign Policy* (Boulder, CO: Westview Press, 1988), 47; Raskin, *Notes on the Old System*, 135; Marcus Raskin, "The Kennedy Hawks Assume Power from the Eisenhower Vultures," in *The Pentagon Watchers: Students Report on the National Security State*, ed. Leonard S. Rodberg and Derek Shearer (Garden City, NY: Doubleday, 1970), 96.

22. Richard J. Barnet and Marcus G. Raskin, *An American Manifesto: What's Wrong with America and What Can We Do About It* (New York: Signet, 1970), 30; Richard J. Barnet, "The Future of Democracy," *Yale Review* 72 (Autumn 1982), 26–28; Marcus G. Raskin, "The American Political Deadlock" (Paper presented at "Colloquium on Latin America and the United States: Present and Future of Their Economic and Political Relations," Oaxtepec, Mexico, November 1975), 15.

23. Neil Sheehan, "Should We Have War Crimes Trials?" *NYT*, March 28, 1971, BR 1–2.

24. Richard J. Barnet, "Testing the Legality of the Viet-Nam War," undated [1966], IPSR, Box 15, Folder 70.

25. Barnet, "Testing the Legality of the Viet-Nam War."

26. Richard J. Barnet and Richard A. Falk, "United States of America vs. Captain Howard B. Levy, Court Martial, Fort Jackson, NC, May 10, 1967," IPSR, Box 1, Folder 1.

27. Leonard Rodberg to Marcus Raskin, Richard Barnet, and Ralph Stavins, "Some Troubled Thoughts on War Crimes," February 12, 1970, AWP, Box 7, Folder 25.

28. Philip Nobile, "Raskin: A Code for War Crimes," *Baltimore Sun*, January 10, 1972. Though a relatively minor episode, it is worth mentioning how the issue of war criminality led to Barnet's opposition to the selection of William Bundy as the editor of *Foreign Affairs*, the premier foreign policy establishment journal published by the Council on Foreign Relations. Explaining his position, Barnet wrote that "it is a disgrace for an organization to select a man for its most important position without even raising or considering the question of whether the man is a war criminal, especially when there is much affirmative evidence spread over the public record." Besides Barnet, Princeton professor of international law Richard Falk, author Ronald Steel, and Princeton professor of international affairs Richard Ullman "raised strong objection[s]" to Bundy's selection. Schulzinger, *The Wise Men of Foreign Affairs*, 210–11; Richard Barnet to David G. Nathan, January 3, 1972, IPSR, Box 3, Folder 5; David Rockefeller to Council on Foreign Relations Members, August 9, 1971, IPSR, Box 7, Folder 11.

29. See Sandra Scanlon, *The Pro-War Movement: Domestic Support for the Vietnam War and the Making of Modern American Conservatism* (Amherst: University of Massachusetts Press, 2013).

30. David Riesman to Richard Barnet, January 4, 1972, IPSR, Box 3, Folder 7.

31. Gary Jonathan Bass, *Stay the Hand of Vengeance: The Politics of War Crimes Tribunals* (Princeton, NJ: Princeton University Press, 2000), 147–73; Howard Ball, *Prosecuting War*

Crimes and Genocide: The Twentieth-Century Experience (Lawrence: University Press of Kansas, 1999), 35–85.

32. *Principles of International Law Recognized in the Charter of the Nuremberg Tribunal and in the Judgment of the Tribunal* (New York: United Nations, 1950), http://legal.un.org/ilc/texts /instruments/english/commentaries/7_1_1950.pdf.

33. Bass, *Stay the Hand of Vengeance*, 174–76.

34. Marcus G. Raskin, "From Imperial War-Making to a Code of Personal Responsibility," in *Washington Plans an Aggressive War*, ed. Ralph Stavins, Richard J. Barnet, and Marcus G. Raskin (New York: Random House, 1971), 298–99, 302–3, 306, 316.

35. Patricia A. Krause, ed., *Anatomy of an Undeclared War: Congressional Conference on the Pentagon Papers* (New York: International Universities Press, 1972), 162–63.

36. Krause, *Anatomy of an Undeclared War*, 167–68; Richard J. Barnet, "The War Planners: The Trouble with 'The Best and the Brightest,'" *Progressive* (December 1971), 16.

37. Raskin, "From Imperial War-Making to a Code of Personal Responsibility," 318.

38. Marcus Raskin, "A Proposed Amendment to National Security Act of 1947," undated [1972], IPSR, Box 62, Folder 23.

39. J. William Fulbright to Marcus Raskin, September 15, 1972, IPSR, Box 62, Folder 23.

40. "Official Accountability Act H.R. 8388" (Washington, DC: GPO, 1976), 1–2.

41. Robert Kastenmeier, "Introduction of the Official Accountability Act," July 8, 1975, IPSR, Box 62, Folder 23.

42. Michael R. Belknap, *The Vietnam War on Trial: The My Lai Massacre and the Court-Martial of Lieutenant Calley* (Lawrence: University Press of Kansas, 2002), 191–99, 206–7, 212–13.

43. Richard Overy, "The Nuremberg Trials: International Law in the Making," in *From Nuremberg to The Hague: The Future of International Criminal Justice*, ed. Philippe Sands (New York: Cambridge University Press, 2003), 10.

44. Chris af Jochnik and Roger Normand, "The Legitimation of Violence: A Critical History of the Laws of War," *Harvard International Law Journal* 35 (1994), 50–51, 91–95.

45. Pfeffer, *No More Vietnams?* 77.

46. Bruce J. Schulman, "Restraining the Imperial Presidency: Congress and Watergate," in *The American Congress: The Building of Democracy*, ed. Julian E. Zelizer (Boston: Houghton Mifflin, 2004), 644–46; Julian E. Zelizer, *On Capitol Hill: The Struggle to Reform Congress and Its Consequences, 1948–2000* (New York: Cambridge University Press, 2004), 156–76.

47. Marcus Raskin, "Memorandum," undated, IPSR, Box 70, Folder 47; Raskin, "Nuremberg and Vietnam," 4.

48. Raskin, *Notes on the Old System*, 90–94; Raskin, *The Politics of National Security*, 199–200.

49. Raskin, *Notes on the Old System*, 149–52, 155–56.

50. Reinhold Niebuhr, *The Children of Light and the Children of Darkness* (1944; reprint, Chicago: University of Chicago Press, 2011), 10.

51. George McGovern to Marcus Raskin, November 19, 1974, IPSR, Box 71, Folder 56.

52. Raskin, "From Imperial War-Making to a Code of Personal Responsibility," 282.

53. Marcus Raskin, "Testimony Before Senate Subcommittee on Separation of Powers," March 11, 1976, IPSR, Box 62, Folder 18; Marcus Raskin, "The Crisis and Responsibility of Congress to Tell the Truth," July 15, 1975, IPSR, Box 70, Folder 4; Barnet, *The Economy of Death*, 137.

Chapter 5

1. CIA, "Pinochet's Role in the Letelier Assassination and Subsequent Coverup," Intelligence Assessment, May 1, 1987, National Security Archive, https://nsarchive.gwu.edu/briefing -book/chile/2016-09-23/cia-pinochet-personally-ordered-letelier-bombing. On the long campaign to bring Letelier's murderers to justice, see Alan McPherson, *Ghosts of Sheridan Circle: How a Washington Assassination Brought Pinochet's Terror State to Justice* (Chapel Hill: University of North Carolina Press, 2019).

2. David P. Forsythe, *Human Rights and U.S. Foreign Policy: Congress Reconsidered* (Gainesville: University Press of Florida, 1988), 29, 43, 49–50.

3. Richard J. Barnet, "Preface to *Workers Against the Gulag*," in *First Harvest: The Institute for Policy Studies, 1963–1983*, ed. John S. Friedman (New York: Grove Press, 1983), 47; *Congressional Record*, U.S. Congress, Senate, 95th Cong., 1st Sess., March 3, 1977, 123, pt. 5, 6137.

4. On Tyson's statement and Carter's response, see Peter Kornbluh, *The Pinochet File: A Declassified Dossier on Atrocity and Accountability* (2003; reprint, New York: New Press, 2013), 43. Peter Weiss to Jimmy Carter, March 10, 1977, Institute for Policy Studies Records, Wisconsin Historical Society, Madison (hereafter IPSR), Box 70, Folder 26.

5. On the role the United States and counterrevolutionaries played in the downfall of Allende, see Lubna Z. Qureshi, *Nixon, Kissinger, and Allende: U.S. Involvement in the 1973 Coup in Chile* (Lanham, MD: Lexington Books, 2009); Tanya Harmer, *Allende's Chile and the Inter-American Cold War* (Chapel Hill: University of North Carolina Press, 2011), especially 190–275.

6. John Gittings, introduction to *The Lessons of Chile: The Chilean Coup and the Future of Socialism*, ed. John Gittings (Nottingham: Bertrand Russell Peace Foundation, 1975), 7–8.

7. On the Chilean solidarity movement, see Margaret Power, "The U.S. Movement in Solidarity with Chile in the 1970s," *Latin American Perspectives* 36 (November 2009), 46–66; Kelly, *Sovereign Emergencies*, 61–133.

8. For Letelier's experiences following the coup, see Ted Szulc, "A Very Quiet Horror," *Playboy* (February 1977), IPSR, Box 54, Folder 2; Orlando Letelier to Richard Barnet, October 16, 1974, IPSR, Box 13, Folder 12; John Dinges and Saul Landau, *Assassination on Embassy Row* (New York: Pantheon Books, 1980), 82–87.

9. Juan Gabriel Valdés, *Pinochet's Economists: The Chicago School in Chile* (New York: Cambridge University Press, 1995), 236–38, 243–47, 26. See also Naomi Klein, *The Shock Doctrine: The Rise of Disaster Capitalism* (New York: Picador, 2008), 59–88.

10. Orlando Letelier, "The 'Chicago Boys' in Chile: Economic 'Freedom's' Awful Toll," *Nation*, August 28, 1976, 137.

11. Letelier, "The 'Chicago Boys' in Chile," 138–42.

12. Landau, *They Educated the Crows*, 13–15; "Affidavit of Michael Moffitt," undated, IPSR, Box 43, Folder 2; memorandum of conversation between Henry Kissinger and Augusto Pinochet, "U.S.-Chilean Relations," June 8, 1976, reprinted in Kornbluh, *The Pinochet File*, 259.

13. Editorial, "Terror in Washington," *NYT*, September 22, 1976, 40; Patrick Symmes, "The Man Who Would Not Disappear," *Washington City Paper*, September 22, 1995.

14. Jack Anderson, "'Condor': South American Assassins," *WP*, August 2, 1979, DC9; John Dinges, *The Condor Years: How Pinochet and His Allies Brought Terrorism to Three Continents* (New York: New Press, 2004), 164–89.

15. Richard J. Barnet, "Dirty Tricks and the Intelligence Underworld," *Society* 12 (March/April 1975), 52–53.

16. "Senate Resolution 561," 94th Cong., 2nd Sess., September 21, 1976, IPSR, Box 38, Folder 28. Toby Moffett and twenty-four other members of Congress put forth the same resolution in the House. See "House Resolution 1559," 94th Cong., 2nd Sess., September 21, 1976, IPSR, Box 38, Folder 28.

17. Richard J. Barnet and Marcus G. Raskin to Daniel Inouye, September 23, 1976, IPSR, Box 38, Folder 42.

18. Landau, *They Educated the Crows*, 1–2; Dinges and Landau, *Assassination on Embassy Row*, 389–90. On September 15, 1980, the United States Court of Appeals, while not questioning the outcome of the trial, overturned the 1979 convictions of the three Cubans accused of murdering Letelier and Moffitt. Virgilio Paz Romero and Jose Dionisio Suarez Esqivel escaped capture. For this and future legal battles, see "Chronology of Events: Letelier-Moffitt Assassination, Investigation, and Trials," April 22, 1983, updated August 1983, IPSR, Box 38, Folder 25; "Letelier's Kin to Receive Compensation," *WP*, January 12, 1992, A10.

19. Robert Borosage, "Dear Friend" letter, undated, IPSR, Box 24, Folder 11.

20. Dinges and Landau, *Assassination on Embassy Row*, 389–90.

21. Robert A. Strong, *Working in the World: Jimmy Carter and the Making of American Foreign Policy* (Baton Rouge: Louisiana State University Press, 2000), 75.

22. Isabel Letelier, "Politics and Ethics of Liberation: An Agenda for the Eighties," speech given at the Society of Christian Ethics in Iowa, January 18, 1981, IPSR, Box 52, Folder 38.

23. Policy Alternatives for the Caribbean and Central America, *Changing Course: Blueprint for Peace in Central America and the Caribbean* (Washington, DC: IPS, 1984), 23.

24. Alan McPherson, "Letelier Diplomacy: Nonstate Actors and U.S.-Chilean Relations," *Diplomatic History* 43, no. 3 (June 2019), 458.

25. Richard J. Barnet, review of *Assassination on Embassy Row*, *New Republic*, June 21, 1980, 30. Vanessa Walker offers a more generous perspective of Carter's handling of the Letelier assassination. See her "At the End of Influence: The Letelier Assassination, Human Rights, and Rethinking Intervention in U.S.-Latin American Relations," *Journal of Contemporary History* 46, no. 1 (2011), 110–11, 116.

26. "Dear Member of Congress Letter," June 29, 1977, IPSR, Box 48, Folder 3; Peter Kornbluh to Hodding Carter III, October 24, 1979, IPSR, Box 46, Folder 49.

27. Peter [Kornbluh] to Robert Borosage, Saul Landau, John Cavanagh, Isabel Letelier, and Michael Moffitt, "Off-the-Record Conversation with Robert Pastor," undated, IPSR, Box 24, Folder 11.

28. Walker, "At the End of Influence," 131.

29. Robert S. Steven, interview by Charles Stuart Kennedy, August 3, 2001, Association for Diplomatic Studies and Training Foreign Affairs Oral History Project, 102, https://adst.org/oral-history/oral-history-interviews/; McPherson, "Letelier Diplomacy," 446–47.

30. "Congressional Conference on Southern Cone of Latin America," *Chile Legislative Center Bulletin* 2, no. 2 (October 1977), IPSR, Box 47, Folder 2; "Report on Activities: 1978–1979," undated, Field Foundation Archives, Dolph Briscoe Center for American History, University of Texas at Austin (hereafter FFA), Part 1, Box 2T25, Folder Institute for Policy Studies, 1979; "News from Congressman Tom Harkin," August 1, 1979, IPSR, Box 38, Folder 28.

31. Tom Harkin, Toby Moffett, and George Miller to Jimmy Carter, October 16, 1979, IPSR, Box 38, Folder 28.

32. Walker, "At the End of Influence," 131–32. For the response from Harkin and Kennedy to Carter's November 30 actions, see "Harkin Blasts 'Despicably Weak' Carter Response to

Chile," Tom Harkin Statement, November 30, 1979, and "From the Office of Senator Edward Kennedy," November 30, 1979, both in IPSR, Box 38, Folder 28.

33. Edward Kennedy to Joanne Wallmark, March 22, 1988, IPSR, Box 38, Folder 28.

34. Chile Committee for Human Rights Statement of Purpose, May 19, 1983, IPSR, Box 47, Folder 9; Lars Schoultz, *Human Rights and United States Policy Toward Latin America* (Princeton, NJ: Princeton University Press, 1981), 87–88; "Isabel Letelier and the Human Rights Project," undated, IPSR, Box 47, Folder 58.

35. Gar Alperovitz, Richard Barnet, Howard Wachtel, and Richard F. Kaufman to the editors of *Wall Street Journal*, September 30, 1976, IPSR, Box 13, Folder 12.

36. Ad Hoc Working Group on Latin America, *The Southern Connection*, 5–6; Isabel Letelier, "Overview of Human Rights," in *Chile: Ten Years and Beyond: The Proceedings of a Conference* (Washington, DC: Washington Office on Latin America, 1984), 24–25. The Washington Office on Latin America and the Letelier-Moffitt Memorial Fund for Human Rights sponsored the conference in Washington, D.C., on September 15, 1983. Both Senator Edward Kennedy and Congressman Ted Weiss spoke at the conference after introducing a congressional bill, "Calling for the Restoration of Democracy in Chile." Other participants included former Mexican president Luis Echeverria, Chilean exiles, and Representative George Miller.

37. IPS News Release, September 19, 1977, IPSR, Box 48, Folder 22.

38. Landau, *The Dangerous Doctrine*, 165–67.

39. Isabel Letelier and Michael Moffitt, *Human Rights, Economic Aid and Private Banks: The Case for Chile* (Washington, DC: IPS, 1978), 1, 10.

40. Jeffrey Stein, "Banks Under Attack for Chile Loans," *In These Times*, April 26–May 2, 1978; John M. Goshko, "Several U.S. Banks Accused of Undercutting Policy on Chile," *WP*, April 12, 1978, A9; Michael Moffitt to Robert Borosage, Saul Landau, and Peter Weiss, December 18, 1978, IPSR, Box 23, Folder 31.

41. "Dear Friends" letter, June 18, 1979, IPSR, Box 46, Folder 49; Robert Borosage and Saul Landau to Vincent Burke, June 15, 1979, IPSR, Box 24, Folder 11.

42. Edward J. Laurance, "Political Implications of Illegal Arms Exports from the United States," *Political Science Quarterly* 107 (Autumn 1992), 503n7.

43. Michael T. Klare, "Pathology of a Plague," *Sojourners* (October 1981).

44. "Militarism and Disarmament Project Research Proposal (for Stern Foundation): Arms Sales and Regional Conflict—The Military Implications of U.S. Weapons Transfers to the Less-Developed Nations," undated [1977], IPSR, Box 13, Folder 35; Gaddis Smith, *Morality, Reason, and Power: American Diplomacy in the Carter Years* (New York: Hill and Wang, 1986), 63–64.

45. Michael T. Klare and Max Holland, *Conventional Arms Restraint: An Unfulfilled Promise* (Washington, DC: IPS, 1978), 5–7.

46. Cynthia Arnson and Michael Klare, "Law or No Law, the Arms Flow," *Nation*, April 29, 1978, 502–3.

47. The most thorough examination of America's role in training foreign police forces, going back to "colonial policing" in the early twentieth century in the Philippines, is Jeremy Kuzmarov, *Modernizing Repression: Police Training and Nation-Building in the American Century* (Amherst: University of Massachusetts Press, 2012). See also Stuart Schrader, *Badges Without Borders: How Global Counterinsurgency Transformed American Policing* (Oakland: University of California Press, 2019).

48. Michael T. Klare and Cynthia Arnson, *Supplying Repression: U.S. Support for Authoritarian Regimes Abroad* (Washington, DC: IPS, 1981), 4–7, 17–19.

49. Vincent McGee to Leslie Dunbar, May 20, 1980, FFA, Part 2, Box 2T73, Folder Institute for Policy Studies, Militarism; Michael Klare, "Proposal to the Field Foundation on Research and Organizing American Trade in Repressive Technology," 1978, FFA, Part 2, Box 2T71, Folder Institute for Policy Studies, 1978–1980; "Report on Activities: 1978–1979," undated, FFA, Part 1, Box 2T25, Folder Institute for Policy Studies, 1979; Michael Klare to Leslie Dunbar, October 20, 1978, FFA, Part 2, Box 2T71, Folder Institute for Policy Studies, 1978–1980.

50. Michael Moffitt, "The Global Banking Empire: From Pretoria to Santiago," speech given at Columbia University Law School for the Committee to Oppose Bank Loans to South Africa, February 24, 1979, IPSR, Box 56, Folder 4.

51. George P. Shultz, "Pinochet and the Letelier-Moffitt Murders: Implications for U.S. Policy," October 6, 1987, National Security Archive, https://nsarchive.gwu.edu/briefing-book/chile/2016-09-23/cia-pinochet-personally-ordered-letelier-bombing; Morris Morley and Chris McGillion, *Reagan and Pinochet: The Struggle over US Policy Toward Chile* (New York: Cambridge University Press, 2015), 317.

52. Saul Landau and Peter Kornbluh, "Chile: The Ambassador Has Forgotten What Happened," *WP*, October 1, 1983, A13.

Chapter 6

1. *Land of My Birth*, directed by Saul Landau (San Francisco: Round World Productions, 2003). According to Landau, the campaign used the film "extensively," showing it to voters across Jamaica "to explain Michael's policy and platform." The film, Landau suggested, played an important part in Manley's reelection. See Dennis Schaefer and Larry Salvato, *Masters of Light: Conversations with Contemporary Cinematographers* (1984; reprint, Berkeley: University of California Press, 2013), 253.

2. On some of the events discussed in this chapter, see Paul Adler, "'The Basis of a New Internationalism?': The Institute for Policy Studies and North-South Politics from the NIEO to Neoliberalism," *Diplomatic History* 41, no. 4 (September 2017), 665–93.

3. On the connections between liberalism and multinational corporations, see Jason Scott Smith, "The Liberal Invention of the Multinational Corporation: David Lilienthal and Postwar Capitalism" in *What's Good for Business: Business and American Politics Since World War II*, ed. Kim Phillips-Fein and Julian E. Zelizer (New York: Oxford University Press, 2012), 107–22.

4. Liberals and socialists in the midcentury United States put forth their own "post-capitalist" vision, which in certain ways mirrored the thinking of IPS intellectuals. On these debates among social theorists, see Howard Brick, *Transcending Capitalism: Visions of a New Society in Modern American Thought* (Ithaca, NY: Cornell University Press, 2006).

5. Susan George to Friends and Colleagues of the North-South Food Roundtable, December 28, 1981, Institute for Policy Studies Records, Wisconsin Historical Society, Madison (hereafter IPSR), Box 23, Folder 30.

6. Susan George to Friends and Colleagues of the North-South Food Roundtable, December 28, 1981.

7. Susan George, "An Issues Paper," 1979, IPSR, Box 93, Folder 53.

8. Barnet, Dellinger, and Falk, "Symposium: U.S. Foreign Policy in the Middle East," 29–30.

9. Richard Barnet and Orlando Letelier, "International Economic Order Program," undated [1975], IPSR, Box 12, Folder 32.

10. Michael Moffitt to Robert Borosage, "Draft on the Planning Paper IPS/TNI Program on International Economic Order," January 18, 1978, IPSR, Box 23, Folder 31.

11. "International Economic Order Project Proposal for Fiscal Year 1985–1986 and Report on Activities for Fiscal Year 1984–1985," 1985, IPSR, Box 30, Folder 39.

12. Nils Gilman, "The New International Economic Order: A Reintroduction," *Humanity* 6 (Spring 2015), 4. For a similar argument, see Vanessa Ogle, "State Rights Against Private Capital: The 'New International Economic Order' and the Struggle over Aid, Trade, and Foreign Investment, 1962–1981," *Humanity* 5 (Summer 2014), 211–34.

13. Michael Moffitt to Bob Borosage and Howard Wachtel, Fall 1977, IPSR, Box 23, Folder 31; Susan George to International Economic Order Project, May 1982, IPSR, Box 23, Folder 30.

14. On these efforts to secure improved trade agreements, see John Toye and Richard Toye, "From New Era to Neo-Liberalism: U.S. Strategy on Trade, Finance and Development in the United Nations, 1964–1982," *Forum for Development Studies* 32 (2005), 151–80.

15. Susan George, *Feeding the Few: Corporate Control of Food* (Washington, DC: IPS, 1979), 5–7. See also Patricia Perkins and Matthew Rothschild, "Interview: Susan George," *Multinational Monitor* (March 1982), 13.

16. Michael Moffitt to Peter G. Bourne, October 21, 1977, IPSR, Box 56, Folder 5.

17. Richard J. Barnet, *The Lean Years: Politics in the Age of Scarcity* (New York: Simon and Schuster, 1980), 159.

18. Garrett Hardin, "Lifeboat Ethics: The Case Against Helping the Poor," *Psychology Today* (September 1974), 38, 40–41.

19. Barnet, *The Lean Years*, 162.

20. "The Universal Declaration of Human Rights," http://www.un.org/en/documents/udhr/.

21. Robert E. Wood, *From Marshall Plan to Debt Crisis: Foreign Aid and Development Choices in the World Economy* (Berkeley: University of California Press, 1986); Patrick Allan Sharma, *Robert McNamara's Other War: The World Bank and International Development* (Philadelphia: University of Pennsylvania Press, 2017), 202–7, 68–71, 118–20, 123–24.

22. Samuel Moyn, *Not Enough: Human Rights in an Unequal World* (Cambridge, MA: Belknap Press, 2018), 2–6, 126–28, 133–38.

23. Richard Barnet, "U.S. Needs Modest, Uniform Stand on Human Rights," *Los Angeles Times*, March 13, 1977, G2; IPS News Release, September 19, 1977, IPSR, Box 48, Folder 22.

24. Paul R. Ehrlich, *The Population Bomb* (1968; reprint, New York: Ballantine Books, 1971), xi; Club of Rome, *The Limits to Growth: A Report for the Club of Rome's Project on the Predicament of Mankind* (New York: Universe Books, 1972), 86. On the various population control measures, see Matthew Connelly, *Fatal Misconception: The Struggle to Control World Population* (Cambridge, MA: Belknap Press, 2008).

25. D. John Shaw, *World Food Security: A History Since 1945* (New York: Palgrave Macmillan, 2007), 130–36, 147, 149.

26. "Progress Report on Program of TNI for 1974–1975," September 1974, IPSR, Box 15, Folder 42; Joe Collins to Richard Barnet, Marcus Raskin, Eqbal Ahmad, and Peter Weiss, November 30, 1974, IPSR, Box 6, Folder 44; Edmundo Flores to Joe Collins, December 4, 1974, Box 6, Folder 44.

27. Transnational Institute Report, *World Hunger: Causes and Remedies* (Washington, DC: IPS, 1975), 135.

28. Jack Anderson, "Memos Bare ITT Try for Chile Coup," *WP*, March 21, 1972, B13.

29. Tehila Sasson, "Milking the Third World? Humanitarianism, Capitalism, and the Moral Economy of the Nestlé Boycott," *American Historical Review* 121 (October 2016), 1220; Vernie Alison Oliveiro, "The United States, Multinational Corporations and the Politics of

Globalization in the 1970s" (PhD diss., Harvard University, 2010), 77–78, 97, 100, 122, 126–27; Bair, "From the Politics of Development to the Challenges of Globalization," 493–95.

30. Brick and Phelps, *Radicals in America*, 212–13. On fears of a corporate takeover of America's government, see People's Bicentennial Commission, *Common Sense II: The Case Against Corporate Tyranny* (New York: Bantam, 1975).

31. Paul Baran and Paul Sweezy, "Notes on the Theory of Imperialism," *Monthly Review* (March 1966), 18, 30–31; Robert Scheer, *America After Nixon: The Age of the Multinationals* (New York: McGraw-Hill, 1974), 65–82.

32. Richard J. Barnet and Ronald E. Müller, *Global Reach: The Power of the Multinational Corporations* (New York: Touchstone, 1974), 78–80.

33. Richard J. Barnet, "The Corporation Nation," *WP*, January 31, 1975, B6; "Richard Barnet on Multinational Corporations," *Sojourners* (February 1976), 16.

34. On the Global South's response to multinational corporations, see Daniel J. Sargent, "North/South: The United States Responds to the New International Economic Order," *Humanity* 6 (Spring 2015), 206.

35. "Richard Barnet on Multinational Corporations," 17.

36. George, *Feeding the Few*, 47.

37. Richard J. Barnet, "The Profits of Hunger," *Nation*, February 9, 1980, 147.

38. Barnet and Müller, *Global Reach*, 261, 263.

39. Richard J. Barnet, "Policy Paper for Carter/Mondale," 1976, IPSR, Box 1, Folder 27.

40. Jennifer Bair, "Corporations at the United Nations: Echoes of the New International Economic Order?" *Humanity* 6 (Spring 2015), 164–66, 169.

41. Susan George, Personal Memo to the July 27 Meeting Participants, undated [likely mid-1980s], IPSR, Box 93, Folder 53; Susan George to Friends and Colleagues of the North-South Food Roundtable, December 28, 1981.

42. For an overview of the radical critique of foreign aid, see Lynn Richards, "The Context of Foreign Aid: Modern Imperialism," *Review of Radical Political Economics* 9 (December 1977), 43–75.

43. Marcus Raskin and Richard Barnet to Bradford Morse, January 10, 1966, IPSR, Box 57, Folder 36.

44. Barnet, *The Lean Years*, 188; Susan George, "Report to INRA-CIERA, Managua Nicaraguan Libre: Prospects for Nicaraguan Exports of Basic Grains in the Present World Agricultural and Political Context," March 1981, IPSR, Box 93, Folder 51.

45. Susan George, *Ill Fares the Land: Essays on Food, Hunger, and Power* (Washington, DC: IPS, 1984), 23–24.

46. Stephen J. Macekura, *Of Limits and Growth: The Rise of Global Sustainable Development in the Twentieth Century* (New York: Cambridge University Press, 2015), 142–45, 138–39.

47. Susan George, *How the Other Half Dies: The Real Reasons for World Hunger* (Montclair, NJ: Allanheld, Osmun, 1977), 73.

48. George, *How the Other Half Dies*, 78–83; George, "An Issues Paper." A key later text on self-reliance is Samir Amin, *Delinking: Towards a Polycentric World* (London: Zed Books, 1990).

49. Hollis Chenery, introduction to *Redistribution with Growth*, ed. Hollis Chenery et al. (New York: Oxford University Press, 1974), xiii.

50. George, "An Issues Paper."

51. Susan George, "World Hunger: Asking the Right Questions," *Educational Leadership* (September 1983), 60.

52. Mark Hertsgaard to Robert Borosage, "Economic Human Rights Newsletter," July 3, 1978, IPSR, Box 23, Folder 7.

53. Hertsgaard to Borosage, "Economic Human Rights Newsletter."

54. Susan George, telephone interview by the author, August 14, 2018.

55. For background information on Ahmad, see Justin Jackson, "Kissinger's Kidnapper: Eqbal Ahmad, the U.S. New Left, and the Transnational Romance of Revolutionary War," *Journal for the Study of Radicalism* 4 (2010), 75–119; Stuart Schaar, *Eqbal Ahmad: Critical Outsider in a Turbulent Age* (New York: Columbia University Press, 2015).

56. Minutes of Meeting of Executive Committee, Institute for Policy Studies, May 4, 1973, IPSR, Box 82, Folder 11; "TNI: History," http://www.tni.org/page/history.

57. Draft of Proposed New Constitution for the Transnational Institute for Policy Studies, 1975, IPSR, Box 82, Folder 15; Minutes of Meeting of the Board of Trustees, Institute for Policy Studies, May 24, 1987, IPSR, Box 84, Folder 8; John [Cavanagh] to IPS Staff and Program Council, "TNI, 1986: The Challenge," May 15, 1986, IPSR, Box 86, Folder 4.

58. Richard Barnet to Marcus Raskin, February 28, 1974, IPSR, Box 106, Folder 42; Robert Borosage to Ariane Van Buren, November 11, 1986, IPSR, Box 16, Folder 41.

59. Eqbal Ahmad to Richard J. Barnet and Marcus G. Raskin, February 13, 1974, IPSR, Box 5, Folder 20.

60. Draft Proposal to the Samuel Rubin Foundation for the Establishment of the Transnational Institute, May 3, 1974, IPSR, Box 106, Folder 42.

61. Richard J. Barnet and Marcus G. Raskin to Eqbal Ahmad, July 22, 1974, IPSR, Box 5, Folder 20; Minutes: TNI Planning Board, October 20–23, 1975, IPSR, Box 106, Folder 27.

62. Saul Landau to Samuel Rubin, August 8, 1977, IPSR, Box 36, Folder 15.

63. Nils Gilman, "Modernization Theory: The Highest Stage of American Intellectual History," in *Staging Growth: Modernization, Development, and the Global Cold War*, ed. David C. Engerman et al. (Amherst: University of Massachusetts Press, 2003), 63–69.

64. Andre Gunder Frank, *Capitalism and Underdevelopment in Latin America: Historical Studies of Chile and Brazil* (New York: Monthly Review Press, 1967), vii–viii, xi, 11–12, 16.

65. Isabel Letelier to Dick Barnet, Marcus Raskin, Saul Landau, and Eqbal Ahmad, October 1, 1976, IPSR, Box 47, Folder 51; Orlando Letelier and Michael Moffitt, *The International Economic Order (Part 1)* (Washington, DC: Transnational Institute, 1977), 52.

66. Craig Murphy, *The Emergence of the NIEO Ideology* (Boulder, CO: Westview Press, 1984), 108–10; Gilbert Rist, *The History of Development: From Western Origins to Global Faith*, 4th ed. (New York: Zed Books, 2014), 148–52.

67. Susan George to International Economic Order Project, May 1982, IPSR, Box 23, Folder 30.

68. Howard M. Wachtel, *The New Gnomes: Multinational Banks in the Third World* (Washington, DC: Transnational Institute, 1977), 13–17, 20–22, 29.

69. Howard Wachtel, "IEO Project Planning Meeting Agenda," undated [likely early 1979], IPSR, Box 38, Folder 9.

70. Howard M. Wachtel and Michael Moffitt, "House Balks at IMF Bank Bailout," *In These Times*, April 5–11, 1978, 2; Howard Wachtel and Michael Moffitt to Michael Harrington, April 19, 1977, Box 23, Folder 31.

71. Dan Morgan, "Much IMF Help Goes to Repay Commercial Loans, Study Finds," *WP*, June 25, 1977, A2; Howard M. Wachtel, "Dancing for the IMF: He Who Pays the Piper Calls the Tune," July 1978, IPSR, Box 97, Folder 48.

72. Mazower, *Governing the World*, 349–50, 358–59.

73. Michael Moffitt to Robert Borosage, "Draft of the Planning Paper IPS/TNI Program on International Economic Order," January 18, 1978, IPSR, Box 23, Folder 31. Harkin introduced and passed several such amendments in 1975 and 1976. These earlier measures ended U.S. economic assistance to known human rights violators and instructed U.S. representatives in the Inter-American Development Bank and the African Development Fund to veto loans intended for countries with poor human rights records.

74. Sargent, *A Superpower Transformed*, 178–82; Brands, *Making the Unipolar Moment*, 63–66.

75. Michael Moffitt to International Economic Order Meeting, June 22, 1978, IPSR, Box 54, Folder 29.

76. Adom Getachew, *Worldmaking After Empire: The Rise and Fall of Self-Determination* (Princeton, NJ: Princeton University Press, 2019), 2–4, 8–9, 168–73. On the centrality of democracy to Manley's vision for Jamaica, see Anna Kasafi Perkins, *Justice as Equality: Michael Manley's Caribbean Vision of Justice* (New York: Peter Lang, 2010); F. S. J. Ledgister, *Michael Manley and Jamaican Democracy, 1972–1980: The Word Is Love* (Lanham, MD: Lexington Books, 2014).

77. Michael Moffitt, "Forum: Buddy, Can You Spare a Dime?" *New Internationalist* (November 1978), 19–20.

78. Saul Landau, "Jamaica's Hot Politics," *Mother Jones* (September/October 1980), 20, 22; Michael Moffitt, "Manley Fights for His Life," *Nation*, May 31, 1980, 651.

79. Michael Manley to Howard Wachtel, September 27, 1978, IPSR, Box 54, Folder 31; Michael Moffitt, "De-Railing Development: The IMF in Jamaica," March 1979, IPSR, Box 54, Folder 33, 56–57, 59.

80. "The Terra Nova Statement: Report on a Working Group Meeting on the International Monetary System and the Third World," October 5–7, 1979, IPSR, Box 54, Folder 36, 2–6, 9. Also found in *Development Dialogue* 1 (1980), 29–30.

81. Michael Moffitt and Robert Borosage to Planning Group, "Thoughts on International Monetary Reform: Draft," March 25, 1980, IPSR, Box 54, Folder 39.

82. Michael Moffitt to Henry Ruiz, May 20, 1980, IPSR, Box 54, Folder 39.

83. "The Arusha Initiative: A Call for a United Nations Conference on International Money and Finance," 1980, IPSR, Box 54, Folder 37. Also found in *Development Dialogue* 2 (1980), 11–23.

84. "The Arusha Initiative."

85. "Solidarity with Jamaica: Resolution Adopted by the South-North Conference," *International Foundation for Development Alternatives Dossier* 19 (September/October 1980), 11.

86. Paul Fabra, "Third World Shakes Up the Monetary Fund," *Le Monde*, July 10, 1980; "Introductory Note," *International Foundation for Development Alternatives Dossier* 20 (November/December 1980), 2; Martha Honey, "Tanzania, IMF Reach Accord on $200 Million Loan," *WP*, August 9, 1980; Ann Crittenden, "Tanzania Reportedly About to Get Major I.M.F. Loan," *NYT*, September 4, 1980, D6; Michael Moffitt, "IMF, Tanzania Bury Hatchet," *Multinational Monitor* (July 1980). In the end, Nyerere refused to cut government spending, which led to the deal coming undone after Tanzania received only $25 million. The two sides resumed negotiations, but when the IMF demanded strict conditionality terms, Tanzania ended the talks. See Horace Campbell and Howard Stein, "Introduction: The Dynamics of Liberalization in Tanzania," in *Tanzania and the IMF: The Dynamics of Liberalization*, ed. Horace Campbell and Howard Stein (Boulder, CO: Westview Press, 1992), 64–65.

87. Malcolm S. Adiseshiah, "The Next Step on International Financial and Monetary Issues," *Foreign Trade Review* 17 (July 1982), 272; Vijay Prashad, *The Darker Nations: A People's History of the Third World* (New York: New Press, 2007), 209, 220.

88. On the ascendency of neoliberalism in the 1980s, see John Toye and Richard Toye, *The UN and Global Political Economy: Trade, Finance, and Development* (Bloomington: Indiana University Press, 2004), 254–75; Greta R. Krippner, *Capitalizing on Crisis: The Political Origins of the Rise of Finance* (Cambridge, MA: Harvard University Press, 2001), 86–105; Quinn Slobodian, *Globalists: The End of Empire and the Birth of Neoliberalism* (Cambridge, MA: Harvard University Press, 2018).

89. Barnet, "Reflections: The Four Pillars," 76.

Chapter 7

1. Arnaud de Borchgrave and Robert Moss, *The Spike* (New York: Crown, 1980), 301, 331–32, 344. After IPS threatened a libel lawsuit, Crown Publishers changed the name of the think tank in the paperback edition of *The Spike*. One of the authors, Borchgrave, called the revision "absolute nonsense." See Curt Suplee, "Fictional or Not, IPS Says IPR with a Branch in Amsterdam Is Too Close to Home," *WP*, May 17, 1981, C1–C2.

2. Williams, *The Tragedy of American Diplomacy*, 15; Emily S. Rosenberg, "Economic Interest and United States Foreign Policy," *American Foreign Relations Reconsidered, 1890–1993*, ed. Gordon Martel (New York: Routledge, 1994), 43–45; Curt Caldwell, "The Cold War," in *America in the World: The Historiography of American Foreign Relations Since 1941*, ed. Frank Costigliola and Michal J. Hogan, 2nd ed. (New York: Cambridge University Press, 2013), 105–12.

3. Gar Alperovitz, *Atomic Diplomacy: Hiroshima and Potsdam: The Use of the Atomic Bomb and the American Confrontation with Soviet Power* (New York: Simon and Schuster, 1965).

4. Quote comes from *Foreign Policy* article reprinted in Barnet, "The Illusion of Security," 278–79.

5. Barnet, "The Illusion of Security," 279.

6. Rael Jean Isaac, "The Institute for Policy Studies: Empire on the Left," *Midstream* (June/July 1980), 7, 9, 15; Paul Hollander, "Clipping," February 12, 1985, Institute for Policy Studies Records, Wisconsin Historical Society, Madison (hereafter IPSR), Box 92, Folder 11.

7. "Expert on Russia Questions Policy," *WP*, February 27, 1972, A12; Nicholas Von Hoffman, "Brain Power to the Disaffected," *Washington Post Potomac*, March 17, 1968, 17.

8. Alan Wolfe, *The Rise and Fall of the "Soviet Threat": Domestic Sources of the Cold War Consensus* (Washington, DC: IPS, 1979), 7–8, 20; Richard J. Barnet, "The Last White Paper," *Chicago Tribune*, January 11, 1970.

9. For a detailed account of Team B's efforts, see Anne Hessing Cahn, *Killing Détente: The Right Attacks the CIA* (University Park: Pennsylvania State University Press, 1998), 122–85.

10. Marcus Raskin to Theodore Sorensen, January 17, 1977, IPSR, Box 64, Folder 7.

11. Richard J. Barnet, "The Present Danger: American Security and the U.S.-Soviet Military Balance," *Libertarian Review* (November 1977), 11, 14–15.

12. Invitation to a Working Conference: The Myths and Realities of the "Soviet Threat," Washington, DC, May 14–15, 1979, IPSR, Box 24, Folder 37; Wolfe, *The Rise and Fall of the "Soviet Threat,"* 2.

13. Marcus Raskin, "U.S.-Soviet Relations: The New Realism," in *Winning America: Ideas and Leadership for the 1990s*, ed. Marcus Raskin and Chester Hartman (Boston: South End Press, 1988), 292.

14. William C. Indoden, "The Prophetic Conflict: Reinhold Niebuhr, Christian Realism, and World War II," *Diplomatic History* 38, no. 1 (2014), 55–56; Mark Edwards, "'God Has Chosen Us': Re-Membering Christian Realism, Rescuing Christendom, and the Contest of Responsibilities During the Cold War," *Diplomatic History* 33, no. 1 (2009), 81, 87–91; Mark Edwards, "Cold War Transgressions: Christian Realism, Conservative Socialism, and the Longer 1960s," *Religions* 6 (2015), 269–73.

15. Richard Barnet, "Battling This Present Darkness," *Sojourners* (October 1981). On the progressive strain of religion in post–World War II America, see David R. Swartz, *Moral Minority: The Evangelical Left in an Age of Conservatism* (Philadelphia: University of Pennsylvania Press, 2012).

16. Jim Wallis, "Against the Consensus," *Sojourners* (October 1981).

17. Second Meeting of the Group on Foreign Policy: Summary, January 7, 1980, IPSR, Box 11, Folder 23.

18. Fred Halliday to Robert Borosage, November 24, 1981, IPSR, Box 94, Folder 20.

19. Fred Halliday, *Soviet Policy in the Arc of Crisis* (Washington, DC: IPS, 1981), 88, 108–9; Eqbal Ahmad and Richard J. Barnet, "Bloody Games," *New Yorker*, April 11, 1988, 62.

20. On the debates over economic conversion between the 1940s and early 1970s, see Derek Shearer, "Conversion to Peace: Reorganizing the Lines of Power," *Nation*, May 17, 1971, 618–22; Derek Shearer, "Converting the War Machine," *Southern Exposure* 1 (1973), 37–48. Seymour Melman, *Our Depleted Society* (New York: Holt, Rinehart, and Winston, 1965); Seymour Melman, *Pentagon Capitalism: The Political Economy of War* (New York: McGraw-Hill, 1970); Seymour Melman, *The Permanent War Economy: American Capitalism in Decline* (New York: Simon and Schuster, 1974).

21. Richard J. Barnet, *Real Security: Restoring American Power in a Dangerous Decade* (New York: Simon and Schuster, 1981), 113–18.

22. Richard Barnet, "A Reporter at Large: The Search for National Security," *New Yorker*, April 27, 1981, 120, 140.

23. Barnet, *The Economy of Death*, 153–58.

24. Barnet, *The Economy of Death*, 161–63.

25. Barbara Wien, telephone interview by the author, February 8, 2018; "Unitarian Universalist Social Concerns Grants Panel," undated, IPSR, Box 27, Folder 32.

26. Wien interview; Katz, *Ban the Bomb*, 142–44; "1989 Real Security Schedule," undated, IPSR, Box 79, Folder 50; "Accomplishments: Real Security Education Project: The First Two Years," undated, IPSR, Box 14, Folder 48.

27. Wien interview; Barbara Wien, "Evaluation of the Real Security Education Project: The First Fifteen Months," April 1989, IPSR, Box 14, Folder 49.

28. Wien, "Evaluation of the Real Security Education Project"; Andrew Douglas to Barbara Wien, March 28, 1988, Field Foundation Archives, Dolph Briscoe Center for American History, University of Texas at Austin (hereafter FFA), Part 2, 1940–1990, Box 4X104, Folder Institute for Policy Studies, Real Security Education Project.

29. Katz, *Ban the Bomb*, 160–61; Henry Richard Maar, "The Lost Years: The American Peace Movement, from Vietnam to Nuclear Freeze," *Peace & Change: A Journal of Peace Research* 44, no. 3 (July 2019), 389–97; David S. Meyer, *A Winter of Discontent: The Nuclear Freeze and American Politics* (New York: Praeger, 1990), 217–18; David Cortright, *Peace Works: The Citizen's Role in Ending the Cold War* (Boulder, CO: Westview Press, 1993), 133–58.

30. "Program on Real Security, Proposal for Funding: 1982–1983," IPSR, Box 14, Folder 47; Marcus Raskin to Betsy [?], undated, IPSR, Box 60, Folder 5.

31. Ronald Dellums to Marcus Raskin, January 15, 1986, SANE, Inc. Records, Swarthmore College Peace Collection, Swarthmore, PA (hereafter SR), Series G, Box 6, Folder National Board Meeting, January 18–19, 1986; Jonathan Fuerbringer, "1987 Budget Plan with Military Cut Approved in House," *NYT*, May 16, 1986, A1.

32. Minutes of National Commission for Economic Conversion and Disarmament, October 12, 1988; Robert Krinsky, "Briefing Paper Two: An Introduction to Disarmament," May 1988, both in IPSR, Box 72, Folder 37.

33. Seymour Melman and Marcus Raskin, "The Money for Economic Fix Is There," *Los Angeles Times*, December 9, 1991, B11.

34. Gretchen Heefner, *The Missile Next Door: The Minuteman in the American Heartland* (Cambridge, MA: Harvard University Press, 2012), 8, 79, 87, 93–99, 109; Matthew Class, *Citizens Against the MX: Public Languages in the Nuclear Age* (Urbana: University of Illinois Press, 1993), 64, 103–4, 146, 78.

35. Heefner, *The Missile Next Door*, 163–64.

36. Angie Blake, "Up in Arms: An Interview with William Arkin," *In Progress: Newsletter of the Institute for Policy Studies* 1 (Spring 1988), 4, FFA, Part 2, Box 4X104, Folder Institute for Policy Studies, Real Security Education Project; William Arkin, "Nuclear Security: The Enemy May Be Us," *Bulletin of the Atomic Scientists* (November 1983), 4; William Arkin, "Waging Secrecy," *Bulletin of the Atomic Scientists* (March 1985), 6.

37. William Arkin, telephone interview by the author, March 1, 2018.

38. Arkin interview; Kathleen Clark, telephone interview by the author, May 30, 2018.

39. Arkin interview; William Arkin to Bob Borosage and Larry Bostian, undated, IPSR, Box 79, Folder 50; William Arkin, "Arms Race and Nuclear Weapons Research Project: Proposal for Funding (1985–1986)," June 1985, FFA, Part 2, Box 2T150, Folder Institute for Policy Studies; William M. Arkin and Richard W. Fieldhouse, *Nuclear Battlefields: Global Links in the Arms Race* (New York: Ballinger, 1985).

40. Arkin interview; Jeffrey Schmalz, "A Question of Nuclear Weapons on S.I.," *NYT*, October 8, 1985, B1.

41. "Program on National Security and Foreign Policy Budget," undated, IPSR, Box 84, Folder 5; William Arkin and Richard Fieldhouse, "Focus on the Nuclear Infrastructure," *Bulletin of the Atomic Scientists* (June/July 1985), 11–12.

42. Fred Hiatt, "Building a Force for World War IV," *WP*, July 27, 1986, A1; Kathleen Clark, "A Radio Network for the Weeks—or Months—of Nuclear War," *Baltimore Sun*, July 18, 1986.

43. Nancy Foster, "Should Amherst Resist Air Force Tower? Yes," *Amherst Bulletin*, January 23, 1985, GWEN Project Records, Swarthmore College Peace Collection, Swarthmore, PA (hereafter GPR), Box 5, Folder GWEN Project Documents, 1987–1989.

44. Foster, "Should Amherst Resist Air Force Tower? Yes."

45. William Arkin, "Preparing for World War IV," *Bulletin of the Atomic Scientists* (May 1985), 6.

46. Paul Hollander, "IPS Testimony Certain to Be Anti-U.S.," *Daily Hampshire Gazette*, February 12, 1985, GPR, Box 4, Folder Institute for Policy Studies, Bill Arkin, and Kathleen Clark; Deborah McDermott, "Air Force Backs out of Forum," *Daily Hampshire Gazette*, February 12, 1985, GPR, Box 5, Folder Information Packets, 1985.

47. Leslie H. Gelb, "U.S. Has Contingency Plan to Put A-Arms in 4 Countries, Aides Say," *NYT*, February 13, 1985, A1, A12. As Arkin explained to one philanthropic foundation, his research led to "front page stories in *The New York Times* and over 300 newspaper articles throughout the

world" covering the breaking news. See William Arkin, "Impact Through the Media: A Report to the Field Foundation," April 2, 1986, FFR, Part 2, Box 2T149, Folder IPS, Arkin.

48. Lois Barber, "Nuclear Warfare Planning Comes Home," *Progressive Review*, May–June, 1986, GPR, Box 5, Folder Mainstream Press and Wire Stories; Lois Barber, telephone interview by the author, May 28, 2018; Lois Barber, "GWEN Across America: Preparing for Nuclear War," *SANE World* (Spring 1987), 12–13, GPR, Box 5, Folder GWEN Project Documents, 1986. It was Arkin, in fact, who encouraged Foster and Barber to take their campaign national. He even helped them secure a small grant from Carol and W. H. "Ping" Ferry. See Barber interview.

49. David Morrison, "Fuses Are Short over Tall Towers," *National Journal*, May 31, 1986, 1325–26; "Remarks by Kathleen Clark," Gettysburg, PA, December 17, 1985, GPR, Box 4, Folder Institute for Policy Studies, Bill Arkin, and Kathleen Clark.

50. Kathleen Clark, "Presentation About the Ground Wave Emergency Network (GWEN)," Elmira, NY, November 18, 1986, GPR, Box 4, Folder Institute for Policy Studies, Bill Arkin, and Kathleen Clark.

51. Nancy Foster and Lois Barber to Bill Arkin and Kathleen Clark, January 23, 1987; Nancy Foster to Bill Arkin, September 17, 1987; Lois Barber to Bill Arkin and Kathleen Clark, January 16, 1987, all in GPR, Box 4, Folder Institute for Policy Studies, Bill Arkin, and Kathleen Clark.

52. Nancy Foster, "Kathleen Clark Conversation Notes," May 2, 1986; Nancy Foster, "Kathleen Clark Conversation Notes," March 20, 1986 and March 28, 1986 all in GPR, Box 4, Folder Institute for Policy Studies, Bill Arkin, and Kathleen Clark; Kathleen Clark to Silvio Conte, July 29, 1986, GPR, Box 5, Folder GWEN Project Documents, 1986.

53. Nancy Foster, "Bill Arkin Conversation Notes," May 31, 1988, GPR, Box 4, Folder Institute for Policy Studies, Bill Arkin, and Kathleen Clark; "U.S. to Complete Emergency Radio Network," *NYT*, September 12, 1988, A14; Ronald Fraser, "If Congress Can't Cut This . . . Then It Can't Make Headway on the Pentagon Budget," *NYT*, January 31, 1990, A27; Sarah Johansson, "Congress Turns down the Radio," *Bulletin of the Atomic Scientists* (January/February 1994), 5–6.

Chapter 8

1. John Rees, "Freezers Meet with Soviets to Make Plans," *Review of the News*, June 15, 1983, Institute for Policy Studies Records, Wisconsin Historical Society, Madison (hereafter IPSR), Box 23, Folder 1.

2. Abella, *Soldiers of Reason*, 117–19; Lawrence Freedman, *The Evolution of Nuclear War Strategy*, 2nd ed. (London: Macmillan, 1989), 169–70, 193–95; Robert Ayson, *Thomas Schelling and the Nuclear Age: Strategy as Social Science* (New York: Routledge, 2004), 59–61.

3. Richard J. Barnet, "Speech: Nuclear Deterrence: Confronting the Dilemma," Second Biennial Conference on the Fate of the Earth, September 1984, IPSR, Box 2, Folder 42.

4. Arthur Waskow to the *New York Review* editors, December 11, 1963, Arthur Waskow Papers, Wisconsin Historical Society, Madison (hereafter AWP), Box 3, Folder 11.

5. Marcus Raskin, "Speech: Problems of Peace," March 24, 1964, IPSR, Box 62, Folder 11.

6. Richard J. Barnet, "Some Problems of Government-Sponsored Disarmament Research: The United States Arms Control and Disarmament Agency," undated [likely 1965], IPSR, Box 1, Folder 45. While working for Representative Kastenmeier, Raskin and Waskow pushed for a National Peace Agency. Congress, however, preferred a bill drafted by John F. Kennedy's disarmament advisor, John J. McCloy, one of the famed establishment figures who made up "The Wise Men," that called for the creation of the ACDA. As McCloy's aide, Barnet worked closely with the ACDA, but he quickly soured on the agency due to its unwillingness to move beyond

arms control. Raskin shared Barnet's sentiments regarding the ACDA. He considered "the ACDA's original vision" to have "been very badly corrupted within the government to the point where it is alarming." This led the IPS cofounder to "feel rather betrayed." See Marcus Raskin to Bradford Morse, November 23, 1971, ISPR, Box 57, Folder 37.

7. Barnet, "Some Problems of Government-Sponsored Disarmament Research."

8. Richard J. Barnet, "Research on Disarmament," *Background* 6 (Winter 1963), 6.

9. DeBenedetti and Chatfield, *An American Ordeal*, 37–38. The story of liberal support for arms control is also told in Duncan C. Clarke, *Politics of Arms Control: The Role and Effectiveness of the U.S. Arms Control and Disarmament Agency* (New York: Free Press, 1979); Freedman, *The Evolution of Nuclear War Strategy*, 95–103, 191–207; and Robin Ranger, *Arms and Politics, 1958–1978: Arms Control in a Changing Political Context* (Toronto: Gage, 1979), 3–49.

10. Shane J. Maddock, *Nuclear Apartheid: The Quest for American Atomic Supremacy from World War II to the Present* (Chapel Hill: University of North Carolina Press, 2010), 208–9, 259–60; Francis J. Gavin, *Nuclear Statecraft: History and Strategy in America's Atomic Age* (Ithaca, NY: Cornell University Press, 2012), 78–80, 99–100. On the importance of Lyndon Johnson's arms control policies to détente, see Hal Brands, "Progress Unseen: U.S. Arms Control Policy and the Origins of Détente, 1963–1968," *Diplomatic History* 30, no. 2 (April 2006): 253–85.

11. Richard J. Barnet, "The Current Disarmament Impasse," in *Arms Control for the Late Sixties*, ed. James E. Dougherty and J. F. Lehman Jr. (Princeton, NJ: D. Van Nostrand C., 1967), 9–11.

12. John Newhouse, *Cold Dawn: The Story of SALT* (New York: Holt, Rinehart and Winston, 1973), 18, 69.

13. Gavin, *Nuclear Statecraft*, 108–16; Gregg Herken, *Counsels of War* (New York: Knopf, 1985), 256–64; Fred Kaplan, *The Wizards of Armageddon* (New York: Simon and Schuster, 1983), 369–70, 382–87.

14. Strobe Talbott, *Deadly Gambits: The Reagan Administration and the Stalemate in Nuclear Arms Control* (New York: Knopf, 1984), 211–18.

15. Fred M. Kaplan, *Dubious Specter: A Skeptical Look at the Soviet Nuclear Threat* (Washington, DC: IPS, 1980), 61–63.

16. Richard J. Barnet, *The Giants: Russia and America* (New York: Simon and Schuster, 1977), 104–5.

17. Untitled speech given by Marcus Raskin at Columbia University, January 26, 1985, IPSR, Box 59, Folder 27. On Reagan's initial unwillingness to seek negotiations, see Wittner, *Toward Nuclear Abolition*, 313–18, 322–25.

18. Marcus Raskin to Betsy [?], undated, IPSR, Box 60, Folder 5.

19. William M. Arkin, "National Security Program: Thoughts on the Next Decade of Work at IPS," November 3, 1986, IPSR, Box 14, Folder 48.

20. Arthur Waskow, "A Vision of the Possible Society: Creative Disorder, 1999," address to Convention of the War Resisters International, Rome, Italy, April 7, 1966, AWP, Box 3, Folder 5.

21. Richard J. Barnet, "On Living in an Arsenal," *Science*, April 19, 1968, 293–94.

22. Richard Barnet to James R. Newman, January 25, 1965, IPSR, Box 88, Folder 11.

23. Barnet, "The Current Disarmament Impasse," 15.

24. Brick, *Age of Contradiction*, 150.

25. Richard Barnet, "Russian Roulette," *Working Papers for a New Society* 6 (May/June 1978), 77.

26. James Warburg and Richard Barnet, "New Era for American Policy and Statecraft," transcript of a seminar for members of Congress, February 17, 1965, IPSR, Box 11, Folder 28.

For the bugaboo over whether the freeze advocated unilateral disarmament and its effect on the proposed freeze resolution, see Douglas C. Waller, *Congress and the Nuclear Freeze: An Inside Look at the Politics of a Mass Movement* (Amherst: University of Massachusetts Press, 1987), 206–10, 221–25, 264–66.

27. Marcus Raskin, "Towards a Modern National Security Policy," in *The Federal Budget and Social Reconstruction*, ed. Marcus G. Raskin (Washington, DC: IPS, 1978), 66–67.

28. Michael Klare to Marcus Raskin, Saul Landau, Richard Barnet, Eqbal Ahmad, and Robert Borosage, October 17, 1977; "Current Militarism/Disarmament Project Activities," November 3, 1977; "Some Comments on the Oct 8th 'Cram Session,'" October 11, 1977, all in IPSR, Box 12, Folder 52.

29. "Some Comments on the Oct 8th 'Cram Session.'"

30. Marcus Raskin to Seymour Melman, September 13, 1977, IPSR, Box 72, Folder 1; David Cortright to Marcus Raskin, August 28, 1978, SANE, Inc. Records, Swarthmore College Peace Collection, Swarthmore, PA (hereafter SR), Series H, Box 10, Folder D, Cortright Correspondence, July–September 1978; David Cortright to Robert Borosage, May 13, 1983, SR, Series H, Box 14, Folder D, Cortright Correspondence, April–June 1983; David Cortright, telephone interview by the author, June 12, 2018.

31. National Board Meeting Minutes, January 18–19, 1986, SR, Series G, Box 6, Folder National Board Meeting, January 18–19, 1986; David Cortright to Stanley Platt, July 14, 1986, SR, Series G, Box 75, Folder Files of David Cortright.

32. Leonard Rodberg, "How Can We Make Progress in the Next Round?" June 16, 1972, IPSR, Box 75, Folder 40.

33. Richard J. Barnet, "History of the Arms Race, 1945–1978," in *Peace in Search of Makers: Riverside Church Reverse the Arms Race* Convocation, ed. Jane Rockman (Valley Forge: Judson Press, 1979), 13; Marcus Raskin, "Arms Control Versus General Security and Disarmament," 1983, IPSR, Box 67, Folder 3.

34. Raskin, "Towards a Modern National Security Policy," 65.

35. Rees, "Freezers Meet with Soviets to Make Plans."

36. Marcus Raskin to Henry Kendall, November 14, 1983, IPSR, Box 94, Folder 33; "Program on National Security General Support Proposal," 1986, IPSR, Box 14, Folder 47.

37. Minutes of Meeting of the Board of Trustees, Institute for Policy Studies, March 15, 1983, "Institute for Policy Studies in 1983: A Summary of Projected Work," IPSR, Box 83, Folder 12; Marcus Raskin to Dr. A. A. Vasiliev, October 16, 1985, IPSR, Box 59, Folder 30.

38. Larry McDonald to George P. Schultz, May 12, 1983, IPSR, Box 28, Folder 18; "The Minneapolis Dialogue on Security and Disarmament: A Report," July 29, 1983, IPSR, Box 94, Folder 33. Only two Soviet academics did not receive a visa, most notably Nikolai Mostovets, who served as Head of Section, International Department CPSU Central Committee.

39. Rees, "Freezers Meet with Soviets to Make Plans."

40. For instance, according to the *Washington Post*, the most significant information to come out of the first meeting was the acknowledgment by one of the Soviet participants that his nation might institute a launch-on-warning strategy to counter Reagan's arms buildup. See Dusko Doder, "Soviets Said to Consider Faster Nuclear Missile Launch in Crisis," *WP*, April 11, 1982, A5.

41. Seymour Melman introduced the idea of a "peace race" in his 1961 book, *The Peace Race*. The book advocated major cuts to defense spending to allow for a greater focus on domestic issues and economic foreign aid. Even President John Kennedy spoke in favor of a "peace race." Just five days after the United Nations received the McCloy-Zorin Accords, which the UN

General Assembly adopted unanimously in December 1961, Kennedy addressed the body on September 25, 1961. In his speech, Kennedy declared the desire of the United States "to challenge the Soviet Union, not to an arms race, but to a peace race" in pursuit of general and complete disarmament. The U.S. government drafted an official proposal the following year, *Blueprint for the Peace Race*, which offered an "outline" for general and complete disarmament. See Seymour Melman, *The Peace Race* (New York: G. Braziller, 1961); John F. Kennedy, "Address in New York City Before the General Assembly of the United Nations," Gerhard Peters and John T. Woolley, American Presidency Project, https://www.presidency.ucsb.edu/node/235679; U.S. Arms Control and Disarmament Agency, *Blueprint for the Peace Race: Outline of Basic Provisions of a Treaty on General and Complete Disarmament in a Peaceful World* (Washington, DC: U.S. Arms Control and Disarmament Agency, 1962).

42. Marcus Raskin, "Arms Control Versus General Security and Disarmament," 1983, IPSR, Box 67, Folder 3.

43. David Cortright, *Peace: A History of Movements and Ideas* (New York: Cambridge University Press, 2008), 141.

44. Richard J. Barnet, "U.S.-Soviet Relations: The Need for a Comprehensive Approach," *Foreign Affairs* 57 (Spring 1979), 786.

45. Marcus Raskin to Cora Weiss, July 14, 1982, IPSR, Box 59, Folder 13.

46. Meyer, *A Winter of Discontent*, 222–31, 236–37.

47. David Cortright to Marcus Raskin, December 19, 1983, SR, Series H, Box 15, Folder D. Cortright Correspondence, October–December 1983.

48. Cortright interview.

49. Russ Hoyle, "Friendly Overtures in Minneapolis," *Time*, June 6, 1983, 10.

50. William Greider, "The Russians One on One," *Rolling Stone*, July 7, 1983, 7, 28.

51. "The Minneapolis Dialogue on Security and Disarmament: A Report."

52. Marcus Raskin, "Report on the Third Annual IPS US/Soviet Exchange," November 1984; George McGovern, "Report on IPS Discussions in USSR—Summer 1984," both in IPSR, Box 77, Folder 40.

53. Patricia Derian, "Talking to Russians: Why Bother?" *WP*, June 9, 1983, A19.

54. For Gorbachev's disarmament proposal, see Mikhail S. Gorbachev, *Nuclear Disarmament by the Year 2000: A Soviet Program* (New York: Richardson and Steirman, 1986). Marcus G. Raskin, "Towards a Program for Common Security and General Disarmament: A U.S.-Soviet Exchange," March 1986, IPSR, Box 78, Folder 5. Arbatov served as an advisor to both Leonid Brezhnev and Gorbachev. His influence grew under the latter premier as he encouraged reforms within the Soviet Union. On Arbatov's involvement in discussions related to SALT and later Soviet foreign policy, see Raymond L. Garthoff, *Détente and Confrontation: American-Soviet Relations from Nixon to Reagan*, 2nd ed. (Washington, DC: Brookings Institution, 1994), 210; Melvyn P. Leffler, *For the Soul of Mankind: The United States, the Soviet Union, and the Cold War* (New York: Hill and Wang, 2007), 404.

55. Cortright, *Peace Works*, 211; Evangelista, *Unarmed Forces*, 7–8; Marcus Raskin to Neil Kinnock, June 23, 1986, IPSR, Box 60, Folder 4; George Caldwell to Marcus Raskin, December 12, 1986, SR, Series G, Box 147, Folder SANE, Press Department.

56. Marcus Raskin, "MDP Study Group," October 13, 1977, ISPR, Box 13, Folder 35.

57. Marcus G. Raskin, "Draft Treaty for a Comprehensive Program for Common Security and General Disarmament," in *Essays of a Citizen: From National Security State to Democracy* (Armonk, NY: M. E. Sharpe, 1991), 232–33, 267.

58. Marcus G. Raskin, "The McCloy-Zorin Correspondence," *Bulletin of the Atomic Scientists* (February 1983), 34–36.

59. Raskin, "The McCloy-Zorin Correspondence."

60. Marcus Raskin to Robert Kastenmeier, February 25, 1986, IPSR, Box 71, Folder 18.

61. Marcus Raskin to Paul Simon, March 3, 1987, IPSR, Box 66, Folder 34.

62. John Newhouse, *War and Peace in the Nuclear Age* (New York: Knopf, 1989), 402.

Epilogue

1. Editors, "Happy 50th Anniversary, IPS!" *Nation*, October 14, 2013.

2. Richard Barnet, "The Challenge of Change," *Sojourners* (June 1989).

3. Hubert Humphrey to Marcus Raskin, November 18, 1963, Institute for Policy Studies Records, Wisconsin Historical Society, Madison (hereafter IPSR), Box 70, Folder 28.

4. William Schneider, "The Democrats in '88," *Atlantic* (April 1987); Ray Moseley, "Dukakis to Focus on Foreign Policy," *Chicago Tribune*, September 12, 1988; Lily Geismer, *Don't Blame Us: Suburban Liberals and the Transformation of the Democratic Party* (Princeton, NJ: Princeton University Press, 2015), 251–79.

5. Sidney Blumenthal, "Jackson and the Braintrust," *WP*, April 5, 1988, D1, D3; Charles Krauthammer, "The Democrats Move Left," *WP*, April 8, 1988, A21.

6. On the erosion of democracy and its links to the ascendancy of neoliberalism, see David Harvey, *A Brief History of Neoliberalism* (New York: Oxford University Press, 2005); Nancy MacLean, *Democracy in Chains: The Deep History of the Radical Right's Stealth Plan for America* (New York: Viking, 2017); Wendy Brown, *Undoing the Demos: Neoliberalism's Stealth Revolution* (Brooklyn, NY: Zone Books, 2015); Stephanie L. Mudge, *Leftism Reinvented: Western Parties from Socialism to Neoliberalism* (Cambridge, MA: Harvard University Press, 2018).

7. Brick and Phelps, *Radicals in America*, 266–68.

8. Stephen J. Kobrin, "Multinational Corporations, the Protest Movement, and the Future of Global Governance," in *Leviathans: Multinational Corporations and the New Global History*, ed. Alfred D. Chandler Jr. and Bruce Mazlish (New York: Cambridge University Press, 2005), 224–26.

9. Andrew J. Bacevich, *American Empire: The Realities and Consequences of U.S. Diplomacy* (Cambridge, MA: Harvard University Press, 2002), 53; Al From, "Hey, Mom—What's a New Democrat?" *WP*, June 6, 1993, C1; Thomas B. Edsall, "NAFTA Debate Reopens Wounds in the Body of the Democratic Party," *WP*, October 24, 1993, A4.

10. Sarah Anderson and John Cavanagh, eds., *NAFTA's First Two Years: The Myths and Realities* (Washington, DC: IPS, 1996), i–ii; DAN statement quoted in Jeremy Brecher, *Strike!*, rev. ed. (Oakland, CA: PM Press, 2014); John Cavanagh, e-mail communication to the author, July 25, 2019.

11. Tony Judt, "Bush's Useful Idiots," *London Review of Books*, September 21, 2006, 3–5; Maria Ryan, "Bush's 'Useful Idiots': 9/11, the Liberal Hawks and the Cooption of the 'War on Terror,'" *Journal of American Studies* 45, no. 4 (2011), 667–93.

12. David Cortright, "The Peaceful Superpower: The Movement Against War in Iraq," in *Charting Transnational Democracy: Beyond Global Arrogance*, ed. Janie Leatherman and Julie A. Weber (New York: Palgrave Macmillan, 2005), 75–80.

13. Phyllis Bennis and John Cavanagh, "Response I: An Agenda for Peace," *Nation*, April 21, 2003, 13; Phyllis Bennis, "How to Get out of Iraq: A Forum," *Nation*, May 24, 2004, 16–17.

14. Lloyd Grove, "A Liberal Dose of Idealism: Think Tank Fetes 30 Years on the Left," *WP*, October 4, 1993, B7.

15. James McGann, *2018 Global Go To Think Tank Index Report* (Philadelphia: University of Pennsylvania Think Tanks and Civil Societies Program, 2019), 78–80.

16. Stahl, *Right Moves*, 182–94; Lawrence J. Korb and Brian Katulis, *Strategic Redeployment: A Progressive Plan for Iraq and the Struggle Against Violent Extremists* (Washington, DC: Center for American Progress, 2005); Brian Katulis, Hardin Lang, and Vikram Singh, *On the Brink: Managing the ISIS Threat in Iraq* (Washington, DC: Center for American Progress, 2014); Lawrence Korb, Caroline Wadhams, Colin Cookman, and Sean Duggan, *Sustainable Security in Afghanistan: Crafting an Effective and Responsible Strategy for the Forgotten Front* (Washington, DC: Center for American Progress, 2009).

17. Daniel Bessner and Stephen Wertheim, "Democratizing U.S. Foreign Policy: Bringing Experts and the Public Back Together," *Foreign Affairs*, April 5, 2017, https://www.foreignaffairs.com/articles/united-states/2017-04-05/democratizing-us-foreign-policy.

18. Bessner and Wertheim, "Democratizing U.S. Foreign Policy"; Daniel Bessner, "What Does Alexandria Ocasio-Cortez Think About the South China Sea," *NYT*, September 17, 2018, https://www.nytimes.com/2018/09/17/opinion/democratic-party-cortez-foreign-policy.html.

ACKNOWLEDGMENTS

Robert Lockhart saw the potential in this project at an early stage. I am indebted to him for reaching out and encouraging me to submit my manuscript to the University of Pennsylvania Press. His unflagging encouragement gave me the inspiration to finish the book despite the often hectic teaching schedule I kept over the last several years. The readers enlisted by the Press strengthened the book immeasurably, forcing me to rethink its central argument and expand the scope of the project. This book also benefited from incredible feedback from several scholars whom I greatly admire. I thank Paul Adler, Daniel Bessner, Daniel Geary, Vanessa Walker, and Sandy Zipp for taking the time away from their own research and writing to read and comment on chapters.

At the University of Wisconsin–Milwaukee (UWM) I had the good fortune of working with a stellar group of scholars who provided the perfect mix of guidance, encouragement, and rigorous feedback, which influenced how I approached the writing of this book. I consider myself lucky to have had the opportunity to have as my advisor David Hoeveler, whose scholarly accomplishments are surpassed only by his genuine kindness. In addition to being generous with his time and always willing to read drafts of my work, he also provided me with the intellectual freedom to develop as a scholar. More than anything else, he taught me how to write clearly. I also owe a tremendous debt of gratitude to Howard Brick. It was through Howard's work that I first became interested in studying radicalism and intellectual history, so his continued support, whether writing letters of recommendation or offering advice, means the world to me. To this day, Joseph Rodriguez remains one of my strongest advocates in the Department of History at UWM. Marc Levine and Joe Austin also deserve thanks for supporting me throughout graduate school.

I am grateful for the assistance of archivists at the Wisconsin Historical Society, the University of Wisconsin–Milwaukee Archives, the Swarthmore College Peace Collection, the Dolph Briscoe Center for American History at the University of Texas, the John F. Kennedy Library, and the Special

Collections Research Center at George Washington University. Portions of Chapters 3 and 4 appeared in the September 2017 issue of *Diplomatic History*, under the title "Confronting America's National Security State: The Institute for Policy Studies and the Vietnam War." I thank the editors of *Diplomatic History* for permission to republish this material.

Academic life can often feel all-compassing, so it is a relief to have people around me who have no connection to academia. My nieces, Izzy and Evelyn, and nephew, Austin, offered countless moments of unmatched fun and entertainment. Their youthful energy never failed to brighten my day. My sister, Lisa, and my brother-in-law, John, offered their unwavering support. Finally, my parents, Randy and Jenny, who never questioned my decision to pursue a Ph.D. in history, have given me much more than I can ever repay.